AFTER ALEXANDER

The Time of the Diadochi (323–281 BC)

edited by

Víctor Alonso Troncoso and Edward M. Anson

Oxbow Books
Oxford and Oakville

I0894436

First published in the United Kingdom in 2013. Reprinted in 2016 by
OXBOW BOOKS
The Old Music Hall, 106-108 Cowley Road, Oxford, OX4 1JE

and in the United States by
OXBOW BOOKS
1950 Lawrence Road, Havertown, PA 19083

© Oxbow Books and the individual authors 2013

Paperback Edition: ISBN 978-1-78570-512-0
Digital Edition: ISBN 978-1-78297-063-7 (ePub)

A CIP record for this book is available from the British Library

Library of Congress Cataloging-in-Publication Data

After Alexander : the time of the Diadochi (323-281 bc) / edited by Víctor Alonso Troncoso and Edward M. Anson.
pages cm
"This volume contains the revised proceedings of an international symposium on "The Time of the Diadochi (323-281 BC)", held at the University of La Coruña (Spain), in September 2010."
Includes bibliographical references and index.
ISBN 978-1-84217-512-5
1. Greece--History--Macedonian Hegemony, 323-281 B.C.--Congresses. 2. Macedonia--History--Diadochi, 323-276 B.C.--Congresses. I. Alonso Troncoso, V. (Víctor), author, editor of compilation. II. Anson, Edward, author, editor of compilation.
DF235.4.A47 2013
938'.08--dc23
2012048608

All rights reserved. No part of this book may be reproduced or transmitted in any form or by any means, electronic or mechanical including photocopying, recording or by any information storage and retrieval system, without permission from the publisher in writing.

For a complete list of Oxbow titles, please contact:

UNITED KINGDOM
Oxbow Books
Telephone (01865) 241249, Fax (01865) 794449
Email: oxbow@oxbowbooks.com
www.oxbowbooks.com

UNITED STATES OF AMERICA
Oxbow Books
Telephone (800) 791-9354, Fax (610) 853-9146
Email: queries@casemateacademic.com
www.casemateacademic.com/oxbow

Oxbow Books is part of the Casemate Group

Front cover: Fortress of Kurganzol, Uzbekistan (Photo M. J. Olbrycht), and busts of Philetairus, 'Craterus', Seleucus, and Demetrius Poliorcetes, with tetradrachm of Lysimachus (Photos V. Alonso Troncoso).
Back cover: Bisotun, Iran (Photo M. J. Olbrycht).

Harry J. Dell
Fritz Gschnitzer
In memoriam

NOTE ON THE ABBREVIATIONS AND THE CHRONOLOGY

Following Oxbow Books' norms of publication, all journal titles are given in full in the bibliography provided by each contributor at the end of his/her paper. As regards the abbreviations of ancient sources, Greek authors and titles of works, as well as Greek inscriptions, papyri and ostraca, and collections of fragments (v.g., Jacoby *FGH*, Müller *FHG*), are cited according to the new edition of the *Diccionario Griego-Español* Canon Lists, vol. I (2nd ed.), Madrid 2008 (with English version on line: http://dge.cchs.csic.es/index2.htm). For the Latin sources the *Oxford Latin Dictionary* (Oxford 1968) has been used and, only for the missing abbreviations in the latter's list, we have resorted to the *Thesaurus Linguae Latinae. Index* (5th ed.), Leipzig 1990. In some special cases, however, the contributors have given their own list of abbreviations alongside their bibliography.

Concerning the chronological references, the dates are generally before Christ. Only in dubious cases the indication BC appears, while the years of the Era are explicitly referred as AD.

CONTENTS

LIST OF CONTRIBUTORS

Víctor Alonso Troncoso is Professor of Ancient History at the University of La Coruña (Spain) and currently Visiting Research Scholar at ISAW (New York University)
v.alonso.troncoso@udc.es

Edward M. Anson is Professor of History at the University of Arkansas at Little Rock (United States of America)
emanson@ualr.edu

Luis Ballesteros Pastor is Professor of Ancient History at the University of Seville (Spain)
lbpastor@us.es

Elizabeth Baynham is Senior Lecturer in Classics and Ancient History at the University of Newcastle (Australia)
elizabeth.baynham@newcastle.edu.au

Tom Boiy is Post-Doctoral Researcher in Near Eastern Studies at the Catholic University of Leuven (Belgium)
tom.boiy@arts.kuleuven.be

Brian Bosworth is Professor of Classics and Ancient History at Macquarie University, Sydney (Australia)
brian.bosworth@mq.edu.au

Timothy Howe is Associate Professor of History and Ancient Studies at St. Olaf College, Northfield (United States of America)
howe@stolaf.edu

Franca Landucci Gatinnoni is Associate Professor of Ancient Greek History at the Catholic University of Milan (Italy)
franca.landucci@unicatt.it

Alexander Meeus is Post-Doctoral Fellow in Ancient History of the Research Foundation – Flanders (FWO) at the Catholic University of Leuven (Belgium)
alexander.meeus@arts.kuleuven.be

Sabine Müller is Visiting Professor of Ancient History at the University of Siegen and Lecturer in Ancient History at Kiel University (Germany)
mueller@geschichte.uni-siegen.de

Daniel Ogden is Professor of Ancient History at the University of Exeter (United Kingdom) and Research Fellow in the University of South Africa
d.ogden@exeter.ac.uk

Marek Jan Olbrycht is Professor of Ancient History and Oriental Studies at the University of Rzeszów (Poland)
marekolbrycht@wp.pl

Paschalis Paschidis is Senior Researcher at the Institute for Greek and Roman Antiquity of the National Hellenic Research Foundation, Athens (Greece)
paspas@eie.gr

Elisabetta Poddighe is Senior Researcher of Greek History at the University of Cagliari (Italy)
poddighe@unica.it

Frances Pownall is Professor of Classics at the University of Alberta, Edmonton (Canada)
frances.pownall@ualberta.ca

Giuseppe Squillace is Senior Lecturer in Ancient Greek History at the University of Calabria, Rende (Italy)
giuseppesquillace@libero.it

Shane Wallace is Walsh Family Lecturer in Classics and Ancient History at Trinity College, Dublin (Ireland)
shane.wallace@hotmail.co.uk

Pat Wheatley is Senior Lecturer in Classics and Ancient History at the University of Otago, Dunedin (New Zealand)
pat.wheatley@otago.ac.nz

PREFACE

Víctor Alonso Troncoso

This volume contains the revised proceedings of an international symposium on 'The Time of the Diadochi (323–281 BC)', held at the University of La Coruña (Spain), in September 2010. The meeting was the fifth in a regular series of international conferences that began in 2002 at the University of Calgary (Canada), when Waldemar Heckel convened the first symposium. The convener and Lawrence Tritle then edited a selection of papers from the conference, *Crossroads of History: The Age of Alexander* (Claremont, CA 2003). Three years later, Waldemar Heckel renewed the initiative by hosting a second symposium in Calgary, whose proceedings were edited by the convener, along with Lawrence Tritle and Pat Wheatley, under the title *Alexander's Empire: Formulation to Decay* (Claremont, CA 2007). In 2006 the third conference was organized by Pat Wheatley at the University of Otago, Dunedin (New Zealand), the result of which was the volume *Alexander and his Successors: Essays from the Antipodes* (Claremont, CA 2009), edited by the organizer of the symposium and Robert Hannah. The fourth event in this series took place in spring 2008, now four years ago, at Clemson University, South Carolina (USA), sponsored by Elizabeth Carney, who took the responsibility of publishing the proceedings alongside Daniel Ogden: *Philip II and Alexander the Great: Father and Son, Lives and Afterlives* (Oxford 2010). Each symposium, therefore, has produced a publication, thus showing the scientific commitment of both organizers and participants. As I write, another conference, this time on 'Alexander the Great and his Successors: The Art of King and Court', is planned for January 2013 and hosted by Macquaire University and the University of Newcastle (Australia), being the conveners Ken Sheedy, Blanch Menadier and Elizabeth Baynham.

Readers can judge for themselves the quality of each of the proceedings and, in them, of the different papers. For my part, I would like to point out some common features of all these symposia. First, from the outset they have been truly international meetings, not only summoning colleagues from the traditionally leading continents in classical studies, Europe and America, but also attracting researchers from Australia and New Zealand. In that respect, it is also worth observing that in 1997 Brian Bosworth and Elizabeth Baynham hosted a seminal conference on Alexander the Great at the University of Newcastle, with the title *Alexander the Great in Fact and Fiction* (Oxford 2000). If we ask why this genuine international style of our symposia, the answer is easy to supply: Alexander the Great is too universal a phenomenon – like Greek civilisation or canonical literature – to be monopolized by any country or any ideology. Secondly, ever since the series commenced ten years ago, it became clear to the organizers that the chronological frame should not be restricted to the reign of the Macedonian conqueror, but should include the monarchy of his father Philip as well as the time of the Successors, in other words a coherent period of three quarters of a century and at least two generations of rulers. Thirdly, each symposium has differed slightly from the others in focus, or composition, but the traditional research fields have occupied a place in all the conference programmes. I refer to source-critical research, chronography, political and military history, prosopography, or religious studies. At the same time, new thematic interests and approaches have entered our agenda, such as ethnicity, invention of tradition, iconography and the power of images, gender history, Iranian studies, etc. The Successors period has been the chronological frame chosen for the present meeting, this being the first time that one of our symposia has been monographically devoted to the *Diadochenzeit*. Yet, if it is true that we exclude Alexander's lifetime, it is no less so that the Macedonian conqueror remains an immanent presence during these critical years.

This fifth conference was the first to take place in the old continent, and therefore the first to assemble a majority of European delegates. They came from Belgium, Germany, Greece, Ireland, Italy, Poland, Spain, and the United Kingdom. If the Americas contributed to the meeting with scholars from Canada and the United States, Oceania was still present in the persons of two Australian colleagues. In addition, two invited colleagues who at the last minute were unable to attend the conference have agreed to send their papers for inclusion in this volume.

Gratus animus societatis – the motto could also be that of our society of symposiasts, and I do not want to betray it. As the convener of the fifth symposium it is my pleasure to thank the principal sponsors whose generosity made it possible to hold the conference, namely the Spanish Ministry of Science and Innovation, through the medium of the grant *acción complementaria* HAR2009-08390-E/HIST, and the Office of the Pro Vice-Chancellor for Research of La Coruña University, directed by Professor Concepción Herrero López. There are other people who should not be overlooked either. My thanks also go to the contributors themselves, who travelled to this Atlantic *finis terrae* not only to present their own papers, but also to participate actively in the long and vivid discussions that characterized all the working sessions. Clare Litt, publishing director at Oxbow Books (Oxford), deserves mention for her interest in the project and her constant advice. Some postgraduate students were of great assistance with the logistics of the conference, while Alma Díaz Valerio at the Faculty of Humanities was again of invaluable help in dealing with the nightmare of bureaucracy. Moreover, it no longer came as a surprise that my wife, Aurora Lasagabáster Latorre, once again saved me when the symposium attained its true meaning at home. Lastly, I am especially grateful to Professor Edward M. Anson, my co-editor. His superb knowledge of the Diadochi period and his capacity for work have enormously facilitated the preparation of these proceedings.

INTRODUCTION

Edward M. Anson

The papers here presented were with two exceptions delivered at 'The Time of the Diadochi (323–281 BC)' conference held in La Coruña, Spain, from September 9–11, 2010. This conference, organized by Víctor Alonso Troncoso and the faculty of the Humanities of the University of La Coruña, represents the fifth symposium of what is generally and affectionately come to be called by its participants 'the Alexander group'. While the 'group' has a significant percentage of regular attendees, the requirements for membership are not onerous. Thoughtful papers and a willingness to participate in lively discussions are all that is required. At these conferences everyone attends every session and participates in the discussions, which tend to carry over into breaks, lunches, and dinners.

Our conferences and publications typically, and this current collection is certainly no exception, represent a fairly eclectic collection of studies, with the result that this assemblage is organized around four separate, but Diadochan themes: The Sources and their Use; The Struggle for Power among the Diadochi; The Role of the Iranians in the Age of the Diadochi; The Use of Image and Slogan in the Time of the Diadochi. One of the joys of these conferences is that they are reflective of the current trends in the scholarship. These particular papers, while containing a number of what might be called traditional studies, show an emphasis on source criticism, the role of Iranians in the world created by Alexander's conquests, and the propagandistic use of themes, myths, and symbols in the presentation and the appropriation of authority.

The period of the Diadochi relies on a very limited number of narrative sources. One of the major difficulties faced by historians studying the time of the Diadochi, usually defined as beginning with the death of Alexander the Great in 323 and ending with the deaths of the last two Successors in 281, is the dearth of surviving narrative materials. For example, most of our information for the first half of this period comes from Books 18 through 20 of Diodorus of Sicily's universal history, written in the last century of the Roman Republic. This basic narrative is supplemented by the fragments of Byzantine summaries of the second-century AD, *Events after Alexander*, written by Lucius Flavius Arrianus (Arrian), which covers the immediate aftermath of Alexander's death down to early 319. Additional information from the Roman period is provided by the biographers Nepos and Plutarch and the *Strategems* of war collected by Polyaenus.

Marcus Junianius (or Junianus) Justin's, perhaps, late second-century AD, *Epitome* of Pompeius Trogus' universal history, Books 13–17, is the only extant work that presents a continuous narrative of the entire period. Justin's books cover less than thirty pages of Latin text. Given the limited number of available sources and these survivors' rather abbreviated treatment of the period, to paraphrase the words of one of our contributors, Pat Wheatley, we need to take advantage of every scrap of evidence we can find. Our sources, moreover, are not only limited in number, but written long after the events being described and therefore are dependent on other works now lost and seldom referenced by our survivals. Recent scholarship has both postulated the identity of these underlying sources and pointedly insisted that the surviving works are not mere ciphers of the earlier sources. In particular, with respect to the latter point, the importance of understanding the milieu, purposes, contemporary issues, and style of these remaining historians has been emphasized. For example, in the case of our major source for the Diadochi, Diodorus of Sicily, this involves thinking about the politics and culture of the late Roman Republic generally and even that of contemporary Sicily specifically.

In the search for additional materials, Tom Boiy presents an examination of the available cuneiform documents for our period. These have proven most useful in adding to our knowledge of the chronology of the early Hellenistic Age and have filled in a number of the many lacunae that abound in our narrative sources. Pat Wheatley also joins in the effort to expand our knowledge of the Successors through, in his case, a fresh examination of the authorship and historiographical tradition of the so-called *Heidelberg Epitome*, a surviving collection of excerpts from a number of unnamed authors dating from the Byzantine period. While, as Wheatley states, this is an oft cited source, it has escaped a 'thorough going-over' since its original publication in 1914. His paper, 'The *Heidelberg Epitome*: A Neglected Diadoch Source', calls much of the earlier analysis into question.

Three of the studies in this section are devoted to attempts to unravel the source history of our remaining narrative accounts. These extant sources are most often unclear in the attribution of their material. Moreover, other intermediate authors may stand between those original sources and our surviving histories. Franca Landucci Gattinoni argues that the now lost history of Macedonian affairs by Duris of Samos is just such an intermediate source between an earlier favorable Seleucid historian and the narrative of the Third Diadoch War found in Diodorus. Frances Pownall examines the thirty-six extant fragments of this same Duris' Macedonian history and concludes that he was hostile to all of Alexander's Macedonian Successors chiefly on moral grounds. She finds only Eumenes of Cardia, the Greek Diadoch supposedly overwhelmed by Macedonian prejudice, of all of those who contended for power after Alexander's death was viewed favorably.

Timothy Howe reviews the sources regarding Alexander the Great's supposed, self-proclaimed, divinity in light of the political milieu of the period of the Diadochi, asking the question: 'To what extent is Alexander's living divinity an invented tradition?' Howe argues that the Successors attempted to create a tradition of rule through their association of divine kingship and their close connection to the Conqueror, thus legitimizing their own kingships. Consequently, for Howe, Alexander's supposed divinity was part of an evolving history and invented tradition which began during the Diadoch period.

Brian Bosworth focuses on the early first century AD geographer Strabo's commentary on Indian Brahmans and compares his account of a delegation who met with the Roman emperor Augustus to the description regarding Alexander the Great's encounter with them over three centuries earlier, as a means of gaining insights into the Roman geographer's analysis and use of sources. The study in particular examines two immolation accounts from the two separate encounters. The study highlights the complexity of tradition on Alexander, while observing that like so much of the extant material, and all of the narrative accounts, Strabo writes in the political and intellectual context of the Roman Empire. This section concludes with a paper reminding all of us who study this period of the limits that must be placed on our use of sources. Alexander Meeus offers a corrective for what might be unflatteringly called our occasional flights of fantasy in pursuit of narrative. He insists that despite our scarcity of sources our analysis must be based on rigorous logic and scrutiny of what does survive.

The second section of the book includes five studies looking at specific historical issues relating to the Age of the Diadochi. These include my attempt to explain Eumenes of Cardia's strategy in his final battle when he faced not only a formidable opponent in the person of Antigonus Monophthalmus and the real possibility of defeat, but also the risk of assassination by his own allies, if victorious; an analysis by Elizabeth Baynham of the claimed old age of the Argyraspids, Alexander's old infantry guard and the best infantry unit serving in Asia after Alexander's death, these troops were all reportedly in their 60s and 70s, in which she notes that reports of vigorous individuals in their 50s, 60s, 70s, and beyond, occur not only in our sources, but in modern firsthand accounts, and even in a piece of forensic evidence from the fourth century BC; Paschalis Paschidis examines the dating of the awarding of royal titles to Antigonus and his son Demetrius by the Athenians to 307, as declared by Plutarch, and concludes after an analysis of the evidence that Plutarch is in error; Shane Wallace through a study of the career of Adeimantus of Lampsacus examines the role of *philoi,* royal 'friends', as intermediaries between the Hellenistic kings and the Greek cities. These individuals often referred to as 'royal flatterers' were, concludes Wallace, in fact, powerful royal officials whose relationship with their respective monarchs was 'predominantly personal'.

The third section in its overall theme represents a change which has developed in recent years in our perspective on Persia and Persian cultural survivals in the Age of Alexander and the Diadochi. Put simply there has been a conscious effort by many to break away from the Hellenocentric view of our predominantly Greek sources. Where once the decadence of the Achaemenid Empire and the inevitable collapse of Persia before the advance of the Greeks and Macedonians were commonplace, now scholars speak of the vitality, resilience, and continuity of Persian traditions through the reign of Alexander and well into the Hellenistic Age. Here, three papers examine the role of the 'conquered' in the realms that emerged after the death of the great conqueror. In 'Iranians in the Diadochi Period', Marek Jan Olbrycht points out the prominent roles played by Iranians in the administration and military of Alexander and his Successors. Along these same lines Luis Ballesteros Pastor examines the evidence for Iranian continuity in Anatolia and finds that pockets of resistance remained which eventually blossomed into Hellenistic kingdoms ruled by sovereigns proclaiming their direct connection to an Iranian past. In the last study in this group, Sabine Müller tracts a continuation of Iranian influence through an examination of the roles played by certain of the Diadochi's Iranian wives, and in particular that of Apama, the wife of Seleucus and the mother of his heir Antiochus. For Müller, Apama served as a prominent figure cementing Seleucus and his new Asiatic subjects.

In the fourth and final division, the papers are joined by their analysis of the use of varying forms of propaganda. These studies, in particular, represent one of the newer trends in modern studies of the ancient Greek and Roman worlds in general, that is the application of theories and techniques from other disciplines to the explication of events and actions in our field of study. The importance of symbols and ideas has been applied to the study of the ancient world for more than a century, but these studies have been rooted mostly in the pursuit of the origin of these systems of meaning rather than the creation and/or the manipulation of symbols, images, ideals, and myths, as part of contemporary attempts to incline people to particular beliefs and/or actions. In this collection are four studies which in different ways look at ancient attempts to manipulate populations through the use of these various forms of propaganda. Giuseppe Squillace explores the employment of the 'Greek Freedom' motif with respect to the island of Rhodes, connecting similar offerings by Alexander and Ptolemy I to the common theme of freedom, and additionally pointing to the propaganda value for the latter of emphasizing a connection to the former. Likewise, Elisabetta Poddighe examines the use of this same concept of 'Freedom of the Greeks' as a means of manipulating the opinion in the Greek world. In her analysis of Philip III's *Diagramma* of 319, which proclaimed 'the restoration of the governments enjoyed under Philip and Alexander', she examines both the ideology and the symbolic content of the decree, arguing that the proclamation was a repudiation of Antipater's policies and an affirmation of those of Philip II. Consequently, this was a not too subtle attack on the dead regent's son Cassander, the heir to those of his father's actions perceived to be opposed to 'Greek freedom'.

Daniel Ogden investigates the origins of the cult of Agathos Daimon, a *genius loci*, a snake cult associated with the foundation of Alexandria in Egypt and with the conqueror/founder himself, connecting the cult to Ptolemy's transfer of Alexander's body to his Egyptian namesake city. This and other actions are then associated with Ptolemy's attempts to link his kingship with that of Alexander. In the last paper in this section, Víctor Alonso Troncoso shows how the employment of images, in this case elephants, was used to advertise the authority of particular rulers. The author demonstrates that such symbols could be associated with long-standing interpretations, or as in the case of elephants in the Age of the Diadochi, with particular incidents of recent memory in the expectation that the image would both evoke the particular action and also be seen as emblematic of the valor and power of the specific individual.

Let me conclude this introduction with a warm thank you to my co-editor, Professor Víctor Alonso Troncoso, for hosting what proved to be a most enjoyable conference, with our colleague in addition to feasting us most magnificently, even conducting tours for the conferees. These included the oldest still functioning light house in Europe, dating from the time of the emperor Hadrian, and a pilgrimage to the city of Santiago de Compostela, where we spent a most enjoyable day, including a trip onto the roof of the cathedral. I have toured many cathedrals, but have never been escorted onto the roof. I speak for all of the attendees when I again thank our most gracious host and his institution.

THE DIADOCHI HISTORY IN CUNEIFORM DOCUMENTATION

Tom Boiy

The deplorable situation of the sources for the Diadochi period is a well-known fact. Diodorus' books 18–20 of his Universal History form the only history survey that is entirely preserved. Recent studies and discussions have clearly shown that the use of his sources (as far as we know them), methods and chronological framework of this first century compilator were perhaps not always what we hoped for or what we wanted them to be. The aim of this contribution is to see what Babylonia has to offer to add to our knowledge of the Diadochi period.

Worth mentioning in the first place is Berossus, a Babylonian priest who lived in Babylon during Alexander's lifetime and who wrote a history of Babylonia from the beginning until his own time in Greek, the so-called *Babyloniaca* or *Chaldaica* (*FGH* 680 T 1–2). He dedicated his work to the Seleucid king Antiochus I (*FGH* 680 T 2). As an eye-witness he is without doubt a very attractive source, but unfortunately his work is not completely preserved, and the surviving fragments deal with Babylonia's prehistory, with Neo-Babylonian kings and some episodes on the Achaemenid dynasty (especially Cyrus and his conquest of Babylon). The preserved fragments of Berossus' *Babyloniaca* do not deal with the Diadochi period and they add therefore nothing whatsoever to our knowledge of this period (see De Breucker 2010).

There is nothing comparable to Berossus, Diodorus or Greek historiography in cuneiform literature. A first category of Babylonian historiographical works derived from lexical sciences, making lists of related subjects (see e.g. von Soden 1985, 150–51). King lists mentioned all Babylonian kings in their chronological order with their number of regnal years. The entire history was divided into dynasties. Since the Babylonian dating system used the king's regnal years as a central reference point, these king lists obviously served a practical purpose. Although king lists were superfluous in the Seleucid period once the Seleucid era was in use, we still have two king lists from that period that also include the Diadochi period: the Babylon King List Iraq 16 pl. 53 (BKL) and the Uruk King List BaM Beih. 2 88 (UKL). BKL begins with the reign of Alexander the Great and UKL also includes earlier kings (earliest preserved kings date from the Neo-Assyrian period). If we compare the information from both sources, it is clear that they do not give exactly the same historical data:

	UKL	BKL
Philip Arrhidaeus	6	[ ]
Antigonus	6	no king for [ ] years, Antigonus ruled
Alexander IV	not listed	6
Seleucus	31	25

The differences in BKL and UKL are caused by different definitions of a reign and the complicated political situation of the Diadochi period. In BKL a purely legal point of view was adopted: the scribe indicated the period when Antigonus ruled the region as 'kingless' years because Antigonus chose to ignore the regnal years of the official king in the date formulas in favour of his years as *stratēgos*. At the return of Seleucus to Babylonia in 311 the scribe of BKL accepts Alexander the Great's son Alexander IV as Babylonian king: while Alexander IV was indeed theoretically king of his father's empire, he never actually ruled and for all but part of the first year of his life he did not reside in Babylon. The scribe of UKL, however, chose a more pragmatic point of view: the *stratēgos* Antigonus is accepted as effective ruler instead of the titular king Alexander IV and after Seleucus' return the restoration of Alexander IV in the date formulas is ignored in favour of the later dynast and in 311 already de facto ruler Seleucus I. The differences between both lists can therefore be harmonised easily and both are confirmed by the information on the basis of the date formulas of legal and administrative cuneiform tablets from the Diadochi period (Boiy 2007, 93–94).

The chronicles constitute another type of historiographical cuneiform tablets. In the first published edition of all Assyrian and Babylonian chronicles, Grayson (1975a, 22) presumed that there was one continuous series of Babylonian chronicles starting from Nabonassar in the eighth century until the Hellenistic period (the last copy, ABC 13b, dates to Seleucus III).[1] This series includes the famous Chronicle of the Diadochi (ABC 10), but also two other chronicles dealing with the Diadochi period: ABC 11 (BM 32440+32581+32585) on Antiochus I as – according to Babylonian conception – 'crown prince' and ABC 12 (BM 32235 and 32957) on the last years of Seleucus I.

The Chronicle of the Diadochi (BM 34660+36313; ABC 10) is the most informative cuneiform chronicle dealing with the Diadochi period and has been studied regularly. After the editio princeps by Smith (1924, 124–49), several transliterations and translations have appeared.[2] The only autograph copy of the text was published in the editio princeps and Grayson added (hardly readable) photographs. The chronology of the chronicle has been studied intensively together with the chronology of the early Hellenistic period in general.[3] The most urgent desideratum for further study and research of the Diadochi Chronicle now is a new line drawing copy to check the new readings in the recent transliterations and a full and up-to-date historical commentary.[4]

The new online publication *Babylonian Chronicles of the Hellenistic Period* (BCHP) by Finkel and van der Spek (2006) also offers, apart from a new edition of the known chronicles, several new chronicles dating to the Hellenistic period, half of them dating to the Diadochi period:

BCHP 1: Alexander chronicle (BM 36304; as ABC 8 originally dated by Grayson in the Late Achaemenid period; Glassner 1993, 206 redated it because of the appearance of Ḫanû, 'Greeks'; van der Spek recognized Alexander in m*a-lek-sa*)[5]
BCHP 2: Alexander and Arabia (BM 41080)
BCHP 4: Arses and Alexander (BM 36613, published for the first time by Sachs (1977)
BCHP 6: ruin of Esagila (BM 32248+32456+32477+32543 + an unnumbered fragment in the collection 76–11–17; not dated; Antiochus mentioned as prince)
BCHP 7: Antiochus, Bactria and India (BM 32310+32398+32384)[6]
BCHP 8: juniper garden (BM 32266)[7]

Another genre, closely related to historiography, is the so-called 'prophecy' texts. Although these texts use the omen terminology and they pretend to foretell events, they are rather post factum foretelling or *vaticinium ex eventu* (Biggs 1967, 117). There is one example of a Babylonian prophecy dealing with the period of Alexander: the so-called dynastic prophecy (BM 40623; Grayson 1975b, 24–37). The text foretells/describes the reigns of Babylonian kings starting from the Neo-Babylonian period until at least the arrival of Alexander in Babylonia;[8] the rise and fall of each king is mentioned and the number of his regnal years. The end contains a problematic passage mentioning the defeat of Greek troops. Since Darius III obviously never defeated Alexander the Great, several solutions have been proposed for this enigma: an emendation from 'Hanû' into 'Guti' to make it a defeat of Persian troops instead of Greek troops, relating the passage to a different political situation by skipping two decades (which means that it refers to the wars between Antigonus and Seleucus during the Diadochi period) and the change from a *vaticinium ex eventu* into a real prophecy (possibly a warning for Alexander that he might lose all if he does not pay attention to the prediction of the Babylonian astronomers).[9]

There are no royal inscriptions or building inscriptions, an important source for the reconstruction of Mesopotamian political history until that time, preserved from the Diadochi period.[10]

A final genre of historiographical literature are the historical notes at the end of the Astronomical Diaries (AD). The Astronomical Diaries collect daily observations of the sky with special attention for the positions of the moon, for eclipses, for solstices and equinoxes, for the position of the planets and phenomena of Sirius. Apart from the astronomical observations some other topics are also treated at the end of each paragraph: weather conditions, the prices of basic commodities, the level of the River Euphrates in Babylon and some historical notes (see Slotsky 1997, 23–42). These notes provide us with valuable information on the history of Mesopotamia in the first millennium.

The Astronomical Diaries are now available in an accessible edition by Hunger based on a manuscript by the late A. Sachs.[11] The Diadochi period is covered in AD 1 (Sachs and Hunger 1988). Not every single year is represented in the Astronomical Diaries, the passages are often fragmentarily preserved, and, compared to the later periods, the Diadochi period is especially underrepresented: there are a number of diaries from the reign of Alexander the Great, but after the second year of Philip Arrhidaeus not a single diary is preserved for more than a decade. In addition, the historical notes are rather small compared to those from, for instance, the Parthian period. The historical notes not only provide us with valuable information on Babylonia during the Diadochi period, but also the prices of commodities can be used for historical research: the high prices in 309, for instance, clearly demonstrate the hardship of life in Babylon and Babylonia during the years when Antigonus Monophthalmus waged war in Babylonia against Seleucus' troops.[12] In addition, some extra information appears in the enumeration of prices of the month Ayaru (May-June) 325: 'the sale of barley and everything else was cut off in the streets of Babylon' (AD 1-324B 'Obv. 12'–13'). Finally, there sometimes appears a historical note in the middle of the astronomical observations. The most famous example of this technique is the death date of Alexander the Great: AD 1–322B 'Obv.' 8' simply mentions '29: the king died', but this small remark allows us to date Alexander's death on 11 June 323.[13]

Legal and administrative documents are direct witnesses from the Diadochi period itself and are therefore also a potentially important source of information on Babylonia during the period. For the Hellenistic age in general there are only two cities from which a substantial number of cuneiform legal and administrative documents are preserved: the traditional capital Babylon (mainly administrative texts) and the southern centre Uruk (almost exclusively legal documents). While Borsippa, in the neighbourhood of Babylon, provides about one hundred cuneiform documents, other Babylonian towns, such as Cutha, Kish, Nippur, Larsa, Ur and Marad have not left us more than a handful of cuneiform tablets each.

As far as the Diadochi period is concerned, the situation with respect to cuneiform sources is quite similar: a substantial amount of tablets is preserved from Babylon, more or less 100 from Borsippa and a handful from the other Babylonian cities.[14] The only exception appears to be Uruk: not more than 3 documents predate the Seleucid dynasty (305 BC), placing the city in the group of cities that have left us only a handful of documents. Compared to the relative wealth of tablets from Uruk in the later periods this is rather meagre and Uruk is, as far as the number of preserved documents is concerned, surpassed by Borsippa.

If we look at the content of these preserved tablets, there are also differences to be discerned. In Babylon most texts are administrative tablets belonging to the so-called 'Esagil archive' starting in the Late Achaemenid period until the beginning of the Seleucid period (Jursa 2005, 73–74). The majority of these texts are ration lists mentioning temple personnel with the amount of rations provided. In a header (repeated at the end of the reverse) the nature of the ration (barley, date or wool) is explained, the period for which the ration was intended and the person responsible for the rations of that group of personnel. As far as other tablets are concerned, especially ex-votos, donations given to Bēl and Bēltīya to prolong the life of the donor, are famous. These texts often stipulate that the money donated was intended to pay for 'clearing the rubble of the temple Esagil' (Boiy 2004, 110–11).

From Borsippa almost all preserved tablets are part of the so-called 'brewers' archive' (Jursa 2005, 97). They are letter-orders and receipts dealing with the payment of rations and materials to brewers by their paymasters. The earliest texts date to the Late Achaemenid period and the bulk of the tablets originate from the period of Antigonus Monophthalmus and Alexander IV.

The cuneiform tablets from the other Babylonian cities are, as is the case for Uruk during the Hellenistic period, legal tablets dealing with daily transactions such as debt notices, marriage contracts and home sales.

The first and foremost use of legal and administrative documents for the reconstruction of history is the information from the date formulas. Especially for the extremely complicated political and military situation of the early Diadochi period, this first-hand information is an important historical source (for an overview, see Boiy 2007, 22–27). A first caveat is that not all dates mentioned in the cuneiform tablets are real date formulas in the sense that they note the time of writing of the tablet. The date in the heading of the Esagil ration lists for instance mentions the period for which the rations were intended. Therefore no days, but only months (and the year) are registered. A problem with dating these ration lists is that we do not know when exactly they were written: before, during or after the time span for which the rations were meant. Apart from the lack of an indication for the date of composition, there is no verb indicating whether the rations had already been given or were to be given in the (near) future. We have argued elsewhere (Boiy 2011) that, since the text describes a long period for which every individual is named, it is in our view more likely that an exact account of expenses was given and not an estimation of future costs. The letter-orders of the Borsippa brewers' archive do mention a date of composition in the date formula at the end of the text, and in the body of the text the period for which the rations were intended is mentioned. In some cases the time span between these two moments was quite long and, if the name of the ruler is not mentioned in the date formula, this situation has been the cause of different chronological interpretations (for the date of CT 49 50 and its problems, see Boiy 2007, 115–16). Finally, also some year numbers mentioned may seem odd or problematical because rulers did not always start counting from year 1 onwards. For Antigonus Monophthalmus – already an anomaly because he dated in his own name as *stratēgos* of Asia instead of dating in the name of the official king – no first year is attested, probably because he wanted to link his own epoch with the time of death of Philip Arrhidaeus.[15] Another, more famous example is, of course, the beginning of the Seleucid Era: in 305 Seleucus took the royal title and he dropped the name of Alexander IV in the date formulas, but he redated his reign from the moment he returned to Babylonia and took the title *stratēgos* of Asia in 311. Because the date formulas mentioned king Alexander IV from 311 until 306 (partly when Alexander IV was already murdered), the first six years of Seleucus' regnal period are never attested in contemporary date formulas.

A specific dating problem is caused by the legal document BRM 2 51 from Larsa because it mentions the sixth year of an unknown king. The original editor interpreted the name ^{m}*ar-ʾ-si-uq-qa* as king Arsaces and he dated the tablet to the Parthian period, but newly published tablets from the British Museum originating from the same archive make clear that they belong to the Diadochi period (Joannès 2001). A more exact date of this tablet is at present not possible.[16]

Apart from some incidental references to events important for the reconstruction of the political history of Babylonia during the Diadochi period, the content of the legal and administrative tablets inform us especially on the social and economic situation of the Babylonians at that time and their daily lives.

The colophons of literary tablets give the same information as the date formulas of the legal and administrative tablets.[17] Apart from the historiographical literature treated above, there are lexical lists, hymns, incantations, rituals, cultic songs, epics, *omina*, mathematical and astronomical tablets, school texts, etc. preserved from the Hellenistic period. Like the legal and administrative documents, most tablets originate from Babylon and Uruk. In addition to the chronological information preserved in the dates in the colophons, these literary tablets inform us mainly on the religious and intellectual life of the Babylonians during that period.

In Babylon a group of incantation tablets written by a scribe called Tanittu-Bēl/Bēl-ab-uṣur//Ša-nāšišu from the beginning of the Hellenistic period is preserved. Some of these tablets were dated by the colophon to the 13th year of Alexander the Great (Finkel 1991). From Late Achaemenid/Early Hellenistic Uruk we have the so-called 'Iqīšâ-library': astronomical/astrological texts, *omina* and incantations owned by someone called Iqīšâ/Ištar-šum-ereš//Ekur-zakir. The first tablets from this library became known from copies on the antiquities market, published by Thureau-Dangin in TCL 6, and later new texts from the same library were excavated by the German Orient-Gesellschaft in situ in 1969 (Hunger 1970).

Beyond supplying the chronological information, colophons are sometimes much more instructive. TCL 6 38, for instance, a tablet dealing with rituals of the Anu cult and the tasks of the priests during these rituals, has a colophon of not less than eight lines explaining that it is a copy of a text that was stolen by king Nabopolassar (first king of the Neo-Babylonian dynasty, last quarter of the 7th century), that it was found in Elam by the āšipu priest Kidin-Anu of the Ekur-zakir family, who copied it and brought it back to Uruk during the reign of Seleucus and Antiochus (which can only be the coregency of Seleucus I and Antiochus I, 294–281).[18] An āšipu priest called Kidin-Anu of the Ekur-zakir family who lived during the Diadochi period can be retraced (Wallenfels 1994, 29), but the actions described in the colophon are more doubtful. To explain this doubt, a few words on the religious history of Uruk in the first millennium are necessary. During the 7th century the love goddess Ištar was Uruk's patron deity and the cult of Anu was not important yet in Uruk (Beaulieu 2003, 330). It is only during the Achaemenid period that we see Anu taking over from Ištar (see especially Kessler 2004). The information from the colophon of TCL 6 38 therefore rather looks like a propaganda stunt from the Anu priesthood to make its cult look older and more prestigious than it actually was.

Apart from the historical notes in Astronomical Diaries (see above), a lot more astronomical tablets can be used for the reconstruction of the history of the Diadochi period. Several kinds of astronomical tablets furnish chronological information. Especially astronomical texts that supply a year-by-year survey have proved to be extremely useful for the reconstruction of a chronological framework. For the early Hellenistic period, the so-called 'Saros Cycle texts' presenting a year-by-year survey of months during which solar or lunar eclipses could occur, have enabled us to unravel the chronological mysteries (Boiy 2007, 30–31, 77–80). Also astronomical tablets presenting periodically returning phenomena, the so-called goal-year texts (Sachs 1948, 285 and Hunger 2006), can be handy to link some year date from the early Hellenistic period in a fixed and known relation to a year from the Seleucid era (Boiy 2007, 28–30).

The classical historiographical tradition, defective though it is, remains the main source for a more or less continuous reconstruction of the history of the Diadochi period. The cuneiform sources mainly add to a better knowledge of the chronology of events, contribute some details and fill a few of the numerous lacunas.

Bibliography

Beaulieu, P. (2003) *The Pantheon of Uruk during the Neo-Babylonian Period*. Leiden.

Beloch, K. J. (1927) *Griechische Geschichte*. IV.2. Berlin-Leipzig.

Biggs, R. D. (1967) More Babylonian 'Prophecies', *Iraq* 29, 117–32.

Boiy, T. (2001) Dating Problems in Cuneiform Tablets concerning the Reign of Antigonus Monophthalmus, *Journal of the American Oriental Society* 121, 645–49.

Boiy, T. (2004) *Late Achaemenid and Hellenistic Babylon*. Leuven.

Boiy, T. (2007) *Between High and Low. A Chronology of the Early Hellenistic Period*. Frankfurt.

Boiy, T. (2009) Date Formulas in Cuneiform Tablets and Antigonus Monophthalmus, again, *Journal of the American Oriental Society* 129, 467–76.

Boiy, T. (2010) Royal and Satrapal Armies in Babylonia during the Second Diadoch War. The Chronicle of the Successors on the Events during the Seventh Year of Philip Arrhidaeus (= 317/6 BC), *Journal of Hellenic Studies* 130, 1–13.

Boiy, T. (2010a) 8.1. An Inscription of Antiochus I (Seleucid King, First Half of the Third Century BC). In M. J. Boda and J. R. Novotny (eds) *From the Foundations to the Crenellations: Essays on Temple Building in the Ancient Near East and Hebrew Bible*, 473, Münster.

Boiy, T. (2010b) 8.2. An Inscription of Anu-uballiṭ (Nikarchos) (Governor of Uruk, Middle of the Third Century BC). In M. J. Boda and J. R. Novotny (eds) *From the Foundations to the Crenellations: Essays on Temple Building in the Ancient Near East and Hebrew Bible*, 473, Münster.

Boiy, T. (2010c) 8.3. An Inscription of Anu-uballiṭ (Kephalon) (Governor of Uruk, End of the Third Century BC). In M. J. Boda and J. R. Novotny (eds) *From the Foundations to the Crenellations: Essays on Temple Building in the Ancient Near East and Hebrew Bible*, 474, Münster.

Boiy, T. (2011) The Reigns of the Seleucid Kings according to the Babylon King List, *Journal of Ancient Near Eastern Studies* (in print).

De Breucker, G. (2010) Berossos of Babylon (680). In I. Worthington (ed.) *Brill's New Jacoby*. Available at: http://www.brillonline.nl/subscriber/uid=2017/entry?entry= bnj_a680 [Accessed November 4, 2010].

Del Monte, G. F. (1997) *Testi Dalla Babilonia Ellenistica*. Pisa.

Depuydt, L. (1997) The Time of Death of Alexander the Great: 11 June 323 BC (-322), ca. 4:00–5:00 PM, *Welt des Orients* 28, 117–35.

Errington, R. M. (1970) From Babylon to Triparadeisos: 323–320 BC, *Journal of Hellenic Studies* 90, 49–77.

Finkel, I. L. (1991) Muššu'u, Qutāru, and the Scribe Tanittu-Bēl, *Aula Orientalis* 9, 91–104.

Finkel, I. L. and R. J. van der Spek (2006) Babylonian Chronicles of the Hellenistic Period, Available at: http://www.livius.org/cg-cm/chronicles/chron00.html [Accessed November 4, 2010].

Glassner, J. (1993) *Chroniques mésopotamiennes*. Paris.

Glassner, J. (2005) *Mesopotamian Chronicles*. Atlanta.

Grayson, A. K. (1975a) *Assyrian and Babylonian Chronicles*. Locust Valley, NY.

Grayson, A. K. (1975b) *Babylonian Historical-Literary Texts*. Toronto and Buffalo.

Hunger, H. (1968) *Babylonische und Assyrische Kolophone*. Kevelaer.

Hunger, H. (1970) Die Tafeln des Iqišâ, *Welt des Orients* 6, 163–65.

Hunger, H. (2006) *Astronomical Diaries and Related Texts from Babylonia VI*. Vienna.

Joannès, F. (2001) Les débuts de l'époque hellénistique à Larsa. In C. Breniquet and C. Kepinski (eds) *Études mésopotamiennes. Recueil de textes offert à Jean-Louis Huot*, 249–64, Paris.

Jursa, M. (2005) *Neo-Babylonian Legal and Administrative Documents: Typology, Contents, and Archives*. Münster.

Kessler, K. (2004) Urukäische Familien versus babylonische Familien. Die Namengebung in Uruk, die Degradierung der Kulte von Eanna und der Aufstieg des Gottes Anu, *Altorientalische Forschungen* 31, 237–62.

Linssen, M. J. H. (2004) *The Cults of Uruk and Babylon: The Temple Ritual Texts as Evidence for Hellenistic Cult Practises*. Leiden.

Manni, E. (1949) Tre note di cronologia ellenistica, *Atti della Academia Nazionale dei Lincei. Rendiconti. Classe di Scienza morale, storiche e filologiche* 8, 53–85.

Oelsner, J. (2003) Zur Datierung von BRM 2,51, *Nouvelles Assyriologiques Brèves et Utilitaires* 2003 no. 83.

Otto, W. (1925) Die Bedeutung der von Sidney Smith, Babylonian historical texts veröffentlichten Diadochenchronik, *Sitzungsberichte der Bayerischen Akademie der Wissenschaften. Philosophisch-philologische und historische Klasse*, Schlußheft, 9–12.

Renger, J. (1980–1983) Königsinschriften B. Akkadisch, *Reallexikon der Assyriologie* 7, 65–77.

Sachs, A. (1948) A Classification of the Babylonian Astronomical Tablets of the Seleucid Period, *Journal of Cuneiform Studies* 2, 271–90.

Sachs, A. (1977) Achaemenid Royal Names in Babylonian Astronomical Texts, *American Journal of Ancient History* 2, 129–47.

Sachs, A. and H. Hunger (1988) *Astronomical Diaries and Related Texts from Babylonia I*. Vienna.

Sachs, A. and H. Hunger (1989) *Astronomical Diaries and Related Texts from Babylonia II*. Vienna.

Sachs, A. and H. Hunger (1996) *Astronomical Diaries and Related Texts from Babylonia III*. Vienna.

Sherwin-White, S. (1991) Aspects of Seleucid Royal Ideology: The Cylinder of Antiochus I from Borsippa, *Journal of Hellenic Studies* 111, 71–86.

Slotsky, A. L. (1997) *The Bourse of Babylon. Market Quotations in the Astronomical Diaries of Babylonia*. Bethesda.

Smith, S. (1924) *Babylonian Historical Texts Relating to the Capture and Downfall of Babylon*. London.

van der Spek, R. J. (2000) The Effect of War on the Prices of Barley and Agricultural Land in Hellenistic Babylonia. In J. Andreau, P. Briant and R. Descat (eds) *Économie antique. La guerre dans les économies*, 293–313, Saint-Bertrand-de-Comminges.

van der Spek, R. J. (2003) Darius III, Alexander the Great and Babylonian Scholarship. In W. Henkelman and A. Kuhrt (eds) *A Persian Perspective. Essays in Memory of Heleen Sancisi-Weerdenburg*, 289–346, Leiden.

Von Soden, W. (1985) *Einführung in die Altorientalistik*. Darmstadt.

Wallenfels, R. (1994) *Uruk: Hellenistic Seal Impressions in the Yale Babylonian Collection*. Mainz.

Wiseman, D. J. (1985) *Nebuchadrezzar and Babylon*. Oxford.

Notes

1 Caroline Waerzeggers presented the paper 'The Babylonian Chronicles Reconsidered' at the Rencontre Assyriologique Internationale in July 2010 in Barcelona, where she studied the provenance of the tablets (all texts are at present preserved in the British Museum). On the basis of the entry numbers and the British Museum collections, she could prove that there are actually two traditions: one from Borsippa, with the tablets describing the Neo-Babylonian and first half of the Achaemenid period, and one from Babylon, with the tablets describing the Late Achaemenid and Hellenistic period. It is therefore safe to conclude that all cuneiform chronicles dealing with the Diadochi period originate from Babylon.

2 See Grayson 1975a, 115–19; Glassner 1993, 207–09; 2005, 242–46; Del Monte 1997, 193–94; Finkel and van der Spek 2006. A preliminary online edition of all Babylonian chronicles of the Hellenistic period (BCHP). In this edition they added an additional small fragment (BM 35930) that might have been a part of the third column of the Diadochi Chronicle dealing with Seleucus' return to Babylonia.

3 The original interpretation of the chronology and its implication by Smith 1924, 126–29 were heavily criticized by Beloch 1927, 616–17 and further adapted by Otto 1925. The chronicle played an important role in the genesis of the so-called 'Low Chronology' by Manni 1949 and Errington 1970. For a full *status quaestionis* of the chronology of the early Hellenistic period and the role the Diadochi Chronicle played in this research, see Boiy 2007, 111–29.

4 See Boiy 2010 for a full historical commentary on the passage Obv. 33–37 dealing with the seventh year of Philip Arrhidaeus. This work is needed for the whole chronicle.

5 See the commentary on l. 3' in http://www.livius.org/cg-cm/chronicles/bchp-alexander /alexander_03.html.

6 BM 32310 was already published as a chronicle fragment of the Seleucid period (ABC 13a, Grayson 1975a, 124). It was joined with BM 32398 and 32384 by Finkel and interpreted by Finkel and van der Spek 2006 as a text dealing with prince Antiochus I. Antiochus is mentioned in Rev.' 10' (partly broken, his title is not preserved) and king Seleucus in Obv. 13'. The title prince is not mentioned (the editors reconstruct it in the lacuna of Obv. 5'), but the editors refer to the same crude handwriting of the other tablets concerning the prince (ABC 11 and BCHP 8).

7 A prince is mentioned and because the script has a resemblance with the other tablets dealing with the prince (ABC 11, BCHP 6 and 7) it is interpreted by Finkel and van der Spek 2006 as belonging to the same group.

8 Most commentators agree that Nabopolassar, the founder of the Neo-Babylonian dynasty, is the first king who was described in the Dynastic Prophecy, but also Nebuchadnezzar has been suggested (Wiseman 1985, 96).

9 For a full commentary and survey of opinions, see van der Spek 2003, 311–32.

10 See Renger 1980–1983, 70–71. For the entire Hellenistic period the number of royal inscriptions and building inscriptions is very restricted: one royal cylinder from Borsippa dating from the period immediately following the Diadochi period (Antiochus I, 281–261; V R 66; see Sherwin-White 1991

and Boiy 2010a) and a few building inscriptions from Hellenistic Uruk (middle and end of the third century; YOS I 52 and WVDOG 51 pl. 108; see Boiy 2010b and 2010c).

11 Sachs and Hunger 1988, 1989 and 1996. Each text is indicated with a number that gives the (astronomical) year treated in the text. The astronomical year reckoning differs one year from the historical year reckoning BC (-1 = 2 BC) because, contrary to the historical era, the astronomical era uses the year 0. An additional complication is the use of the Babylonian year, a luni-solar calendar starting in spring, in the edition of the Astronomical Diaries. This means that events mentioned in for instance AD 1–322 must be dated between spring 323 and spring 322.

12 AD 1–308 Obv.’ 17 and ‘Rev. 6’ and 15’; see van der Spek 2000.

13 The Babylonian day 29 Ayaru started the evening of 10 June, but if Alexander had died during the night of 10/11 June, the passage in the astronomical observations would have been ‘night of 29: the king died’. For a more detailed study of the moment of Alexander’s death, see Depuydt 1997.

14 This means that from Cutha, Kish, Nippur, Larsa, Ur and Borsippa most Hellenistic tablets that are preserved date from the Diadochi period and that for later periods we are almost exclusively dependant on Babylon and Uruk.

15 For more information on the date formulas naming Antigonus Monophthalmus, see Boiy 2001 and 2009.

16 Oelsner 2003 proposed to read Arrhidaeus in ^{m}*ar-ʾ-si-uq-qa*, but this theory is untenable: the second part of the name cannot be interpreted as Arrhidaeus and Philip Arrhidaeus was always indicated with his dynastic names in date formulas. No other known royal name can at present be linked with the reading ^{m}*ar-ʾ-si-uq-qa*. For a more detailed description of tablet’s date, see Boiy 2007, 26.

17 For an overview of colophons of literary cuneiform tablets in Mesopotamia in general, see Hunger 1968.

18 The copy itself is not dated in the colophon. Because the name of the scribe (Šamaš-ēṭir/Ina-qibīt-Anu/Šipqāt-Anu//Ekur-zakir) is mentioned however, we know that the copy has to be dated at least a century later than the copy made in Elam according to the colophon. The scribe is known as the scribe of several other literary cuneiform tablets, some of which are dated 118 SE, and as the scribe of some legal texts dated between 119 SE and 150 SE (see Linssen 2004, 172).

THE *HEIDELBERG EPITOME*: A NEGLECTED DIADOCH SOURCE

Pat Wheatley

Introduction

I first became curious about the *Heidelberg Epitome* because of its relative inaccessibility and because (aside from Felix Jacoby's short commentary accompanying *Die Fragmente der griechischen Historiker* [*FGH*] 155), it had not been the subject of any sort of study to my knowledge since Georg Bauer's inaugural-dissertation, *Die Heidelberger Epitome. Eine Quelle zur Diadochengeschichte*, presented at Leipzig in 1914. It seemed extraordinary to me that, nearly a century later when every scrap and fragment pertaining to the Successors seems to have received a thorough going-over, no attention at all had been paid to this document. My curiosity was further piqued when I realised that, although no-one paid any *direct* attention to it, the *Heidelberg Epitome* has been cited almost continually by researchers over the decades.[1] It is especially cited where scholars want to glean just one more shred of source evidence for a matter they are dealing with, or to toss one more gram of evidence onto the scales in promoting a tricky solution to a problem. Finally, my curiosity turned practically to astonishment when I looked more closely at Bauer's dissertation, the sole extensive work of analysis on the *Epitome*, and realised that his historiographical analysis of it is quite contrived and, I think, misleading: his historical asseverations are quite shaky, and his attempts to reify the document by defending some of the patent errors in it are strained and implausible.

This paper, therefore, will first discuss the authorship and the historiographic tradition behind the *Epitome*, and attempt some tentative speculations on its pedigree, in the process perhaps remedying some of Bauer's misapprehensions. Following this, I shall make some specific historical comments on a few entries in the *Epitome* to illustrate my historiographic musings.

Text and Translation

[Text from F. Jacoby, *FGH* 155; trans. J. C. Yardley, 2011, mod.][2]

1.

(1) ὅτι Ἀλεξάνδρου τελευτήσαντος ἐναπελείφθησαν αἱ γυναῖκες αὐτοῦ καὶ παῖς ἀτελής, ὃν ἐγέννησεν ἐκ τῆς Ῥωξάνης. στασιαζόντων δὲ τῶν περὶ αὐτὸν περὶ τῆς βασιλείας ἐτάχθη βασιλεύειν ὁ ὁμοπάτριος ἀδελφὸς Ἀλεξάνδρου ὁ Ἀρριδαῖος,

ὁ καὶ Φίλιππος ὕστερον ὀνομασθείς, μέχρις οὗ φθάσηι εἰς ἀνήκουσαν ἡλικίαν ὁ Ἀλεξάνδρου παῖς. (2) ἐπεὶ δὲ ἦν νωθρὸς ὁ Ἀρριδαῖος, ἔτι δὲ καὶ ἐπιληπτικός, ἡιρέθη ἐπίτροπος καὶ ἐπιμελητὴς τῶν βασιλικῶν πραγμάτων ὁ Περδίκκας, ὧι δέδωκεν ὁ Ἀλέξανδρος τελευτῶν τὸν ἑαυτοῦ δακτύλιον ὡς πιστοτέρωι τῶν ἄλλων στρατηγῶν. (3) ὃς συνδιασκεψάμενος δέδωκεν ἑκάστωι στρατηγῶι σατραπείαν διεξάγειν, μερίσας ἁπάσας οὔσας πλείους τῶν κδ. ἀπελθόντες δὲ οὕτως εἰς τὰς ὁρισθείσας ἑκάστωι σατραπείας ἤρξαντο ὑπερβάθμιον τείνειν πόδα ὡς ἠδύνατο ἕκαστος. ὅθεν μεγάλας δυνάμεις λαβὼν ὁ Περδίκκας ἀπῆλθεν εἰς Αἴγυπτον πολεμήσων Πτολεμαίωι. ἔνθα καὶ ἐπιβουλευθεὶς ἐφονεύθη ὑπὸ τῶν ἑαυτοῦ οἰκείων. (4) εἶτα διεδέξατο τὴν ἐπιμέλειαν τῶν βασιλέων ὁ Ἀντίπατρος, ὃς καὶ αὐτὸς συνδιασκεψάμενος ἐνήλλαξε τὰς δοθείσας παρὰ τοῦ Περδίκκου σατραπείας ἄλλην ἄλλωι δούς, πλὴν Πτολεμαίου καὶ Λυσιμάχου· τούτους γὰρ οὐκ ἠδυνήθη μεταστῆσαι. δέδωκε δὲ ἄλλοις μὲν ἄλλας, Ἀντιγόνωι δὲ τὴν Σουσιανὴν σατραπείαν, Σελεύκωι δὲ τὴν τῆς Βαβυλῶνος· τὸν δὲ ἑαυτοῦ υἱὸν Κάσανδρον ἀπέδειξε χιλίαρχον. (5) εἶτα μετὰ καιρὸν τελευτήσαντος καὶ τοῦ Ἀντιπάτρου διεδέξατο τὴν ἐπιτροπὴν καὶ ἐπιμέλειαν τῶν βασιλικῶν πραγμάτων ὁ Πολυσπέρχων ἐφ' οὗ ἡ Ὀλυμπιὰς ἐδολοφόνησε τὸν Ἀρριδαῖον καὶ τὴν γυναῖκα αὐτοῦ Εὐρυδίκην. (6) εἶτα ὁ Κάσανδρος μισθωσάμενός τινας τῶν βασιλικῶν διακόνων ἐδολοφόνησε τήν τε Ὀλυμπιάδα καὶ Ῥωξάνην καὶ τὸν υἱὸν αὐτῆς τὸν Ἀλέξανδρον τὸν υἱὸν Ἀλεξάνδρου, ὃς ἔμελλεν εἶναι διάδοχος τῆς ὅλης βασιλείας. ἐγένετο δὲ ταῦτα ἐν Μακεδονίαι [[τῆς Ὀλυμπιάδος τῆς μητρὸς Ἀλεξάνδρου]]. (7) ἐντεῦθεν σύγχυσις ἐγένετο τῶν σατραπειῶν, καὶ ἐπεβούλευον ἄλλοι ἄλλοις καὶ προσετίθουν ταῖς ἑαυτῶν καὶ μείζονας περιεβάλλοντο δυνάμεις οἱ πανουργότεροι καὶ ἐφόνευον τοὺς ἀσθενεστέρους. ἐμεγαλύνθη δὲ ὑπὲρ τοὺς πολλοὺς ὁ Ἀντίγονος μετὰ τοῦ αὐτοῦ υἱοῦ τοῦ Πολιορκητοῦ Δημητρίου. διὸ καὶ ὠνόμασεν ἑαυτὸν βασιλέα καὶ ἐφόρεσε διάδημα. ἰδόντες δὲ καὶ οἱ ἕτεροι, ὅσοι οὐκ ἠλαττοῦντο αὐτοῦ, ἐφόρεσαν κἀκεῖνοι διάδημα καὶ ὠνόμασαν ἑαυτοὺς βασιλεῖς, ὅ τε Πτολεμαῖος ἐν Αἰγύπτωι καὶ Συρίαι καὶ ὁ Λυσίμαχος ἐν Θράικηι καὶ ὁ Σέλευκος ἐν Βαβυλῶνι, ὃς ἀποθανόντος Ἀντιγόνου ἦρξε πάσης Ἀσίας· καὶ κατὰ διαδοχὴν οἱ αὐτοῦ υἱοί.

1.2 πιστοτέρον MS. 1.4 Ἀντιγόνωι is an error for Ἀντιγένει. 1.5 Following 'Polyperchon' is a deletion of some 28 letters. Over it, in the same hand, is the following: ἐφ' οὗ ἡ Ὀλυμπιὰς ἐδολοφόνησε τὸν Ἀρριδαῖον καὶ τὴν γυναῖκα αὐτοῦ Εὐρυδίκην, 'During his rule Olympias murdered Arrhidaeus and his wife, Eurydice'. 1.6 Following 'royal servants' there are about 11 letters erased. Over them the same hand has noted: 'he killed Olympias and...'; Following 'in Macedonia' there is a lacuna of eight letters. 'Of Olympias, mother of Alexander' is crossed out in the text.

(1) How, on Alexander's death, his wives were left behind as well as the - as yet unborn - child he had with Rhoxane. There ensued a dispute amongst his men regarding the kingship, and it was decided that Arrhidaeus, Alexander's brother by the same father - Arrhidaeus was also later given the name 'Philip' - should have the throne until Alexander's son came of age. (2) Arrhidaeus was slow-witted, and he was also an epileptic; and so a guardian and manager of the king's affairs was chosen – Perdiccas, to whom Alexander on his death-bed gave his ring as being the most loyal of his

officers. (3) After due consideration, Perdiccas gave each of the officers a satrapy to administer, distributing all the satrapies amongst them, a total of more than 24. After departing for the satrapies they had each been assigned, they all began to overstep their boundaries as much as they could. And so Perdiccas, having thus acquired great power, went off to Egypt to make war on Ptolemy. But there he became the target of a conspiracy and was assassinated by his own subjects. (4) Antipater then succeeded to the administration of royal affairs, and he, after also giving the matter due consideration, changed the satrapies assigned by Perdiccas, giving each officer a different one, except in the case of Ptolemy and Lysimachus, whom he could not remove. He did, however, make changes in the distribution of the others, giving the satrapy of Susiana to Antigonus, and that of Babylon to Seleucus, while he also appointed his own son Cassander to a chiliarchy. (5) Then, later on, when Antipater also died, it was Polyperchon who succeeded to the stewardship and management of the king's affairs. During his rule Olympias murdered Arrhidaeus and his wife, Eurydice. (6) Then Cassander bribed some of the royal servants ... Rhoxane and her son Alexander, the son of Alexander, who was going to succeed to the whole realm. These events took place in Macedonia ... [[of Olympias, mother of Alexander]]. (7) There followed chaos in the satrapies, with rulers plotting against each other and adding to their own territories, and with the more unconscionable of them surrounding themselves with great forces and murdering the weaker satraps. Antigonus - and, along with him, his son Demetrius Poliorcetes - gained ascendancy over most of them. Accordingly, he called himself 'king' and wore a diadem. When the others who were not weaker than he was saw this, they too wore a diadem and called themselves kings. These were Ptolemy in Egypt and Syria, Lysimachus in Thrace, and Seleucus in Babylon. (Seleucus ruled all of Asia after Antigonus' death, as did his sons when they succeeded him).

2.

(1) ὅτι τὸ σῶμα τοῦ Ἀλεξάνδρου μετὰ <τὸν> θάνατον κατήγαγον οἱ Μακεδόνες εἰς Ἀλεξάνδρειαν ἐκ Βαβυλῶνος, κοσμήσαντες αὐτὸ πάνυ πολυτελῶς καὶ πλείστου χρυσοῦ καὶ ἀργύρου περιθέντες ἀναλώματα καὶ καλλωπισμόν· κατήγαγον δὲ μετὰ πολλῆς καὶ πεπληθυσμένης δορυφορίας. (2) εἶτα ἐκεῖθεν διεβίβασαν εἰς Μακεδονίαν τὴν Ῥωξάνην μετὰ τοῦ σὺν Ἀλεξάνδρωι γενομένου αὐτῆι παιδὸς ὀνομαζομένου Ἀλεξάνδρου καὶ αὐτοῦ. διεβίβασαν δὲ καὶ Φίλιππον τὸν Ἀρριδαῖον, ὃς βασιλεύσας ὑπὸ ἐπιτρόποις ἔτη ς′ καὶ μῆνας δ′ ἐφονεύθη μετὰ τῆς γυναικὸς αὐτοῦ Εὐρυδίκης ἀπηνῶς παρὰ τῆς [[Κλεοπάτρας]] μητρυιᾶς αὐτοῦ τῆς Ὀλυμπιάδος. (3) ὕστερον δὲ μετὰ καιρὸν ὀλίγον ἐφονεύθη καὶ αὐτὴ ἡ Ὀλυμπιὰς σὺν τῆι νύμφηι Ῥωξάνηι καὶ τῶι ἐγγόνωι Ἀλεξάνδρωι ἀπηνῶς παρὰ τοῦ υἱοῦ τοῦ Ἀντιπάτρου τοῦ Κασάνδρου. (4) ὃς Κάσανδρος μετὰ τοὺς τοιούτους φόνους ἔγημε τὴν Θεσσαλονίκην τὴν ὁμοπάτριον ἀδελφὴν τοῦ μεγάλου Ἀλεξάνδρου. ἥτις Θεσσαλονίκη ἔκτισεν ὕστερον τὴν Θεσσαλονίκην· ὁ δὲ ἀνὴρ αὐτῆς ὁ Κάσανδρος ἔκτισεν τὴν Κασάνδρειαν.

2.1 τὸν Reitzenstein; δοφυφορίας Jacoby 2.2 Κλεοπάτρας is crossed out. 2.3 Ρωξάνηι Jacoby.

(1) How the Macedonians, after his death, took Alexander's corpse from Babylon to Alexandria, having decked it out in a very costly manner and set around it a great deal of gold and silver as a lavish form of adornment; and how they escorted it with a large and numerous retinue of guards. (2) Then they conveyed Rhoxane to Macedonia along with the son that she had with Alexander, whose name was also Alexander. They also conveyed there Philip Arrhidaeus who, after ruling through trustees for six years and four months, was cruelly murdered, along with his wife Eurydice, by his stepmother Olympias. (3) A short time afterwards Olympias herself was also cruelly murdered (and with her Alexander's wife Rhoxane and Olympias' grandson Alexander) by Antipater's son, Cassander. (4) After such horrific murders Cassander married Thessalonice, who was the sister of Alexander the Great, born of the same father. This Thessalonice later founded Thessalonica, and her husband Cassander founded Cassandreia.

3.

(1) ὅτι ὁ Εὐμένης σοφὸς ὢν ἐκ τῶν στρατηγῶν καὶ διαδόχων Ἀλεξάνδρου ἐτήρησε στοργὴν ἀδολωτάτην πρὸς τὸν Ἀλέξανδρον καὶ τεθνεῶτα, καὶ ἐπολέμησεν πολλάκις πρὸς τοὺς ἐπεμβαίνοντας τοῖς βασιλικοῖς πράγμασι, καὶ ἐνίκησε μεγάλους πολέμους καὶ στρατηγοὺς μεγάλους ἐκ τῶν Μακεδόνων. (2) εἶτα ἐπεὶ ὁ Ἀντίγονος πλεονεκτῶν καὶ αὐξανόμενος ἐβούλετο νοσφίζεσθαι καὶ τὸ τῆς βασιλείας ὄνομα, ἐδεήθησαν οἱ βασιλεῖς τοῦ Εὐμένους εἰς βοήθειαν ἥ τε Ὀλυμπιὰς καὶ ὁ Ἀρριδαῖος ὁ Φίλιππος καὶ ἡ Ῥωξάνη διὰ γραμμάτων βασιλικῶν. ὃς καὶ ἐπικαμφθεὶς ταῖς ἐκείνων δεήσεσιν ἀνῆλθεν εἰς τὰς ἐπέκεινα τῆς Βαβυλωνίας σατραπείας, καὶ συναγαγὼν μεγάλας ἐκεῖθεν δυνάμεις ἐπολέμησε τῶι Ἀντιγόνωι. καὶ δὶς καὶ τρὶς καὶ νενίκηκε, τάχα δ' ἂν καὶ ἐς τὸ παντελὲς ἠφάνιζεν, εἰ μή τινες τῶν περὶ αὐτὸν φίλων ἐπιβουλεύσαντες συνέλαβον καὶ δεδώκασι τῶι Ἀντιγόνωι. τούτου δὲ γενομένου ηὐξήθη ἐς μέγιστον ὁ Ἀντίγονος καὶ ἦν τοῖς ὅλοις ἀπρόσμαχος.

3.2 ἀριδαῖος MS.

(1) How, of the generals and successors of Alexander, Eumenes, who was a wise man, maintained genuine affection for Alexander even after his death; how he fought many wars against those who rode roughshod over the king's settlements; and how he was victorious in some great wars and over great generals of the Macedonians. (2) Then, when Antigonus became greedy and grew in strength, and wanted to appropriate for himself the royal prerogative, the Royal family - Olympias, Philip Arrhidaeus and Rhoxane - asked Eumenes by means of court dispatches to come to their aid. Swayed by their pleas, Eumenes marched inland to the satrapies that lay beyond Babylonia, where, marshalling great forces from the area, he fought a war with Antigonus. He defeated him two or three times, and would soon have done away with him altogether had not some of the friends who were with him plotted against him, seized him and surrendered him to Antigonus. When this happened, Antigonus rose to the apex of his power and was irresistible to everybody.

4.

ὅτι νικήσας, ὡς εἴρηται, ὁ Πτολεμαῖος ἐν Αἰγύπτωι τὸν Περδίκκαν ἔλαβε τὰ αὐτοῦ στρατεύματα ὅσα ἤθελεν, ἔλαβε δὲ καὶ τὴν αὐτοῦ γυναῖκα Κλεοπάτραν τὴν ὁμοπάτριον ἀδελφὴν τοῦ μεγάλου Ἀλεξάνδρου καὶ εἶχεν αὐτὴν εἰς γάμου κοινωνίαν σὺν ταῖς ἄλλαις αὐτοῦ γυναιξίν. ἦν δὲ ἡ Κλεοπάτρα αὕτη θυγάτηρ μὲν τοῦ Φιλίππου, ἀλλ' ἐξ ἄλλης γυναικός, Κλεοπάτρας κἀκείνης λεγομένης.

4. the number 4 is written in paler ink; ἤθελεν above ἔχρηζε.

How Ptolemy, after defeating Perdiccas in Egypt (as has been recounted), took as much of Perdiccas' troops as he wanted, and also took as his wife Cleopatra (Alexander the Great's sister, by the same father) and kept her married to him along with his other wives. Cleopatra was Philip's daughter, but by another woman, she too called Cleopatra.

Authorship

The *Heidelberg Epitome* comprises four excerpts concerning Diadoch history contained in Codex Palatinus Graecus 129.[3] The complete codex runs to 141 pages and contains numerous excerpts of other authors made by a Byzantine scholar for private use. Various additions to the main text appear in the margin or leaf of the manuscript sometimes in the same handwriting, but at other times in different handwriting (see some of the notes to the Greek text, taken mainly from Jacoby). It seems likely, then, that the original epitomator either was assisted by another scribe, or his work was supplemented by a later writer (Reitzenstein 1904, 311). The purpose of the whole manuscript is unclear, and the order and content of all the excerpts do not conform to any coherent plan. Codex Palatinus Graecus 129 was discovered in the late 19th century by Max Treu, who published excerpts from the codex containing collections of Greek proverbs (Treu 1889, 193–201). The codex had been held at the Bibliotheca Palatina, the Palatinate Library of Heidelberg, since the 16th century, but little is known about the author. One should stress that as a collection of short snippets of Diadoch history made for private reading or study (and perhaps even edited by another writer), the text's quality is clearly not of the same order as other sources for events after Alexander's death.

The four excerpts now known as the *Heidelberg Epitome* begin on sheet 137 and are preceded by text from Josephus. The first edition of the text was published in a collection by Richard Reitzenstein in 1904 in an essay about the *Alexander Romance* (308–15), but the epitome was initially thought to contain little material of any real historical value since some peculiar traditions in it pointed to a relationship with the *Alexander Romance* itself. It was in fact Reitzenstein who coined the name *Heidelberg Epitome*. Bauer also consulted the manuscript and produced an edition in his dissertation (2–4), but did not alter the text or change Reitzenstein's earlier reading. Felix Jacoby subsequently reproduced the text in *FGH* 155, with minor changes in the critical apparatus.

Bauer concluded (92–101) that a Byzantine writer produced the epitome in order to summarise historical information about the Diadoch period, and in particular to discuss the history of Alexander's empire after his death until the formation of independent kingdoms. The author was therefore a Byzantine epitomator who had access to a wealth of ancient sources mainly through earlier Byzantine collections and epitomes, which he probably used for his excerpts in the *Heidelberg Epitome*.[4]

Important evidence for the date when the *Epitome* was made can be found by examination of other authors represented in the codex. Treu made a list of 74 authors he could detect in Codex Palatinus Graecus 129 in the 19th century, ranging chronologically from the 6th century BC (Theognis, Aeschylus) through the 12th century (Eustathius, Constantine Manasses).[5] The latest Byzantine writers cited are Theodoros Metochites (1270–1332) and Manuel Philes (1275–1345), and this provides a *terminus post quem* for authorship of the document. Therefore, Reitzenstein (1904, 311) suggested that the codex was written towards the end of the 13th century, but the manuscript itself has been dated on paleographical grounds to about the middle of the 15th century by Victor Emil Gardthausen, the 19th century German palaeographer, and this conclusion was followed by Bauer (1914, 96–97).

As to the source of the Heidelberg excerpts on Diadoch history, Bauer also concluded that the Greek of the sources was essentially the *koine* - in his own words 'der Wortschatz von Diodor und Polybios' (1914, 98). Thus the post-Classical use of such terms as *numphe* ('bride, young wife, lady') was probably already present in the source of the *Epitome*, and by analogy, is likely to have also been found in Trogus' *Philippic History* by Justin.[6] However, the *Epitome* also shows elements of intrusive Byzantine Greek. The use of *kai* in καὶ δὶς καὶ τρὶς καὶ νενίκηκε,[7] and the expression ὑπερβάθμιον τείνειν πόδα ('stretch a foot over the threshold', translated here as 'overstep their boundaries') show the influence of Byzantine Greek.[8] It is notable here that this expression (ὑπερβάθμιον πόδα ῥιπτῶν) also appears as an entry in the *Suda*.[9] The mixture of vocabulary and idioms from both Hellenistic and Byzantine Greek strongly suggests that the author was a Byzantine epitomator who revised an earlier source which used Hellenistic Greek, and indeed Bauer himself says: 'The occurrence of Byzantine linguistic material next to Hellenistic words - the mixture of simplicity of diction, with ornate, often clumsy turns of phrase - confirms my opinion that the epitome is based on a Byzantine revision, that is, that the epitomator was a Byzantine'.[10]

Reitzenstein was initially inclined to believe that the source of the *Heidelberg Epitome* was Dexippus' *Events after Alexander* (*FGH* 100 T 5, F 8), written in the third century AD, but preserved only in abbreviated form by Photius. This was a history in four books that began with the death of the king and covered the first satrapy distribution at Babylon (F 8; cf. F 31), the preliminaries to the Lamian war (F 32–36), and according to Photius, a good deal more material parallel to Arrian's *Events after Alexander*, which itself chronicled events up to the winter of 320/19.[11] Moreover, the *Epitome*'s remarks about Eumenes (3.1: ὅτι ὁ Εὐμένης σοφὸς ὢν ἐκ τῶν στρατηγῶν καὶ διαδόχων Ἀλεξάνδρου) also bear some resemblance to the entry on Eumenes in the *Suda*.[12] Since Ulrich Köhler argued (1890, 560–88) that the lives of Leonnatus, Perdiccas, Craterus, and Eumenes in the *Suda* may have been based on Dexippus, this might suggest a connection between

Dexippus and the *Epitome*. However, Reitzenstein eventually rejected this thesis on the grounds that the epitomator had already excerpted three passages on Diadoch history on sheet 129 of Codex Palatinus Graecus 129 from Josephus and Dexippus, though in the latter case indirectly via the 14th century scholia to Lucian (F 31). He concluded that earlier Byzantine excerpts of poor quality may have been the source of the *Epitome*, though their identity is obscure.[13] One might also add the observation that the scope of the *Heidelberg Epitome* is somewhat greater than either Dexippus or Arrian, running as it does to the founding of Cassandreia and Thessalonica after 316 (F 2.4), and any case for sourcing the *Epitome* entirely in Dexippus' work is liable to be unsustainable.

Because of variations between the text of the *Epitome* and the corresponding historical passages of Diodorus, Bauer (1914, 88–92) concluded that the Byzantine epitomator mainly used Agatharchides of Cnidus as a source, supplemented by another writer who he thought may have been Timagenes of Alexandria.[14] Agatharchides was a second century geographer and historian, who was active in Ptolemaic Egypt. His best known work, *On the Erythraean Sea*, is geographical in nature, but he also produced two large histories: *Affairs in Asia* in 10 books, which, according to Josephus (*AJ* 12.5), certainly dealt with the history of the Diadochi, and *Affairs in Europe* in 49 books.[15] However, Bauer's theory is rendered problematic by the uncertainty as to whether the historical works of Agatharchides, which were not popular in antiquity, survived into the Byzantine era. Even though the treatise *On the Erythraean Sea* was extensively excerpted by Photius, the only remaining citations of Agatharchides' historical works are by Athenaeus, Phlegon, Diodorus, Pliny, Aelian, and Josephus,[16] and their very scantiness tends to predicate that the originals were long gone by the time the epitomator penned his recollections.

It seems to me that the principle of Occam's razor should be brought to bear on the *Epitome*. Bauer's arguments that Agatharchides and Timagenes were used by the Heidelberg epitomator must be considered highly speculative and should be rejected categorically. The historiographic pedigree of the document is liable to be the same as that of nearly all the sources for the Diadochi, and it is simple and obvious: *it derives ultimately from Hieronymus of Cardia*.[17] This conclusion does not mean that it is necessary to absolutely rule out Reitzenstein's surmise that unknown earlier Byzantine epitomes had some influence on the Heidelberg extracts, nor that there may be some resonance with the late *Liber de Morte* and *Alexander Romance* traditions. It is quite likely that our epitomator was influenced by any number of (theoretical) earlier writers, and that multiple sources contaminated the final text, but fundamentally, the historical narrative originates from Hieronymus, perhaps even sometimes via Diodorus, and it is the Cardian's book which underpins the document. This can be demonstrated by even a brief analysis of the historical content.

Some Historical Remarks

Several entries and characteristics of the *Epitome* are notably Hieronymean.

1. *The murder of Philip III Arrhidaeus* (F 2.2). The *Heidelberg Epitome* here transmits a rare

and critical chronographic fixed point for the early period of the Successors, recording that Arrhidaeus reigned for exactly six years and four months before he was murdered on the orders of Olympias. The specificity echoes Diodorus (19.11.5), who supplies a detailed narrative of events in Macedonia in 316 which is generally agreed to be based on Hieronymus, and it is certain that such a precise chronographic peg was embedded in the primary source tradition (Bosworth 1992, 56). That a source as late as the *Epitome* should transmit this data, when all other source traditions are imprecise,[18] can only mean that the epitomator, at some remove, had access to a Hieronymean document, be it a rag of the original, or perhaps Diodorus. The precise pointer is of incalculable value to historians, as it provides a solid chronological equation: since Alexander died on 11 June 323 (Depuydt 1997), and the accession of Arrhidaeus occurred within a month of that event, the deaths of Eurydice and Philip Arrhidaeus can be dated to October (or at the latest, November) 317.[19]

2. *The treatment of Eumenes* (F 3). The tone of the *Epitome* shows remarkable empathy with Eumenes, and here we must surely perceive the shadow of Hieronymus, supposedly Eumenes' kinsman.[20] The links may be lateral, but are evident when comparisons are made to Plutarch's and Nepos' *Lives* of Eumenes, and Diodorus, all liable to be based on Hieronymus fairly directly, and also Justin 14.1–4 (not to mention the *Suda*, and sundry other peripheral sources). His wisdom is remarked by the *Epitome*,[21] as is his integrity and loyalty, especially to the Argead house, and his military expertise.[22] Finally the ironic and undeserved nature of his downfall - a favourite *topos* in the ancient tradition - completes the cameo (cf. Anson 2004, 188–90). Admittedly, this is standard grist for the historiographic mill, but there can be no doubt that all transmissions of the events immediately after the battle of Gabiene in 316 derive from the pen of Hieronymus, who was eyewitness to the betrayal, and then taken in by Antigonus in the aftermath (D.S. 19.44.3).

3. *Alexander gives his ring to Perdiccas* (F 1.2). A detail which is common to Curtius, Diodorus, Justin, Nepos, and the *Liber de Morte*,[23] in fact, to all of the main sources except Arrian and Plutarch, but it comes as something of a surprise to find that this element is also plucked out for preservation in an epitome as late as the *Heidelberg*.[24] The epitomator, when abbreviating the extremely complex manoeuvrings in Babylon after Alexander's death, probably found the ring motif a convenient way to explain Perdiccas' early pre-eminence, but there can be no doubt that the detail was embedded in the Hieronymean tradition.[25]

4. *The structure of the epitome* (F 1). Although it is chronologically the latest and easily the most far-removed historical source dealing with matters after Alexander's death, the actual order of the events recounted by the Heidelberg document is redolent of all the other surviving epitomes and scraps of evidence. In particular, the *Heidelberg Epitome* follows the order of Justin 13 and Arrian F 1 quite closely (if in an even more abbreviated fashion), and the narrative that unfolds, when matched against Diodorus' detailed account, must be deemed remarkably accurate.[26] Nothing is added, but the

pattern is quite clear: the Marshals quarrel, but eventually reach the compromise of a dual kingship; Arrhidaeus' suitability is commented on; Perdiccas, who was given Alexander's ring, becomes regent; the first satrapy distribution is performed; Perdiccas attacks Ptolemy but is assassinated; Antipater succeeds to the regency and reassigns the satrapies, and is succeeded himself by Polyperchon. The structural similarities of the *Epitome* to the earlier tier of Hieronymus-based sources appears to extend even further in fragment 1.7, where the epitomator intensifies his compression with a leap in continuity from the Antigonid victory in Iran in 317/16 to the arrogation of the kingship in 306. This closely follows the pattern of first, Justin, and next, Pausanias and Appian (who are more truncated still).[27] One might even suggest that the *Heidelberg Epitome* appears to represent an intermediate stage in abbreviation between, say, Justin's and Photius' epitomes of Trogus and Arrian, and the miscellaneous summary 'skipping' sources such as Pausanias and Appian. Such matters cannot be pressed too far, but it would seem inescapable that the tendrils of Hieronymus are systematically insinuated into the Heidelberg text, and this is reflected by a structural correspondence to the earlier, 'mainstream' sources.

The above list is far from exhaustive, though sufficient within the parameters of the present essay to postulate with confidence the historiographic tradition behind the *Epitome*. But not all entries are demonstrably accurate or reinforced by consensus. The notorious error in the *Heidelberg Epitome* is the assertion (F 4) that after defeating Perdiccas, Ptolemy married Alexander's sister, Cleopatra.[28] Ptolemy did indeed pursue Cleopatra much later, in 308, but Antigonus had her murdered (D.S. 20.37.3–6). The tradition that Ptolemy was to marry Cleopatra is not found elsewhere except in the *Liber de Morte* and its related *Alexander Romance* testament texts.[29] Now, this is not the time to essay into the labyrinth of that source tradition, but it would appear that here the *Heidelberg Epitome* was indeed influenced by the *Liber de Morte* or traditions related to it, as Reitzenstein suspected long ago.[30] But this is the only place. Bauer's (1914, 82–88) attempts to rationalise the entry historically are tendentious, and are decisively refuted by Heckel (1988, 57–58). Nor is there a clear way to explain the entry historiographically, unless one were to suppose that the epitomator tacked the final fragment onto the *Epitome* from an entirely different source. If this was the case, fragment 4 could be viewed as a quite separate document from fragments 1–3. But further speculation of this nature would be futile.

Conclusion

The only egregious historical error in the *Epitome* is the assertion (F 4) that Ptolemy actually married Alexander's sister, Cleopatra. Other discernable mistakes such as the compression of Cassander's extermination of Alexander's family members (F 2.3), the statement that Thessalonice, instead of Cassander, founded Thessalonica (F 2.4), and the assignation of Susiana to Antigonus instead of Antigenes (F 1.4) can be reasonably attributed to the compressed nature of the genre, or simple copyists' 'typo' errors. So the bottom line is that the *Heidelberg Epitome* is generally reasonably accurate – or at least as reliable as any other source for the Successors, but its pedigree is nebulous. It is reminiscent of Hieronymus of Cardia, most obviously through its affinity with Diodorus, but also in its favorable treatment of Eumenes, and it contains some very precise historical details. How much use the text is to the historian of the Diadochi is another question altogether, perhaps answered to some degree by the fact that the foregoing is the first essay devoted entirely to this document since 1914.

Bibliography

Alonso-Núñez, J. M. (1997) Approaches to World History in the Hellenistic Period: Dicearchus and Agatharchides, *Athenaeum* 85, 53–67.

Ameling, W. (2008) Ethnography and Universal History in Agatharchides. In T. Corey Brennan and H. J. Flower (eds) *East and West. Papers in Ancient History presented to Glen W. Bowersock*, 13–59, Cambridge, MA.

Anson, E. M. (2004) *Eumenes of Cardia. A Greek among Macedonians*. Leiden.

Atkinson, J. E. and J. C. Yardley (2009) *Curtius Rufus: Histories of Alexander the Great, Book 10*. Oxford.

Badian, E. (1968) A King's Notebooks, *Harvard Studies in Classical Philology* 72, 183–204.

Badian, E. (1987) The Ring and the Book. In W. Will (ed.) *Zu Alexander d. Gr. Festschrift G. Wirth zum 60. Geburtstag am 9.12.86*, vol. I, 605–25, Amsterdam.

Bauer, G. (1914) *Die Heidelberger Epitome. Eine Quelle zur Diadochengeschichte*. Greifswald.

Billows, R. A. (1990) *Antigonus the One-Eyed and the Creation of the Hellenistic State*. Berkeley.

Bosworth, A. B. (1971) The Death of Alexander the Great: Rumour and Propaganda, *Classical Quarterly* 21, 112–36.

Bosworth, A. B. (1992) Philip III Arrhidaeus and the Chronology of the Successors, *Chiron* 22, 55–81.

Bosworth, A. B. (2000) Ptolemy and the Will of Alexander. In A. B. Bosworth and E. J. Baynham (eds) *Alexander the Great in Fact and Fiction*, 207–41, Oxford.

Bosworth, A. B. (2002) *The Legacy of Alexander. Politics, Warfare, and Propaganda under the Successors*. Oxford.

Burstein, S. M. (1989) *Agatharchides of Cnidus: On the Erythraean Sea*. London.

Depuydt, L. (1997) The Time of Death of Alexander the Great: 11 June 323 BC (–322), ca. 4:00–5:00 PM, *Die Welt des Orients* 28, 117–35.

Errington, R. M. (1970) From Babylon to Triparadeisos: 323–320, *Journal of Hellenic Studies* 90, 49–77.

Fraser, P. M. (1996) *Cities of Alexander the Great*. Oxford.

Goralski, W. (1989) Arrian's *Events after Alexander*: Summary of Photius and Selected Fragments, *Ancient World* 19, 81–108.

Hammond, N. G. L. (1985) Some Macedonian Offices *c*. 336–309 BC, *Journal of Hellenic Studies* 105, 156–60.

Hammond, N. G. L. (1989) Aspects of Alexander's Journal and Ring in His Last Days, *American Journal of Philology* 110, 155–60.

Heckel, W. (1988) *The Last Days and Testament of Alexander the Great: A Prosopographic Study*. Stuttgart.

Heckel, W. (2006) *Who's Who in the Age of Alexander the Great*. Malden, MA.
Heckel, W. (2007) The Earliest Evidence for the Plot to Poison Alexander. In W. Heckel, L. Tritle and P. Wheatley (eds) *Alexander's Empire. Formulation to Decay*, 265–75, Claremont, CA.
Heckel, W. and J. C. Yardley (2004) *Alexander the Great: Historical Sources in Translation*. Malden, MA.
Hornblower, J. (1981) *Hieronymus of Cardia*. Oxford.
Köhler, U. (1890) Über die Diadochengeschichte Arrians, *Sitzungsberichte der Preussischen Akademie der Wissenschaften, Phil.-hist. Klasse*, 557–88.
Landucci Gattinoni, F. (2008) *Diodoro Siculo: Biblioteca storica Libro XVIII. Commento storico*. Milan.
Marcotte, D. (2001) Structure et caractère de l'oeuvre historique d'Agatharchide, *Historia* 50.4, 385–435.
Martin, G. (2005) Antipater after the Lamian War: New Readings in Vat. Gr. 73 (Dexippus Fr. 33), *Classical Quarterly* 55.1, 301–05.
Martin, G. (2006) *Dexipp von Athen. Edition, Übersetzung und begleitende Studien*. Tübingen.
Meeus, A. (2008) The Power Struggle of the Diadochoi in Babylon, 323 BC, *Ancient Society* 38, 39–82.
Meeus, A. (2009a) Some Institutional Problems Concerning the Succession to Alexander the Great: *Prostasia* and Chiliarchy, *Historia* 58.3, 287–310.
Meeus, A. (2009b) Kleopatra and the Diadochoi, in P. Van Nuffelen (ed.) *Faces of Hellenism. Studies in the History of the Eastern Mediterranean*, 63–92, Leuven.
Rathmann, M. (2005) *Perdikkas zwischen 323 und 320. Nachlassverwalter des Alexanderreiches oder Autokrat?* Vienna.
Reitzenstein, R. (1904) *Poimandres: Studien zur griechisch-ägyptischen und frühchristlichen Literatur*. Leipzig.
Roos, A. G. (1967) *Flavius Arrianus* II, *Scripta minora et fragmenta*. Leipzig.
Rosen, K. (1967) Political Documents in Hieronymus of Cardia (323–302 BC), *Acta Classica* 10, 41–94.
Seibert, J. (1969) *Untersuchungen zur Geschichte Ptolemaios' I*. Munich.
Seibert, J. (1983) *Das Zeitalter der Diadochen*. Darmstadt.
Simonetti Agostinetti, A. (1993) *Flavio Arriano, gli eventi dopo Alessandro*. Rome.
Stoneman, R. (2008) *Alexander the Great. A Life in Legend*. New Haven.
Tarn, W. W. (1948) *Alexander the Great*. vol. II. Cambridge.
Treu, M. (1889) Griechische Sprichwörter, *Philologus* 47 (n.f. 1), 193–201.
Wheatley, P. V. (2009) The Besieger in Syria, 314–312 B.C. Historiographic and Chronological Notes. In P. V. Wheatley and R. Hannah (eds) *Alexander and His Successors. Essays from the Antipodes*, 323–33. Claremont, CA.
Yardley, J. C. and W. Heckel (1997) *Justin: Epitome of the Philippic History of Pompeius Trogus*. Vol. I. Oxford.
Yardley, J. C., P. V. Wheatley, and W. Heckel (2011) *Justin: Epitome of the Philippic History of Pompeius Trogus*. Vol. II. Oxford.

Notes

1 See, for instance, Tarn 1948, 262; Rosen 1967, 41, 45–46, 61, 69–71; Badian 1968, 185; Seibert 1969, 31, 33–34, 93–94, 106–07, 124; Errington 1970, 72; Bosworth 1971, 130–31; 2000, 219, 239; 2002, 23, 56–57; Hammond 1985, 158; Heckel 1988, 57–58; 2006, 90; Fraser 1996, 226; Rathmann 2005, 9, 31, 35, 43; Martin 2005, 301; Landucci Gattinoni 2008, 18–19; Meeus 2008, 54, 61, 82; 2009a, 293–94, 300.

2 I thank Professor Yardley for kindly allowing me to use his translation, which has also appeared in

Appendix II of Yardley, Wheatley and Heckel 2011, 316–18; additionally, I am very grateful for his advice and discussion of various contextual points arising from the translation.

3 See, in general, Bauer 1914, 1–2; Seibert 1983, 53–54; Heckel and Yardley 2004, xxv.

4 Bauer 1914, 97: 'Auch die vier Exzerpte der Diadochengeschichte dürfte der Schreiber aus einem Sammelwerke nur kopiert haben. Der Verfasser wird ein byzantinischer Autor gewesen sein, dem das Erbe der Alten noch in reicherem Maße zu Gebote stand'.

5 Treu's 1889 list is preserved by Bauer (1914, 96), and includes an even representation of writers across a 19 century timespan.

6 Just. 14.6.2: *cum nuru Roxane et nepote Hercule*, 'with her daughter-in-law Rhoxane and her grandson Hercules'; cf. *Heidelberg Epit.* 2.3: σὺν τῆι νύμφηι Ῥωξάνηι καὶ τῶι ἐγγόνωι Ἀλεξάνδρωι: 'and with her Alexander's wife Rhoxane and Olympias' grandson Alexander'; see Bauer 1914, 99.

7 3.2: 'he defeated him 2 or 3 times'. This usage occurs only 6 times in Classical literature (Hdt. 2.121b; 3.148; Pl. *Phd.* 63e; *Phlb.* 60a; *Lg.* 957a; Ar. Byz. *Epit.* 2.563), but frequently in Byzantine works.

8 Bauer 1914, 99–100; Hornblower 1981, 89. τείνω = stretch, extend, draw tight; ὑπερβάθμιος -ον 'stepping over the threshold; metaph: going beyond bounds, transgressing' (*LSJ*). The first example in the lexicon is the present *Heidelberg Epitome* entry; also cited are Asclepius Philosophus, *in Metaph.* 98.11; Marinus, *Procl.* 13; Agathias Historicus 2.29; Philoponus Joannes, *in Cat.* 6.13, all sixth century AD writers.

9 *Suda* Y234: Ὑπερβάθμιον πόδα ῥιπτῶν: ἀντὶ τοῦ ἀτάκτως, ἀπρεπῶς διαπραττόμενος, 'Casting a foot over the threshold, meaning behaving in a disorderly [and/or] inappropriate manner' (trans. Roth, *Suda Online*).

10 Bauer 1914, 101: 'Das Auftreten von byzantinischem Sprachgut neben hellenistischen Wörtern, die Vermischung von Einfachheit der Diktion mit verschnörkelten, oft ungeschickten Wendungen, spricht meines Erachtens dafür, daß der Epitome eine byzantinische Überarbeitung zugrunde liegt; das heißt, daß der Epitomator ein Byzantiner war'.

11 *FGH* 100 F 8.8: καὶ τὰ ἄλλα διέξεισι ἐν πολλοῖς, ὡς κἀν τούτοις, Ἀρριανῶι κατὰ τὸ πλεῖστον σύμφωνα γράφων. On Dexippus, see now Martin 2006. Arrian's *Events after Alexander* is still best consulted in Roos 1967, 253–86; cf. Goralski 1989; Simonetti Agostinetti 1993; Bosworth 2002, 22–23.

12 *Suda* E3579: ὁ δὲ Εὐμένης οὗτος ὑπὸ Ἀντιγόνου ἀναιρεῖται, ἀνὴρ σοφώτερος ἢ κατὰ τοὺς λοιποὺς τῶν Μακεδόνων δόξας εἶναι καὶ ἀνεπίληπτος ἐν στρατηγίαις, ὡς καὶ τῷ ἔπειτα χρόνῳ παρασχεῖν ὄνομα, 'This Eumenes is put to death by Antigonus, [and was] a man with a greater reputation for wisdom than the rest of the Macedonians, and beyond criticism in matters of strategy, so that he has handed on his name even to later times' (trans. Shipley, *Suda Online*). The compiler has spliced this sentence, clearly referring to Eumenes of Cardia, onto the end of an entry on Eumenes II of Pergamon. Cf. Reitzenstein 1904, 311.

13 Reitzenstein 1904, 311–12: 'Allein unser Exzerptor kann Dexipp nicht mehr gesehen haben, denn schon Blatt 129 bietet er drei Angaben über Diadochengeschichte aus Josephos und Dexippos, entlehnt aber die Angabe letzteren wörtlich aus den Scholien zu Lukian (vgl. Fr. 1 Müller). Auch sachlich ist es unmöglich, daß der Exzerptor Dexipp noch las. Er hätte dann nach seiner bei allen übrigen Historikern durchgeführten Sitte eine ganz andere Fülle von einzelnen Geschichten herausgehoben und nimmermehr glauben können, der Tod der Olympias und Roxane sei zusammengefallen. Dürftige byzantinische Exzerpte lagen ihm vor, deren Ursprung kaum mehr zu bestimmen ist'.

14 Bauer 1914, 92: 'Der Verfasser des epitomierten Werkes hätte dann ohne Zweifel Agatharchides zwar stark benutzt, daneben aber auch eine andere Quelle herangezogen, oder selbst die Tatsachen umgestaltet. Denn die genannten Entstellungen finden sich nicht bei Diodor und sind auch dem wahrheitsliebenden Agatharchides nicht zuzutrauen. Eher könnte man hier an Timagenes denken, durch den, wie gesagt, die Überlieferung der Diadochengeschichte eine lokalpatriotische Färbung erhalten zu haben scheint, und für den es sehr nahe lag, Agatharchides als Quelle zu benutzen'. Cf. Seibert 1983, 54; Heckel 2004, xxv.

15 On Agatharchides, see Burstein 1989; Alonso-Núñez 1997, 53–67; Marcotte 2001, 385–435; Ameling 2008.

16 For the fragments of the historical works, see *FGH* 86 F 1–22; with Burstein 1989, 18–21.

17 Already presumed by, for instance, Rosen 1967, 41; Errington 1970, 72; cf. Heckel 2004, xxv.

18 Justin gives six years straight (14.5.10); Porphyry (*FGH* 260 F 3.2), relaying the Armenian version of

Eusebius' *Chronicle*, has eight years, though the Greek versions have seven; cf. *FGH* 260 F 2.1; Syncellus, *Chron.* 320 ('seventh') and 325. Thus there is a rough consensus among the Greek sources that Arrhidaeus was murdered in his seventh regnal year, but only Diodorus and the *Heidelberg Epitome* preserve the precise duration of his reign.

19 However, it should be noted that Egyptian and Near-Eastern sources variously accord Arrhidaeus six, seven, or eight regnal years from his accession year in 323/22, and it is possible that a recently published cuneiform astronomical tablet (BM 32238 = *Astronomical Diary* V, p. 7, No. 2 V′ 12′) gives an even more precise date for Philip's death: 26 December 317. The discrepancy between the Classical and Babylonian sources is likely to be due to a time lapse between the murder of Philip and arrival of the news in the east. For detailed discussion and sources, see now Yardley, Wheatley and Heckel 2011, 204–06.

20 Eumenes' father was named Hieronymus (Arr. *Ind.* 18.7; cf. D.S. 18.50.4; Nep. *Eum.* 1.3), and a family relationship has long been hypothesised by scholars: Hornblower 1981, 8, 154; Billows 1990, 390–91; but cautionary, Anson 2004, 5.

21 Plu. *Eum.* 1.4; 8.1; *Suda* E3579; Just. 14.1.11; cf. Bauer 1914, 72.

22 D.S. 18.42.2; 58.4; 19.44.2; Nep. *Eum.* 1.6; 2.3; Plu. *Eum.* 1. 4. On Eumenes' loyalty, and his military skill, with comprehensive source lists, see Anson 2004, via index.

23 Curt. 10.5.4; 6.4; 6.17; D.S. 17.117.3; 18.2.4; Just. 12.15.12; Nep. *Eum.* 2.1; *LM* 112; cf. Lucian, *Dial.mort.* 13 (391); with Rathmann 2005, 9–26.

24 Badian 1968, 185 (cf. 204), is the first to note the oddity of this detail surviving into the *Epitome*; see also Badian 1987, 605–08. The leading discussions of recent historical commentaries are essential: Yardley and Heckel 1997, 292; Landucci Gattinoni 2008, 17–22; Atkinson and Yardley 2009, 145 (who, importantly, remind us that the ring anecdote was perhaps a Roman *topos*).

25 Bosworth (2002, 56) notes that F 1.2 of the *Heidelberg Epitome* mirrors Diodorus 18.2.4, and Badian (1987, 607) admits that Hieronymus very probably recorded the ring story. The matter of whether Curtius used Hieronymus, and indeed, whether the latter addressed the settlement at Babylon at any length at all, is a vexed one: see Errington 1970, 72–75; Hornblower 1981, 88–89; Hammond 1989, 159; Meeus 2008, 45–46; Atkinson and Yardley 2009, 172–73, 195–96. It hardly needs to be said that Trogus, decanted through Justin, himself used, among others, Hieronymus: Hornblower 1981, 65–66; Yardley and Heckel 1997, 30; Atkinson and Yardley 2009, 218–19; and the similarities between Curtius' and Justin's accounts of the Babylonian settlement indicate frequent recourse to a common source, see Meeus 2008, 45–46. It is likely that Nepos also used Hieronymus for his *Life of Eumenes*, see Hornblower 1981, 67, 90; Hammond 1989, 159–60; cf. Heckel 2007, 274.

26 Bosworth observes (2002, 23, 56–57; cf. 1971, 130–31) that the *Heidelberg Epitome* has affinities with Diodorus (but adds little of historical worth); cf. similar remarks by Seibert 1983, 53–54; and Heckel, 2004, xxv. Rosen also demonstrated the congruence between the sources for the succession over 40 years ago: 1967, 45–46.

27 Just. 15.2.6; Paus. 1.6.5; App. *Syr.* 54.272; Wheatley 2009, 328–29. It is debatable whether Polyaenus 4.6–14 (whose entries are also often based on snippets from Hieronymus) should be included with these sources: the nature of the genre in this case precludes continuity of narrative altogether.

28 On Cleopatra's relations with the Diadochi, see now Meeus 2009b, who thoroughly investigates the modern treatments, though he surprisingly fails to connect the Heidelberg fragment with the *Romance* tradition for Cleopatra's alliance with Ptolemy (83).

29 The *LM* is generally consulted as appended to the *Metz Epitome*: *Aegyptiorum regnum Ptolemaeo trado et Cleopatram, sororem meam, uxorum do* (117); cf. Ps.-Callisthenes (rec. A) 3.33.15 and variants. On the *LM* and its historical background, which need not concern us here, see now Bosworth 2000 (textual tradition outlined 207); cf. Heckel 1988 (trans. 16; texts of both *LM* and *Romance* versions of the Testament 86–107); and 2007. On the *Alexander Romance*, see now the magisterial synthesis of Stoneman 2008.

30 Reitzenstein 1904, 308–15; cf. Bauer 1914, 1–2, 87–88; and note Jacoby's commentary to *FGH* 155 F 1.4: 'Auch hier ist wahrscheinlicher, daß E[pitome] dem Testament Einfluß auf seine Darstellung gestattete'. Fraser (1996, 213, 226) regards the *Epitome* as one of the 'floating fragments of the Romance', a refreshing analysis, based on the Cleopatra link; but it is telling that Stoneman does not mention the *Epitome* at all in his exhaustive assembly of *Romance* texts (2008, 230–45).

SELEUCUS *vs.* ANTIGONUS: A STUDY ON THE SOURCES

Franca Landucci Gattinoni

In the complex and articulated historical framework of the early Hellenistic age, among Alexander's Diadochi there soon emerged strong tensions aimed to redesign the geography of power, tensions which resulted in a long series of wars. Because of the breadth of the topic, an in-depth investigation of the first two post-Alexander decades is beyond the scope of this study.

Instead, the paper focuses on the issues related to the interconnections of two figures who, albeit different, were among the protagonists of the events of those two decades, namely Antigonus Monophthalmus and Seleucus Nicator.[1] In effect, these connections frame indeed a fundamental paradigm in the key political and military dynamics of early Hellenism, as Seleucus very cleverly built his power at the expense of Antigonus in particular, who in 301 was defeated and killed at the battle of Ipsus (Anatolia) by a coalition in which Seleucus himself was *magna pars* (Plu. *Demetr.* 29.7–8; App. *Syr.* 55.279–280).

In this perspective, the examination of the historiographical tradition about the events in which the still-young Seleucus, after full and loyal cooperation, claimed his autonomy and independence from the then-old Antigonus, is especially valuable. This tradition stands out in the books 18–20 of the *Historical Library* of Diodorus which, for their detailed coverage and articulation, have become a touchstone for the investigation of the issues related to Alexander's Diadochi.[2] In these books Seleucus, for the first time, plays a leading role with respect to the conference at Triparadisus in the summer of 320,[3] when, according to Diodorus (18.39.5–6), he was nominated as the satrap of Babylon, one of the core regions of what had been Alexander's empire. Diodorus furnishes no explanation for the reasons why at Triparadisus Seleucus, one of the closest military associates of the deceased Perdiccas, was appointed satrap of Babylon by the head of the coalition that had just eliminated the old regent. Differently, Cornelius Nepos (*Eum.* 5.1) explicitly states that Seleucus had been one of the assassins of Perdiccas, thus legitimizing the hypothesis that sees Babylon as the reward to Seleucus for his act of betrayal.[4] Finally, there are no explicit references to Seleucus's participation in the murder of Perdiccas in Photius's brief epitome of Arrian's *Successors*; however, Arrian (*Post Alex.* 1.33) puts great emphasis on the role played at Triparadisus by Seleucus himself, who sided with Antigonus in favour of Antipater before the latter officially proceeded with the division of the satrapies. Thus, unlike Diodorus, Arrian highlights the excellent results achieved, for the benefit of Antipater, by the joint action of both Seleucus and Antigonus, implying the existence of 'prior' agreements between the two, who, until then, had officially militated in opposite factions – as Antigonus had been among the foremost and most bitter opponents of Perdiccas (D.S. 18.25.3–6).

On his part, Diodorus highlights harmony and cooperation between Seleucus and Antigonus also with respect to the war led by the latter against Eumenes of Cardia who, for his loyalty to Perdiccas, had been sentenced to death by the Macedonians in Egypt.[5] In particular, in chapters 12–48 of Diodorus's book 19, devoted to the war between Antigonus and Eumenes, Seleucus always acts in accordance with Monophthalmus'orders, but he is a deuteragonist, who takes the scene only when Antigonus and Eumenes, who were marching from west to east, enter the geo-political space of Babylon, where Seleucus had just installed himself as satrap.[6]

In detail, at 19.2–14 Diodorus reports the battle between Eumenes and Selecus near Babylon (see also D.S. 18.73.3–4; commentary in Landucci Gattinoni 2008, 267–69), and proves intent on highlighting both the former's great strategic capabilities and the 'Macedonianness' of Seleucus. With Peithon, the satrap of Media, the governor of Babylon was trying to incite the Macedonians recruited by the Greek Eumenes against the latter by emphasizing his foreignness to their *ethnos*.[7] In addition to that, at 19.17–18 Diodorus seems to insist on the hierarchical nature of the relationship between Antigonus and Seleucus: chapter 17 mentions a 'common enterprise' (*koinopragia*), proposed by Monophthalmus and accepted by Seleucus and Peithon, aimed to strengthen opposition against Eumenes thanks to the latter's substantial military reinforcements.[8] Chapter 18 narrates that Antigonus, once in Susa, entrusted Seleucus with the satrapy of the region and ordered him (*prosetaxe*) to besiege the acropolis of the city.[9] Seleucus's obedience to Monophthalmus is implied by the soldiers Seleucus himself (with Peithon) had sent to Antigonus (D.S. 19.27.1); it also is explicitly reaffirmed at 19.48.6, where Diodorus highlights that Seleucus had sent Xenophilus, who had charge of the treasures at Susa, to join Monophthalmus and had directed him to be at the latter's command.[10] Thus, throughout this part of book 19, the future Seleucus Nicator exists merely because his path is intertwined with Antigonus; furthermore, his subordination to Monophthalmus appears to be predictable since the latter is presented as the supreme chief of the war against Eumenes, fought for and on behalf of the Macedonians who had sentenced the Cardian to death.[11] These Diodorean elements evidence the historiographical intention of emphasizing the importance of Antigonus while remaining essentially 'neutral' with respect to Seleucus, who is considered to be one of the many prominent figures of the Macedonian establishment subject to Antigonus, who had been created 'commander-in-chief of the royal army' (*stratēgos tēs basilikēs dunameōs*) in Asia at Triparadisus.

In this part of book 19, Diodorus emphasizes not only the subordination of Seleucus to Antigonus, but also the former's free-willing acceptance of the situation. Conversely, the chapters devoted to Seleucus in the section dedicated to the first phase of the so-called Third Diadoch War (D.S. 19.49–92) adopt a significantly different perspective in describing his exploits and his relationship with Monophthalmus.[12] In effect, the historiographical reconstruction provided in these chapters seems to be aimed at highlighting the greatness of Seleucus's personality: being endowed with exceptional strategic, administrative and relational skills, Seleucus seems here determined to play his part in full autonomy, neither acknowledging nor accepting any authoritarian 'tutelage'.

In detail, in book 19 this aspect is particularly evident as, first of all, Diodorus informs us that by the time of the events narrated Seleucus and Monophthalmus militated in two opposing factions; he also sets the breakdown of cooperation between the two and Seleucus's escape to Egypt as the cause of subsequent events.[13] Secondly, Diodorus describes Seleucus as a close associate of Ptolemy with no hint at any hierarchical standing of the two.[14] Thirdly, by framing an actual paean, Diodorus (19.90–92) finally reconstructs Seleucus's triumphant return to Babylon, this being the acknowledged turning-point in his life, so much so that it officially became the first year of the Seleucid era so named after him (on the issues connected with Hellenistic chronology, see most recently Grzybek 1990).

In particular, with regard to the fracture between Antigonus and Seleucus,[15] Diodorus's text (19.55–57) furnishes a reconstruction of the events that differs from Appian's (*Syr.* 53.268) in its more openly pro-Seleucid tones.[16] On his part, Appian tries to 'justify' Antigonus's irritation against Seleucus by pointing out that the latter had arrogated to himself the right to punish an officer (perhaps of Monophthalmus?) without consulting Antigonus, who was also present on the spot.[17] Differently, Diodorus confines himself to stating that Monophthalmus, after having been welcomed to Babylon with royal honours, asked Seleucus for an administrative account of the wealth of the satrapy *ex abrupto,* with the arrogance of one who addresses a lowest-rank collaborator.[18] Besides, in these same chapters, Diodorus's interest in the figure of Seleucus is also evidenced by the unprecedented choice of reporting, indirectly yet exhaustively, the thoughts and words of Seleucus, who is no longer a subordinate but *the* protagonist of the events. In this respect, it may be noted that, when facing the intimidations of Antigonus, Seleucus first reaffirmed the legitimacy of his position; later, having considered the personal risks of confronting Monophthalmus in Babylon, Seleucus decided to flee to Egypt,[19] where he was welcomed and protected by Ptolemy, portrayed in fully positive terms (on this characterization, see Landucci-Gattinoni 1987, 37–42). There, the refugee committed himself to denouncing the misdeeds of Antigonus and his inordinate ambitions, which convinced not only Ptolemy but also Cassander and Lysimachus to begin the so-called Third Diadoch War.[20]

Strong, original and diversified stances of a pro-Seleucid (and pro-Ptolemaic) perspective also underlie Diodorus's impassioned narration of the military cooperation between Seleucus and Ptolemy,[21] and foremostly, of their great victory in Gaza against Demetrius, the young son of Antigonus.[22] In detail, in chapter 81 Diodorus celebrates the two Diadochi as if they were to be considered the greatest commanders of their time, making explicit reference to their famous invincibility, a reputation earned over two decades at least, in events related to Alexander's expedition and in subsequent military endeavours. In chapters 83–84, Diodorus also emphasizes their tactical skills through a detailed description of the military manoeuvres by which they defeated Demetrius's army. Finally, in chapter 85 Diodorus praises the generosity of the two victorious generals, who had fought not for greed for booty but to restore legality after Monophthalmus's violations, so much so that they allowed the defeated to bury their dead and returned the enemy's baggage without ransom along with prisoners 'who had been accustomed to be in attendance at the court' (of Demetrius and his father Antigonus).[23]

Most remarkably, however, Diodorus's pro-Seleucid perspective climaxes in chapters 90–92, devoted to Seleucus's return to Babylon, which are so devised as to lead readers towards an increasingly evident admiration of his personality. In the narration, Seleucus, destined *ab origine* to achieve the highest peaks of power (on his *omina imperii* see above n. 19), succeeds in galvanizing the few comrades who had followed him in the long march from Gaza to Babylon;[24] then, he immediately obtains the support of the local populations, who were still bound to the memory of Seleucus's good-government between 319 and 315;[25] finally, he re-conquers Babylon and, after fighting off the counterattack led by the general Nicanor, who was still loyal to Antigonus, he expands his control over the neighbouring satrapies: in this way, he gained a king's stature and a reputation worthy of royal power.[26]

In the light of these elements, in book 19 the description of Seleucus's exploits and of his connection with Monophthalmus reveals an open pro-Seleucid tone on the part of Diodorus. In addition to that, in the same book there also emerges a constant and punctual reference to Alexander who seems to embody a specific ideal model for the future king of Syria (so too Primo 2009, 181–83). In effect, according to the Siceliot historian, as early as during his first clashes with Antigonus, Seleucus claimed that Babylon had been awarded to him for the merits he had acquired during the reign of Alexander;[27] besides, once in Egypt Seleucus accused Monophthalmus of pursuing the elimination, first and foremost, of those who had fought heroically alongside the son of Philip II.[28] Furthermore, while describing the battle of Gaza, Diodorus highlights Ptolemy's and Seleucus's military reputation, and reminds readers that both had fought alongside Alexander.[29] Finally, in the speech held by Seleucus on the eve of his return to Babylon, to alleviate the fears of his most faithful collaborators, the name of Alexander is cited twice, almost as if its mere evocation were able to dispel any possible danger.[30]

Thus, these passages of Diodorus's book 19 display a fully pro-Seleucus perspective as well as the constant reminder of the figure of Alexander. This is a clear sign of discontinuity if compared to the way in which Seleucus is presented in the passages about the war between Antigonus and Eumenes. The same discontinuity is also evidenced in the final chapters of book 19 and in the whole of book 20, where the name of Seleucus is mentioned seldom and without special emphasis. In effect, on the basis of irrefutable facts he could not but be presented as one of the Diadochi, which he was, yet his actions seem to become relevant only when they intersect those of other Successors of Alexander.[31]

In this respect, a further specific element fits the picture, namely the lack of any hint, in Diodorus's account, at Seleucus's possible participation in the 311 general peace.[32] Without entering the *vexata quaestio* of the veracity of Seleucus's exclusion from the treaty,[33] the fact that Diodorus, in his narration of the end of the Third Diadoch War, seems to 'ignore' Seleucus sharply contrasts with his version of the breaking out of the war, where the drift between Antigonus and Seleucus, with the latter's escape to Egypt, is his focus of interest and is presented as the real *casus belli* that triggered the subsequent events (see above note 13).

Thus, in Diodorus's book 19 readers are confronted with two different historiographical stances. Of these, only the chronicle of the first phase of the Third Diadoch War pays homage to Seleucus, portrayed as the true and heroic antagonist of Monophthalmus. The latter, instead, stands out as an arrogant person determined, with Demetrius his son, to prevail over the legitimate aspirations of the other Diadochi of Alexander. The historiographical perspective of these passages, given their strong anti-Antigonid orientation, cannot be attributed to Hieronymus of Cardia, who is generally considered to be the sole source for books 18–20 of Diodorus's *Library*: as known and now confirmed by a recently published papyrus (*POxy*. 71.4808), he wrote his main work, *History of the Diadochi*, during his very long stay at the court of the Antigonids, which would not tolerate hostile attitudes against the ruling dynasty, let alone inclinations favourable to other dynasts like Seleucus (on this subject, see most recently Landucci Gattinoni 2008, xii–xxiv). Instead, these passages seem to derive from the specific anti-Antigonid source that left ample traces in books 18–20, and that I have already proposed to identify, albeit in a purely hypothetical manner, with Duris of Samos (Landucci Gattinoni 1997, 194–203; 2008, xii–xxiv).

Diodorus appears particularly well-informed on Seleucus's moves and on his thoughts and propaganda too, yet only with respect to the first phase of the Third Diadoch War. About these events Diodorus seems likely to have referred to a tradition that preserved wide-ranging and fully articulated details; this leads to hypothesize the existence of an authoritative intermediary guaranteeing first-hand information which neither Duris nor Hieronymus could know directly, because they were 'friends' neither of Seleucus nor of his son and heir Antiochus. With regard to this intermediary, though in the silence of the sources any assumption is highly speculative, I think it is possible to propose the name of Demodamas of Miletus,[34] whom the scholarly tradition portrays as a loyal collaborator of Seleucus I and of his son Antiochus I. Demodamas, who was a general and in charge of a series of voyages of exploration in the north-eastern regions of the Seleucid empire, was also the author of at least two works: a history of Halicarnassus and a geo-ethnographic monograph based on his voyages to the East. Therefore, Demodamas appears as a typical representative of a historiographical tradition interested both in the cultural heritage of the ancient 'city-states' (*poleis*) and in the more or less alien characteristics of the peoples encountered by the Greeks thanks to Alexander's conquests. In particular, the close relations between Demodamas and the first two Seleucid kings are proven, beyond any reasonable doubt, by two

Milesian inscriptions, found in the sanctuary of Apollo Didymeus, in honour of prince Antiochus and of queen Apama respectively – the former being Seleucus I's eldest son, the latter his wife (as well as Antiochus's mother).[35] In both texts the proponent is Demodamas himself, who, shortly after the battle of Ipsus,[36] wished to demonstrate the loyal alignment of his native city to Seleucus, his political patron: for this, he mentions with emphasis and solemnity the merits of all the members of the dynasty in favour of his own fellow citizens.[37]

This issue has also been recently re-addressed by a young Italian scholar, Andrea Primo (2009, 181–90), who, after dealing briefly with Diodorus's account of the origin and developments of the Third Diadoch War, investigates in depth the contents of book 19.90–92, and appraises their wholly pro-Seleucus tone. In this respect, Primo (2009, 186) concludes his analysis by stating that:

> All the elements that appear in chapters 90–92 contribute to granting Seleucus the stature of a legitimate 'king' (*basileús*): in the presence of his staff, Seleucus reiterates his ideological connection with Alexander; he gains the support of the population of Babylon thanks to his previous good government; he wins consensus from his own and his rivals' troops thanks to his humanity and, foremostly, his military value; finally, he is on equal terms with the other 'kings' (*basileĩs*). Here [...] it is clear that Diodorus incorporated some of the historiographical motives elaborated at the Syrian court.

Shortly after this statement, however, Primo (2009, 186, 113 n. 28) challenges my assumption that the work of Demodamas may be the primary source of Diodorus's chapters under investigation, underlining that 'no element may lead to a similar conclusion'; instead, he proposes Patrocles as a source. However, he overlooks the fact that this hypothesis has been formulated on the basis of an indirect – not direct – reference of Diodorus to the work by Demodamas through an intermediate source, Duris of Samos, a much more famous author than the unknown Demodamas, and thus a certainly much more accessible source, than the original, for Diodorus.

The origins of Patrocles are unknown; like Demodamas, he was a close associate of Seleucus, as often reported in historical and/or geographical literary tradition (Primo 2009, 72–78). In particular, Diodorus (19.100.5 = *FGH* 712 T 1) states that in 312–311, when Babylon was besieged by Demetrius Poliorcetes (see Landucci Gattinoni 2007, 29–54), Patrocles was the general of the city (appointed by Seleucus himself).[38] As for Patrocles's 'intellectual' activity, it is fully attested by Strabo, who not only praises his geographical and topographical knowledge in a long methodological passage (2.1.2–7 C68–69 = *FGH* 712 F 1–4a), but also frequently cites his *auctoritas* about the easternmost territories of the Seleucid kingdom (11.7.1–3 C508–509 and 11.11.5–6 C518 = *FGH* 712 F 5,7 and F 4b,6).

Strabo's words legitimate the hypothesis, widely shared by modern scholars, of Patrocles as the author of a geo-ethnographic work based on the vast amount of data and information accumulated in the long years he spent fighting and ruling in the eastern regions of the kingdom. On these bases, on a purely hypothetical manner, Primo assumes first that Patrocles in his work described his own actions to defend Babylon from the attack of Demetrius Poliorcetes in 312–311, and secondly that his autobiographical account was subsequently used – directly or indirectly – by Diodorus.

All these elements considered, I think it is now clear and evident that Diodorus's text on the Seleucus/Antigonus contest at the time of the Third Diadoch War encapsulates arguments typical of the propaganda of the Seleucid court. Differently, it is more controversial to determine the primary source through which – directly or indirectly – Diodorus came to know these arguments after nearly three centuries. This, all the more so, since the works of both Demodamas and Patrocles, who certainly were spokesmen of Seleucid propaganda, quickly fell into oblivion, like most Greek post-classical literature condemned as decadent by the purists of the Hellenistic period.

In conclusion, the current state of our knowledge attests the legitimacy of two elements only:

1) Diodorus's text on the Seleucus/Antigonus contest at the time of the Third Diadoch War is favourable to Seleucus and hostile to Antigonus and his son Demetrius; with regard to this aspect, it seems unlikely that Hieronymus of Cardia would appropriate and use arguments deeply critical of Antigonus and his son Demetrius, respectively the grandfather and father of king Antigonus Gonatas, at whose court in Pella he lived and wrote;[39]
2) the two honorary inscriptions made in Miletus at the request of Demodamas in 300–299 (see above note 37) prove that he maintained close ties with his country of origin, which was contiguous, in terms of geography, language and traditions, to Duris of Samos's homeland; conversely, no information is available on any possible relations of Patrocles with the Aegean cultural world.

Sic stantibus rebus, then, Demodamas of Miletus remains the ideal candidate to give a face and an identity to the blatantly pro-Seleucid primary source of the passages on the first phase of the Third Diadoch War in Diodorus's *Library*. Demodamas's work, produced at the court of Seleucus and Antiochus, can be believed to have circulated widely in his homeland, near which, in that same period, lived and worked Duris of Samos (cf. Landucci Gattinoni 1997, 9–28), who, in my opinion, must be considered the most reliable intermediary between Demodamas and Diodorus: as a matter of fact, to reach Diodorus's lifetime, this pro-Seleucid primary source must have been filtered through an undoubtedly consolidated historiographical strand, like Duris's certainly was. In the attempt of building a tradition independent from Antigonid propaganda, Duris was indeed to put to good use all the alternative voices that came from the *entourage* of the other Diadochi, especially with respect to events occurring in the East which were, even physically, very remote from his own personal reality.

Bibliography

Anson, E. M. (2004) *Eumenes of Cardia. A Greek among Macedonians*. Leiden.

Bearzot, C. (1983) A proposito di alcuni prodigi relativi a Seleuco I Nicatore, *Giornale filologico ferrarese* 6, 3–15.

Bearzot, C. (1984) Il santuario di Apollo Didimeo e la spedizione di Seleuco I a Babilonia. In M. Sordi (ed.) *I santuari e la guerra*, 51–81, Milan.

Billows, R. A. (1990) *Antigonos the One-Eyed and the Creation of the Hellenistic State*. Berkeley and Los Angeles.

Bosworth, A. B. (2002) *The Legacy of Alexander: Politics, Warfare, and Propaganda under the Successors*. Oxford.

Brodersen, K. (1989) *Appians Abriss der Seleukidengeschichte* (Syriake *45, 232–70, 369). Text und Kommentar*. Munich.

Del Monte, G. F. (1997) *Testi dalla Babilonia Ellenistica. Volume I. Testi Cronografici*. Pisa and Rome.

Goukowsky, P. (ed.) (2007) *Appien. Histoire romaine. V: Livre XI. Le livre syriaque*. Paris.

Grainger, J. D. (1990) *Seleukos Nikator. Constructing a Hellenistic Kingdom*. London and New York.

Grzybek, E. (1990) *Du calendrier macédonien au calendrier ptolémaïque: Problèmes de chronologie hellénistique*. Basel.

Hadley, R. A. (1969) Hieronymus of Cardia and Early Seleucid Mythology, *Historia* 17, 142–52.

Hadley, R. A. (1974) Royal Propaganda of Seleucus I and Lysimachus, *Journal of Hellenic Studies* 94, 50–65.

Haussoullier, B. (1902) *Etudes sur l'histoire de Milet et du Didymeion*. Paris.

Heckel, W. (2006) *Who's Who in the Age of Alexander the Great. Prosopography of Alexander's Empire*. Malden, MA.

Isager, S. (1998) The Pride of Halikarnassos: Editio Princeps of an Inscription from Salmakis, *Zeitschrift für Papyrologie und Epigraphik* 123, 1–23.

Isager, S. and P. Pedersen (eds) (2004) *The Salmakis Inscription and Hellenistic Halikarnassos*. Odense.

Landucci Gattinoni, F. (1985) La pace del 311 a. C. In M. Sordi (ed.) *La pace nel mondo antico*, 108–18, Milan.

Landucci Gattinoni, F. (1987) La figura di Tolomeo nei libri XVIII–XX di Diodoro, *Aevum* 61, 37–42.

Landucci Gattinoni, F. (1992) *Lisimaco di Tracia nella prospettiva del primo ellenismo*. Milan.

Landucci Gattinoni, F. (1997) *Duride di Samo*. Rome.

Landucci Gattinoni, F. (2003) *L'arte del potere: vita e opere di Cassandro di Macedonia*. Stuttgart.

Landucci Gattinoni, F. (2005) La tradizione su Seleuco in Diodoro XVIII–XX. In C. Bearzot and F. Landucci (eds) *Diodoro e l'altra Grecia. Macedonia, Occidente, Ellenismo nella Biblioteca storica. Atti del Convegno. Milano, 15–16 gennaio 2004*, 155–81, Milan.

Landucci Gattinoni, F. (2007) Babilonia e i Diadochi di Alessandro: staticità asiatica e dinamismo macedone. In T. Gnoli and F. M. Muccioli (eds) *Incontri tra culture nell'Oriente Ellenistico e Romano. Atti del Convegno di Studi. Ravenna, 11-12 marzo 2005*, 29–54, Milan.

Landucci Gattinoni, F. (2008) *Diodoro Siculo. Biblioteca storica. Libro XVIII. Commento storico*. Milan.

Landucci Gattinoni, F. [and C. F. Konrad] (eds) (2004) *Plutarco. Vite parallele: Sertorio - Eumene*. Milan.

Marasco, G. (1984) La fondazione dell'Impero di Seleuco I: espansione territoriale e indirizzi politici, *Rivista storica italiana* 96, 310–37.

Marasco, G (1985) *Appiano e la storia dei Seleucidi fino all'ascesa al trono di Antioco III*. Florence.

McCabe, D. F. (1985) *Didyma Inscriptions. Texts and List*. Princeton.

Meeus, A. (forthcoming) Diodorus and the Chronology of the Third Diadoch War, *Phoenix*.

Mehl, A. (1986) *Seleukos Nikator und sein Reich. I. Teil. Seleukos' Leben und die Entwicklung seiner Machtposition*. Leuven.

Musti, D. (1968) Lo Stato dei Seleucidi, *Studi classici e orientali* 15, 61–197.
Orth, W. (1977) *Königlicher Machtanspruch und städtische Freiheit*. Munich.
Primo, A. (2009) *La storiografia sui Seleucidi: da Megastene a Eusebio di Cesarea*. Pisa and Rome.
Richter, H. D. (1987) *Untersuchungen zur hellenistischen Historiographie. Die Vorlagen des Pompeius Trogus für die Darstellung der nachalexandrischen hellenistischen Geschichte (Iust.13 -40)*. Frankfurt.
Robert, L. (1984) Pline VI. 49, Démodamas de Milet et la reine Apamé, *Bulletin de correspondance hellénique* 108, 467–72.
Schäfer, Ch. (2002) *Eumenes von Kardia und der Kampf um die Macht im Alexanderreich*. Frankfurt.
Scharrer, U. (1999) Seleukos I. und das babylonische Königtum. In K. Brodersen (ed.) *Zwischen West und Ost. Studien zur Geschichte des Seleukidenreichs*, 95–128, Hamburg.
Schmitt, H. H. (ed.) (1969) *Die Staatsverträge des Altertums*. III. Munich.
Seibert, J. (1971) Review: W. Günther, *Das Orakel von Didyma in hellenistischer Zeit*, Tübingen 1971, *Göttingische Gelehrte Anzeigen* 226, 186–212.
Seibert, J. (1983) *Das Zeitalter der Diadochen*. Darmstadt.
Sherwin-White, S. (1987) Seleucid Babylonia: A Case Study for the Installation and Development of Greek Rule. In A. Kuhrt and S. Sherwin-White (eds) *Hellenism in the East. The Interaction of Greek and non-Greek Civilizations from Syria to Central Asia after Alexander*, 1–31, Berkeley and Los Angeles.
Sherwin-White, S. and A. Kuhrt (1993) *From Samarkhand to Sardis. A New Approach to the Seleucid Empire*. London.
Thornton, J. (1995) Al di qua e al di là del Tauro: una nozione geografica da Alessandro Magno alla tarda antichità, *Rivista di cultura classica e medievale* 37, 97–126.
Walton, F. R. (ed.) (1957) *Diodorus of Sicily. Vol. XI. Books XXI-XXXII*. Cambridge, MA.
Welles, C. B. (ed.) (1934) *Royal Correspondence in the Hellenistic Period*. New Haven.
Zecchini. G. (1998) Nosso di Alicarnasso, *Zeitschrift für Papyrologie und Epigraphik* 128, 60–62.

Notes

1 For a broad update on Antigonus and Seleucus, see Heckel 2006, 32–34, 246–48. On Seleucus in particular, see Landucci Gattinoni 2005, 155–81; 2007, 29–54. All dates in this paper, unless differently specified, are BC.

2 Vast bibliography on the history of early Hellenism in Diodorus is available. For an initial systematic approach, see Seibert 1983, 27–36; for a global update, see in general Landucci Gattinoni 2008.

3 The in-depth discussion of the chronological issues concerning the age of the Diadochi is beyond the scope of the present study. For a systematic approach on this topic, see Landucci Gattinoni 2008, xxiv–xlvi, li–liii. A careful analysis of the chronology of the Third Diadoch War is in Meeus, forthcoming.

4 See Mehl 1986, 27–28; Grainger 1990, 33. For explicit emphasis on Seleucus's participation in the murder of Perdiccas, see Sherwin-White and Kuhrt 1993, 10.

5 D.S. 18.37.2. See Landucci Gattinoni 2008, 162–63. On Eumenes, see the recent monograph studies by Schäfer 2002 and by Anson 2004.

6 Diodorus's book 19 consists of 110 chapters, of which, however, 26 are dedicated to the history of the western Mediterranean area, whereas Book 18, which includes 75 chapters, is entirely devoted to the events of Greece, Macedonia and Asia. In book 19, apart from the numerous chapters dedicated to the western Greek world and, albeit minimally, to the Roman world, two large sections can be identified. One is devoted to the long and exhausting duel between Antigonus and Eumenes which took place in

the western provinces of the empire (on the importance of Diodorus's Book 19 in the reconstruction of the final duel between Antigonus and Eumenes, see most recently Schäfer 2002, 131–66). The other section deals with the so-called Third Diadoch War, which, after Eumenes's death, broke out in the entire territory administered by Alexander's Successors, who were all personally involved in the military operations (on this aspect, see Landucci Gattinoni 2003, 124–26). The first section extends through chapters 12–48, with no solution of continuity, and concludes not with the capture and murder of Eumenes (see D.S. 19.44.1–5), but rather with the elimination, by Monophthalmus, of all possible rebellious effects on the part of the generals who had sided with the Cardian (the description of the 'clearance' operation led by Antigonus after Eumenes's death concludes at D.S. 19.48.8, with the lapidary expression: καὶ τὰ μὲν περὶ Ἀντίγονον ἐν τούτοις ἦν. In the following chapter Diodorus explicitly highlights the shift to the European area, to narrate Cassander's definitive establishment in Macedonia). The second section, which extends from chapter 49 to chapter 105, is sometimes interrupted by chapters about the western world (see, in particular, chapters 65; 70–72; 76; 101–104), and concludes with the news of the signing of the 311 peace treaty (on this peace, see Landucci Gattinoni 2003, 124 and note 181), rightly presented as the necessary antecedent of the murder of the last Argead king, the young Alexander IV, and of the subsequent accession of the Diadochi to royal power (see D.S. 19.105.1–4, which is the last chapter in Book 19 dedicated to the Greek and eastern Greek world: in effect, chapters 106–110 exclusively focus on the western Greek world, after a passing hint at contemporary Roman events, at 105.5).

7 See D.S. 19.13.1: (*sc.* Σέλευκος καὶ Πίθων) ἐπεχείρουν τοὺς Μακεδόνας πείθειν ἀποστῆσαι τὸν Εὐμενῆ τῆς στρατηγίας καὶ μὴ προάγειν καθ' αὐτῶν ἄνδρα ξένον καὶ πλείστους Μακεδόνας ἀνῃρηκότα. On the importance of Macedonian ethnic prejudice against the Greek Eumenes, see my remarks in Landucci Gattinoni 2004. With regard to this aspect Schäfer 2002, 15–18 is rather doubtful: in the wake of the generally accepted critical views, he tends to underestimate this element for exquisitely historiographical reasons.

8 See D.S. 19.17.2. On the meaning of the term κοινοπραγία, in the sense of unofficial joint action, which evokes spectres of civil war, almost in ideal opposition to συμμαχία, which is the word commonly used to identify an alliance among the legitimate rulers of sovereign and independent communities, see Landucci Gattinoni 1985, 108–18; Mehl 1986, 49 and note 61.

9 See D.S. 19.18.1. Grainger 1990, 51–53, raises doubts about Seleucus's actual willingness to 'obey' Antigonus when carrying out the latter's orders, as emerging in Diodorus. I am inclined to think, however, that these remarks are rather *ex post*, and that in the text by Diodorus under examination no element legitimizes controversial interpretations.

10 See D.S. 19.48.6: ἀπήντησεν αὐτῷ (= Ἀντιγόνῳ) ἐπὶ τῷ Πασιτίγρι ποταμῷ Ξενόφιλος ὁ κυριεύων τῶν ἐν Σούσοις χρημάτων, ἀπεσταλμένος ὑπὸ Σελεύκου πᾶν ποιῆσαι τὸ προστασσόμενον.

11 Once again, Grainger 1990, 53, rightly highlights the substantial ambiguity of the position of Antigonus who, in order to reaffirm his right to lead the war against Eumenes, referred back to the decisions made by Antipater at Triparadisus thus, however, denying any legitimacy to the orders issued by the regent nominated by Antipater himself before dying; this was Polyperchon who, in order to fight his own war against Cassander, officially annulled the capital sentence inflicted to Eumenes and declared him to be a loyal servant of the Argead kings (on the issues arising in the post-Antipater age, see most recently Landucci Gattinoni 2003, 27–43). No hint at such an ambiguity is evident in Diodorus's text.

12 For a recap of the various phases of the Third Diadoch War along a specifically Seleucid perspective, see Mehl 1986, 62–103, and Grainger 1990, 60–91.

13 See D.S. 19.55–57: these chapters narrate the clashes between Antigonus and Seleucus; the latter's escape to Egypt; and the means by which Seleucus managed to convince Ptolemy, first, and then the other Diadochi of the dangerousness of Monophthalmus.

14 See D.S. 19.58.5; 60.3–4; 62.4–6; 64.4; 68.2–4; 75.2, which mention Seleucus's name in connection with his military endeavours between 315 and 312, and in particular D.S. 19.80–86, with the long description of the battle of Gaza, where both Seleucus and Ptolemy, with no distinction, are given merit for their

victory over the son of Antigonus, the young (and inexperienced) Demetrius, who was to become Demetrius Poliorcetes (the Besieger): see remarks in Bosworth 2002, 214–16, which emphasize the relevance of Seleucus's role in the war against Antigonus, yet avoiding mentioning the possible pro-Seleucid partisanship of Diodorus's source.

15 Grainger 1990, 272 n. 46 (note indicated at page 62) underlines that on this topic 'debate by modern historians ... is scanty and brief'.

16 See, in particular, the sharp remarks by Mehl 1986, 52–55; less strong yet not conflicting with the former is the position expressed by Marasco 1985, 48–51. *Contra*, but with unconvincing arguments, Brodersen 1989, 104–05.

17 See App. *Syr.* 53.268: ὑβρίσαντος δέ τινα τῶν ἡγεμόνων τοῦ Σελεύκου καὶ οὐ κοινώσαντος Ἀντιγόνῳ παρόντι, χαλεπήνας ὁ Ἀντίγονος ᾔτει λογισμοὺς χρημάτων τε καὶ κτημάτων.

18 See D.S. 19.55.3: τοῦ δ' Ἀντιγόνου λόγους ἀπαιτοῦντος τῶν προσόδων οὐκ ἔφησεν ὀφείλειν ὑπὲρ ταύτης τῆς χώρας ὑπέχειν εὐθύνας.

19 See D.S. 19.55.3–8, where the historian expands on the oracle reported to Antigonus by the Chaldeans that informed him that, had he allowed Selecus to flee, the latter would become the master of Asia, and Antigonus himself would find death fighting him. The chapter closes with a reference to that part of Diodorus's *Library* that deals with the events prophesied by the Chaldeans, i.e. with a cross-reference to the narration of the battle of Ipsus, contained in the now lost book 21: according to Diodorus's words in the passage under investigation, the possibility cannot be ruled out that in book 21 there was an *excursus* devoted to the *omina imperii* framed by Seleucus's propaganda, an *excursus* similar to those in Iust. 15.4.1–12 and in App. *Syr.* 56.283–292 (for a commentary on these passages, see, respectively, Richter 1987, 67–71; Brodersen 1989, 131–42; Goukowsky 2007, 150–51). For a more thorough investigation of pro-Seleucus *omina imperii*, a widely-debated topic in scholarly criticism, see Hadley 1969, 142–52; 1974, 50–65; Bearzot 1983, 3–15; 1984, 51–81; Marasco 1985, 69–84.

20 See D.S. 19.56.2: (Seleucus) διεξῄει δὲ ... τὰς προσφάτους εὐτυχίας, ἐξ ὧν ὑπεδείκνυεν ὑπερήφανον γεγενημένον καὶ ταῖς ἐλπίσι περιειληφότα πᾶσαν τὴν Μακεδόνων βασιλείαν.

21 See Mehl 1986, 83 n. 55, which underlines that the conciseness of the parallel sources (Plu. *Demetr.* 5.2–4; App. *Syr.* 54.272; Paus. 1.6.5; Iust. 15.1.6) prevents any detailed comparison of their respective historiographical orientations.

22 On this topic, besides commentary in Mehl 1986, 62–103 and in Grainger 1990, 60–91, see also remarks in Billows 1990, 124–29, which reads the events from the perspective of the Antigonids.

23 D.S. 19.85.3. For brevity's sake, all passages 'in favour' of Seleucus and Ptolemy (which amount to whole chapters) cannot be reported in this study. In this respect, I believe that the partisanship of Diodorus's source can be appraised even from a small set of lines, see, by way of example, D.S. 19.81.5: (Demetrius) οὐ μόνον γὰρ πρὸς πλείονας ἤμελλε διακινδυνεύειν, ἀλλὰ καὶ πρὸς ἡγεμόνας σχεδὸν μεγίστους, Πτολεμαῖον καὶ Σέλευκον.

24 See D.S. 19.90.1–5, and in particular the words by which Diodorus concludes the chapter: ἐπολιτεύετο δὲ καὶ πρὸς τοὺς συστρατεύοντας καὶ κατεσκεύαζεν αὑτὸν ἴσον ἅπασιν, ὥσθ' ἕκαστον αἰδεῖσθαι καὶ τὸ παράβολον τῆς τόλμης ἑκουσίως ὑπομένειν.

25 See D.S. 19.91.1–5. Most remarkably, in book 18 Diodorus never mentions Seleucus' good government in Babylon, proving to be uninterested in the topic; on Seleucus' relations with local populations, see Sherwin-White 1987, 1–31; Sherwin-White and Kuhrt 1993, 7–14; Scharrer 1999, 95–128.

26 See D.S. 19.92.5: (Seleucus) περί τε τῶν διῳκημένων ἔγραψε πρὸς Πτολεμαῖον καὶ τοὺς ἄλλους φίλους, ἔχων ἤδη βασιλικὸν ἀνάστημα καὶ δόξαν ἀξίαν ἡγεμονίας.

27 See D.S. 19.55.3: (Seleucus) οὐκ ἔφησεν ὀφείλειν ὑπὲρ ταύτης τῆς χώρας ὑπέχειν εὐθύνας, ἣν Μακεδόνες αὐτῷ δεδώκασι διὰ τὰς γεγενημένας ἐξ αὐτοῦ χρείας Ἀλεξάνδρου ζῶντος.

28 See D.S. 19.56.1: (Seleucus) κατηγορίαν ἐποιεῖτο πικρὰν Ἀντιγόνου, λέγων ὅτι διέγνωκεν πάντας τοὺς ἐν ἀξιώμασιν ὄντας καὶ μάλιστα τοὺς Ἀλεξάνδρῳ συνεστρατευκότας ἐκβαλεῖν ἐκ τῶν σατραπειῶν.

29 See D.S. 19.81.5: (Ptolemy and Seleucus) πάντας τοὺς πολέμους Ἀλεξάνδρῳ συστρατευσάμενοι καὶ πολλάκις καθ' αὑτοὺς δυνάμεων ἡγησάμενοι μέχρι τῶν καιρῶν τούτων ὑπῆρχον ἀνίκητοι.

30 See D.S. 19.90.3–5: Seleucus underlines that men like Ptolemy and himself, who had collaborated with

Alexander (first occurrence), had accumulated crucial experience; later, referring to the *omina imperii* that foretold his own bright destiny, Seleucus mentions the fact that Alexander (second occurrence) had appeared to him in a dream and had given him a clear sign of his future power.

31 To mention only one example: book 20 of Diodorus' *Library* wholly omits mentioning Seleucus' expedition to India against Chandragupta (see Mehl 1986, 156–91; Grainger 1990, 128–36); interest in Seleucus' actions only re-emerges in connection with his westward march to join the new coalition against Antigonus and Demetrius on the eve of the battle of Ipsus (see D.S. 20.106–113). Differently, hypotheses are hardly possible on the contents and perspectives of book 21, now wholly lost, if not for a little number of fragments from different and often fortuitous traditions (on this aspect, see the dated, yet still interesting, remarks by Walton 1957, vii–xxiv); two of these fragments narrate episodes with Seleucus as protagonist, respectively connected to his relations with Ptolemy I after the battle of Ipsus in 301 (D.S. 21.1.5) and with his conduct at the time of Demetrius' imprisonment in Syria after 285 (D.S. 21.20). As rightly pointed out by Grainger 1990, 211, in both cases Seleucus is described as conflicting with both allies (Ptolemy and Lysimachus) – whom he had long sided with when fighting against Monophthalmus and Poliorcetes – almost as if Diodorus wished to emphasize the seriousness of the fracture existing in the coalition hostile to the Antigonids. *Sic stantibus rebus*, although prudence is crucial due to the miserable state of the preserved fragments, I would not rule out the presence, in these fragments, of traces from Hieronymous of Cardia, all the more so since Diodorus's narration of Demetrius's imprisonment, at least, re-echoes some features of the parallel passage in Plu. *Demetr.* 51.1–4, inserted in a clearly pro-Antigonid context, that has to be attributed to Hieronymous of Cardia (on these fragments from D.S. 21, see also the important remarks by Mehl 1986, 207–12, 278–82, although not particularly concerned with historiographical issues).

32 See D.S. 19.105.1, which, when mentioning the contents of the 311 peace treaty, makes no reference to the name of Seleucus, while affirming that Cassander, Ptolemy and Lysimachus found an agreement with Antigonus and signed it. The name of Seleucus is also absent in the letter, preserved via epigraphic remains, sent by Antigonus to the inhabitants of Scepsis to announce the signing of the peace (see Welles 1934, no. 1 = Schmitt 1969, no. 428). Differently, the so-called *Diadochi Chronicle* or *Chronicle of the Successors* (see Del Monte 1997, 183–94) seems to hint at a peace treaty between Seleucus and the Gutian army: the latter's identification with the army of Antigonus is however controversial and disputable (see Landucci Gattinoni 2007, 29–54, for bibliographical references on this issue). On the peace in general, see Landucci Gattinoni 1985, 108–18; Billows 1990, 131–34; Landucci Gattinoni 1992, 119–21; 2003, 124–26.

33 For a *status quaestionis* updated to the end of the 1960s, see Seibert 1983, 123–29; on more recent years, Marasco 1984, 308–10, which favours the hypothesis of Seleucus's exclusion from the peace treaty; Mehl 1986, 120–28, is more cautious and believes no definitive conclusions can be drawn; Grainger 1990, 104–14, gives for granted Seleucus' total exclusion from the peace treaty; Bosworth 2002, 240–45, proposes the existence of a clause in the peace treaty to award Seleucus the control of the satrapy of Babylon, yet under Antigonus' patronage.

34 The same hypothesis already in Landucci Gattinoni 2005, 155–81. On testimonies about Demodamas and on the fragments of his works, see *FGH* 428 T 1–3; F 1–3; for a recap note, see Primo 2009, 79–82. That Demodamas was from Miletus – as sustained by Stephanus of Byzantium (*Ethn.* s.v. 'Antissa') – and not from Halicarnassus – as supposed by Athenaeus (15.30 [682E]) – seems to be confirmed by the II–I century Salmakis inscription (*editio princeps* in Isager 1998, 1–23; further discussion in Isager and Pedersen 2004, passim). In fact, the inscription, which displays a catalogue of celebrities of Halicarnassus beginning from Herodotus, does not list the name of Demodamas, which legitimizes the hypotheses that Demodamas was neither a citizen of Halicarnassus, nor was he considered to be a famous local figure in the II century (see Zecchini 1998, 60–62).

35 On the inscription in honour of prince Antiochus, see *OGIS* 213 = *Didyma* 479 = McCabe 1985, 7; on the inscription in honour of Apama, see *Didyma* 480 = McCabe 1985, 8.

36 As recently re-affirmed by Robert 1984, 467–72, the two inscriptions are basically contemporaneous: the decree for Apama is datable to the beginning of the year 299/8 (see line 19 with the indication

of the *stephanophoros*, eponymous of Miletus), and the decree for Antiochus is datable to the end of the year 300/299 (both decrees, then, can be set in the Iulian year 299).

37 Yet, the fact that as early as 300/299 Demodamas was the consolidated intermediary of the ties between Miletus on the one hand, and Seleucus and his allies on the other, credits the hypothesis that dates the origins of the relations between Demodamas and Seleucus Nicator at least to the last decade of the IV century: see in particular Bearzot 1984, 51–81, and Robert 1984, 467–72, who, independently one from the other, both reject the scholarly *communis opinio* which, since the early 20th century, has post-dated these relations to the first decades of the III century (see e.g. Haussoullier 1902, 33–37; Musti 1968, 148–49; Orth 1977, 17–32). In effect, also Seibert 1971, 200–04, has long pointed out that the span 315–12, during which Seleucus as Ptolemy's admiral sailed extensively in the waters facing Miletus (see Landucci Gattinoni 2005, 155–81), is to be considered the most credible for the establishment of ties among Seleucus Nicator, Miletus and the Milesians – among whom Demodamas in particular – also because between the re-conquest of Babylon and the battle of Ipsus Seleucus carried out all his activities in the East, with no direct contact with the coasts of Asia Minor.

38 Plutarch (*Demetr.* 47.3–5 = Patrocles *FGH* 712 T 2), on his part, narrates that Patrocles, as a faithful friend, was still at the side of Seleucus in 286/85, when the latter was pursuing the fugitive Demetrius in the region of the Taurus. According to Strabo (2.1.17 C 74 = *FGH* 712 T 3a), Patrocles was the governor of Bactria and Sogdiana in the last years of Seleucus's reign; furthermore, according to Plinius (*Nat.* 6.58 = *FGH* 712 T 3b), Patrocles served as *praefectus classis* under the kings Seleucus and Antiochus. Finally, Memnon (*FGH* 434 F 1.9.1–3 = *FGH* 712 T 4) reports that Patrocles played an important role even after the death of Seleucus – killed by Ptolemy Ceraunus at Lysimachia in September 281 – since he had been sent by Antiochus I with a strong military contingent to the territories 'beyond the Taurus', in the hope of saving the shortly inherited kingdom that was stirred by dangerous unrest (on the expression 'on this side of' and 'beyond' the Taurus Mountains, see the exhaustive remarks by Thornton 1995, 97–126).

39 The same opinion seems to be shared also by Primo 2009, 113–14. It is noteworthy that the Italian scholar does not rule out the possibility that Diodorus might have 'taken advantage' of other sources besides his main reference corpus, which Primo in any case refers back to Hieronymus of Cardia; in this respect, according to Primo 2009, 113 note 28, one has to consider the 'possibility that Diodorus might have had access to a multiplicity of sources unknown to us': facing the unknown, silence is golden...

DURIS OF SAMOS AND THE DIADOCHI

Frances Pownall

The exiguous remains from the once-extensive Macedonian history of Duris of Samos have rendered his political views frustratingly obscure.[1] While scarcity of evidence is naturally a limiting factor in the study of all fragmentary historians, in the case of Duris, the sensationalism and almost baroque nature of the narrative of the surviving fragments of his Macedonian history (cf. Pédech 1989, 389), as well as his political career and his alleged connection with the generally pro-Macedonian Peripatetic school, have intensified the problem. Not surprisingly, therefore, modern scholars have attributed to the Samian a variety of (often mutually contradictory) political convictions, particularly with regard to his views on the Diadochi, both as a group and individually. Over the last few decades, for example, it has been argued that Duris and his family (who served politically as tyrants of their native Samos) enjoyed a close relationship with the Antigonids (Kebric 1977, 4–9; refuted by Billows 1990, 335–56), Lysimachus (Shipley 1987, 175–81; refuted by Lund 1992, 15–17), or the Ptolemies (suggested more tentatively by Billows 1990, 335–36, esp. n. 15 and 17). At the same time, however, the following conclusions have been reached on Duris' overall political convictions: (1) thanks to his association with the Peripatetic school, he was philo-Macedonian (Bearzot 1985, esp. 37–40); (2) he was a Greek patriot with a definitively anti-Macedonian bias (Kebric 1977, 19–35; Shipley 1987, 80–81; cf. 'la sua visione ellenocentrica della storia' in Landucci Gattinoni 1997, 81–82); (3) no political views can be discerned at all in his work, which is simply moralistic (Billows 1990, 234 n. 10; cf. Pédech 1989, 347).

Furthermore, the entire question of Duris' political views stands in need of a thorough re-evaluation in light of Andrew Dalby's demonstration that the widely-held belief that Duris was a student of Theophrastus, who succeeded Aristotle as head of the Lyceum, rests on nothing more than a nineteenth-century emendation of the text of Athenaeus (4.128a = T 1), which suggests that there is not necessarily any connection at all between Duris and the Peripatetic School.[2] The foundations of this alleged connection have already been weakened by F. W. Walbank's magisterial refutation of the once-conventional viewpoint that Duris was the first to apply the Aristotelian properties of tragedy to historical narrative, thus inventing so-called 'tragic history'.[3] Walbank's demonstration that many of the characteristics of this supposed new style of history had been present in Greek historiography since its beginnings, revealing that Duris did not invent a new style of history based on the teachings of Aristotle, renders the foundations of the assumption that he had a close connection with the Peripatetic school shaky indeed. The whole edifice collapses with Dalby's demonstration that it was only Duris' brother Lynceus, a comic poet and writer of letters offering humorous remarks on contemporary *mores* (now beginning to come into his own in modern scholarship: cf. Dalby 2000, 372–94; Funaioli 2004, 197–208), whom Athenaeus claimed to have been a pupil of Theophrastus, and not the historian himself.[4] With any association of Duris with the Peripatetic School now effectively removed, it is time to re-consider his political views.

Although Duris is attested to have written a number of other historical works, his political views on the Diadochi are found in what was apparently his *magnum opus*, his Macedonian history of at least twenty-three books. Only thirty-six fragments survive that can definitely be attributed to Duris' Macedonian history (F 1–15 and 35–55), once evidently an extensive work, and so I must preface my discussion with three caveats. The first is that more than half of the extant fragments come from Athenaeus or Plutarch (sixteen and seven respectively), writers who systematically mined the works of earlier authorities to collect anecdotal (and often salacious) material. The passages cited by the later authors, or 'cover-texts' according to the useful term coined by Guido Schepens (1997, 166 n. 66), may not, therefore, provide an entirely accurate representation of the character of the original, which must have contained a higher proportion of straight historical narrative (see the cautionary remarks of Billows 1990, 333–35); Cicero, at least, considered Duris a meticulous historian (*Att.* 6.1.18 = T 6). On the other hand, the *testimonia* indicate that Duris certainly had a reputation in antiquity for sensationalism (T 7 and 8), which is precisely why he appealed to both Athenaeus and Plutarch.[5] A second, but related, problem in assessing the fragments through the filter of their cover-texts is determining the extent to which the cited material actually derives from the lost source. In other words, where does the cited portion of the passage end (and similarly, transitions from verbatim quotation to paraphrase, and vice versa, are not always clearly signalled either), and original commentary by the author of the cover-text, who often has his own agenda, begin?[6] Finally, while there may be material in other works, such as Plutarch's *Life of Demetrius*, which derives either directly or indirectly from Duris,[7] I confine my discussion to passages in which he is explicitly cited in order to ensure that the relevant material is indeed Durian without contamination by other sources.

With these caveats in mind, I proceed to a discussion of the passages in which Duris' political views can be discerned. I begin with a lengthy passage in which Duris expresses his opinion of Demetrius of Phalerum, the Peripatetic philosopher and pro-Macedonian politician, appointed by Cassander in 317 to absolute rule in Athens, a position he held for ten years until he was expelled by Demetrius Poliorcetes (Athen. 12.542b-e = F 10):[8]

> Demetrius of Phalerum, as Duris says in the sixteenth book of his *Histories*, gained control of 1200 talents a year, and from these funds little was expended upon the troops and

> the management of the city, but all the rest were spent on his innate indulgence, for he celebrated magnificent feasts every day with a large number of guests. He even surpassed the Macedonians with the expenses of his dinners, and the Cypriotes and Phoenicians in his elegance. Showers of perfume fell to the ground, and flowered patterns of various sorts were built into the floors of the banqueting-halls by craftsmen. Assignations with women were held in secret, as were nocturnal love-affairs with youths, and the Demetrius who laid down rules and regulated the lives of other people conducted his own life with the utmost disregard for the law. He was also attentive to his appearance, dyeing the hair of his head blond, painting his face with rouge, and anointing himself with other unguents, for he wished to appear cheerful in his appearance and handsome to those he met. In the procession at the Dionysia, which he marshalled when he was archon (309/8), the chorus sang in his honour the following verse of Seiron (?) of Soli,[9] in which he was addressed as sun-like: 'The most noble archon, sun-like, celebrates you (i.e., Dionysus), with divine honours'.[10]

As I shall argue, this passage is very representative of Duris' overall political views, and also, as it is in direct quotation, offers a lesser chance of contamination by its cover-text.

First of all, it is important to observe that the overall tenor of the passage is distinctly hostile to Demetrius. The context in Book 12 of Athenaeus is a general denunciation of the deleterious effects of luxury, particularly as manifested in political rulers (cf. Giovannelli-Jouanna 2007, 228), and Duris' negative portrayal of Demetrius fits very well into his own narrative purposes; there is no reason, therefore, to doubt his ascription of these views to the Samian. Duris portrays Demetrius as extravagant, sexually dissolute, and vain, and what is more, highlights his hypocrisy, for his strict sumptuary legislation stood in strong contrast to his daily displays of private wealth and extravagance.[11] In fact, Duris alleges that Demetrius' extravagance exceeded even that of the Macedonians, who as individuals are the target of criticism elsewhere in his Macedonian history for the dissolute luxury and excessive drinking of their banquets (F 12, 15, and 37a-b), a common topos in contemporary Greek historiography (Pownall 2010, 55–65). Duris further alleges that Demetrius' 'elegance' (*kathareiotēs*), a term clearly used with a negative connotation in this context of hedonism and extravagance, surpassed that of the Cypriotes and the Phoenicians. The use of these particular peoples as negative comparanda corroborates statements that Duris makes in other parts of his history, where he alludes to the profligacy of the Cypriote king Pasicyprus (F 4, with Pownall 2009–), and denies to the Phoenicians their usual attribution (e.g., Herodotus 5.58) of the introduction of alphabetic writing to Greece (F 6). It can perhaps be assumed that Duris viewed the Phoenicians and Cypriotes, both major commercial powers in the Mediterranean world, as purveyors of luxury goods by sea to wealthy and hedonistic markets.[12] In light of his views on the Macedonians, Phoenicians, and Cypriotes, Duris' contention that Demetrius surpassed them all suggests that his intent was discredit him, by highlighting his luxury and extravagance, which to the Greeks represented hallmarks of tyranny.[13]

What lies behind Duris' portrayal of Demetrius as a flamboyant dandy? It is worth noting that Duris' depiction of Demetrius' decadent symposia, with their unrestrained sexual license including homosexuality, is reminiscent of the description of the Macedonian court found in Theopompus (Athen. 260–261a = *FGH* 115 F 225b). While the allegations of homosexual practices at Philip's court can most likely be attributed to the topos of the sexual intemperance of the tyrant (*pace* Flower 1994, 108–11), there may also be another explanation at play in this passage. Duris carefully describes Demetrius as dyeing his hair, and applying cosmetics and perfume. This description suggests that he was both long-haired and clean-shaven, in keeping with the re-invention of the royal image by Alexander himself, modelled after the iconographic images of beardless, long-haired androgynous figures such as Apollo, Achilles, or Dionysus (Alonso 2010, esp. 16–18; cf. Stewart 1993, esp. 72–86 and Mihalopoulos 2009).[14] Demetrius' androgyny probably represents a deliberate cultivation of the royal image, enhanced by his association with Dionysus, whose rituals were imbued with both luxury and effeminacy (cf. D.S. 4.4.2–4 and Pentheus' famous cross-dressing scene in Euripides' *Bacchae*). Imitating Alexander, the Successors often assimilated themselves with Dionysus as an integral part of their self-fashioning as embodiments of wealth, bounty, and power, culminating in the deliberate cultivation of *tryphē* by the Ptolemies (Ager 2005, 22–28; Müller 2009a, 159–72), but this association was construed by Duris and the Greek sources as another topos of tyranny.[15]

Finally, this passage demonstrates that Duris did indeed link the moral with the political, for he explicitly states that Demetrius' extravagance and taste for luxury prevented him from the proper political management of Athens. Furthermore, it is likely no coincidence that the Athenian politician Demochares, Demosthenes' nephew, offers a very similar portrayal of Demetrius, emphasizing his hypocrisy by contrasting the frugality of his financial administration with the lavishness of this same celebration of the Dionysia, with its procession headed by a giant mechanical slime-spitting snail (Plb. 12.13.8–11 = *FGH* 75 F 4). Demochares' political views were virulently anti-Macedonian, not surprisingly in light of his own political career, and extended naturally to those who abetted their occupation of his native Athens, including Cassander, the Peripatetics, and Demetrius of Phalerum.[16] Given the similarity in their portrayals of Demetrius, it is not an unreasonable hypothesis that Duris' criticisms spring from similar political attitudes.[17] If so, not only does Duris express explicit disapproval of Demetrius of Phalerum, whose decadent lifestyle marked him out as a tyrant, but we can perhaps infer that his negative judgment extended also to the Peripatetic School, of which Demetrius was a member, and to Cassander, by whom he was appointed. Likewise, Duris hints that the Athenians' reference to Demetrius as 'sun-like', with its connotations of divinity, in the poem sung to Dionysus during this notorious procession should be considered offensive flattery to their Macedonian-imposed oppressor.

The Athenians' flattery of Demetrius of Phalerum pales in comparison with the effusive praise which they lavished a few years later upon his namesake and successor, the Besieger, in an ithyphallic hymn (a metre usually reserved for Dionysiac processions) sung on the occasion of the Eleusinia (Athen. 6.253d–f = F 13):[18]

> This is what Demochares has said on the subject of the flattery of the Athenians. Duris of Samos, in the twenty-second book of his *Histories*, quotes the actual ithyphallic hymn: 'The greatest of the gods and those dearest to our city are here, for the occasion brought both Demeter and Demetrius to this place. She comes to celebrate the holy mysteries of the Maiden (i.e., Persephone), and he is joyful in his presence here, as is proper for a god, and is handsome and laughing. His appearance is something majestic, with his friends all around him, and he himself in their midst, and his friends are like the stars, while he is like the sun. Hail son of most powerful Poseidon and Aphrodite! The other gods are either far away or they do not have ears or they do not exist or they do not pay any attention to us at all, but we see that you are present, not made of wood or stone, but here in reality. And so we pray to you. First bring about peace, o dearest one, for you have the power ...

Once again Athenaeus links Duris' criticism of the Athenians for their obsequious flattery of Demetrius, and their attribution of divine honours to him, to a similar criticism by Demochares (6.252f–253d = *FGH* 75 F 1–2), whose paraphrase of the same hymn he cites just prior to this passage. But unlike Demochares, who was likely embarrassed by the obsequious attitude of his native city, Duris did not refrain from quoting the ithyphallic hymn verbatim (cf. Olson 2008, 162 n. 262). While the sarcastic comment contrasting the fawning contemporary conduct of the Athenians with their glorious past at Marathon immediately after the ithyphallic hymn has now been demonstrated to have come from Athenaeus himself (Baron 2011, 100–04),[19] rather than from Duris, there is no reason to doubt his negative attitude towards the Athenians, who were responsible for uprooting the Samian people, including his own family, for nearly forty-five years during their occupation of the island in the fourth century; a number of remarks hostile to Athens in general, and Pericles in particular, are extant from his work on Samian local history (esp. F 65–67; cf. Shipley 1987, 181; Knoepfler 2001, 30–31; Landucci Gattinoni 2005, 225–45).

Duris' criticism of Macedonian flatterers is not limited to Athens alone. In a later context in Book 6 (the topic of which is parasites), Athenaeus cites Duris (6.249c–d = F 3) on a certain Achaean by the name of Arcadion (probably the same Arcadion described at 10.436d as a bitter enemy of Philip) in order to provide an antithesis to the stock figure of the hypocrite flatterer (Giovannelli-Jouanna 2007, 231):

> Arcadion the Achaean, however, was not a flatterer. Theopompos includes him in his narrative (*FGH* 115 F 280), as does Duris in the fifth book of his *Macedonian History*. This Arcadion hated Philip and went into voluntary exile from his homeland. He was very clever, and a large number of his sayings are recorded. On one occasion Arcadion happened to be visiting Delphi at the same time as Philip. When the Macedonian caught sight of him, he summoned him and asked: 'How long, Arcadion, will you continue your exile?' He replied: 'Until I come to people who do not know Philip'. Phylarchus (*FGH* 81 F 37), in the twenty-first book of his histories, says that Philip laughed at this and invited Arcadion to dinner; in this way he put an end to his enmity.

Arcadion's witticism plays upon Tiresias' prophecy to Odysseus in the underworld, that his homecoming will not be a happy one until he encounters people who do not know the sea (Hom. *Od.* 11.122; cf. 23.269); so too will Arcadion thoroughly reject

Philip. Athenaeus' citation implies that this anecdote could be found in the narratives of Theopompus, Duris, and Phylarchus, which suggests that it became a topos (not surprisingly, as the original Homeric passage was itself adapted from a folktale; Hansen 1990, 241–72). What is more interesting, however, is that only Phylarchus (if we can trust Athenaeus' citation) preserves the sequel to Arcadion's remark (cf. Plu. *Mor.* 457e–f), the sole portion of the anecdote that could be construed as at all favourable to Philip (cf. Pownall 2009–, Commentary to F 3). As we have seen, Theopompus portrayed Philip as a stereotypical tyrant, and we can extrapolate from Duris' citation of the Arcadion topos that he did so too.

Duris refers to Philip's own drinking habits in contexts of criticism of the extravagant and often riotous Macedonian symposia (Athen. 6.231b–c = F 37a; 4.155d = F 37b), in which the Macedonian kings simultaneously displayed their royal power and cemented their ties with the elite of their court and potential allies.[20] In these citations, Duris' reference to Philip's habitual use of a small gold drinking cup, which he kept under his pillow, does not suggest that he viewed the Macedonian king as a model of simplicity (so Giovannelli-Jouanna 2007, 231–32), but on the contrary as a full participant in the notorious banquets of the Macedonian court (Pliny the Elder at least certainly understood this anecdote to be a criticism of luxury, *Nat.* 33.50), in which the characteristically small Macedonian drinking cup represented a symbol of largesse, transferred by the Greek sources into the drinking of unmixed wine, the hallmark of a barbarian (Pownall 2010, 64–65). Duris also comments on the lavishness of Alexander's banquets (F 49), at which the guests were seated on silver couches covered with purple cloaks; the purple dye of the shellfish murex was the only colourfast dye in antiquity, and its use denoted both extravagance and luxury. Furthermore, Duris' choice of the year 370/69 as the starting point for his Macedonian history implies that he viewed the death of Amyntas III, the father of Philip II, as the impetus for the chain of events which eventually culminated in the political domination of the Greeks by Philip and Alexander (D.S. 16.60.6 = T 5, with Pownall 2009–, Commentary to T 5). Taken together, these passages suggest that Duris' criticism of Macedonian flatterers was levied not only against the Athenians, against whom he had a personal axe to grind, but against all those who flattered the successive Macedonian rulers, beginning with Philip II. Conversely, Duris, like Theopompus (cf. Flower 1994, 98–155), appears to have portrayed the extreme luxury and decadence (including the sexual license) of the Macedonian courts of both Philip and Alexander in terms of the stereotypical topoi of tyranny.

Returning to Duris' citation of the ithyphallic hymn sung in celebration of Demetrius Poliorcetes, Athens is not the only target of his criticism, for the Besieger himself is also represented in a very negative light, in his hubristic acceptance of the divine honours bestowed upon him by the Athenians and his adoption of solar imagery, which represented his self-proclaimed role as conqueror of the world (Mikalson 1998, 96–97). In fact, it is interesting to note that the deification and solar imagery which were implicit in Duris' criticism of Demetrius of Phalerum now become explicit in the hymn to Demetrius Poliorcetes, a comparison made even more invidious by their shared names; it is surely no coincidence that our sources for the hubristic behaviour of both homonyms are Demochares and Duris (O'Sullivan 2009a, 300). Demochares' political views have been demonstrated to have been not only anti-Macedonian in general (as noted above), but anti-Antigonid in particular (Marasco 1984; Billows 1990, 337–38); Duris' very similar condemnation of the Besieger suggests that he had no particular love for Demetrius, or by extension, the Antigonids.

Another fragment preserved by Athenaeus (12.535e-536a = F 14) in direct quotation confirms this hypothesis:

> In the twenty-second book of his *Histories*, Duris says: '... Demetrius, however, exceeded them all (i.e., Pausanias, Dionysius I of Syracuse, and Alexander). He had his footwear specially made at great expense. With respect to the shape in which it was constructed it was almost a half-boot, with a felt covering of the most expensive purple. Upon it, the craftsmen had woven a large intricate pattern of gold in the back and in the front. His miltary cloaks had a lustrous sheen of brownish grey, and the universe with golden stars and the twelve signs of the zodiac were woven in. His head-dress was studded with gold, and it held fast his felt hat, made of genuine purple dye, and the fringed edges of its material went down to his back. When the festival in honour of Demetrius was held in Athens, he was depicted on the stage as riding on the world'.[21]

In this passage, Duris emphasizes the extravagance and theatricality of Demetrius' attire, which surpassed that of Pausanias, Dionysius, and Alexander. The adoption of Persian attire (redolent to the Greeks of both luxury and barbarism) was considered the outward sign of tyranny in the other examples Duris cites, and presumably this was the point that he wished to make in the case of Demetrius too (cf. Plu. *Demetr.* 42.1). The golden head-dress (*mitra*) was a characteristically Persian garment, as well as a festal adornment of Dionysus (D.S. 4.4.4).[22] The luxury and effeminacy of Demetrius' festal attire suggest that he, like his namesake, was attempting to adopt the new royal image, inaugurated by Alexander, by associating himself with Dionysus;[23] it is unlikely to be a coincidence that his portraiture represents him as beardless (cf. Alonso 2010, 23). Duris, like Theopompus, highlights the flamboyancy, effeminacy, and luxury of Demetrius' image in order to discredit him as a tyrant, as shown in this passage by his deliberate association of the Besieger's Dionysiac attire with his hubris in his self-proclaimed role as ruler of the world and his acceptance of divine honours from the Athenians.[24]

Duris appears to offer a third reference to the dissipation of Demetrius Poliorcetes in the context of a generalizing comment on the proclivity of rulers to excessive drinking (Athen. 12.546c–d = F 15):

> And Duris of Samos says in the twenty-third book of his *Histories* that in ancient times rulers had a passion for drinking. Therefore Homer makes Achilles say the following abusive words to Agamemnon (*Il.* 1.225): 'You wine-soaked man, with the eyes of a dog'. And when he alludes to the death of the king, he says (*Od.* 11.419–20): 'How we lay grouped around the mixing bowl and the laden tables'. Thus Homer shows that his death happened at the very moment of his passion for drinking.

As Athenaeus shows in this paraphrase, Duris employed *exempla* from Homeric saga to condemn the moral weaknesses of contemporary rulers, naturally enough for the writer of a work entitled *Homeric Problems* (F 30). Duris was not averse to manipulating these Homeric citations to suit his own moralistic purposes, however, for Agamemnon's drinking was not the focus of either of the original Homeric passages (the quarrel between Achilles and Agamemnon and Odysseus' encounter with the shade of Agamemnon in the underworld). This citation is taken from Book 23 of Duris' Macedonian history, that is, immediately following his descriptions of Demetrius' dissipation and hubris in Book 22 (F 13 and 14). Therefore, it is hard not to associate this comment upon the destructive effects of excessive drinking with Demetrius Poliorcetes, who drank himself to death while in the custody of Seleucus in 283 (cf. Pownall 2009–, Commentary to F 15).

Thus far, we have established that Duris was hostile to the Macedonians and their instruments in general, and to the Antigonids in particular, at the very least. But what of the other Successors? Another Macedonian leader who is the target of explicit criticism is Polyperchon (Athen. 4.155c = F 12):

> In the seventeenth book of his *Histories*, Duris of Samos says that Polysperchon[25] used to dance if he became drunk, even though he was a rather elderly man and second to none of the Macedonians in both his military command and reputation. He used to put on a saffron-coloured robe and Sicyonian shoes and dance incessantly.

Here, Duris accuses Polyperchon of excessive drinking, as well as inappropriate and indecorous dancing; it is worth noting that the association of these two vices had been a topos in Greek literature since Hippocleides' notorious dance in Herodotus (5.129). Furthermore, the incongruous image of an old man dancing is generally associated with both symposiastic contexts and Dionysiac rituals (cf. the Cadmus-Tiresias scene in Euripides' *Bacchae*),[26] both of which, of course, involve the consumption of wine. Sicyonian shoes are women's shoes (Herod. *Mim.* 7.57), while the saffron-coloured robe is associated with Dionysus (Herod. *Mim.* 8.28–34; Athen. 5.198c), with all the overtones of luxury and effeminacy implied by Dionysiac ritual (Eur. *Bacch.* 453–9; Zanker 2009, 229). Interestingly, while Polyperchon shows no evidence of any particular intelligence in the other ancient sources, Duris is the only one to portray him as intemperate and effeminate, which suggests that Duris deliberately imbued Polyperchon's attempts at royal posturing with the stereotypical topoi of tyranny, culminating with the implication that he, like Demetrius, modelled himself upon Dionysus, an association he perhaps deduced (or invented) as a result of Polyperchon's notorious alliance with Olympias, whose Dionysiac activities were well known (cf. F 52).

Unfortunately, after this our trail starts to get cold, as no explicit comment on any of the other Macedonian Successors is extant, apart from a touching anecdote on the loyalty of Lysimachus' dog, which threw itself onto the funeral pyre of its master (Plin. *Nat.* 8.143 = F 55). While it has been deduced from this 'affectionate piece about his favourite dog' that Duris must have been favourable towards Lysimachus (Shipley 1987, 180–81), it seems far more likely, particularly in light of its context in Pliny, that this anecdote represents a 'wonders' tale about the connection between humans and animals (cf. the very similar anecdote in an earlier context, F 7, on the mutual affection between a boy and a dolphin which is reminiscent of the famous Arion episode in Herodotus

1.24), and in fact it became a topos in antiquity.[27] Therefore the anecdote on the loyalty of Lysimachus' dog tells us little about Duris' attitude to Lysimachus himself.

In fact, the only Successor who receives explicit praise from Duris in the extant fragments is Eumenes of Cardia, who was the lone Greek among their number (Plu. *Eum.* 1 = F 53):

> Duris of Samos narrates that Eumenes of Cardia was the son of a man who became a wagon-driver in the Chersonese as the result of his poverty, but he was reared with a liberal education in literature and athletic training. While he was still a boy, Philip, who was visiting there and had some free time, watched the youths of Cardia training in the *pankration* and the boys in wrestling, in which Eumenes was successful and proved himself to be intelligent and brave. Philip was pleased by him and received him into his entourage.

While Duris does praise Eumenes for his intelligence and courage, the main point of the anecdote is the rags-to-riches story of Duris' rise to prominence as a member of Philip's entourage from his obscure origins; both Nepos (*Eum.* 1.4) and Plutarch (*Eum.* 1) agree with the much more likely tradition in which he was a member of the Cardian elite (Anson 2004, 35 n. 4). Because the focus of Duris' narrative is Eumenes' dramatic rags-to-riches metamorphosis, this fragment does not indicate in any explicit way if Duris continued to approve of Eumenes as an adult (although the tenor of the anecdote in which he comes to Philip's favour suggests that he does), or, if he did so, whether he was motivated by patriotic reasons (like Hieronymus of Cardia, whose eulogistic treatment of his relative served as the main source for most of the later historians; Hornblower 1981, 196–211; Anson 2004, 3–25; Roisman 2010, 135–48), or, conversely, by dislike of Eumenes' opponent, Antigonus Monophthalmus.

Finally, in two separate fragments, both from Plutarch (*Phoc.* 4 = F 50 and *Phoc.* 17 = F 51), Duris offers praise of the Athenian politician Phocion. Because Plutarch emphasizes his subject's incorruptible character in his *Life*, his use of Duris as a source suggests that the Samian's general portrayal of Phocion was favourable.[28] In the first passage (F 50), Plutarch cites Duris on the ascetic and self-controlled nature of Phocion, attributing to him the comment that Phocion customarily, whether at home in Attica or on campaign, went around barefoot and without a cloak, so that the men under his command used to joke that whenever Phocion actually got dressed it was a sign of very extreme cold weather. In his quasi-Socratic asceticism (Tritle 1988, 21–22, 32, 45), then, Phocion represents the antithesis of the dissolute and depraved Macedonian Successors we find peopling Duris' Macedonian history (cf. Gehrke 1976, 190 n. 44). In the second passage (F 51), Plutarch cites Duris for the statement that after Alexander had become great and conquered Darius, he omitted the word 'greetings' (*chairein*) from his letters, except for those to Phocion and Antipater. The purpose of the citation is to illustrate the special esteem in which he was held by Alexander, but in the overall context of Phocion's incorruptibility, for Plutarch immediately proceeds to emphasize how he rejected large gifts of money from Alexander (*Phoc.* 18). As Larry Tritle (1988, 114–15, 118) has demonstrated, Phocion managed to preserve his political independence from the Macedonians by his refusal to accept their gifts, and his policies, even when they involved the avoidance of war with Macedon and collaboration with the Macedonians, were motivated by patriotism and concern for Athens' continued survival. Plutarch's citations suggest that Duris favoured Phocion as a patriot, and consequently portrayed him as ascetic and self-controlled in order to highlight his distance from the luxury and extravagance of the Macedonian rulers.[29]

Three other considerations on his portrayal of Phocion may be relevant, in light of the fragments previously discussed, assuming that Duris underlies much of the narratives of Plutarch and Diodorus (so Bearzot 1985, 16–50, 148–56). First, Phocion's condemnation and death occurred in 318 during the brief democratic revolution in Athens incited by Polyperchon in his rivalry with Cassander. When Phocion appealed to Polyperchon for help, the Macedonian, in the words of Christian Habicht (1997, 48), 'demonstrated both a lack of political skill and the extent of his perfidy: he dropped all pretence of support for Phocion and his party, handing them over to their opponents to deal with as they saw fit'. Duris' favourable treatment of Phocion, therefore, dovetails with his hostile treatment of Polyperchon (cf. Bearzot 1985, 44–45, 49–50). Second, the Athenian democracy does not come off much better, in that the mob would not allow Phocion to speak in his own defense when Polyperchon sent him to Athens for trial, but sentenced him to drink hemlock, and would not even allow him a proper burial in Attica (Plu. *Phoc.* 34–37; D.S. 18.66–67). It is a pity that Duris' thoughts on the condemnation and death of Phocion are not extant, but disapproval of the radical democracy in Athens fits with derogatory comments on contemporary Athenians in other contexts, and is a trait which is common to the moralistic narratives of numerous fourth-century and Hellenistic historians (cf. Pownall 2004). Third, Cinzia Bearzot has suggested that Duris lies behind the hostile traditions on both Demades and Antipater (1985, 41–42, 148–49, 156); this suggestion is attractive because Demades' venality would provide an excellent foil for Phocion's incorruptibility, and Antipater is represented explicitly as a tyrant (Plu. *Phoc.* 19.2).

What conclusions can we draw from the few fragments extant from Duris' Macedonian history in which any glimpse of his political views can be gleaned? First, all of the Macedonian Successors who are mentioned by name receive hostile treatment from Duris, particularly on moral grounds, as do the Macedonians in general, and those who flatter them. This of course includes not only the Athenians, whom Duris had further grounds to dislike because of Athens' fourth-century exile of the Samians from their homeland, but also Demetrius of Phalerum, and (by extension) the Peripatetic School, the successive heads of which made a point of remaining on good terms with their Macedonian overlords. The only Successor whom Duris treats favourably, in the extant fragments at least, is Eumenes, who was a Greek. It is likely (although in no way provable) that Duris joined the other ancient authorities who, under the influence of Hieronymus, attributed Eumenes' downfall to Macedonian prejudice against a Greek. As a Greek patriot, Phocion too receives praise from Duris. The surviving fragments, therefore, do not indicate that Duris favoured any one particular set of

Diadochi, but rather that he offered a blanket condemnation of all the Macedonian rulers, beginning with Philip and Alexander, using moral criteria to criticize their political administrations; like Theopompus, he turned the luxury and extravagance through which they displayed their power and prestige into evidence of their tyranny. Furthermore, the fragments extant from his narrative suggest that he, in alignment with the historiographical tradition of the late fourth century and the early Hellenistic period (cf. Pownall 2004), overtly viewed luxury and extravagance not only as symbols of tyranny, but also as causal factors for political and military decline. Consequently, the Diadochi, with their incessant internecine warfare and ensuing inability of any one ruler to remain in a dominant position for very long, offered an attractive subject for Duris' moralistic history. Given the somewhat sensationalistic nature of many of the surviving fragments, it is tempting to suggest that he exaggerated both the perceived vices of the Successors and their declines and falls so that they might serve as more effective moral *exempla*. In any case, with his moralistic interpretation of history, Duris was very much the intellectual product of his times.

Bibliography

Ager, S. L. (2005) Familiarity Breeds: Incest and the Ptolemaic Dynasty, *Journal of Hellenic Studies* 125, 1–34.

Alonso Troncoso, V. (2010) The Bearded King and the Beardless Hero. In E. Carney and D. Ogden (eds) (2010) *Philip II and Alexander the Great: Father and Son, Lives and Afterlives*, 13–24, Oxford and New York.

Anson, E. M. (1977) The Siege of Nora: A Source Conflict, *Greek, Roman, and Byzantine Studies* 18, 251–56.

Anson, E. M. (2004) *Eumenes of Cardia: A Greek Among Macedonians*. Boston and Leiden.

Ballesteros Pastor, L. (2005) Atenión, Tirano de Atenas, *Historia Antigua* 23, 385–400.

Baron, C. A. (2011) The Delimitation of Fragments in Jacoby's *FGrHist*: Some Examples from Duris of Samos, *Greek, Roman, and Byzantine Studies* 51, 86–110.

Bearzot, C. (1985) *Focione tra storia e trasfigurazione ideale*. Milan.

Billows, R. A. (1990) *Antigonos the One-Eyed and the Creation of the Hellenistic State*. Berkeley and Los Angeles.

Carney, E. (2007) Symposia and the Macedonian Elite: The Unmixed Life, *Syllecta Classica* 18, 129–80.

Cooper, C. (2009) (Re)Making Demosthenes: Demochares and Demetrius of Phalerum on Demosthenes. In P. Wheatley and R. Hannah (eds) *Alexander and His Successors: Essays from the Antipodes*, 310–22. Claremont, CA.

Dalby, A. (1991) The Curriculum Vitae of Duris of Samos, *Classical Quarterly* 41, 539–41.

Dalby, A. (2000) Lynceus and the Anecdotists. In D. Braund and J. Wilkins (eds) (2000) *Athenaeus and his World*, 372–94, Exeter.

Flower, M. A. (1994) *Theopompus of Chios: History and Rhetoric in the Fourth Century BC*. Oxford.

Fromentin, V. (2001) L'histoire tragique a-t-elle existé? In A. Billaut and C. Mauduit (eds) *Lectures antiques de la tragédie grecque*, 77–92, Lyon.

Funaioli, M. P. (2004) Linceo di Samo. In E. Cavallini (ed.) *Samo: storia, letteratura, scienza*, 197–208, Pisa and Rome.

Gehrke, H.-J. (1976) *Phokion. Studien zur Erfassung seiner historischen Gestalt*. Munich.
Giovannelli-Jouanna, P. (2007) Les fragments de Douris de Samos chez Athénée. In D. Lenfant (ed.) *Athénée et les fragments d'historiens*, 215–37, Paris.
Habicht, C. (1997) *Athens from Alexander to Antony*. Cambridge, MA and London (transl. from German).
Hansen, W. F. (1990) Odysseus and the Oar: A Folkloric Approach. In L. Edmunds (ed.) *Approaches to Greek Myth*, 241–42, Baltimore and London.
Heckel, W. (2006) *Who's Who in the Age of Alexander the Great: Prosopography of Alexander's Empire*. Oxford.
Hornblower, J. (1981) *Hieronymus of Cardia*. Oxford.
Hornblower, S. (1994) Introduction. In S. Hornblower (ed.) *Greek Historiography*, 1–72, Oxford.
Kebric, R. B. (1977) *In the Shadow of Macedon: Duris of Samos*. Wiesbaden.
Knoepfler, D. (2001) Trois historiens hellénistiques: Douris de Samos, Hiéronymos de Cardia, Philochore d'Athènes. In F. Chamoux (ed.) *Histoire et historiographie dans l'antiquité*, 25–44, Paris.
Landucci Gattinoni, F. (1997) *Duride di Samo*. Rome.
Landucci Gattinoni, F. (2005) Duride di Samo e l'imperialismo ateniense. In L. Breglia and M. Lupi (eds) *Da Elea a Samo: Filosofi e politici di fronte all'impero ateniense*, 222–45, Naples.
Lund, H. S. (1992) *Lysimachus: A Study in Early Hellenistic Kingship*. London and New York.
Marasco, G. (1984) *Democare di Leuconoe. Politica e cultura in Atene fra IV e III sec. a. C.* Florence.
Marincola, J. (2003) Beyond Pity and Fear: The Emotions of History, *Ancient Society* 33, 285– 315.
Mihalopoulos, C. (2009) The Construction of a New Ideal: The Official Portraiture of Alexander the Great. In W. Heckel and L. A. Tritle (eds) *Alexander the Great: A New History*, 275–93, Malden, MA.
Mikalson, J. D. (1998) *Religion in Hellenistic Athens*. Berkeley.
Müller, S. (2009a) *Das Hellenistische Königspaar in der medialen Repräsentation. Ptolemaios II. und Arsinoe II*. Berlin and New York.
Müller, S. (2009b) In Favour of Aphrodite: Sulla, Demetrios Poliorcetes, and the Symbolic Value of the Hetaira, *Ancient History Bulletin* 23, 38–49.
Olson, S. D. (ed.) (2006–08–10) *Athenaeus: The Learned Banqueters*. Vols 2, 3, and 6. Cambridge, MA and London.
O' Sullivan, L. (2009a) *The Regime of Demetrius of Phalerum in Athens, 317–307 BCE: A Philosopher in Politics*. Leiden and Boston.
O' Sullivan, L. (2009b) Macedonians, Heroes and Athenian Burial Laws. In P. Wheatley and R. Hannah (eds) *Alexander and His Successors: Essays from the Antipodes*, 118–35, Claremont, CA.
Pédech, P. (1989) *Trois historiens méconnus: Théopompe - Duris - Phylarque*. Paris.
Pelling, C. B. R. (1980) Plutarch's Adaption of his Source-Material, *Journal of Hellenic Studies* 100, 127–40; reprinted in B. Scardigli (ed.) (1995) *Essays on Plutarch's Lives*, 125–54, Oxford.
Pelling, C. B. R. (2000) Fun with Fragments: Athenaeus and the Historians. In D. Braund and J. Wilkins (eds) *Athenaeus and his World*, 171–90, Exeter.
Pownall, F. (2004) *Lessons from the Past: The Moral Use of History in Fourth-Century Prose*. Ann Arbor.
Pownall, F. (2008) Critias' Commemoration of Athens, *Mouseion* 8, 333–54.
Pownall, F. (2009–) Duris of Samos (76). In I. Worthington (ed.) *Brill's New Jacoby* (on-line).
Pownall, F. (2010) The Symposia of Philip II and Alexander III of Macedon: The View from Greece. In E. Carney and D. Ogden (eds) *Philip II and Alexander the Great: Father and Son, Lives and Afterlives*, 55–65, Oxford.
Roisman, J. (2010) Hieronymus of Cardia: Causation and Bias from Alexander to his Successors.

In E. Carney and D. Ogden (eds) *Philip II and Alexander the Great: Father and Son, Lives and Afterlives*, 135–48, Oxford.

Schepens, G. (1997) Jacoby's *FGrHist*: Problems, Methods, Prospects. In G. W. Most (ed.) *Collecting Fragments/Fragmente sammeln*, 144–72, Göttingen.

Shipley, G. (1987) *A History of Samos 800-188 BC*. Oxford.

Slater, W. J. (2000) Gnomology and Criticism, *Greek, Roman, and Byzantine Studies*, 41, 99–121.

Stewart, A. (1993) *Faces of Power: Alexander's Image and Hellenistic Politics*. Berkeley and Los Angeles.

Sweet, W. E. (1951) Sources of Plutarch's *Demetrius*, *Classical Weekly* 44, 177–81.

Tritle, L. A. (1988) *Phocion the Good*. London, New York and Sydney.

Walbank, F. W. (1960) History and Tragedy, *Historia* 9, 216–34; reprinted in F. Walbank (1985) *Selected Papers*, 224–41, Cambridge.

Walbank, F. W. (2000) Athenaeus and Polybius. In D. Braund and J. Wilkins (eds) *Athenaeus and his World*, 161–70, Exeter.

Zanker, G. (2009) *Herodas*: Mimiambs. Oxford.

Zanker, P. (1995) *The Mask of Socrates: The Image of the Intellectual in Antiquity*. Berkeley (trans. from German).

Notes

1 Translations and commentaries on the extant fragments of Duris of Samos (*FGH* 76) can be found in Landucci Gattinoni 1997 and Pownall 2009–. All further references to the *testimonia* and fragments of Duris are to *FGH* 76 (now available on-line in *Brill's New Jacoby*).

2 Dalby 1991, 539–41; with discussions by Landucci Gattinoni 1997, 36–38; Pownall 2009–, commentary to T 1; Baron 2011, 91–93. Nevertheless, the most recent translation of Athenaeus retains the misleading emended text (Olson 2006, 110–11).

3 Walbank 1960, 216–34; see also Fromentin 2001, 77–92; Landucci Gattinoni 1997, 51–55; Pownall 2009–, commentary to F 1; Baron 2001, 93. The term 'tragic history' should probably be jettisoned altogether, for it impedes a proper understanding of Hellenistic historiography (Hornblower 1994, 44–45; Marincola 2003, 285–315).

4 Athen. 3.100e; 4.130d; 8.337d = T 2; *Suda*, s.v. 'Lynceus', with the discussions of Dalby, 1991, 539–41; Pownall 2009–, Commentary to T 2; Baron 2011, 93 n. 16.

5 On the appeal to Athenaeus of Hellenistic historians in general, and Duris in particular, see Walbank 2000, 163–64 and Giovannelli-Jouanna (2007, 215–37). As both Walbank (2000, esp. 166–69) and Giovannelli-Jouanna (2007, esp. 235: 'connivence intellectuelle et morale entre le citateur et sa source') suggest, the moralistic nature of Duris' historiography is likely what drew Athenaeus to him.

6 On this problem in general, see Schepens 1997, 166 n. 66; on Athenaeus' tendency to include independent material in a passage attributed to a single dominant source, see Pelling 2000, 171–90; on the difficulty in determining the boundaries of fragments of Duris in particular, see Baron 2011, 86–110. And while Plutarch's adaptation of his sources as needed to produce the narrative needed for the context is well known (see, e.g., Pelling 1980, 127–40), a similar tendency is increasingly being recognized in Athenaeus, previously dismissed as a 'plodding transcriber, faithfully preserving whatever he found' (Pelling 2000, 187). Giovannelli-Jouanna (2007, 215–37) analyzes the specific practices of Athenaeus in citing Duris, and concludes it is generally possible to ascertain the limits of the material that is directly from Duris, but that the fragments themselves, with their moral emphasis, offer a skewed view of the Macedonian history as a whole.

7 Plutarch is generally thought to have used Duris extensively in the *Demetrius*, although he nowhere cites him: cf. Sweet 1951, 177–81; Kebric 1977, 55–60; Billows 1990, 334 and n. 11. Plutarch cites Duris in a number of his other *Lives* and was evidently familiar with his work, which suggests that unattributed Durian material may underlie his narrative in other places (e.g., in the *Pyrrhus*, Kebric 1977, 59 n.

31; in the *Eumenes*, Anson 1977, 254–55; 2004, 27 n. 169); obviously, it is impossible to determine the extent to which this is the case. It is also likely that Diodorus used Duris as a source for his narrative of this period in Books 18–20 (Landucci Gattinoni 1997, 169–204; *contra* Kebric 1977, 60–66).

8 On the political career of Demetrius of Phalerum, see O'Sullivan 2009a. She provides a useful corrective to the view that Demetrius' philosophical education as a Peripatetic underlay his reforms (2009a, 5–7, 197–240).

9 Seiron of Soli is otherwise unknown; on this problematic emendation of the text of Athenaeus (not mentioned by Olson 2010, 156–57), see Landucci Gattinoni 1997, 124–25.

10 This, and all other translations of Duris, are taken from Pownall 2009–.

11 A virtually identical passage appears in Aelian *VH* 9.9, but in reference to Demetrius Poliorcetes (resulting most likely from a confusion of the two homonyms). O'Sullivan (2009b, 118–35) has recently argued that the real aim of Demetrius of Phalerum's sumptuary legislation was to distance Athens from Macdonian excesses.

12 On this theme in another, equally moralistic, literary context, cf. Pownall 2008, 333–54.

13 Cf. Ager 2005, 26: 'Unrestrained luxury and unlimited power, bringing with them a complete (and frequently perverse) sexual license, were associated with tyranny'.

14 Cf. the elegant hairstyle and effeminate clothing of the comic poet Menander, who was an associate of Demetrius of Phalerum in the Peripatetic School (Zanker 1995, 80–81).

15 Cf. Athenaeus' descriptions of the Athenian tyrant Athenion's return to Athens under the patronage of Mithridates of Pontus, the 'new Dionysus' (5.212 = Posidon. *FGH* 87 F 36), and of the assimilation to Dionysus of both Mark Antony (4.148b-c = Socr.Rhod. *FGH* 192 F 1–2) and Caligula (4.148d); on the negative topoi of tyranny in these passages, see Ballesteros Pastor 2005, 385–400.

16 Kebric 1977, 23–24; Marasco 1984, 99–109; Billows 1990, 337–39; Cooper 2009, 320–21.

17 Similarity of viewpoint, however, does not necessarily entail a personal connection between Demochares and Duris, as posited by Kebric (1977, 25–26) and O'Sullivan (2009a, 307), both of whom accept the now untenable presumption that Duris spent time in Athens as the student of Theophrastus.

18 For commentary on the ithyphallic hymn, see Mikalson 1998, 94–97.

19 Cf. Athenaeus' very similar description of the reception of Athenion by the Athenians (5.212a-e, with Ballesteros Pastor 2005, 389–90).

20 On the political reasons for the excess of Macedonian symposia, see Carney 2007; on the Greek sources' deliberate misconstruction of the important role they played in Macedonian society into evidence of their barbarism and tyranny, see Pownall 2010, 55–65.

21 After this sentence, Athenaeus switches to a new source, which implies that Duris is responsible for the totality of this citation.

22 Cf. Athenaeus' description of the statue of Dionysus draped in purple and gold garments during the famous procession of Ptolemy II in Alexandria at (5.198c = Callix. *FGH* 627 F 2).

23 Cf. Plu. *Demetr.* 2.3, but this statement is doubted by Müller (2009b, 42–43), as representing Plutarch's view, rather than Demetrius' intent.

24 The festival mentioned in this passage is the City Dionysia, which according to Plutarch (*Demetr.* 12.1) was renamed the Demetria in his honour, presumably for Duris yet another example of the Athenians' obsequious flattery (although he does not criticize his native Samians for paying divine honours to Lysander and renaming the Samian festival of Hera the Lysandreia (F 71).

25 An inauthentic variant spelling for Polyperchon; cf. Heckel 2006, 'Polyperchon' n. 618.

26 Cf. Slater 2000, 117–21 on the dancing old man as a proverbial image.

27 Plu. *Mor.* 970c and Ael. *NA* 6.25, with slightly different versions preserved by Phlegon of Tralles *FGH* 257 F 9 and App. *Syr.* 64.

28 Cf. Bearzot 1985, 16–34, 148–56, who argues that Duris was the major source for Plutarch's *Phocion*, but for very different reasons than I have proposed.

29 Plutarch's citation of Chares of Mytilene as a second source for F 51 (= *FGH* 125 F 10) supports this hypothesis, for, as I have argued previously (2010, 60–61), 'it is likely ... that his *Histories of Alexander* highlighted the luxury and excessive drinking of Alexander's symposia in order to discredit the king and his un-Hellenic behavior'.

THE DIADOCHI, INVENTED TRADITION, AND ALEXANDER'S EXPEDITION TO SIWAH

Timothy Howe

The tradition of Alexander the Great's divinity has puzzled historians and biographers since Antiquity. Certainly all of our major ancient authors attest to Alexander's engagement with divine kingship to varying degrees, and this has facilitated numerous modern interpretations.[1] Indeed, so far is our view of Alexander influenced by the Roman-era sources that Diana Spencer (2009, 251) states: 'thinking about Alexander the Great means thinking about a character generated by the cultural politics of the Roman world'. I would argue that it means thinking about a character generated by the cultural politics of the world created by the Diadochi as well. While scholars have adopted a variety of innovative and effective methodologies for dealing with the source problems concerning Alexander's divinity, they have viewed the subject only in 'Alexander-centred' ways. That is, Alexander thought he was a god or did not think he was a god. Consequently, one highly crucial question has received little focused attention: to what extent is the very concept of Alexander's living divinity a product of the distortions and agendas of the Diodochi? To put it another way: to what extent is Alexander's living divinity an invented tradition?

Eric Hobsbawm (1983, 9), in his now classic introduction to the subject, has argued that 'invented traditions' belong to three overlapping types:

> a) those establishing or symbolizing social cohesion or the memberships of groups, real or artificial communities, b) those establishing or legitimizing institutions, status or relations of authority, and c) those whose main purpose was socialization, the inculcation of beliefs, value systems and conventions of behaviour.

The living divinity of Alexander the Great seems to fit all three of these, and as Bosworth (1971) notes, the Diadochi were not above manipulating traditions when they saw fit.[2] Alexander Meeus (2009, 235) has argued persuasively that the Diadochi elaborated both their personal connections to and similarities with Alexander: 'the history of Alexander the Great did not end with his death. His generals, striving for personal power in the vacuum he left, immediately saw the benefit of exploiting his name'. Sociologist Catherine Bell (1992, 191) describes the dynamic the Diadochi faced as they strove to weave their own political narratives with Alexander's story and create lasting control: 'ideological strategies are particular forms of power struggling, effective when sheer violence would dissolve the society, when people are open to the rhetoric of collectivity and unity because it is in their interests to be so united'.[3] In this light, what we are left with when examining the divinity of Alexander is a pastiche of historical agendas, very few portions of which are original. Very few portions of which are unaffected and unembellished by the events occurring between the death of Alexander and their encoding in the surviving Roman-era authors. If we can confront the Roman baggage, as Spencer (2002; 2009; cf. Dreyer 2009b, 56–57) has done, then I suggest we also grapple with the baggage of the Diadochi. From this perspective, the most interesting aspect of Alexander's religiosity then becomes: how and why is this theme so present to the Alexander authors? Why was Alexander's divinity important to them and in what ways was it important?

Immediately after Alexander's death in June of 323, there was no clear path to succession, but there were plenty of highly ambitious and capable Macedonians who coveted the position. Indeed, Bosworth (2002, 6) may have put it best when he described the period of the successor kings as 'frankly baffling, a kaleidoscope of exotic individuals engaged in complex military and diplomatic maneuvers on several fronts simultaneously'. At this time there were no obvious successors for the kingship, for Alexander's Sogdian wife was still pregnant at the time and the king's only living child, Heracles, had never been officially acknowledged. Additionally, he left behind one half brother, Arrhidaeus, with an attested psychological disorder, and one legitimate full sister, Cleopatra. In the end, the shaky solution was to give Arrhidaeus and Alexander's legitimate son, Alexander IV, joint kingship. Yet, given his son's infancy and the various physical and mental handicaps of his half brother, the true power of Alexander's rule fell to the regent Perdiccas and to a lesser extent Antipater as they secured custody of the royal wards (Kincaid 1980, 11–12). In the Babylon Settlement, Perdiccas doled out the vast satrapies of Alexander's Empire to several of the most highly capable marshals: Egypt to Ptolemy, Media to Peithon, Thrace to Lysimachus, and Hellespontine Phrygia to Leonnatus. With no strong Argead heir it is not surprising that deadly rivalries were quick to evolve. After more than a dozen years of perpetual warfare between the inheritors of Alexander's empire, no less than five distinct kingdoms emerged, with the ruler of each declaring his rightful inheritance of Alexander's legacy by at least the mid 310s.

In this politically complex situation, the Macedonians faced a succession crisis like no other in their history. In the past, problems had arisen from the *oversupply* of legitimate Argeads. Moreover, the struggles for succession had always played out within the limited boundaries of Macedon; Alexander and his father Philip had been able to eliminate potential rivals in order to achieve at least the appearance of a united army and nobility.[4] The succession crisis of 323 was more complicated in every way. Each of the Successors commanded contingents of loyal Macedonians, and all of the leaders desired to appeal to the largest possible audiences, in order to gain the widest possible support (Bosworth 2002, 64–98, 279–84; Kincaid 1980, 1–52; Anson 2004, 35–51). As Bosworth (2002, 4) shrewdly notes, 'the new rulers were Macedonians, commanders under Alexander, but their courts were more cosmopolitan, their friends recruited from the entire Greek world and their armies still more heterogeneous... In other words the rulers were all things to all men'.

For a Diadoch to thrive in this environment he must both protect and expand his power base without risking overextension. Manipulation of tradition was a highly useful weapon in the Diadoch arsenal because, as Ton Otto (2009, 38) observes, 'traditions inculcate certain values and norms of behaviour by repetition; thus, they are devices for socialization and the production of consensus... Traditions have the capacity to symbolize and establish social cohesion and membership of a group or community'. Truly there was no precedent in established custom for these new regimes, and a ruler's authority depended not only on the respect and loyalty of his army but more importantly on the goodwill of the locals whose taxes and crops supported and made possible that army. According to Otto, during times of social stress, traditions are often exchanged with neighbouring or newly subordinate groups, in order to stabilize social structures and create new, unifying, social identities (Otto 2009, 40–46). And in the Near East the Diadochi encountered a wide variety of traditions, traditions that were necessarily absorbed and modified as part of their new administrations, divine kingship being just one of many. But above all, the Successors relied on promoting a connection to Alexander in order to justify their rule. Through imitation, political propaganda, and outright theft they strove to surpass each other in being connected to Alexander (Meeus 2009; Stewart 1993, 229–323). Indeed, Ptolemy I went so far as to steal Alexander's corpse! Repeated attempts to gain legitimacy through marriage, manipulation or murder of the surviving members of the Argead dynasty ended in the slaying of Alexander's half brother, full sister, mother, and both his legitimate and illegitimate sons at the hands of various Diadochi (Kincaid 1980, 26–27).

This politically competitive climate provided the perfect environment for story creation and invented tradition.[5] As a result, we see the first direct and undeniable steps towards divine kingship: nine cults for Seleucus, five for Ptolemy and at least ten for the Antigonids, along with several each for Lysimachus, and Cassander.[6] The Diadochi seem not unwilling to add such honours to their acclaim, legitimacy, and power.[7] Indeed, any sort of divine confirmation of a successor king by a particular group was used as a tool of political legitimization, a means of more effective governance in an effort to push ahead of the rest. But since each ruler was relying on a connection to Alexander in order to legitimate his rule, a divinely acknowledged successor should not accept such honours unless it had first been established that Alexander himself had received corresponding or greater acclaim (Dreyer 2009a).

Here, the question must be addressed that if Alexander's own soldiers and countrymen were so admittedly opposed to – or at least tentative in accepting – his own aspirations for divinity (as we see repeatedly in the Vulgate: e.g. Curt. 4.7.30; Just. 11.11.12), why did they accept the unquestionable declarations of divinity in regards to the Diadochi? Moreover, if Alexander had not been openly – or at least not widely or authoritatively – declared as divine within his lifetime, how could this happen to his successors so quickly after his death? It is probable that many participants (and many non-participants) in Alexander's campaigns were trying to make sense of why (and how) Alexander was able to achieve what he did – the conquest of Persia, and, in grappling with these seemingly superhuman achievements, a tradition was constructed. As Bruce Lincoln explains, humans use myth, often spontaneously in times of stress, to make sense of unusual or extraordinary actions and behaviours. Superhuman achievements require superhuman narratives and myth serves to alter reality so the impossible can become possible and therefore less unsettling. 'This misrepresentation ... is an ideological move characteristic of myth, as in the projection of the narrator's ideals, desires, and favoured ranking of categories into a fictive prehistory that purportedly establishes how things are and must be' (Lincoln 1999, 149).

Scholars may be tempted to chalk up the divine honours paid to the Diadochi as mere empty flattery of cities (and individuals) motivated by fear or self-interest, yet we must consider the nature of Greek religion as defined on one side by the prayer and sacrifice of the worshiper, and by the aid and protection given in return by the gods on the other. In a very real sense, the Diadochi have divine-scale power either to help or to harm. From the perspective of the average Greek, Macedonian, Babylonian or Egyptian, the rise of Alexander and his Successors represented an entirely new scale of 'god-like' rulers who were immensely powerful, unpredictable, and appeared to maintain ultimate power to destroy, protect, or save virtually any thing or person. This is clearly shown in the Ithyphallic composed at Athens for Demetrius Poliorcetes early in the third century: 'other gods are far away or have no ears or don't exist or are devoid of concern for us, but you we see ... in real presence' (Athen. 6.253 = Duris *FGH* 76 F 13).[8] The desire to bring relations with these all-powerful rulers into a well-established and comprehensible framework was a powerful force (Lund 1992, 170–73; Bosworth 2002, 3–5). In many respects, by passing laws honouring the Diadochi as gods, Greek cities were symbolizing their participation and acceptance of this new status. Indeed, as Otto (2009, 52) suggests:

> A particular tradition may serve ideological functions by 'disguising' power inequalities or by 'persuading' those who are subordinated that the inequalities are in their very best interests. The better its persuasive qualities, the more people will accept its content and the greater political power a tradition can muster.

The Diadochi, however, seem not to have gone out of their way to be given divine recognition: independent cities that desired to show their gratitude towards, and loyalty to, a particular dynast bestowed divine honours and the Diadochi accepted.[9] But in order to justify and contextualize their new status the Diadochi also patronized and encouraged cults to Alexander (Dreyer 2009a). In this sense, they facilitated the invention of traditions that accredited Alexander as the first to advance and institute such practices. This was done at least partially out of necessity, as they were clearly men of lesser achievement than their predecessor and essentially relied on the connection with him to secure their authority. Although the Diadochi served as narrators in their own 'divine Alexander' mythologies, they were not the only ones involved in mythmaking. It is during this period of narrative formation, when many of the powerful are solidifying their relationships with Alexander, that the first generation Alexander authors, Ptolemy I Soter, Aristobulus, Nearchus, Onesicritus, Chares, and the only non-participant in Alexander's conquests, Clitarchus,[10] wrote their accounts of the Great King.[11] If it had ever been in their hands, Alexander's story quickly grew beyond Diadoch control and a tradition came into being.

At this point, it might be useful to examine one of the most famous events commonly associated with Alexander's quest for living divinity, his visit to the oracle of Zeus Ammon, in order to demonstrate the ways in which invented tradition in the Age of the Diadochi might explain the evolutionary twists and turns of Alexander's story.[12] Fredricksmeyer (2003, 270) highlights the importance of the visit:

> On the occasion of his occupation of Egypt in 332–1, Alexander made a pilgrimage to the oasis of Siwah in the Libyan desert to consult the oracle of Zeus Ammon. While Darius was readying his forces for the final decision, Alexander took six weeks and several hundred miles to visit the oracle. We should think that his reasons were compelling.[13]

They were; Alexander seems to have been engaging in pragmatic policy building as well as, perhaps some personal security. Alexander was seeking what he often sought - justifications to continue the campaign and confirmation that his actions were of heroic calibre. By going to the sanctuary of Zeus Ammon at Siwah, a relatively nearby, well-known oracle, he could add perspective to his achievements and further legitimate his future conquests. A march across the desert, in emulation of Perseus and Heracles would certainly not damage his heroic credentials. Moreover, a famous oracular response now in the campaign would certainly encourage his Greek and Macedonian troops to carry the fight further into Asia.

But we should not view the trip to Siwah as unique among Alexander's experiences. He had sought out oracular responses before, for much the same reasons. On his way back to Macedonia, after meeting with the Greeks at Corinth, Alexander went out of his way to visit Delphi, and even though the oracular shrine was not receiving visitors and giving prophesies, Alexander forced the priestess to prognosticate about his expedition against Asia.[14] If he were willing to emulate his ancestor Heracles and threaten the Pythia with violence, if he were willing to force an answer out of the Greek world's most prestigious oracle, all just to add credence to his campaign, why would he not consult Siwah, a well-known, Greek-friendly oracle for the same reasons?

There are three main accounts of Alexander's visit, all credited to the first- (or second-) generation authors: Callisthenes (*FGH* 124 F 14 = Str. 17.1.43), the so-called 'court historian of Alexander', Ptolemy I Soter,[15] and Clitarchus, an Alexandrian academic, working under Ptolemaic patronage.[16] According to Callisthenes, Alexander wishes to consult the oracle in order to have matched the glory of his ancestors, Perseus and Heracles, a theme we see many times in Alexander's campaign, most notably at Delphi, Troy and Tyre.[17] In his discussion of Alexander's religious attitudes, Fredricksmeyer observes that Alexander lived by the Homeric ideal, as all nobles in Macedonia still did in the 4th century. This code of conduct stressed competition through excellence in war and conquest. By besting all others in these areas one might approximate the gods and win immortal glory.[18] Such competition certainly plays a role in the visit to Siwah. During the consultation, Callisthenes separates Alexander from the other suppliants. He contrasts how Alexander and then how everyone else is treated by the priests: (1) Alexander does not have to purify himself by changing clothes, everyone else does; (2) Alexander receives his oracle directly from the priest, in plain language, while the rest receive their answers in the traditional mute nods and gestures. Callisthenes takes pains to point out that Alexander is special, Alexander is different, and, above all, Alexander is *better* than other suppliants, perhaps even better than his ancestors, Perseus and Heracles, because he has *his* connection to Zeus revealed to him by the oracle. If viewed from a Homeric context, Callisthenes's presentation makes sense – Alexander has overtopped the competition. The reward: confirmation by Zeus's oracle that he is a son of Zeus (just like Heracles and Perseus were sons of Zeus). In the same section Callisthenes reports that Alexander's tame oracle, which he reestablished at Didyma near Miletus (Arr. *An.* 3.5.), soon confirmed Zeus Ammon's prophesy – Alexander was a son of Zeus. As Lane Fox (1973, 95) has argued, Alexander, as the patron of Callisthenes, was certainly not hostile to this information. Indeed, once Callisthenes began to critique Alexander's policies, his actions were circumscribed.[19]

Callisthenes has embellished the narrative for political effect and Strabo recognized it for what it was – flattery. In this excerpt Strabo comments three times that Callisthenes has exaggerated the account in order to flatter Alexander, to emphasize his 'Homeric' connections. We should note that Callisthenes 'flatters' Alexander in decidedly Greek terms, in the heroic language of tragedy (προστραγῳδεῖ), most certainly for a Greek audience. In the end, I find it significant that Alexander is confirmed as a son of Zeus in Callisthenes's narrative, not a son of Ammon or any other Egyptian or Asian deity.[20] The Greek context is fully, and seemingly solely, engaged. Alexander (and Callisthenes) is playing for a Greek audience.

In Callisthenes's narrative of the Siwah events, then, we can see Alexander's policy: inventing or enhancing a tradition so that he appears as heroic as his demigod ancestors, a son of the most powerful of the gods, Zeus, and as such the very person to lead the Macedonians to victory. Plutarch (*Alex.* 28.1,3) asserts that Alexander was not arrogant about his divine birth and pragmatically used it for the subjugation of his empire. To sum up, through Callisthenes's account of the visit to Siwah, we see Alexander building his own mythos, inventing his tradition, and consolidating a political tool.[21] The Diadochi and the new society they created appropriated, expanded and embellished this mythos, in an effort to do much the same thing as Alexander had done – create a system by which they might consolidate their control and legitimate their rule.

Ptolemy's account (Arr. *An.* 3.3.1–4.5) of the visit to Siwah illustrates the subtle ways in which a Diadoch could build upon the foundation laid by Alexander and Callisthenes. On the surface, the narrative closely resembles the 'court version' given by Callisthenes. Alexander has a longing (πόθος) to visit the oracle because it is infallible. He wants to rival Perseus and Heracles, and like them he is a heroic son of a god (here the son of Ammon).[22] Neither Ptolemy nor Callisthenes is asserting the king *is* a god, nor from these accounts would anyone presume that such was the case. As A. Collins points out in his study of Alexander's Egyptian divinity, 'the proclamation of Alexander as the son of Ammon by the Siwah oasis did not suddenly transform him into a god in Egyptian eyes' (Collins 2009, 204; cf. Anson 2003). Nor does it seem to have done so in Greek eyes. Whatever the oracle may have pronounced, Callisthenes's Alexander did not seem to think it made him markedly different from other Homeric heroes. His conquests allowed him to surpass Heracles and Perseus, not his divine connections, and with that he seems to have been content.

In Ptolemy's account, Alexander appears pragmatic and rational: he wants to consult an infallible oracle 'to secure more exact knowledge of his affairs, or at least *to say he had secured it*' (Arr. *An.* 3.3.2, emphasis added). According to Ptolemy, Alexander went to Siwah for the reason many people consulted oracles, to learn about the future (Bowden 2005). Ptolemy also seems to recognize that Alexander understood the propaganda value inherent in consultation - the king could use the oracle's authority to report whatever he wished, to say that he had in fact secured divine knowledge about his future campaigns. According to Callisthenes, Alexander wished to report his divine sonship, which in Alexander's cultural context put him on par with his Homeric ancestors. Yet Ptolemy holds back in his reporting (and his inventing). He does not relate what Alexander asked the oracle, nor what the oracle answered. Ptolemy merely reports that Alexander received the answer his soul desired. Alexander, after asking his question, received whatever answer he wished and seems not to have told anyone what was said.[23] So far, Ptolemy has followed, and even abbreviated, Callisthenes's account of the visit, so we must examine the events surrounding the oracular consultation to find the Ptolemy's agenda.

On the way to Siwah, Alexander became lost and according to Callisthenes, was guided to the oasis by crows. Ptolemy, alone of the surviving sources, reports that Alexander was redirected onto the proper path by two divine, speaking, snakes (Ptolemy *FGH* 138 F 8). D. Ogden (2009, 156, 160–62) asserts that the episode with the snakes was a deliberate embellishment by Ptolemy. According to Ogden, divine snakes were enmeshed in the symbolism of Ptolemaic rule over Egypt.[24] Consequently, by having snakes save Alexander (and Ptolemy) on the way to Siwah, Ptolemy invents a pedigree for his own divine symbolism. Indeed, he may have gone even farther by connecting divine snakes with Alexander's godly parentage. According to Odgen (2009, 162), 'Ptolemy began the process of merging the tradition of Alexander's sire as a snake with that of Alexander's sire as Ammon'. Indeed, in his account Ptolemy switches Alexander's claim of heroic parentage from Zeus to Ammon.[25] He also does this with the royal coinage he issues after Alexander's death. During Alexander's lifetime, his own coinage commonly bore Heracles on the obverse with Alexander holding a thunderbolt, i.e. portrayed as Zeus-like, on the reverse.[26] After his death the Alexander-as-Zeus reverse image is retired, first by Ptolemy and then by the other Successors, and Alexander as Ammon, with ram's horns, replaced Heracles and his lion skin.[27] Furthermore, under the Ptolemies, and seemingly only under the Ptolemies, Ammon comes to be connected with snakes.[28] It seems clear that once in possession of Egypt Ptolemy strengthened his own connections with the newly invented, continually evolving traditions of both Ammon and Alexander.[29]

If Ptolemy left the Siwah visit largely untouched, apart from the insertion of the guiding snakes, changing the route of the army's return,[30] and shifting Alexander's parentage from Greek Zeus to Egyptian Ammon, the next generation of authors, men like Clitarchus, fleshed out the narrative to a much greater degree, in an attempt to contextualize Alexander's accomplishments. We should remember that Clitarchus was conducting what we today would call 'library research'. Clitarchus combed numerous accounts in order to present the most complete account of Alexander's achievements (Parker 2009). At this point, I would underscore the fact that Clitarchus came from what Ton Otto identified as the pivotal 'new generation' in the evolution of invented traditions. According to Otto (2009, 46), 'it is not enough for the new generation simply to grow up in the institutional context created by the parent generation. The latter wants to ensure the continued validity of their social world by means of legitimations that 'explain' and 'justify' the institutional order and therefore help the new generation internalize these patterns'. The 'new generation' then becomes the next 'parent generation' and begins the process anew (Otto 2009, 46). According to Bosworth (1999, 9), the desire to make sense of the all-powerful Diadochi by 'elevating' them to divine status and at the same time 'lowering' the Egyptian and Olympian gods is particularly Alexandrian, starting before 300 with Hecataeus of Abdera and his propaganda on behalf of Ptolemy I Soter. Some years later Clitarchus reports the Siwah visit (D.S. 17.49.2–52.2; cf. Curt. 4.7.5–8.2; Just. 11.11.2–13).

At first glance we can make some general observations about Clitarchus's agenda. First, we can see that he is trying to sort out and make sense of Alexander's achievements: 'The proof of his [Alexander's] divine birth will reside in the greatness of his deeds; as formerly he has been undefeated, so now he will be unconquerable for all time' (D.S. 17.51.3–4). Here we see an evolution of the mythos Alexander and Callisthenes were at pains to create. The syllogism works in this way: (1) The Homeric ideal asserts that by one's deeds one can achieve divine fame; (2) Alexander has accomplished great deeds; (3) Therefore, Alexander has achieved divine fame, and as Clitarchus puts it, Alexander has proved his divine birth, his living divinity. By extending this logic, those who accomplish deeds on the scale of Alexander (the Diadochi) must therefore also be seen as divine. P. Wheatley (2009, 53–68), in his study of Successor attitudes towards adopting *basileus*, 'king', as a formal title, suggests that this logical framework was, indeed, in play at the time. Demetrius, son of Antigonus Monophthalmus, for example, the first Diadoch to take up the *basileia*, waited until 306 and his first solid military victory. In similar fashion, Ptolemy was given the title Soter by the grateful Rhodians after lifting the siege of Rhodes (conducted by *basileus* Demetrius) in 305. He adopted the diadem and title *basileus* at the same time (Stewart 1993, 231, 243). The other Diadochi seem to have linked their adoption of the title with military success in similar fashion (Wheatley 2009, 63).

Clitarchus's second agenda seems to be connected with the Ptolemies and their capital Alexandria. In Clitarchus's narrative the foundation of Alexandria has been moved *after* the visit to Siwah. By this placement, Clitarchus seems to suggest that Alexander was divinely inspired by his consultation with the priest at Siwah to found Alexandria.[31] Here, Clitarchus has built on the framework constructed by Callisthenes, 'by elaborating and surpassing his panegyrical version, and by adding a justification for Ptolemaic kingship [i.e. the founding of Alexandria]' (Dreyer 2009b, 66; Howe forthcoming). According to Dreyer, such pro-Ptolemaic embellishments are common in Clitarchus's work, the most prominent of which is Ptolemy and his consort Thais's role in the decision to burn Persepolis.[32]

Among the Roman-era authors the story of Alexander's visit to Siwah continued to evolve. Consequently, further layers of mythology were inserted, and over the course of time, the original agendas and actions became obscured. Unfortunately, it is from this later, obscured vantage point that modern historians have sought to understand Alexander's attitudes towards his personal divinity. Scholars such as Ian Worthington argue that Alexander had his personal divinity affirmed at Siwah and that the event marked (directly or indirectly) a fundamental transformation of Alexander's personality. Worthington suggests that because of his experience at Siwah Alexander became increasingly haughty, deluded with and disconnected from his Macedonian friends and soldiers, and more invested in pushing his campaign ruthlessly forward in an irrational quest for divine power.[33] Yet Diana Spencer has argued that this negative, overly moralizing portrayal of Alexander's religiosity, much like his irrational orientalism, can be linked to the Roman-era authors and their own distrust and frustration with nearly-divine, all-powerful despots such as Caligula, Nero, and Domitian (Spencer 2009, 262–65; Dreyer 2009b, 66).

The insertion of a negative bias can be seen clearly in the Siwah narrative. As discussed earlier, Diodorus, writing in the first century, does not attribute arrogance, haughtiness, or grandiose delusions to Alexander when he is at Siwah. The next generation of sources, however, do. According to Curtius (4.7.30), Alexander abuses the content of the oracular response, using its authority to force his Macedonians to address him as Jupiter, so as to increase his fame. Curtius then observes that Alexander's self-promotion had the opposite effect to what he intended: it turned people off the idea that he was divine. Justin (11.11.12) confirms the 'Roman' connections between Alexander's desire for divinity and the resulting Macedonian disapproval: 'this all served to increase the king's vanity and swell his pride to a startling degree, eliminating the geniality which he had acquired from Greek literature and Macedonian upbringing' (transl. Yardley 1997). But as I have hopefully demonstrated these conclusions are not fair to Alexander because they are the product of an evolving narrative. If one returns to Callisthenes, the visit to Siwah appears to have more unity than disconnect with Alexander's wider policies. The king is using an oracle to promote his Hellenic, very Homeric, connections and achievements. We should still keep in mind, however, that even though Callisthenes's account comes the closest to the ways in which Alexander wished to interpret the Siwah incident, it still suffers from myth creation, from invented tradition. In that sense, Callisthenes's Alexander story is no more historically 'accurate' than Justin's.

Bibliography

Anson, E. M. (2003) Alexander at Siwah, *Ancient World* 34, 117–30.

Anson, E. M. (2004) *Eumenes of Cardia: A Greek among Macedonians.* Leiden.

Armstrong, G. A. (2008) Sacrificial Iconography: Creating History, Making Myth, and Negotiating Ideology on the Ara Pacis Augustae, *Religion and Theology* 15, 340–56.

Badian, E. (1971) Alexander the Great, *Classical World* 65, 37–56.

Badian, E. (1981) The Deification of Alexander the Great. In H. J. Dell (ed.) *Ancient Macedonian Studies in Honor of Charles F. Edson*, 48–52, Thessaloniki.

Balsdon, J. P. V. D. (1950) The Divinity of Alexander the Great, *Historia* 1, 363–70.

Bell, C. (1992) *Ritual Theory, Ritual Practice.* Oxford.

Borza, E. N. (1967) Alexander and the Return from Siwah, *Historia* 16, 369.

Borza, E. N. (1981) Anaxarchus and Callisthenes: Intrigue at Alexander's Court. In H. J. Dell (ed.) *Ancient Macedonian Studies in Honor of Charles F. Edson*, 73–86, Thessaloniki.

Borza, E. N. (1992) *The Emergence of Macedon.* Princeton.

Bosworth, A. B. (1971) The Death of Alexander the Great: Rumour and Propaganda, *Classical Quarterly* 21, 112–36.

Bosworth, A. B. (1977) Alexander and Ammon. In K. H. Kintzl (ed.) *Greece and the Eastern Mediterranean in Ancient History and Prehistory*, 52–64, Oxford.

Bosworth, A. B. (1988) *From Arrian to Alexander. Studies in Historical Interpretation.* Oxford.

Bosworth, A. B. (1996) *Alexander and the East: The Tragedy of Triumph.* Oxford.

Bosworth, A. B. (1999) Augustus, the Res Gestae and Hellenistic Theories of Apotheosis, *Journal of Roman Studies* 89, 1–18.

Bosworth, A. B. (2002) *The Legacy of Alexander: Politics, Warfare, and Propaganda under the Successors.* Oxford.

Bowden, H. (2005) *Classical Athens and the Delphic Oracle. Divination and Democracy.* Cambridge.

Burstein, S. (1991) Pharaoh Alexander: A Scholarly Myth, *Ancient Society* 22, 139–45.

Carney, E. (2006) *Olympias. Mother of Alexander the Great.* London.

Carney, E. (2009) Alexander and his 'Terrible Mother'. In W. Heckel and L. A. Tritle (eds) *Alexander the Great: A New History*, 189–202, Malden, MA.

Collins, A. (2009) The Divinity of Alexander in Egypt: A Reassessment. In P. Wheatley and R. Hannah (eds) *Alexander and his Successors: Essays from the Antipodes*, 179–205, Claremont, CA.

Dahmen, K. (2007) *The Legend of Alexander the Great on Greek and Roman Coins.* London.

Dreyer, B. (2009a) Heroes, Cults, and Divinity. In W. Heckel and L. A. Tritle (eds) *Alexander the Great: A New History*, 218–34, Malden, MA.

Dreyer, B. (2009b) Jeder hat Alexander-Bild, das er verdient: The Changing Perceptions of Alexander in Ancient Historiography. In P. Wheatley and R. Hannah (eds) *Alexander and his Successors: Essays from the Antipodes*, 56–71, Claremont, CA.

Edmunds, L. (1971) The Religiosity of Alexander, *Greek, Roman, and Byzantine Studies* 12, 368–91.

Errington, M. R. (1969) Bias in Ptolemy's History, *Classical Quarterly* 19, 233–42.

Errington, M. R. (1990) *A History of Macedonia.* Berkeley and Los Angeles.

Erskine, A. (2002) Life after Death: Alexandria and the Body of Alexander, *Greece and Rome* 49, 163–79.

Fernández Nieto, F. J. (2005) La designación del sucesor en el antiguo reino de Macedonia. In V. Alonso Troncoso (ed.) *Diadochos tes basileias. La figura del sucesor en la realeza helenística*, 29–44, Madrid.
Flower, M. (2002) The Invention of Tradition in Classical and Hellenistic Sparta. In A. Powell and S. Hodkinson (eds) *Sparta: Beyond the Mirage*, 191–217, London.
Fredricksmeyer, E. (1979–1980) Three Notes on Alexander's Deification, *American Journal of Ancient History* 4, 1–9.
Fredricksmeyer, E. (1991) Alexander, Zeus Ammon, and the Conquest of Asia, *Transactions of the American Philological Association* 121, 199–214.
Fredricksmeyer, E. (2003) Alexander's Religion and Divinity. In J. Roisman (ed.) *Brill's Companion to Alexander the Great*, 253–78, Leiden.
Goukowsky, P. (1978) *Essai sur les origines du mythe d'Alexandre*. Vol. I. Nancy.
Grabbe, L. (1992) *Judaism from Cyrus to Hadrian*. Minneapolis.
Greenwalt, W. (1988) Argaeus, Ptolemy II and Alexander's Corpse, *Ancient History Bulletin* 2, 39–41.
Habicht, C. (1956) *Gottmenschentum und griechische Städte*. Munich.
Hammond, N. G. L. (1989) Arms and the King: The Insignia of Alexander the Great, *Phoenix* 43, 217–24.
Hellmann, O. (2000) *Die Schlachtszenen der Ilias*. Stuttgart.
Hogarth, D. G. (1887) The Deification of Alexander the Great, *English Historical Review* 2, no. 6, 317–29.
Houghton, A. and C. Lorber (2002) *Seleucid Coins: A Comprehensive Guide*. New York.
Howe, T. (2008) Alexander in India: Ptolemy as Near Eastern Historiographer. In T. Howe and J. Reames (eds) *Macedonian Legacies: Studies in Ancient Macedonian History and Culture in Honor of Eugene N. Borza*, 215–34, Claremont, CA.
Howe, T. (forthcoming) Founding Alexandria: Alexander the Great and the Politics of Memory. In P. Bosman (ed.) *Alexander in Africa, Acta Classica Suppl. 4*. Pretoria.
Kincaid, C. A. (1980) *Successors of Alexander the Great: Ptolemy I, Pyrrhus of Epirus, Hiero of Syracuse, Antiochus III*. Chicago.
Kuhlmann, K. P. (1988) *Das Ammoneion. Archäologie, Geschichte, und Kultpraxis des Orakels von Siwa*. Cairo.
Lane Fox, R. (1973) *Alexander the Great*. London.
Lincoln, B. (1999) *Theorizing Myth: Narrative, Ideology, and Scholarship*. Chicago.
Lund, S. (1992) *Lysimachus: A Study in Early Hellenistic Kingship*. London.
Meeus, A. (2009) Alexander's Image in the Age of the Successors. In W. Heckel and L. A. Tritle (eds) *Alexander the Great: A New History*, 235–50. Malden, MA.
Mitchell, L. (2007) Born to Rule? Succession in the Argead Royal House. In W. Heckel, L. Tritle and P. Wheatley (eds) *Alexander's Empire: Formulation to Decay*, 61–74, Claremont, CA.
Ogden, D. (2009) Alexander's Snake Sire. In P. Wheatley and R. Hannah (eds) *Alexander and his Successors: Essays from the Antipodes*, 136–78. Claremont, CA.
Otto, T. (2009) Rethinking Tradition: Invention, Cultural Continuity and Agency. In J. Wassmann and K. Stockhaus (eds) *Experiencing New Worlds*, 36–57, London.
Parker, V. (2009) Source-Critical Reflections on Cleitachus' Work. In P. Wheatley and R. Hannah (eds) *Alexander and his Successors: Essays from the Antipodes*, 28–55, Claremont, CA.
Robinson, Jr. C. A. (1943) Alexander's Deification, *American Journal of Philology* 64, no. 3, 287–95.
Roisman, J. (1984) Ptolemy and his Rivals in his History of Alexander, *Classical Quarterly* 34.2, 378–85.
Siebert, J. (1972) *Alexander der Große*. Darmstadt.
Spencer, D. (2002) *The Roman Alexander: Reading a Cultural Myth*. Exeter.

Spencer, D. (2009) Roman Alexanders: Epistemology and Identity. In W. Heckel and L. A. Tritle (eds) *Alexander the Great: A New History*, 251–74, Malden, MA.

Stewart, A. (1993) *Faces of Power: Alexander's Image and Hellenistic Politics*. Berkeley and Los Angeles.

Tarn, W. W. (1948) *Alexander the Great II: Sources and Studies*. Cambridge.

Tritle, L. A. (2003) Alexander and the Killing of Cleitus the Black. In W. Heckel and L. A. Tritle (eds) *Crossroads of History: The Age of Alexander*, 127–46, Claremont, CA.

Wheatley, P. (2009) The Diadochi, or Successors to Alexander. In W. Heckel and L. A. Tritle (eds) *Alexander the Great: A New History*, 53–68. Malden, MA.

Welles, C. B. (1963) The Discovery of Sarapis and the Foundation of Alexandria, *Historia* 11, 271–98.

Worthington, I. (2004) *Alexander the Great: Man and God*. London.

Yardley, J. C. (1997) *Justin: Epitome of the Philipic History of Pompeius Trogus. Books 11-12*. Oxford.

Notes

1 Much early Alexander scholarship sought to combine an intense criticism revolving around the ancient sources with a tendency to portray Alexander the Great as an ambitious, entirely competent, and morally incorruptible leader. Tarn 1948, 350, and Hogarth 1887, 318, for example, have been quick to criticize the ancient sources' references to Alexander's divinity. These scholars link references to divine status with Alexander's notorious 'court flatterers', or from the Successors who possessed a desire to 'record some definite proof or sanction of his divinity'. This approach is further supported and refined by historians like Robinson 1943 and Balsdon 1950, who emphasize that Alexander never personally thought of himself as a god, but was misunderstood as he used this idea to further his political agenda and goals for conquest. In response, scholars such as Habicht 1956 assembled and analyzed the evidence that might support Alexander's divinity, and some, such as Badian 1981, have worked to justify much of the controversial source material (especially the so-called 'Vulgate' tradition of Quintus Curtius Rufus, Plutarch, and Justin). Edmunds 1971, Bosworth 1996, Fredricksmeyer 1979–1980, 1991, 2003 and Worthington 2004 have all contributed substantially to a reconsideration of Alexander's godliness. These scholars have essentially concluded that Alexander actively promoted and pursued deification throughout his rule, and that this was the primary cause of his downfall. Dreyer 2009a concludes that the evidence for Alexander putting himself on a par with the gods during his lifetime cannot be proved to date to *before* the great man's death. Collins 2009 concludes that since Alexander had never been crowned Pharaoh, he never achieved divine status in his lifetime.

2 As Otto 2009, 50, observes, 'invented traditions, though, are intended as innovative forces; they invoke the authority of the past and of repetitive action to legitimate something that, in fact, is new'. The Diadochi certainly did not hold back when appropriating Alexander's legacy. See Goukowsky 1978. Even Alexander's body became a piece in their game for dominance and power. See Greenwalt 1988; Hammond 1989; Erskine 2002; Meeus 2009, 242–43.

3 Otto 2009, 38, suggests that invention of tradition is most likely to happen 'in times of rapid social change, when the strength and legitimacy of old patterns are weakened or destroyed', and often involves an element of 'social engineering'. See Flower 2002, 192 and Armstrong 2008, 340–56, for this phenomenon in Sparta and Augustan Rome, respectively.

4 Errington 1990, 35–59, 103–14; Borza 1992, 133–35, 177–79, 189–97. For further discussion of succession see Fernández Nieto 2005 and Mitchell 2007.

5 'Traditions serve to legitimate customs, providing a reflexive space that confirms the customary patterns. This reflection is both cognitive and normative because it explains, justifies and provides moral authority to the activities concerned' (Otto 2009, 41).

6 Habicht 1956, 82–108 (Seleucids); 109–26 (Ptolemies); 43–81 (Antigonids); 38–41 (Lysimachus); 37–38 (Cassander). See discussion in Lund 1992, 172–73. Cf. Kincaid 1980, 37, 58, who notes the existence of divine ruler cults to Pyrrhus of Epirus also arising at this time.

7 Indeed, the whole effect may have 'snowballed' out of the Successors' immediate control, see Otto 2009, 46.

8 The quotation can have negative as well as positive connotations. According to Grabbe 1992, 211, the Diadochi are portrayed by the Jews of Judaea as the evil semi-divine giants, the offspring of angels and men (*1 Enoch* 7).

9 Much as the Greek cities of Asia Minor have done with Alexander, earlier, when he freed them from Persian rule and established 'democratic' constitutions. See Dreyer 2009a, 223–28. See Kincaid 1980, 35–38, for a discussion of Successor policy. Ptolemy's deification in 304 for his help in lifting the siege of Rhodes is an excellent example of this. See Lund 1992, 169–75. Otto 2009, 47, suggests that we view such actions as attempts to normalize a new relationship and subordinate it to, and integrate it with, existing patterns of behaviour.

10 Parker 2009, 28–55, offers a well-argued analysis of Clitarchus's method and sources and concludes that 'he was much more than a recounter of wild fables, purveyor of salacious gossip, and heedless blunderer.... Cleitarchus' assiduous reading should place him in the first rank for any historian of Alexander who faces one essential difficulty: all of the accounts written by contemporaries have perished' (50–51). He further suggests that 'Cleitarchus is demonstrably working after the publication of those works [i.e. Nearchus, Onesicritus, Callisthenes, and Aristobulus], after the first generation of *Alexander-Historiker*' (36). See Siebert 1972, 17–18, for a discussion and review of the relevant scholarship surrounding the date of Clitarchus's work.

11 Howe 2008, 215–34, argues that Ptolemy I deliberately embellished his narrative of Alexander's Indian campaign, the last important military action of the king's life, to accentuate his, Ptolemy's, role and thereby appear more Alexander-like than the other marshals, such as Perdiccas and Hephaestion.

12 The visit to Siwah has been the focal point of many scholarly debates. Some of the most prominent are: Bosworth 1977; Burstein 1991; Collins 2009; Badian 1981; Fredricksmeyer 1979–1980, 1991, 2003; Edmunds 1971; Tarn 1948, 348–50; Worthington 2004, 203.

13 For Alexander's visit, see Arr. *An.* 3.3.3–4; D.S. 17.49.2–51.4; Curt. 4.7.5–8; Just. 11.11.2–12; Plu. *Alex.* 26.11–27.11; Str. 17.1.43.

14 Plu. *Alex.* 14.6–7. Plutarch, as high priest of Delphi, might have been in unique position to report local Delphic traditions accurately.

15 Arr. *An.* 3.3.1–4.5. Dreyer 2009b, 63, 66, accepts the *communis opinio* that Arrian is reporting Ptolemy here.

16 Dreyer 2009b, 63, suggests that Clitarchus preserved in D.S. 17.49.2–52.1 is the most authoritative; Justin and Curtius have embellished the original narrative with Roman-era material. Parker 2009, 28–55, argues persuasively that Clitarchus was a competent, library-based historian, writing after 280, who used the works of all of the first generation writers, especially Aristobulus and Callisthenes.

17 Arr. *An.* 1.12.1; cf. 7.14.4, where Alexander claims to be in competition with Achilles; Plu. *Alex.* 15.8; D.S. 17.17.3; Just. 11.5.12.

18 Aristotle, Alexander's teacher, imbued in Alexander a love for Homer, and in his *Hymn to Excellence* emphasized Alexander's ancestors, Heracles, Achilles, and Ajax as models of behaviour (Athen. 15.696 b-d). He even gave Alexander an annotated copy of the *Iliad*, so he might continue his studies and master true, heroic, honour (Plu. *Alex.* 15.8–9; 62–5; 72.3; D.S. 17.97.3; Ael. *VH* 7.8). See Fredricksmeyer 2003, 255–56; and Stewart 1993, 78–86, for further discussion. For this 'Homeric' ideal and its implications on later Greeks see Hellmann 2000.

19 Callisthenes opposed the introduction of *proskynesis* (Arr. *An.* 4.11–12; Curt 8.5). Alexander ultimately abandoned the policy, once he saw that it was politically damaging. Tarn 1948, 359–62; Robinson 1943; Borza 1981. For Callisthenes's execution see Arr. *An.* 4.13; Curt. 8.6.1–22. Worthington 2004, 205–06, views Callisthenes's fall as an example of Alexander becoming irrational and fully invested in forcing his living divinity on his subjects.

20 Cf. Plut. *Alex.* 33.1 (Callisthenes *FGH* 124 F 36), where Callisthenes has Alexander pray before Gaugamela, 'that if he really were the son of Zeus they [the gods] should protect and encourage the Greeks'.

21 Whatever he was told at Siwah, Alexander took care to maintain the connection and honour the oracle of Ammon throughout his life. He consulted the oracle about posthumous honours for Hephaistion (Arr. *An.* 7.14.7–10; 7.23.6–8; Plu. *Alex.* 72.2–5; 75.3; Just. 12.12.12; D.S. 17.114–15). He even wanted to

be buried at the oasis (D.S. 18.3.5; 18.28.3; Curt. 10.5.4; Just. 12.15.7), though since this tradition comes from Clitarchus, it seems likely to have been affected by invented tradition and must be interpreted cautiously.

22 Notice the switch in titles. In Callisthenes's account Alexander was a 'son of Zeus'. Ptolemy calls him a 'son of Ammon'. While Alexander was interested in communicating to a Greek audience, through Callisthenes's narrative, and engaging a very Greek Homeric ideal, Ptolemy has a slightly different audience. He must engage the powerful priests of Ammon in Thebes, as well as Greeks and Egyptians in the new city of Alexander. See Howe 2008, 215–233, for a discussion of Ptolemy's historiographic aims and audience. Collins 2009, 179–205, argues that the Egyptian priests developed rituals to legitimate and regularize Macedonia hegemony over Egypt and syncretise Macedonian traditions with native religious beliefs.

23 Alexander was probably led into the inner sanctum of the temple, where he asked his questions. The high priest hid in a secret listening chamber off to the side where he recorded the questions and composed the god's responses in writing. This answer was then given to Alexander. The nature of oracular consultation at Siwah suggests that Alexander could easily keep his answer quiet, if he so wished. See Kuhlmann 1988, 144–46, for a discussion of the layout of the sanctuary and an interpretation of how the oracle operated.

24 Ptolemy's life was saved by a snake in India, and his building projects in Alexandria were connected with snakes. See Ogden 2009, 152–55, 157–60; and also his paper in this volume.

25 See Carney 2006, 102–03, for argument that Olympias did not encourage Alexander into thinking he was son of Zeus Ammon, as Justin 11.11.3–6 asserts: 'Greek women, especially elite or royal Greek women, could not risk the charge of adulterous behavior, whether with a man or a divine snake' (103). Cf. Carney 2009, 200–01. See Carney 2006, 124–37, for discussions of the negative portrayal of Olympias as overly emotional and irrational in the Alexander sources.

26 Originally, it was thought that the so-called 'Elephant Medallions' were the only coins extant that portrayed Alexander as Zeus but a coin hoard from Iraq has yielded 7 similar examples (Dahmen 2007, 6 and 67, n. 3) all dating to within Alexander's lifetime. See Stewart 1993, 191–200, for the many ways Alexander employed the thunderbolt and other Zeus imagery during his lifetime.

27 Dahmen 2007, 6–7 (as Zeus), 13–17 (as Ammon). In Chapter 3 'Making Good use of a Legend', 48–55, Dahmen argues that Successor coinage invariably represented Alexander as divine, in order to strengthen claims to divinity. Not all of the Diadochi, however, replace Heracles with Ammon. The Seleucids long preserve the original forms. See Houghton and Lorber 2002.

28 Until Ptolemy I Soter, neither Greeks nor Egyptians perceived Ammon as a snake (Ogden 2009, 145).

29 When Ptolemy might have begun literary manipulation of the tradition is a matter of some debate. Certainly his own divine honours, offered by the Rhodians in 305 (D.S. 20.11.3), had some impact. Badian 1971, 40, dates Ptolemy's history to the period between the theft of Alexander's body and 308. Errington 1969, 241, connects the work to the war with Perdiccas and thus dates it to not long after 320. Roisman 1984, 385, argues that the date is irrelevant since, '[f]or all we know, Ptolemy could have written his history simply for the sake of writing history. If so, the time of its composition was of little political relevance'. Dreyer 2009b, 56–71, accepts the traditional end of life date (c. 280). I tend to agree with Dreyer.

30 See Howe (forthcoming) where I argue that Ptolemy switched the return from Siwah in order to highlight the importance of Alexandria.

31 Of all the sources, only Clitarchus places the founding of Alexandria after Siwah. See Curt. 4.8.1–3; Just. 11.11.13; Welles 1963; Borza 1967. Dreyer 2009b, 64–66, argues that Clitarchus transposes the chronological order of events to show a divine connection between Ammon and Alexandria and in so doing confer on the Ptolemies, and their rule from Alexandria, divine approval.

32 The destruction of the symbolic, religious capital of the Persians would have great resonance to both Greeks and Egyptians: cf. Dreyer 2009b, 63.

33 Worthington 2004, 203. See also Bosworth 1977, 62–64; 1996, 115–18; Badian 1981, 52–53; Fredricksmeyer 1991, 214; Edmunds 1971, 387–91.

STRABO, INDIA AND BARBEQUED BRAHMANS

Brian Bosworth

'Embassies from kings in India were often sent to me; before that time they had not been seen by any Roman commander' (*R.Gest.div.Aug.* 31.1). This is a famous passage of the *Res Gestae*, eloquent testimony to the imperialist ambitions of the Roman emperor Augustus. In it he declares that he received submission from Indian rulers at the world's eastern rim and did so many times over. The terminology is unambiguous (*ad me ex India regum legationes saepe missae sunt*), and we are to envisage a continuous (*saepe*) diplomatic process. As we shall see, Augustus regarded the Indian ambassadors as embassies and subjects of the Roman imperium. That is clear enough. What is far from clear is the role that the Indian representatives put upon their embassies. They were approaching the world power and must surely have had requests of their own, requests that were pertinent to their military and political milieu. However, diplomatic communications had to be conducted in intelligible language, and – crucially – the interpreters must have the expertise to give a faithful rendering of the terms of any agreement, so that both sides could understand each other.[1] Strabo himself may not have witnessed any of these embassies directly, but he was probably in touch with members of Augustus' entourage in Athens and knew whom to approach for information, written or spoken.[2]

We can now enlarge the focus of the discussion and deal with the general political situation in the Near East. The first recorded embassy dates to 25 BC, when Augustus was in Tarraco, the capital of Nearer Spain. He was convalescing after falling sick during the Cantabrian War, and according to Orosius (*Hist.* 6.21.19–20) he received envoys from India and Scythia in imitation of Alexander, who had been inundated by embassies from the far west during his last days in Babylon. This was an invaluable piece of propaganda. Augustus was able to do what Alexander himself had failed to do, and the lands under his sway extended from Britain to Parthia (*R.Gest.div.Aug.* 32.1). But there was more at issue than simple political propaganda. We should remember that the envoys from India were representatives of their ruler in negotiations with a dynast whom they no doubt considered their equal. They were not subjecting themselves to an overlord.

What, then, were the Indian embassies about? In my opinion the explanation lies in the turbulent history of the Parthian Empire. There had been prolonged civil war, and the reigning king, Phraates IV, had been expelled from his throne around 30 BC, and was replaced – temporarily – by the Parthian noble Tiridates. In his turn Tiridates was deposed thanks to assistance from the Shaka peoples of the north east (the traditional homeland of the Parthian monarchy). He found refuge in Syria, taking a son of the Parthian monarch as hostage, and seeking Augustus' protection (*R. Gest.div.Aug.* 32.1). Not surprisingly Phraates expressed outrage, and demanded the return of his son and 'his slave Tiridates' (Just. 42.5.7), while Augustus cleverly played the two sides off against each other, and observed strict neutrality. In the end there was an impressive hearing in the Roman senate, at which Augustus received representations from Tiridates' and Phraates' envoys. Both parties requested military support, which the Roman emperor roundly refused. He merely offered the return of the Parthian prince, delivering the son back to his father (D.C. 53.33.1–2) – perhaps to an early death, given Phraates' previous ruthless treatment of his relatives, including killing thirty of his brothers, his own father and an adult son (Just. 42.5.1–2).

The Indian embassies now come into the picture. It looks as though there were troubles in the Parthian east as well as the west. The ruling power in Augustus' day was the Shaka peoples who had occupied the lands to the west of the Indus valley, and were in intermittent conflict with the Parthian monarchs. It was the Shaka that supported Phraates in his period of exile and, according to Justin, they were instrumental in his restoration. This was just the time for them to approach Augustus and ask for military assistance. What is more, the arterial road from Gandhara to Mesopotamia was largely in Shaka hands and their embassies could travel to the Roman court without harassment, from the Indus to Spain. There they made their representations and offered what they considered to be the appropriate gifts. It was also natural for Augustus to represent these diplomatic overtures as obeisance from the ends of the world.

Strabo adds a number of details to the general picture. At the beginning of Book 15, he discusses the value of his sources, and lets us know what they are (Str. 15.1.2). He does so in a Thucydidean style, looking for material that is absolutely correct and informants who are totally reliable. He is sceptical, and largely discounts his sources. Above all, and most striking to modern ears, is that he deliberately ignores the reports of the merchants who were active on the South Indian run: 'even these are merely private citizens and of no use as regards the history of the places they have seen' (Str. 15.1.4 C686; trans. H. L. Jones, Loeb).

This ought to be a precious hoard of first hand information, but Strabo is adamant that the material is unreliable. He regards the merchants as rank amateurs with very little geographical knowledge, as indeed does Pliny (*Nat.* 6.160), who treats us to something very rare in his work – a joke! In his eyes even the Roman forces serving under Augustus' grandson Gaius did no more than take a peek at the outer ocean and immediately withdraw. There were clearly entrepreneurs who had direct knowledge of the coastal voyage as far as the Ganges, but they were few in number and their reports were unreliable. Against their scanty notes Strabo sets a detailed report of a colourful episode. The second embassy to Augustus, he claims, came from a single area and a single king (Str. 15.1.4 C686).[3] It showed the magnitude of the task of geographical investigation. There were simply too few potential informants. If a single king could provide the wherewithal for a hugely expensive embassy, how great would the entire population of India be? This gives us a precious insight into the sources of Strabo's information. It clearly came from the ambassadors, who spent several months at Augustus' court, and with judicious use of interpreters could convey a good deal of information about their homeland. The Indian king may also have briefed them well in advance.

This embassy met with Augustus when he was returning from his sensational diplomatic triumph after he recovered the legionary eagles that had been lost with Crassus and Antony. He spent the winter of 20/19 in Syria and gave the area an administrative overhaul. It was there that the Indian embassy arrived. We have a detailed account of its reception, but it was hardly direct transcription. The actual source was the contemporary historian Nicolaus of Damascus, who met the Indian embassy in Antioch and was well placed to report to Augustus (Str. 15.1.73 C719–20). Strabo uses indirect speech, and makes it clear that he bears no responsibility for the veracity of his account, stating explicitly that he is using Nicolaus directly, what was a good choice by current historiographical criteria. Strabo also reports that only three of the ambassadors found their way to the Syrian coast. The rest died of travel fatigue thanks to the length of the journey. That is not surprising. The Danish explorer, Carsten Niebuhr (the father of the historian), set out in January 1761 with a grandiose commission to explore Egypt, Arabia and Syria, and within eighteen months he found himself the sole survivor.[4] The Indians who visited Augustus were more fortunate.

What most fascinated Nicolaus was a letter from the Indian king. He stated that it was written on prepared skin (Str. 15.1.73 C719), a claim that has evoked some scepticism, or did so until the discovery of a tax return from Bactria that was written in Greek on a surface of skin (Rea, Senior, Hollis 1994). It is headed by a dating formula (l. 1), which names three rulers. The first and senior is named *theos Antimachos,* and, as with Ai Khanum, there are a number of subordinate officers with Greek names, and in some cases holding Greek offices. A certain Diodorus was one such official (l. 5), attested controller of revenues, and we also hear of a *nomophylax* (l. 2–3), an official who has some parallels in the Seleucid administration (cf. *OGIS* 240.3, 290.4, 300.2, 483.21). Strabo emphasises that Nicolaus was using documentary evidence and aimed for autopsy. That was the mark of a scrupulous investigator, bent on the establishment of fact. Strabo clearly picked a good source, as far as factual accuracy went. There are other parallels in the letter of Porus, who used parchment as the medium for his official communications and was competent to write in Greek. He identifies himself as Porus, the person who wrote the message, and he adds that he was paramount ruler of six hundred lesser kings. This figure recalls the estimates of Porus' kingdom which were current in Alexander's day. According to Strabo (15.1.33 C701; cf. Arr. *An.* 5.20.4; 6.2.1), the land between the Jhelum and Chenab was immensely populous, boasting some 5,000 cities, each as large as Meropid Cos, although Strabo opines that the numbers are exaggerated. Perhaps the Indian king was aware of the literature relating to Alexander and believed that his domains had comparable resources which would make him a desirable ally. For his part Porus considered it a matter of great concern to acquire the friendship of Caesar.

This brings us to the crux of the matter. The Indian delegation carried proposals for a working alliance. Porus agreed to let Roman forces through his territory wherever they pleased and to collaborate in any enterprise 'that was honourable' (Str. 15.1.73 C719). Strabo's quotation of Porus' alleged language here evokes the Pillar edicts of the Mauryan emperor Asoka, which promote adherence to *Dhamma* (moral purity) 'by being persuaded not to injure living beings and not to take life' (*PE* 7). If Porus also subscribed to Asoka's principles of *Dhamma*, it would have been singularly difficult for him to wage any sort of offensive war. But the Romans had no such scruples. Augustus himself was directly or indirectly responsible for more deaths than that of any single human being of his time, and he may have found it an attractive proposition to use the Indian monarch's treasure chest to increase the imperium of the Roman people. It was a bizarre combination. On the one hand we have the Indian monarch who seems to have belonged to the Jain persuasion and obsessively abstained from the slaughter of practically every living animal. On the other hand, Augustan Rome ran on death and destruction. In the *Res Gestae* (22.3) the emperor proudly claimed to have staged no less that twenty six hunts, with his sons and grandsons, with around 3,500 African beasts slaughtered in the arena. This is hypocrisy on a breathtaking scale. Porus shrank from killing in his own right, but was ready to have the Roman emperor do his dirty work for him.

Was Porus successful? Strabo gives no indication. He simply refers back to Nicolaus as the source for the Indian king's letter and he either does not know the outcome of the embassy or prefers not to mention it. There is, however, a chance that *some* troops were sent to India, and even that they reached their destination. We have some evidence of Roman military units operating in the Far East, in particular what appears to be a detachment of XV Apollinaris, which has left its signature on the cave of Kara-Kamar, far away on the borders of Uzbekistan.[5] This is dubious evidence, given that no single identifiable Latin word can be traced on the cave wall, but it is unlikely that such a *graffito* in such a remote locale would have been a modern forgery. And if the Roman *vexilla* could find their way to the extreme north east, they certainly could do the same for India, and (*exempli gratia*) operate in Porus' interest in the area around the Khyber Pass, where the king's territory was most likely to have been found.

After establishing friendly relations with the Indian embassy (D.C. 54.9.7–9),[6] Augustus spent time in Athens, where the Eleusinian Mysteries were rescheduled in his honour. The royal gifts from India were objects of intense curiosity, particularly the so-called *Hermes*, who had no arms or shoulders and performed all his functions with his feet (Str. 15.1.73 C719). In all probability he remained in Athens after Augustus left for the west and became a tourist attraction. One such tourist was Strabo himself, who insists that he saw the prodigy in person. It is unlikely that he was in Augustus' entourage; otherwise there would have been no need to refer to Nicolaus for an eyewitness description. What is clear is that Strabo learned of the wonders of the embassy through an intermediary (Nicolaus) and supplemented it from his own personal experience. Here he differs from Cassius Dio, who used second hand information and treated it with some scepticism:

like Herodotus, he merely writes what is stated and leaves his sources anonymous (D.C. 54.8–10). He is also inaccurate, when he alleges that the travelling menagerie included Indian tigers, the first to be seen by Romans. This detail does not occur in Nicolaus and Strabo, and it is hard to accept. The exotic beasts in the Indian entourage include snakes and an outsize partridge, but no tigers, and it is hard to see how a beast the size of a tiger could have survived the arduous journey that had killed off the human ambassadors. Admittedly Seleucus I had sent a tiger to Athens (Ath. 13.590a), to the amazement of the populace, but by the time of the Augustan embassies, it was a distant memory. What is more, Dio's embassy supposedly boasted a number of tigers, unlike the single lone beast of Seleucus, and they would have required a prodigious amount of fresh meat merely to stay alive. That consideration alone invalidates the tradition of the Indian tigers.

In contrast, the eyewitness account of Nicolaus seems relatively conservative. It has a profusion of detail, much of it verifiable, and it vindicates Strabo's choice of material. Compare for instance his description of the dress (or undress) of the Indian serving men. There are eight of them, clad in loin cloths which are sprinkled with perfume. That evokes an earlier image, the frieze of the subject peoples at Persepolis. The Indian satrapies show the delegates all wearing loin cloths with the upper parts of their bodies bare (see Badian 1998, 219). That is a reflection of Strabo's description of the Indian embassy, and it appears that the Indian dress was essentially unchanged between the Achaemenid monarchy and the principate of Augustus.

But the most sensational aspect of the affair was the public suicide of a member of the entourage. According to Strabo (15.1.73 C720), the man's name was Zarmanochegas and his tomb was on display, recording his domicile (Bargasa) and adding that 'he sought immortality for himself, following the customs of the Indians (*kata ta patria*)'. This is interesting. Strabo uses direct speech rather than follow Nicolaus. He also claims that the Indian sage was following an Indian custom when he achieved his immortality through his death by fire.[7] This provides us with a rare glimpse of autopsy. It looks as though Strabo himself had viewed the inscription. Cassius Dio (54.9.8–10) is more elaborate. He gives the name as Zarmarus, clearly an abbreviation, and records a number of explanations of his decision to commit suicide: it was either ambition and display, or following ancestral tradition when he was overtaken by old age. He adds that the Indian was initiated into the Eleusinian Mysteries, which were held – extraordinarily – in his honour. There is a tinge of criticism here. Some, according to Dio, maintained that Zarmarus was simply showing off before the emperor, his fellow initiate. Others suggested that he was after immortality. The terminology used certainly implies that there was an element of vain glory in the display. Though a mortal, he was aiming at immortality, and he may have even intended to upstage Augustus himself. In that case, the emperor may have hoped and expected that the Indian sage might disgrace himself. If so, he was singularly disappointed. Whichever tradition one follows, the Indian triumphed over the fire, and his tomb was graced with a deliciously ambiguous epitaph: he had aimed at immortality but failed to achieve godhead.

If immolation by fire was a delicate subject, then Strabo had to be extremely circumspect. His Indian ascetic chose the quickest way to death, leaping directly into the pyre. The slow agony described by some of the earlier accounts has no place here. Death by fire can never be anything other than hideous, but Zarmarus took the easiest way out, as did Proteus Peregrinus when he jumped into the flames at the Olympic Games of 164 (Luc. *Peregr.* 35–36). Zarmarus, of course, was consciously imitating a famous suicide in the reign of Alexander. This was the self-immolation of Calanus, the Brahman courtier of the great king. In this episode there is a fair amount of variation, and Strabo carefully labels his direct sources. We have seen his use of Nicolaus of Damascus. Other authorities that are used for the suicide of Calanus include Onesicritus (*FGH* 134 F 17a) and Megasthenes (*FGH* 715 F 34a), the most influential historians of India during the period of the Diadochi. Strabo (15.1.68 C717) adduces the episode as an example of the variants in the Alexander tradition. There is general agreement that Calanus died by fire, but the means are different, as are the motives. After a passage on the custom of the Brahmans to remain in India lifelong, Strabo turns to the principal variant: one tradition has Calanus lie on a golden couch and remain immovable while the pyre takes its course; another, more problematic, story has him occupy a more elaborate pyre which takes the shape of a house, a wooden structure with its interior filled with dry leaves. The purpose of this somewhat strange arrangement was to produce the greatest possible conflagration in the briefest time.[8] The leaves would provide the initial kindling and the 'house' would collapse into itself, so that a rapid inferno would engulf the funerary couch. Calanus himself leaped into the heart of the flames, where he was consumed along with the rest of the pyre. He was destroyed like the philosopher Empedocles, who had supposedly flung himself into a crater of Mt. Etna to be immediately incinerated (D.L. 8.70–71). He had lost his mortality and his death by fire was his passport to divinity. The story of the wooden house is similar, and Strabo uses appropriately picturesque language: Calanus was burned along with his house, just like one of its main beams. According to this version the scene was sensational, culminating in the death leap of Calanus. The other tradition has that the sage burned with his pyre and remained immovable. Strabo is relatively conservative in his treatment of the great event. He clearly knows several versions, but he selects two which seem to him to be representative. His readers can make up their own minds, and choose whatever branch appeals to them.

The geographer gives us what is arguably a collection of research notes, and apart from the analogy of Calanus and the roof beam, that prose is pedestrian. This contrasts sharply with Arrian's description of the event (*An.* 7.3), which concentrates on the details of the suicide, and in particular the procession to the pyre, with Calanus riding on a royal horse of Nesaean stock. The scene was a colourful medley: gold and silver goblets and rich tapestry, all signs of Alexander's favour, and the assembly performed an exotic display of Indian song. The great ceremony ended appropriately with the procession of the royal elephants, who honoured Calanus with their high pitched war squeal. There could be no more exciting display. Arrian terminates his account with a brief sermon, illustrating the invincibility of the human mind when it is set on its aims. And Arrian deliberately describes the human condition as invincible (*anikētos*), exactly the epithet that is elsewhere applied to Alexander. He himself was uniquely invincible, so Arrian suggests, but his subjects could achieve similar success by sheer force of will. Calanus' suicide now becomes an object lesson. He can burn to death without flinching, without sensational display.

Strabo, it seems, paid particular attention to suicide and Indian attitudes to it. He singled out Megasthenes as a source (Str. 15.1.68 C718) and followed his account of the various types of death. All involve violence and are the mark of an immature and undisciplined temperament. After a virtual typology of suicide Megasthenes ended with Calanus, who was the paradigm of the fiery character, the person who would thrust himself into fire. Calanus was 'a slave to the tables of Alexander' (*FGH* 715 F 34a, 26–27) and, as such, the paradigm of the undisciplined individual. The stage was therefore set for the Indian embassy of 20/19. There in Athens Zarmarus gave a perfect example of the fiery disposition and echoed the display of Calanus. But what display? Which of the two deaths by fire can we accept as authentic? Strabo gives vivid accounts of the two versions. One tradition is common with Arrian (*An.* 7.3.6), who draws upon the contemporary Nearchus (*FGH* 133 F 42.4). This has Calanus victim of a persistent gastric illness, and the sage dies on the pyre, burned to death on a couch. The other has Calanus throw himself into the flames while the fire is at its height. The motives are somewhat different. Calanus kills himself when he is thrall to an incurable disease, whereas Zarmarus in Athens takes preventative action, killing himself before his good fortune ceases: 'he thought it necessary... to depart this life in case something untoward happened to him while he lingered here' (Str. 15.1.73 C720) - a very Herodotean sentiment! The other tradition, based on Onesicritus (*FGH* 134 F 17a), states that Calanus was following the Indian custom, which regarded disease as something shameful and was insistent that the sufferer should commit suicide, even if he merely suspected illness. This tradition is shared by Nearchus (*FGH* 133 F 42.4), who also described Calanus' heroic feat of endurance. Both he and Onesicritus saw illness as an abomination that had to be purged by fire and he refused to compromise his principles, resisting Alexander himself.

Can we go further? I think we can. As has been observed neither Onesicritus nor Nearchus was physically present at Pasargadae where the immolation took place. They were with the ocean fleet on its run from Hormuz to Susa during the winter of 324/3, and were pursuing an unpleasant little vendetta, both accusing the other of incompetence. But both were in a position to question eyewitnesses, and both could claim autopsy at one remove. But what did these eyewitnesses witness? It was probably the leap into the pyre and instantaneous death, as described in the second tradition. This was the story that was passed down to Zarmarus and later still to Proteus Peregrinus. And it is clearly what we should term the authorised version. Against that tradition, Onesicritus and Nearchus represented the Indian sage dying without a motion, a death even more heroic than a violent leap into the flames, which immediately vaporised him. A hostile critic might have considered it cowardice, as did Lucian when he ridiculed Peregrinus for choosing the easiest form of death: 'you just have to open your mouth and you are immediately dead' (Luc. *Per.* 21–2).

Calanus was not the only suicide recorded in the time of Alexander. Diodorus (19.34.3–6) gives a vivid description of an act of *sati* (widow burning), which was perpetrated in the winter of 317/16, when the widow of an Indian prince joined her deceased husband on his funeral pyre. The associated procession is described in detail, and closely matches Arrian's account of Calanus' obsequies. There is the same emphasis on the bride's gold and silver ornaments, an encomium of the lady's virtues sung by her relatives, and, most striking, a ceremonial parade by the Macedonian army, which marched three times round the pyre with full weaponry. The recorded facts are beyond doubt, and they look back to the Achaemenid regime. The great procession included gold and silver vessels as well as royal dress (*esthēta basilikēn*, Arr. *An.* 7.3.2), which was the special prerogative of the Achaemenid monarchs. The *Book of Esther* (6.7–8) is unequivocal on the matter: 'If the king wishes to honour someone, have royal robes brought, which the king has worn, and a horse which the king has ridden, with a royal diadem on his head. The robes and horse should be handed to one of the noblest of the king's officers'. Artefacts which the king had used were treated with special veneration, and their recipients had the status of royal Benefactors (*Book of Esther* 6.7–8; see also Briant 2002, 303).

The story of the Indian princess goes back to the first and best of the earliest Hellenistic historians, Hieronymus of Cardia (cf. D.S. 19.34.1–6), who has given us an extraordinarily vivid picture of the proceedings (cf. also D.S. 19.33). Hieronymus had concentrated on the heroic achievement of the Indian lady, who in 317 braved the onset of the flames and set an impressive example to the Macedonian army.[9] There are parallels from the period, in particular the death of Alexander's mother Olympias (316), who took immense pain to preserve her modesty in the face of her executioners (D.S. 19.51.5: cf. Carney 2006, 85). It is highly unlikely that there was any suggestion of force. What mattered was the preservation of one's dignity in the most extreme circumstances, and Hieronymus described the reactions of the observers to the display of endurance (*karteria*); it inspired some of them to pity, others to a surfeit of praise. The Indian princess proved herself impervious to pain (thanks perhaps to advanced techniques of meditation), and the Brahman sage showed a rare taste for the spectacular. His leap into the unknown would have been galvanic.

According to Arrian (*An.* 7.3.1), Calanus 'told Alexander that it was good for him to bring his life to such an end, before some suffering came to test him and forced him to change his former way of life'. The sentiment is strongly Herodotean, reminiscent of Polycrates of Samos, and Croesus of Lydia, as well as Xerxes himself, whose career can be seen as a steady decline from world empire to military catastrophe. Diodorus (17.107.4–5) also stresses the 'extraordinary' character of the event, which attracted a large audience of soldiers and camp followers. Another factor was Calanus' superhuman power of endurance. Whatever tradition he adopted, it is clear that his behaviour on the pyre had a profound effect upon Alexander's entourage. Calanus was prepared to submit to a hideous death rather than violate his ancestral practices, which included death by fire, as Onesicritus noticed (Str. 15.1.64 = *FGH* 134 F 17a).

Calanus had close connections with Lysimachus the bodyguard and future king, who seems to have had regular discourses with a group of enthusiasts and probed general questions of philosophy (*epi sophia*, Arr. *An.* 7.3.4). What those questions were, is hard to fathom, but the dialogue of Calanus and Onesicritus must preserve something of the truth (Str. 15.1.63–65; Plu. *Alex.* 65 = *FGH* 134 F 17a–b). In this tradition there is a sharp confrontation, which reminds one of Sparta. The source here is the Augustan intellectual Athenaeus of Seleucia, who writes: 'we are not like the Greeks' wise men amongst whom many words are expended on small matters; we are in the habit of giving least advice on the greatest ones, to make them easiest for everyone to remember'. This is the complete opposite of Dandamis, who followed the teaching of Manu and insisted 'that speech and gentle words must be used by a teacher' (Ath.Mech. 5.8–11). Under Brahman ritual the kings had specific duties to discharge, not least the consultation of learned sages and the implementation of their advice (*Laws of Manu*. 7.37–40). There was also an obligation to study in conjunction with recognised authorities. In reality there would have seen precious little time for the Vedas, the oral repository of Brahman lore. Manu (7.39) insists that 'a king who is modest never perishes', and adds that 'he alone who has conquered his own senses can keep his subjects in obedience' (7.44). Brahman rulers duly recognised modesty as the highest virtue of kingship, and came close to the Greek concept of the model king, displaying a general readiness to tolerate Greek thought (cf. Bosworth 1998, 186–90). Calanus, it seems, envisaged himself in competition with the ascetics of the Punjab. Their rivalry was intense, but Calanus had the ultimate trump card of self-immolation. Even before this he was able to view the sophists in what seems to have been an endurance test (Str. 15.1.63 = *FGH* 715 F 17a). It involved fifteen ascetics of Taxila who left the city to demonstrate their powers. There they assume stress position, keeping their posture unchanged from morning to evening. They found the exercise almost intolerable, and it was only the Brahman sage who could cope with the midday sun, naked and motionless.

The role of Ptolemy (the future ruler of Egypt), and Arrian's main primary source, in his capacity as Alexander's *sōmatophylax* and *hipparch* now becomes critical. The pyre was placed under his care, and he was acting on the explicit instructions of Alexander (Arr. *An.* 7.3.2). The nature of these instructions is not known, but it is likely enough that he protected the pyre from marauders. This will have required military protection, and Ptolemy was an expert in the type of skirmishing that would keep robbers at bay (Bosworth 1996, 41–47). The robbers may be identified as the nomadic mountain tribes, specifically the Cossaeans and the Mardians, who had a formidable reputation for brigandage (Curt. 5.6.17–19). One may envisage the tribesmen massing above the mountains and watching the action develop on the plain. In that context Ptolemy's appointment was extremely sensible. He was a cavalry commander, a *hipparch* of long standing, and he had the prestige and military resources to police the plain of Persis.

Diodorus (17.107.4), who was most likely drawing on Cleitarchus' account (Bosworth 1988, 297–98), stresses the enormous size of the audience, including the common soldiers who came down to see the extraordinary sight. This huge mass was crushed together with no room for manoeuvre, and manipulating them would have been an intricate exercise in crowd control. Ptolemy might have used his horses as prototype tanks, applying their considerable weight to create passageways through the mass of observers. This created the so-called wedge formation (*embolon*), which took the shape of an equilateral triangle, pointed at the apex and expanding at the base, so that pressure was maintained on both flanks.

The cavalry was certainly vital if it was a matter of crowd control, but there was also a political factor at work. It is abundantly clear that there was considerable animosity between the infantry and cavalry in the Macedonian army. It surfaced at Babylon at the time of Alexander's death, when the cavalry broke away *en masse* and overran the countryside,[10] where Curtius insists that the cavalry was recruited from the young men of highest nobility. He draws a sharp distinction between the aristocratic cavalry and the humble infantryman, and the distinction was in force at the time of Calanus' suicide. The cavalry enjoyed a privileged and comfortable situation, mounted above the mass of the phalanx men, the groundlings who would have had to be content with an interrupted view of proceedings at the pyre.

Ptolemy's commission to protect the pyre is contrasted with reports of an elaborate procession, in which he led the way, taking the position of honour at its head. As well as protecting the pyre Ptolemy organised the ceremonial proceedings, and was as central to the event as Calanus himself. There would seem to be a unanimous view that the description of the procession comes directly from Ptolemy. In that case he was an eye witness to the sage's triumph over his mortality. But the situation is not as clear-cut as it seems. According to Strabo (15.1.69 C718) a feature of the local festivals of India was the parade of elephants, all decked out in gold and silver, with a good many four-horse chariots and ox carts, 'and then there follows the army in ceremonial dress'. These Indian processions were certainly impressive, but they culminated in animal sacrifice, which some seem to have found repulsive and to be strongly discouraged. Instead we hear of savage predators (leopards, lions and buffaloes), which have been tamed for processional use. It looks as though there was also strong influence from the sect of Jainism, which practised non-violence to an extraordinary degree; no breathing, existing, living, sentient creatures should be slain or treated with violence, or abused (Thapar 2003, 166–67, quoting the *Acharanga-sutra*). The polar opposite would have been the Roman games, in which animals were slaughtered in their thousands.[11] More pertinent for our purposes is the prohibition of festivals, which is mentioned repeatedly in the self-serving documents of Asoka (Thapar 1973, 250–69). We should expect to find encouragement of the festal aspects of community living, particularly when the king had expressed his championship. Asoka seems to have been unusual in his hostility to local festivities. There is no suggestion that the participants were subjected to any formal prohibition; they simply risked incurring the king's displeasure. 'The Beloved of the Gods, the king Piyadassi, sees much evil in festivals, though there are some of which the Beloved of the Gods, the king Piyadassi approves'. Asoka clearly realised that it was impossible to eradicate the sort of gathering that was so vividly described by Strabo, in which the elephants made such a brilliant show of opulence.

According to Strabo (15.1.69 C718), it was Cleitarchus of Alexandria – the major source for Diodorus, Curtius and Justin, the so-called Alexander Vulgate – who described the wheeled wagons used for the transport of large trees at festival times. This does not help us in dating his work, which is one of the most perplexing problems of the age of the Successors (see most recently Parker 2009, who supports the case for a third century date). However, Cleitarchus might give us a pointer, if not a solution. From what he wrote we should infer that there was no central authority in the Ganges and Indus plains, only a plethora of minor states (Bosworth 1996, 199–200). In that case Strabo's source was writing before the establishment of the Mauryan dynasty, which was founded by Chandragupta at the end of the fourth century. That regime was a type of aristocracy under which the commons were held in check by the enlightened rule of the best men, who were in turn supported by a vast collective elephant army. There had been a period of uncertainly under the preceding Nanda dynasty, when a centralised monarchy began to emerge. It was quite feasible for a king to aim for monarchical rule while delegating the administration to the class of counsellors, which in all numbered no less than 5,000 (Thapar 2003, 94–97). On the other hand Chandragupta's regime was as authoritative as one could imagine. That leaves us with a window of opportunity. It looks as though there was a period of comparative tranquillity at the end of Chandragupta's reign, when he was able to send Seleucus his 'gift' of 500 elephants, a present which would have brought both dynasts close to bankruptcy (App. *Syr.* 55; Str. 15.2.9 C724). Otherwise Chandragupta had no major wars to cope with. He did cross the Indus after what seems to have been a fairly desultory campaign, and the result was more a diplomatic settlement than a military victory, concluded by a treaty of friendship and a marriage alliance (*kēdos*).

Strabo has done us the service of delineating some of his primary sources, particularly Onesicritus, who interviewed Calanus face to face through the medium of no less than three interpreters, and recorded the famous dictum. It seems pointless to expect any accurate results from such a procedure: it would be tantamount to fresh water flowing clear through mud. Strabo comes out of this analysis rather well. He does not jump to conclusions, but carefully isolates the various traditions. He tends to leave his sources anonymous, relying on indirect speech to distance himself from the variant traditions. He does occasionally mention sources by name, as when he cites Megasthenes' disquisition on suicide, which leads to the Brahman attack on Calanus. But by and large, his exposition is sober and scrupulous, and provides a sharp contrast to the elaborate literary embroidery that we find in authorities like Arrian. There is, however, more at issue than literature. The interplay of Roman and Parthian imperialism is a fascinating topic, and both sides operate from ideologies that are polar opposites. Augustus was totally ruthless when it came to imperial expansion, whereas the chaotic shambles of the Parthian court did not lend itself to military efficiency. The Romans' attitude to resistance was demonstrated in the chilling pronouncement of Germanicus: 'there was no need for prisoners; only the total extermination of the people would bring the war to an end' (Tac. *Ann.* 2.21.2). So much for the military aspects.

There were other facets to the picture, and they were far from bellicose. One recalls the scene of Calanus' death where two royal bodyguards – and future kings – presided over the staging of the funerary pyre. Lysimachus emerged as a closet philosopher who could exchange arguments with Calanus himself, while Ptolemy could put together his own autobiography, notable for his economy with the truth. This gives some impression of the versatility and richness of the period of the Diadochi, but it is a relatively faint impression. What underpinned the conquest of Sind and the Punjab was the appalling vitality of Alexander.[12]

Bibliography

Badian, E. (1998) The King's Indians. In W. Will (ed.) *Alexander Der Grosse. Eine Welteroberung und ihr Hintergrund*, 205–24, Bonn.

Bosworth, A. B. (1980) *A Historical Commentary on Arrian's History of Alexander*. I. Oxford.

Bosworth, A. B.(1988) *Conquest and Empire: The Reign of Alexander the Great*. Cambridge.

Bosworth, A. B. (1996) *Alexander and the East: The Tragedy of Triumph*. Oxford.

Bosworth, A. B. (1998) Calanus and the Brahman Opposition. In W. Will (ed.) *Alexander der Grosse. Eine Welteroberung und ihr Hintergrund*, 173–203, Bonn.

Bosworth, A. B. (forthcoming) *A Historical Commentary on Arrian's History of Alexander*. III.

Braund, D. C. (1991) New 'Latin' Inscriptions in Central Asia: Legio XV Apollinaris and Mithras?, *ZPE* 89, 188–90.

Briant, P. (2002) *From Cyrus to Alexander. A History of the Persian Empire*. Winona Lake, IN.

Carney, E. (2006) *Olympias*. London.

Casson, L. (1989) *The Periplus Maris Erythraei*. New Jersey.

Hansen, T. (1962) *Arabia Felix: The Danish Expedition of 1761-1767*. Copenhagen (trans. by J. and K. McFarlane).

Heckel, W. (2006) *Who's Who in the Age of Alexander the Great*. Malden, MA.

Parker, V. (2009) Source-Critical Reflections on Cleitarchus' Work. In P. Wheatley and R. Hannah (eds) *Alexander and his Successors*, 28–55, Claremont, CA.

Rea, J. R., R. C. Senior and A. S. Hollis (1994) A Tax Receipt from Hellenistic Bactria, *Zeitschrift für Papyrologie und Epigraphik* 104, 261–80.

Szczurek, P. (2009) Source or Sources of Diodorus' Accounts of Indian *sati* Suttee (Diod. Sic. 19.33–34.6)? In J. Pigon (ed.) *The Children of Herodotus: Greek and Roman Historiography and Related Genres*, 119–43, Newcastle.

Thapar, R. (1973) *Asoka and the Decline of the Mauryas*. Oxford.

Thapar, R. (2003) *The Penguin History of Early India*. London.

Ustinova Y. B. (1990) Naskal'nye latinskie i greceskaya nadpisi iz Kara-Kamara, *Vestnik Drevnej Istorii* 4, 145–47.

Notes

1 According to Arrian (*An.* 7.1.5), interpreters were generally used in dialogues between Alexander and the Brahman ascetics, and Onesicritus apparently claimed to use three intermediaries (Str. 15.1.64).

2 See particularly Str. 15.1.73, where he explicitly states that he saw the armless prodigy who had come to Athens with the second embassy and stayed there as a tourist attraction.

3 The Indian king's name is given as Pandion, with an alternative, Porus. Here we have an instance of cultural assimilation. Strabo, or his source, was faced with two Indian names which had some similarity to Greek. One of the names that should be brought to mind is Porus, the ruler of the Paurava of the Punjab, who was defeated by Alexander and subsequently appointed viceroy of Sind. It looks as though Strabo's Porus was related to the earlier dynast and, as was customary, he assumed his people's name as his formal appellation (Casson 1989, 218–19). The other Indian king (Pandion) was probably the paramount ruler of the Pandyas, one of the most powerful peoples of South India. He may well have been seen as the overlord of the lesser kings of the region, and Porus could have been acting at his behest. For westerners, the name recalled the archaic Athenian king, who had given his name to an Athenian tribe, Pandionis, and the Athenians of Augustus' day were no doubt ready to see a connection between the Pandion of antiquity and the contemporary Indian king.

4 Carsten Niebuhr was a polymath, active in the service of the Danish monarchy. In 1761 he joined the ill-fated expedition commissioned by Frederick V of Denmark to explore sites in Egypt, Arabia and Syria. Its members progressively died away, unable to cope with the extreme conditions that they found in Persia (see Hansen 1962). By May of 1763 Niebuhr was the only member left alive.

5 It was first published by Ustinova 1990 (see Braund 1991, n. 1), but treated with deep suspicion by Braund (1991, 188–90). However, even Braund concedes 'that it seems plausible enough to imagine Roman military scouting-parties pushing that far'.

6 The embassy left Antioch with Augustus' entourage and continued with it to Samos and Athens.

7 Cf. Plutarch (*Alex.* 69.7–8) claiming that the tomb was still called the Indian's tomb in his own time.

8 There is a similar description in Lucian's account of the death of Peregrinus. The pyre was sunk some six feet deep, built of pine and stuffed with dry kindling, so that the fire would catch more quickly and burn more intensely (Luc. *Peregr.* 35–36). Lucianus (*Peregr.* 25) quotes Onesicritus (*FGH* 134 F 18) as a source on Calanus and his way of death.

9 See moreover Szczurek 2009, who examines Diodorus' detailed description of Indian suttee and believes also that he took it from the Cardian, who may well have been an eyewitness to the funeral of Ceteus in 317.

10 Curt. 10.8.13; cf. 10.7.20–1; Nepos *Eum.* 2.2; Heckel 2006, 238; Bosworth, forthcoming; and see the earlier description at Bosworth 1980, 307.

11 See in particular Thapar 1973, 137–45, with *Res Gestae* 22 and compare the *1st Major Rock Edict* (Thapar 1973, 250–51), in which the Indian king boasts that he had reduced the consumption of meat in the royal kitchens from many hundreds of thousands to three (a deer and two peacocks), and even these are not to be killed.

12 I should like to thank Professors Victor Alonso and Edward Anson for their careful editing of this paper, and my partner, Dr Elizabeth Baynham, and research assistant, Ms. Kimberley Davis for their help.

WHAT WE DO NOT KNOW ABOUT THE AGE OF THE DIADOCHI: THE METHODOLOGICAL CONSEQUENCES OF THE GAPS IN THE EVIDENCE

Alexander Meeus

In an article analysing some prosopographical problems of the Successor Era, Wheatley (1997, 61) notes how ancient historians are often 'with some justification' seen as 'purveyors of fantasy' because of their use of sources. Partly this is due to the state of the evidence, but Wheatley also rightly insists on the need for caution and avoiding tendentiousness. While this is mostly a matter of judging individual problems on their own merits, it seems that at least some general principles apply if our conclusions are to be really based on the sources. This has been thoroughly demonstrated by Fischer (1970) in his *Historians' Fallacies. Toward a Logic of Historical Thought*. In spite of certain problems of logic in his own approach, and an overstatement of the extent to which logical precepts can function as the sole tools of historical analysis (Mink 1971; Potter 1971; White 1971), Fischer has aptly shown the need for more methodological rigor in historical scholarship, rigor that can very often be based on (plain) logic. Within the field of Classics, McNeal (1970, 306) has rightly noted that while such 'emphasis on method may seem pedantic (...) only a slow and deliberate approach will yield really valid knowledge'. He goes on to say that 'the modern study of ancient history is full of attempts to pile one hypothesis on another in a desperate effort to gain certainty, often in cases where no certainty is possible. It is sometimes forgotten that the evidence is miserably poor even for the periods which are best documented and that frequently we have to be satisfied with the vaguest scraps of information'.

The first step in this process must be a reflection on the nature of our evidence: besides the constant awareness of the loss of most of the evidence, we need a clear understanding of the specific characteristics of those sources we do have, as I shall argue for Diodorus as a case study.

The Nature of Diodorus' Account

The basic problems of our sources for early Hellenistic history are well known (e.g. Préaux 1978, 88; Walbank 1984, 1–2; Wheatley 2009, 54–55). To compensate for the disappearance of most of the contemporary evidence, however, it is often said that with Diodorus we possess a detailed narrative of the Age of the Successors (e.g. Préaux 1978, 79; Sherwin-White and Kuhrt 1993, 3; Wheatley 2009, 57). Surely, with an average of 7.33 years per book, books 18–20 are among the most detailed ones in the *Bibliotheca* (though 18 is rather brief): the average length of 11–17 is 22.57 years per book. However, Arrian's lost account in 10 books of the years 323 to 319 puts the amount of detail Diodorus provides in a different perspective: this is an average of half a year per book. Furthermore, in book 20 Diodorus' increased interest in the adventures of Agathocles has gravely compressed the information on the Diadochi (not to mention the many digressions in 18–20). Obviously, coins, inscriptions and other documentary and archaeological sources partly fill the lacunas in our knowledge – and often in important ways (Seibert 1983, 54–69; Boiy, this volume), but on the whole such evidence is rather scarce as well.

Many crucial events are missing from Diodorus' account. Cleomenes of Naucratis goes unmentioned, even in what seems a detailed overview of the satrapy distribution (Arr. *Post Alex.* F 1a.5, 1b.2; Dex. *FGH* 100, F 8.2; Iust. 13.4.11); only Pausanias (1.6.3) relates Ptolemy's murder of Cleomenes. Cynnane's Asian adventures with her daughter Eurydice and her murder are only hinted at in the account of her burial in 316 (D.S. 19.52.5; Arr. *Post Alex.* F 1.22–23). Diodorus has completely skipped the war in Asia between Triparadeisus and Antipater's return to Europe (cf. the Gothenburg Arrian palimpsest: Dreyer 2007). Equally absent is the quarrel between Antigonus and Cassander, which induced Antipater not to leave the kings in Asia (Arr. *Post Alex.* F 1.43). Porus' murder is only referred to in passing (D.S. 19.14.8). We get no further context for the plans of both Cassander and Lysimachus to marry Cleopatra (D.S. 20.37.4). In fact we hardly hear anything about Lysimachus before 315. There are important gaps in Diodorus' treatment of Ptolemy, and even of Antigonus we do not get much between 311 and 308. Examples can easily be multiplied. Bosworth (2002, 21) has called Diodorus' silence on the war between Antigonus and Seleucus between 311 and 309, known thanks to the Babylonian tradition (*BCHP* 3, rev.), 'a melancholy indication of how defective our historical knowledge must be'. Indeed, we can be sure that several very important events from the period 323–281 are absolutely unknown to us.

Even when Diodorus provides unique information – as he obviously must, being the most detailed preserved source – he confronts us with the limits of our knowledge. Consider, for instance, the long list of individuals mentioned only in book 19 – most of them only once – and not attested elsewhere: Polycles (11.3), Nicanor (11.8), Eudamus (14.1), Androbazus (14.6), Antipater (16.1), Philotas (16.1), Xenopeithes (16.1), Cephalon (27.4, possibly to be identified with Cebalon of 44.1), Lysanias (29.1), Ceteus (33.1), Callas (35.3, 36.6), Deinias (35.3, 88.6), Orontobates (46.4), Ocranes (47.4), Euitus (48.2), Euagoras (48.2, possibly to be identified with Euagros of 92.4), Thespius (48.5), Molyccus (54.4), Agesilaus (57.4), Idomeneus (57.4), Asclepiodorus (60.2), Myrmidon (62.4), Dioscorides (62.7; 62.9; 68.4), Apollonides (63.1), Alexion (67.1), Aristoteles (68.3), Lycon (73.6), Pausanias (73.6), Agathon (75.2), Agis (79.2), Alexander (88.3), Teucer (88.3), Micythus (88.5), Esioneus (89.3), Nisos (89.3), Polyarchus (91.3), Diphilus (91.3), Athenaeus (94–96), Euteles (100.5).[1] In spite of proposed emendations, Philotas (14.1) and Polemon (14.6) should probably be added as well. Of course, we should be grateful to Diodorus for this rich list, but we would have wanted so much more than mere names. Most of these men obviously were important people: for instance Eurydice's advisor Polycles; Cassander's brother Nicanor; the Indian prince Ceteus; the leading Antigonid diplomats Agesilaus and Idomeneus; the satraps Evitus, Euagoras and Orontobates; Agis, a high Ptolemaic official; the Epeirote princes Alexander, Teucer, Esioneus and Nisus. All of them would have deserved much more than passing references: again it is apparent that Diodorus' account is only comparatively detailed (cf. Simpson 1959).

Writing the history of the world from the beginnings to the time of Caesar in just 40 books, Diodorus obviously had to be selective, but some of the criteria which determined his selection are very different from those of the modern historian.[2] While I do not want to claim that for Diodorus historical significance was not an important criterion of selection, it is not the only one. The amount of attention he pays to certain episodes of lesser historical importance is striking, although the events in question sometimes classify almost as 'fait divers' compared to the many important omissions in the *Bibliotheca*.

Including the *peripeteiai* his audience loved to read (cf. Diodorus' contemporary Cicero, *Fam.* 5.12.4) often seems to have been the rationale. This interest in *peripeteiai* is evident in his treatment of Thibron's adventures in Cyrene (18.19–21). While surely not completely devoid of historical importance, these events are dealt with at disproportionate length. The story's attraction clearly lies in Thibron's many changes of fortune in a short span of time, as Diodorus' moralizing authorial comments explicitly indicate. Except for Ptolemy's involvement at the end, however, this is a local affair which is hardly essential in a universal history. Another good story immediately follows, but again one of limited relevance to world history: the Isaurians burning themselves and their houses, thus putting a tragic end to a city that had been 'prosperous for a great many years' (22).

An entire chapter (19.16) is devoted to the story of the Perdiccan captives at an unidentified fortress in Asia Minor. Attalus, Polemon, and Docimus, Antipater and Philotas had been captured by Antigonus at Cretōn polis (18.45.3). These men had already been defeated and ultimately nothing modified that situation, but Diodorus apparently saw another good story. For a brief moment things seemed to be changing when the captives seized control of the fortress, but very quickly the fickle wheel of fortune rotated again as enemy reinforcements arrived. Furthermore, Docimus, the catalyst of the reversal, experiences a further change of fortune of his own: he manages to escape and wants to betray his friends, but his perfidy is not rewarded, and his short-lived freedom is exchanged for a new prison. These are hardly essential events, but Diodorus loved the *peripeteiai*.

Even when describing important political and military events, Diodorus' interest can lay primarily with fortune's fickleness. The Bactrian revolt is not treated at great length (18.4.8 and 7.1–9), and rather than on the military events, Diodorus focuses on the reversal of Peithon's hopes. He is described as a former bodyguard of Alexander, 'a man full of pride and able to command' (7.3), and 'a man of great ambition' planning to establish his own power in the upper satrapies by getting the settlers on his side (7.4). When Peithon defeated the Greek rebels and convinced them to return to their colonies (7.5–7), Diodorus notes that he was greatly pleased that everything seemed to go according to plan. The Macedonian soldiers, however, in their desire for loot, unexpectedly fell on the Greeks and killed them all. Diodorus (7.9) laconically concludes: 'Peithon then, cheated of his hopes, came back with the Macedonians to Perdiccas'. For Diodorus the focus is not on how the rebellion in the east was ended, but on Peithon's rising hopes after his victory, which very soon afterwards were betrayed altogether.

The same process influences the narrative on a more general level too. Whether this is creative composition or not (Hadley 1996), Diodorus himself is responsible for the decision to reserve so much space for contemplation on Eumenes' changing fortunes. The same interest is evident when we look at the altogether limited concern Diodorus has for Seleucus, the founder of the largest Hellenistic kingdom. He does, however, feature prominently in the narrative at the turning points where he loses everything in 316 (19.55–56) and when he regains it along with more territory at spectacular speed in 312–311 (19.80–85 and 90–92). It could also be a factor in the fascination with Antigonus, a man who did all he could to gain the greatest power, only to lose it all in a single battle. Space forbids me to discuss further examples (see Meeus, forthcoming), but by now the point should be clear.

Apart from Diodorus' interest for the literary quality of his work, carelessness and at times perhaps incompetence affect his account as well. 19.78.5 is a very striking example where the narrative of the campaign of Polemaeus in Greece ends in the following way: 'He also marched against Locris; and, since the Opuntians belonged to the party of Cassander, he began a siege and made continuous attacks'. The typical Diodorean expression 'he made continuous attacks' (συνεχεῖς προσβολὰς ἐποιεῖτο) in this context is hardly meaningful, and merely serves to end a story Diodorus no longer found interesting. We never learn whether Opus was captured. Surely, if this happened in the next archon year, he may have planned to deal with the fate of the city in its appropriate chronological context, but what matters for the historian using his text, is that he did not do so.

That Diodorus' account, comparatively thorough as it may be, remains a brief and uneven summary of the history of the Diadochi, is perfectly in tune with his historical and literary aims, but not with our expectations of a detailed historical source (cf. McKechnie 1994, 304). Similar arguments can be developed concerning our other sources, but space does not allow me to do so here (see e.g. Bosworth 1992 on Plutarch; Stadter 1980, 144–52 on Arrian; Yardley, Wheatley and Heckel 2011 on Justin; cf. in general Pitcher 2009, 113–26).

Methodological Consequences

In the rest of this paper I shall develop four main points about the methodological consequences of the state of the evidence, namely first that we cannot rely on the argument from silence, secondly that the *testis unus testis nullus* principle does not really apply and that on the contrary we may even have very limited evidence for certain important aspects of the period, thirdly that we should be careful in establishing connections between scattered facts or bits of evidence, and fourthly that it is a dangerous practice to emend the ancient texts for merely historical reasons, i.e. to fit our own expectations, if nothing is wrong philologically.

The Argument from Silence

Although it is universally recognized that the argument from silence is a logical fallacy, and most agree that it can therefore not be used in a historical argument, one often encounters it. The most famous case of the argument from silence applied to the Diadochi is undoubtedly to be found at the time of Alexander's death, and it is a particularly striking one. The silence of one source is put against the explicit testimony of more sources than are available for almost any other event: Arrian's silence, which could just as well be due to selection or even to malevolence on behalf of his source (the most popular explanation), has often been considered sufficient reason to reject the historicity of Alexander giving his signet ring to Perdiccas, while in fact there seems no reason whatsoever to doubt it (Rathmann 2005, 9–26).

It has been argued that Polyperchon, when proposing an alliance to Eumenes, did not annul his death sentence (Westlake 1969, 328–29; Hadley 1996, 135, 142; Anson 2008, 144).[3] Indeed, Diodorus does not mention the rescission, and claims by Ptolemy and Seleucus (D.S. 18.62.1; 19.12.2) that he had been condemned by the Macedonians even after Eumenes' appointment as royal general could lend some support to this view (Westlake 1969, 328), but it need not mean more than that Ptolemy and Seleucus did not accept Polyperchon's authority (cf. Grainger 1990, 37). Even if absolution would not have been part of Polyperchon's proposal, it is inconceivable that Eumenes did not ask for it at that moment (he had demanded it before: 18.41.7), and Polyperchon, in need of Eumenes' support, could not but agree. Diodorus has divided the summary of Polyperchon's letter over two archon years, which is a situation that often caused him to forget things. Moreover, it is clear that Diodorus did not report the entire contents of the letter in book 18, where he only mentions that it informed Eumenes of letters to the generals and treasurers in Cilicia and to the commanders of the Silver Shields, while in book 19 (chapter 13) we learn there also were instructions for the commanders in the upper satrapies. Thus, Diodorus' silence about any rescission of Eumenes' death sentence need not be very telling.

Because of the haphazard and fragmentary nature of the evidence I see no problem in accepting that Ptolemy I (and II, III and IV for that matter), who did have Egyptian royal titulature, celebrated the official pharaonic coronation ceremony, even if the coronation is first attested only for Ptolemy V (Huß 2001, 215; Manning 2010, 94–95 n. 85; but see Müller, this volume).

As I have already noted elsewhere (Meeus 2009, 236), the silence of the sources on the fate of all but two of the Asian brides of the Susa mass weddings (one retained, one repudiated) cannot be used to argue that apart from Seleucus all Macedonians divorced them: if the information we had would be a statistically significant sample that allowed us to make any claims on the matter – *quod non*, of course – the conclusion would be that about half of the marriages lasted. Similar problem concerns Alexander's widows. Harders (2012) has recently argued that they were almost completely ignored by the Successors because they are not mentioned in our sources. She is aware of the intrinsic weakness of the argument from silence, and backs-up her claim by arguing that Diodorus is interested in widows on the basis of his interest in the actions of Olympias and Eurydice, so that his silence on Alexander's widows would be telling indeed. However, Diodorus' attention to Eurydice and Olympias was not inspired by a particular interest in widows, but rather by their spectacular reversals of fortune and the opportunity to moralize (esp. 19.11 and 19.49–51). Cynnane was a widow too, and Diodorus did not include her actions, so he certainly did not feel the need to tell us everything he found in his sources about widows. By the same logic we could claim that nothing worth mentioning happened in Athens under Demetrius of Phalerum, because – as we have seen – Diodorus regularly included accounts on local affairs, but Athens is nearly absent from his account between 317 and 307. Silence cannot, therefore, be considered a useful argument in assessing the importance of Alexander's widows. The argument from silence is particularly hazardous when it concerns women (Carney 2005, 73 n. 67), and this must be true *a fortiori* when non-Greek women are concerned. If a specific reason for the sources' unconcern for Alexander's widows is to be found at all, it may be the Greek authors' disinterest in Persian affairs (cf. Briant 2003, 17–18). In any case, we cannot claim that, if someone or something was important, Diodorus – or any other preserved source – would necessarily have said so. Furthermore, Rhoxane's dedications – the combined readings on the stone seem plausible enough – to Athena Polias at the very least show that at some point it seemed useful for her to appear publicly in the Greek world, even if perhaps just by proxy (Kosmetatou 2004). Unfortunately we cannot know whether they belong to the period after Alexander's death, for they could have served the interests of someone like Polyperchon just as well those of Alexander.

The same problem of evidence might affect our understanding of the Macedonian army assembly. Convincing arguments have been put forward for the view that it did not have any constitutionally determined powers, and was only able to exert its influence in a brief period between 330 and 315 (Errington 1978; Anson 1991). Nevertheless, one may wonder whether it is a coincidence that after 315 we only know of a few more assembly meetings in the time of the Diadochi, all of them for the supposed formality of acclaiming a new king (Antigonus and Demetrius in 306 [D.S. 20.53.2; Plu. *Demetr.* 18.1], Demetrius as king of Macedon in 294 [Iust. 16.1.8–18], and Sosthenes in 279 [Iust. 24.5.14]), but apparently never making or confirming any decisions like in the previous years. 315 also happens to be the point when Diodorus' narrative on the Diadochi becomes far less detailed, as the history of Agathocles of Syracuse starts to attract his interest much more strongly. The years from 323 to 315 are treated in 207.5 Teubner pages (18.2–19.65), 190 of which are dedicated to the Diadochi, whereas the much longer period of 314–302 covers 226 Teubner pages (19.66–20.113), only 115 of which deal with the Diadochi. Thus, our knowledge of the army assembly after 315 can only be scantier than for the 15 years before that date, unless it would just be a coincidence that Diodorus becomes less detailed around the time the army assembly loses much of its importance again (cf. Bosworth 1989, 163, on the period before 330). Moreover, in 294 Demetrius (already a king of the whole empire since 306!) apparently has to argue his case in some detail in order to convince the Macedonians, which does not suggest that his acclamation was a mere formality.

The Comparative Weight of Limited Evidence

These few assemblies bring us to the second point, namely that certain aspects of the period may have been more important than our limited evidence would suggest at first sight. We *may* actually be looking at underreported, but important, phenomena more often than we think. In order not to make it into a license to speculate freely, this obviously is a matter of balanced judgement requiring careful analysis and restraint. It is almost generally held that the Successors abandoned Alexander's policy towards the conquered peoples completely: however limited the latter's approach may already have been, the *communis opinio* is that under the Diadochi Asians and Egyptians hardly played any part at all in the government or the army (e.g. Mooren 1978, esp. 54–55; Habicht 2006, 30–31, 39–40). However, even several Diodorean passages seem to contradict such a view. All native satraps in office at the time of Alexander's death saw their positions confirmed, although Atropates did have to cede part of his territory (18.3; Sherwin-White and Kuhrt 1993, 121–122). For Triparadeisus Media Atropatene is no longer mentioned in the list, and we have no idea of what happens to Phrataphernes in Parthia and Hyrcania; Oxyartes, Porus and Taxiles are confirmed apparently despite thoughts of removing the latter two (18.39.6; but see below, *Connecting the Dots*). In 317/6 Antigonus appoints a new native satrap, Orontobates in Media, though perhaps only to avoid a repetition of Peithon's ambitions (19.46.5), and in 316 he installed Aspisas at Susiane. When arriving in Egypt Ptolemy tried to establish good relations with the natives (18.14.1; cf. Just. 13.6.18), as Seleucus seems to have done in Babylonia (19.91.2), and Alcetas in Pisidia (18.46.1–2). Peucestas was very popular with the Persians (19.14.5), and they even protested against his deposition (19.48.5). Tlepolemus in Carmania and Stasanor in Bactria also enjoyed the support of the natives (19.48.1). The Iranian Androbazus commanded a unit in the coalition army fighting against Peithon (19.14.6); Ceteus, an Indian general (and probably his troops too), fought with Eumenes at Paraetacene (19.33.1). Friends of Peithon pasturing their flocks in the hills of Iran informed him of Eumenes' advance after spotting his camp (19.38.4). Alcetas (18.45.5), Arrhidaeus (18.51.1), Antigonus (19.16.3), Peucestas (19.17.6), Meleager and Menoetas (and thus undoubtedly Peithon too) (19.47.2), Ptolemy (19.80.4), Seleucus (19.91.5) and Nicanor (19.92.4) used indigenous soldiers. Again, this is just the evidence from Diodorus: in light of my earlier observations on his account, this seems to be rather abundant evidence that the Successors did anything but neglect the indigenous peoples of their satrapies and kingdoms, and continued Alexander's policies in this respect. That they mostly did so out of self-interest is also clear from Diodorus (18.46.1; 19.91.2; cf. Briant 1996, 890), and hardly surprising.

There had indeed been strong Macedonian resistance to Alexander's orientalising (D.S. 17.77.7–78.1; Curt. 6.6.9–11; Just. 12.4.1), but this does not mean that all of the generals had been opposed to it (Meeus 2009, 236–37), or that they could not expediently change their mind when in power themselves. Ptolemy objected to a half-Asian king when this point of view was to his advantage in the succession debate (cf. Meeus 2008, 48–50), but soon thereafter established good relations with his Egyptian subjects in order to create a solid power base in his satrapy (see above; Huß 2001, 213). The Egyptian priest Manetho advised Ptolemy on the cult of Sarapis (Plu. *Mor.* 362a). Undoubtedly he was thoroughly immersed in Greek culture and historiography when writing his *Aegyptiaca* (Dillery 1999, 97–98; cf. Avenarius 1956, 55–70 on the linguistic and stylistic requirements of such a work). There is evidence for other Egyptians holding positions close to the king in the Ptolemaic administration in these early decades (Thompson 1992, 44–45; Legras 2002; Moyer 2011b, 87–90). The Ptolemaic high commander Philocles probably was a hellenized Phoenician (Hauben 1987, 424–27; 2004, 31 n. 20; *contra* Grainger 1991, 63–64). They may have been exceptions,[4] but it seems likely that the exceptions were more numerous than our predominantly Greek evidence allows us to see, unless one would claim that in this case all individuals would be attested in our fragmentary source record or that non-Greeks are proportionally represented in Greek sources and that we can necessarily recognize them as non-Greeks.[5] There is likewise evidence for Orientals at the court of Antigonus (Billows 1990, 305–08) and under the early Seleucids (Sherwin-White and Kuhrt 1993, 121–25).

Thus, if the Successors seem to have come back from Alexander's policy towards the indigenous peoples, this may well be because for this period we do not have sources with a focus on court life comparable to that of the Alexander sources. Obviously we must not exaggerate (Weber 1997, 34 n. 26): there is no doubt that the conquered peoples were in a subordinate position and that Greeks and Macedonians were privileged, but that should not make us ignore such involvement of indigenous people as there definitely was (cf. Mileta 2012; Olbrycht, this volume). Absent the modern 'tools of empire', it was much more difficult for foreign conquerors to simply oppress their native subjects (cf. Headrick 1981, quote from his title). Perhaps the Diadochi only considered such collaboration with the local elites useful until Macedonian control in their provinces was firmly established (Strootman 2007, 131–32). However, we must – again – bear in mind that the third century presents its own set of problems of evidence, so that it is most difficult to arrive at firm conclusions about the policies of the Epigoni in this respect.

A particular case of limited evidence is of course the *testis unus*. Photius' summary of Arrian (*Post Alex.* F 1.35) calls Amphimachus, appointed satrap of Mesopotamia at Triparadeisus, a 'brother of the king'. Some scholars accept that Amphimachus was a half brother of king Arrhidaeus (Bosworth 2002, 113), while others argue for confusion between Arrhidaeus the satrap of Hellespontine Phrygia and king Arrhidaeus because we have no other sources for the claim (Heckel 2006, 22). Spectacular as the statement that king Arrhidaeus had a half brother may seem, one can wonder whether we really have enough source material to reject it just because it is attested in a single source and because we could think of an alternative explanation, namely that the confusion between both Arrhidaei occurs elsewhere (Just. 13.4.6). That a source has made a mistake has to be proven case by case with proper arguments in each instance, even if it would concern a source that is full of errors. Scholars are very good at finding alternative explanations, so I am not sure whether the fact that an alternative explanation can be found should take precedence over what a source says, even if it is the only source and the statement might seem unlikely to some. Unlikely things do happen, and someone having a brother is not at all that unlikely. The case of Amphimachus is quite comparable with that of Caranus, a brother of Alexander the Great only attested in Justin (11.2.3). The majority of scholars reject his existence (Heckel 1979; 2006, 78; Carney 2000, 77, 279 n. 99), but a good case in favour of it has been made (Unz 1985; Ogden 1999, 26, 39 n. 161–62 with further references). As Unz (1985, 172) has shown with the example of Amyntas Perdicca, the evidence for the first twenty years of Alexander's life is hardly of the nature to allow us to reject explicit statements in one of the sources, whatever its quality may be assumed to be. Justin has recently also been proven largely correct in the matter of Philip's guardianship of Amyntas (Anson 2009), and there is quite a strong tradition in Justin that Alexander had at least one more brother, whom he killed, besides Arrhidaeus (see also 9.7.3 and 9.8.3 where 'multos' might be a rhetorical exaggeration). Given the state of the evidence, I see no problem in accepting that Alexander had another half-brother, and that Arrhidaeus had one too. Another parallel would be Alexander's son Heracles, whose existence Brunt (1975) has conclusively defended against attacks on the basis of the limited evidence.

Of course, this only concerns situations where the only argument for rejecting something and looking for an alternative explanation is that a particular source is our sole source; I am not claiming that we should no longer adopt a critical stance towards our sources, but that must not be used as an excuse to simply reject or modify difficult evidence.

Connecting the Dots

The third principle is the need for caution in working out the relationships between different events that are reported out of context or between different kinds of evidence that may or may not relate to the same reality. In his overview of the troops of the coalition against Peithon Crateua of 318, Diodorus states that Eudamus brought 120 elephants which he had seized after killing Porus (19.14.8). No context is known for the murder, but for some reason scholars usually date it to 318, obviously only the *terminus ante quem*, just because this is when Eudamus shows up with the elephants. Since hardly anything is known of what was going on in the Far East, it could have happened at any time after Triparadeisus (summer 320), when Porus is last attested. The death of Porus and Eudamus' march to the west were two isolated events, the first of which is only mentioned because it explains why Eudamus could bring so many elephants. There is no other connection, and in our ignorance of the context we should not jump to conclusions about the relationship between both events. The same goes for the reason for the murder. Epplett (2007, 222) claims that Diodorus' 'account suggests (...) that certainly one of the motivations was to gain control of Porus' herd of elephants'. The passage merely explains how Eudamus got so many elephants. In our ignorance of the circumstances we can only speculate about the causes of the murder, and getting hold of the elephants may simply have been a welcome side-effect of an action inspired by totally different motives. The murder explains his possession of the elephants, but his possession of the elephants does not necessarily explain the murder. We just do not know whether capturing the elephants was the aim or a result of it (though the latter seems more likely to me). Much as we would like to explain the death of Porus, we should not read in Diodorus' text what is not there, and accept that our sources often just do not give us the information we want. In any case, Porus being killed so soon after Triparadeisus does urge one to reconsider the significance of Diodorus' earlier claim that Porus and Taxiles could not be removed without a royal army and a brilliant general (18.39.6). Had Eudamus received an official murder command (and the required troops), is the claim a grave overstatement or is it an honest assessment of the situation that was later disproved by Eudamus?

Similar problems exist when bringing together scattered indications from various sources, and especially with archaeological and literary evidence which cannot always be integrated as readily as we would wish.[6] It is over three decades now that scholars have been debating the identity of the occupant of Tomb II at Vergina as either Philip II (Musgrave *et al.* 2010) or Philip III (Borza and Palagia 2007), and recently it has been doubted again whether Vergina was Aigai, and whether its tombs were royal rather than just belonging to the elite (Touloumakos 2010). What we definitely need – apart from the complete publication of the excavation results – is more analysis of all Macedonian tombs, comparing architecture, decoration, and grave goods in order to determine whether there is anything distinctively royal about the ones at Vergina (cf. e.g. Andrianou 2009; Tsigarida 2010).

Emending the Sources

The fourth and last point concerns emendations to the ancient texts just because they do not fit our own historical reconstructions, where nothing is necessarily wrong with the grammar or the contents in themselves. In Diodorus 19 for example I found no less than eight such instances. A very striking example occurs at 91.2, striking because the progress of scholarship has now shown conclusively that there is no problem with the passage whatsoever. The τετραετῆ has troubled most scholars because on every reconstruction there were 5 years between Triparadeisus and Seleucus' flight (321–316 or 320–315). In the nineteenth century various emendations have been proposed to solve the presumed problem (Fischer 1906, apparatus ad 19.91.2). Luckily later generations of scholars were more careful and did not emend, but still assumed for instance that by four Diodorus somehow meant five (Errington 1977, 486–87). Thanks to the works of Stylianou (1994) and Boiy (2007), we now know that we have to switch from low to high after Triparadeisus, so that a period of four years between Triparadeisus in 320 and Seleucus' flight in 316 suddenly becomes very exact. Unfortunately, such improved understanding has not yet clarified the other seven passages in book 19, and even Bizière's Budé edition, the most conservative one, has adopted two of them, Tlepolemus for Polemon at 14.6 and *amphippous* for *asthippous* at 29.2. In the case of Polemon-Tlepolemus, the list of persons mentioned only once in Diodorus 19 (see above) means that we should not really be surprised at meeting the unexpected name Polemon in our text. Sometimes, of course, such an emendation may to a certain extent be likely, as with *nomarchias* for *nauarchias* at 85.4, but it is not necessary, and usually it is not even noted that the earliest reference to the cleruchic system in Egypt exists only by virtue of a modern emendation (e.g. Billows 1990, 128). Some still prefer to emend Pydnaeans at 68.2 to Athenians (Huß 2001, 154 n. 467), although it has been shown that we need not doubt that the Pydnaeans could have had the fleet of 36 ships mentioned by Diodorus (Hauben 1978). A fine example from book 18 is the passage on the naval battles of the Lamian War (15.9) mentioning an encounter near the Echinades. Because scholars could not find a reason for a battle to take place in Aetolian waters, they proposed to emend Echinades to Lichades, moving the battle to the Malian Gulf near Lamia. Wrightson (2012) has now argued conclusively that the battle took place near the Echinades off the Aetolian coast.

Conclusion

Although we all know that our evidence is far from abundant, we forget this too often. I have argued that given the fragmentary and haphazard nature of our sources only the most careful methodological approach that constantly takes into account said nature of the evidence can lead to secure results. Thus, it seems that the argument from silence is simply invalid for the study of the Diadochi (and probably the rest of Antiquity as well), and that we have to take into account the comparative weight of limited evidence (including the *testis unus*). Our necessary attempts to create some order through establishing causal or other connections between what in fact can only be largely isolated items for us need to be executed with the most careful restraint, as the many unknown factors involved could easily alter our understanding of such relationships. We should resist the temptation to fill the gaps in our knowledge when the evidence – or rather the lack thereof – clearly prohibits it. Finally, emending the sources for purely historical reasons is an unacceptable practice that only obscures the actual evidence that should be explained. A methodologically rigorous approach will obviously not result in the necessarily true reconstruction of the period: it is always possible that a conclusion reached via the argument from silence is actually correct, but it is a conclusion that cannot be verified as it lacks any basis in the sources. Thus, what methodological rigour will guarantee as much as possible is the proper evidential basis of our conclusions, but misunderstandings obviously can never be ruled out, and often different interpretations of equal value can result from the analysis of the same evidence. History is like that, and if its aim is to try and understand man and society that need not even be a real problem as the debate itself is as useful as the results.[7]

Abbreviations

BCHP *Babylonian Chronicles of the Hellenistic Period* (http://www.livius.org/cg-cm/chronicles/chron00.html)

Bibliography

Andrianou, D. (2009) *The Furniture and Furnishings of Ancient Greek Houses and Tombs.* Cambridge.

Andronikos, M. (1987) *Vergina. The Royal Tombs and the Ancient City*. Athens.

Anson, E. M. (1991) The Evolution of the Macedonian Army Assembly (330–315 BC), *Historia* 40, 230–47.

Anson, E. M. (2008) Macedonian Judicial Assemblies, *Classical Philology* 103, 135–49.

Anson, E. M. (2009) Philip II, Amyntas Perdicca, and Macedonian Royal Succession, *Historia* 58, 276–86.

Avenarius, G. (1956) *Lukians Schrift zur Geschichtsschreibung*. Meisenheim am Glan.

Boiy, T. (2007) *Between High and Low. A Chronology of the Early Hellenistic Period.* Frankfurt.

Borza, E. N. and O. Palagia (2007) The Chronology of the Macedonian Royal Tombs at Vergina, *Jahrbuch des deutschen archäologischen Instituts* 122, 81–125.

Bosworth, A. B. (1989) Review: R. M. Errington, *Geschichte Makedoniens*, *Classical Philology* 84, 160–65.

Bosworth, A. B. (1992) History and Artifice in Plutarch's Eumenes. In P. A. Stadter (ed.) *Plutarch and the Historical Tradition*, 56–89, London.

Bosworth, A. B. (2002) *The Legacy of Alexander. Politics, Warfare, and Propaganda under the Successors.* Oxford.

Briant, P. (1996) *Histoire de l'empire perse de Cyrus à Alexandre*. 2 vols. Leiden.

Briant, P. (2003) *Darius dans l'ombre d'Alexandre*. Paris.

Brixhe, C. (1999) Asie Mineure (*Bulletin Epigraphique*), *Revue des Etudes Grecques* 112,663–87.

Brunt, P. A. (1975) Alexander, Barsine and Heracles, *Rivista di filologia e d'istruzione classica* 103, 22–34.

Carney, E. D. (2000) *Women and Monarchy in Macedonia*. Norman.

Carney, E. D. (2005) Women and *Dunasteia* in Caria, *American Journal of Philology* 126, 65–91.

Dillery, J. (1999) The First Egyptian Narrative History: Manetho and Greek Historiography, *Zeitschrift für Papyrologie und Epigraphik* 127, 93–116.

Dreyer, B. (2007) The Arrian Parchment in Gothenburg. New Digital Processing Methods and Initial Results. In Heckel, W. *et al.* (eds) *Alexander's Empire. Formulation to Decay*, 245–63, Claremont.

Engels, D. (forthcoming) The Achaimenid and the Seleucid Court. Continuity or change? In A. Erskine *et al.* (eds) *The Hellenistic Court*. Swansea.

Epplett, C. (2007) War Elephants in the Hellenistic World. In Heckel, W. *et al.* (eds) *Alexander's Empire. Formulation to Decay*, 209–32, Claremont.
Errington, R. M. (1977) Diodorus Siculus and the Chronology of the Early Diadochoi, 320–311 BC, *Hermes* 105, 478–504.
Errington, R. M. (1978) The Nature of the Macedonian State under the Monarchy, *Chiron* 8, 77–133.
Fischer, C. T. (1906) *Diodori Bibliotheca Historica*. Leipzig.
Fischer, D. H. (1970) *Historians' Fallacies. Toward a Logic of Historical Thought*. New York.
Gehrke, H.-J. (1986) Zur Lage von Salganeus, *Boreas* 9, 83–104.
Gorre, G. (2009) *Les relations du clergé égyptien et des Lagides d'après les sources privées*. Leuven.
Grainger, J. D. (1990) *Seleukos Nikator. Constructing a Hellenistic Kingdom*. London.
Grainger, J. D. (1991) *Hellenistic Phoenicia*. Oxford.
Habicht, C. (2006) *The Hellenistic Monarchies. Selected Papers*. Ann Arbor.
Hadley, R. A. (1996) Diodoros 18.60.1–3: A Case of Remodelled Source Materials, *Ancient History Bulletin* 10, 131–47.
Hadley, R. A. (2001) A Possible Lost Source for the Career of Eumenes of Kardia, *Historia* 50, 3–33.
Harders, A.-C. (2012) Königinnen ohne König. Zur Rolle und Bedeutung der Witwen Alexanders im Zeitalter der Diadochen. In H. Hauben and A. Meeus (eds) *The Age of the Successors (323–276 BC)*. Leuven.
Hauben, H. (1978) The Ships of the Pydnaeans: Remarks on Kassandros' Naval Situation in 314/313 BC, *Ancient Society* 9, 47–54.
Hauben, H. (1987) Philocles, King of the Sidonians and General of the Ptolemies. In E. Lipinski (ed.) *Phoenicia and the East Mediterranean in the First Millennium BC*, 413–27, Leuven.
Hauben, H. (2004) A Phoenician King in the Service of the Ptolemies. Philocles of Sidon Revisited, *Ancient Society* 34, 27–44.
Headrick, D. R. (1981) *The Tools of Empire. Technology and European Imperialism in the Nineteenth Century*. New York.
Heckel, W. (1979) Philip II, Kleopatra and Karanos, *Rivista di filologia e d'istruzione classica* 107, 385–93.
Heckel, W. (2006) *Who's Who in the Age of Alexander the Great. Prosopography of Alexander's Empire*. Oxford.
Huß, W. (2001) *Ägypten in hellenistischer Zeit. 332–30 v.Chr*. Munich.
Kosmetatou, E. (2004) Rhoxane's Dedications to Athena Polias, *Zeitschrift für Papyrologie und Epigraphik* 146, 75–80.
Legras, B. (2002) Les experts égyptiens à la cour des Ptolémées, *Revue Historique* 624, 963–91.
Lloyd, A. B. (2011) From Satrapy to Hellenistic Kingdom: The Case of Egypt. In A. Erskine and L. Llewellyn-Jones (eds) *Creating a Hellenistic World*, 83–105, Swansea.
Manning, J. G. (2010) *The Last Pharaohs. Egypt under the Ptolemies, 305–30 BC*. Princeton.
McKechnie, P. (1994) Greek Mercenary Troops and their Equipment, *Historia* 43, 297– 305.
McNeal, R. A. (1970) Historical Methods and Thucydides 1.103.1, *Historia* 19, 306–25.
Meeus, A. (2008) The Power Struggle of the Diadochoi in Babylon, 323 BC, *Ancient Society* 38, 39–82.
Meeus, A. (2009) Alexander's Image in the Age of the Successors. In W. Heckel and L. A. Tritle (eds) *Alexander the Great. A New History*, 235–50, Malden.
Meeus, A. (forthcoming) The Unexpected in Diodorus' *Bibliotheca*.

Mehl, A. (2003) Gedanken zur 'herrschenden Gesellschaft' und zu den Untertanen im Seleukidenreich, *Historia* 52, 147–60.
Mileta, C. (2012) Überlegungen zur Herrschaft der Diadochen über die Indigenen Kleinasiens. In H. Hauben and A. Meeus (eds) *The Age of the Successors (323-276 BC)*. Leuven.
Mink, L. O. (1971) Review: Fischer 1970, *History and Theory* 10, 107–22.
Mooren, L. (1978) Macht und Nationalität. In H. Maehler and V. M. Strocka (eds) *Das ptolemäische Ägypten*, 51–57, Mainz.
Moyer, I. S. (2011a) Court, *Chora*, and Culture in Late Ptolemaic Egypt, *American Journal of Philology* 132, 15–44.
Moyer, I. S. (2011b) *Egypt and the Limits of Hellenism*. Cambridge.
Musgrave, J. *et al.* (2010) The Occupants of Tomb II at Vergina. Why Arrhidaios and Eurydice must be excluded, *International Journal of Medical Sciences* 7(6), 1–15.
Ogden, D. (1999) *Polygamy, Prostitutes and Death. The Hellenistic Dynasties*. London.
Pitcher, L. (2009) *Writing Ancient History. An Introduction to Classical Historiography*. London.
Potter, D. M. (1971) Review: Fischer 1970, *The Journal of Southern History* 37, 86–90.
Préaux, C. (1978) *Le monde hellénistique. La Grèce et l'Orient de la mort d'Alexandre à la conquête romaine de Grèce (323-146 av. J.-C.)*. I. Paris.
Rathmann, M. (2005) *Perdikkas zwischen 323 und 320. Nachlassverwalter des Alexanderreiches oder Autokrat?* Vienna.
Rowlandson, J. (2007) The Character of Ptolemaic Aristocracy. Problems of Definition and Evidence. In T. Rajak *et al.* (eds) *Jewish Perspectives on Hellenistic Rulers*, 29–49, Berkeley.
Schuler, C. (1999) Kolonisten und Einheimische in einer attalidischen Polisgründung, *Zeitschrift für Papyrologie und Epigraphik* 128, 124–32.
Seibert, J. (1983) *Das Zeitalter der Diadochen*. Darmstadt.
Sherwin-White, S. and A. Kuhrt (1993) *From Samarkhand to Sardis. A New Approach to the Seleucid Empire*. London.
Simpson, R. H. (1959) Abbreviation of Hieronymus in Diodorus, *American Journal of Philology* 80, 370–79.
Snodgrass, A. (1987) *An Archaeology of Greece. The Present State and Future Scope of a Discipline*. Berkeley.
Stadter, P. A. (1980) *Arrian of Nicomedia*. Chapel Hill.
Strootman, R. (2007) *The Hellenistic Royal Court. Court Culture, Ceremonial and Ideology in Greece, Egypt and the Near East, 336-30 BCE*. Diss. Utrecht.
Stylianou, P. J. (1994) The *Pax Macedonica* and the Freedom of the Greeks of Asia (with an Appendix on the Chronology of the Years 323–301), *Epeteris tou Kentrou Epistemonikon Ereunon* 20, 1–84.
Thompson, D. J. (1992) Language and Literacy in Early Hellenistic Egypt. In P. Bilde *et al.* (eds) *Ethnicity in Hellenistic Egypt*, 39–52, Aarhus.
Touloumakos, J. (2010) Die historische Problematik der Gräber von Vergina, *Ancient Society* 40, 15–50.
Tsigarida, B. (2010) A New Gold Myrtle Wreath from Central Macedonia in the Collection of the Archaeological Museum of Thessaloniki, *Annual of the British School at Athens* 105, 305–15.
Unz, R. (1985) Alexander's Brothers, *Journal of Hellenic Studies* 105, 171–74.
Walbank, F. W. (1984) Sources for the Period. In F. W. Walbank *et al.* (eds) *The Cambridge Ancient History* VII^2.1: *The Hellenistic World*, 1–22, Cambridge.

Walton, F. R. (1957) *Diodorus of Sicily* XI, *Fragments of Books XXI–XXXII*. Cambridge, Mass.

Weber, G. (1997) Interaktion, Representation und Herrschaft der Königshof im Hellenismus. In A. Winterling (ed.) *Zwischen 'Haus' und 'Staat'. Antike Höfe im Vergleich*, 27–71, Munich.

Westlake, H. D. (1969) Eumenes of Cardia. In *Essays on the Greek Historians and Greek History*, 313–30, Manchester.

Wheatley, P. V. (1997) Problems in Analysing Source Documents in Ancient History: The Case of Philip, Adviser to Demetrius Poliorcetes, 314–312 BC, and *IG* II^2 561, *Limina* 3, 61–70

Wheatley, P. V. (2009) The *Diadochoi*, or Successors to Alexander. In W. Heckel and L. A. Tritle (eds) *Alexander the Great. A New History*, 53–68, Malden.

White, H. (1971) Review: Fischer 1970, *Pacific Historical Review* 40, 229–30.

Wrightson, G. (2012) The Naval Battles of 322 BCE. In H. Hauben and A. Meeus (eds) *The Age of the Successors (323-276 BC)*. Leuven.

Yardley, J. C., P. Wheatley and W. Heckel (2012) *Justin, Epitome of the Philippic History or Pompeius Trogus*. II. Oxford.

Notes

1 The number would increase if we were to include those only very tentatively identified with homonymous individuals from the time of Alexander (e.g. Atarrhias [36.2], Menoetas [47.1], Meleager [47.1], Glaucias [52.4], Ariston [59.3], Theodotus [64.5]), or those occurring once more in Diodorus' Successor narrative outside of book 19 (e.g. Dionysius [19.68.3; 20.45], Themison [19.62.5; 20.50.4]).

2 For the fragmentary book 21 this effect is even worsened by the interests of the excerptors: Walton 1957, ix.

3 *Pace* Hadley 2001, 12, Diodorus does not claim that the death sentence had been rescinded at 18.59.4: to forget or to ignore (ἐπιλήθω) is by no means the same as to rescind.

4 Hauben 1987, 424–25; Gorre 2009, 482–88. The latter seems to underestimate the significance of the Satrap Stela: cf. his own n. 35–36; Manning 2010, 95–96; Lloyd 2011, 95.

5 On the problems of the evidence: Mehl 2003, 150–51; Rowlandson 2007, 32–34; Moyer 2011a, 23–24. Engels (forthcoming) has strikingly illustrated the problem of onomastic evidence by pointing out that all but one of eleven known Friends of the Arsacids bear Greek names, whereas their court obviously was not almost exclusively Greek; even in the period of the Diadochi onomastics cannot be considered a completely reliable criterion: Billows 1990, 306 n. 32. That scholars can in these questions be misled by the assumption that non-Greeks cannot have been involved, is nicely illustrated by the recently published letter of Eumenes II to Tyriaion granting it the status of a polis. The original editors understood the text to say that it concerned the Graeco-Macedonian colonists and τοῖς συνοικοῦσιν ἐν χωρίοις (those living with them in fortified places) – thus construing a rather strange phrase –, undoubtedly because they could not imagine that in fact the natives living together with them (τοῖς συνοικοῦσιν ἐνχωρίοις) were given citizenship in the new polis, as has been shown independently by Brixhe 1999, no. 509, and Schuler 1999.

6 In the context of the Vergina debate one could think of Andronikos' hypothesis (1987, 227–28) on the genesis of the great tumulus integrating literary and material evidence. On the problems of such an approach, see Snodgrass 1987, 38; cf. Gehrke 1986, 83. One may also wonder how much sense it makes to keep trying to bring the skeletal remains in line with any known physical features of the persons we would like to have found at Vergina (most recently Musgrave et al. 2010).

7 I would like to thank Víctor Alonso Troncoso for inviting me to a most interesting conference, and both him and Ed Anson for their comments on an earlier draft of this paper.

THE BATTLE OF GABENE: EUMENES' INESCAPABLE DOOM?

Edward M. Anson

Plutarch (*Life of Eumenes* 16.1–6) reports that prior to the battle of Gabene most of Eumenes' fellow-commanders, led by Antigenes and Teutamus, decided that after defeating Antigonus they would eliminate Eumenes. The plot, although not mentioned by any other source, appears authentic in light of the earlier problems faced by Eumenes in organizing his command and in the actions taken by Eumenes in preparing for the upcoming Battle of Gabene, as well as that carried out by one of his subordinates during the course of the battle. As I am certain the biographer intended, the conspiracy and Eumenes' reaction to it, when it was revealed to him shortly before the upcoming struggle, gives insights into the character of the Cardian and also raises questions with respect to his strategy in what proved to be his last battle. These scheming commanders were displeased with Eumenes' popularity with the troops. They believed that after the battle, which was assumed would be decisive, a victorious Eumenes with the probable addition of Antigonus' defeated forces, plus those troops already directly under his authority, would, at the least, cease to treat them as equals. If the army of the conspirators was victorious, Eumenes would be killed by his so-called allies; if defeated, he would be killed and the army would retreat to the Upper Satrapies (cf. D.S. 19.43.5). In the end there was a stalemate and Eumenes was surrendered to his enemy Antigonus and the army the Cardian had cobbled together in large part joined Antigonus.

In full realization of the danger, Eumenes, nonetheless, determined to lead his army into battle. His ambition would not let him do otherwise. This paper speculates that Eumenes prepared for victory or defeat by associating himself with his loyal cavalry forces, either to protect himself in the transitional time following a victory, or to accompany him in flight in the case of defeat. The lack of a decisive victory or defeat led Eumenes to expect a continuation of the campaign much as had followed a similar result after the Battle of Paraetacene. This miscalculation cost Eumenes his life.

When Eumenes discovered this plot, he found himself faced with an apparently impossible situation. Defeat would likely mean capture and death at the hands of Antigonus. This commander had trusted Eumenes once before. After defeating the Cardian in the late spring of 319 (D.S. 18.40.5–8; Plu. *Eum.* 9.3),[1] and forcing him to take refuge in the fortress of Nora (D.S. 18.41.1–2; Plu. *Eum.* 10.1; Nep. *Eum.* 5.3; Just. 14.2.2–3), the following year he had released Eumenes after the latter agreed to be his subordinate (see Anson 1977, 251–56; 2004, 136–37). This alliance lasted until Polyperchon, the new regent in Macedonia, offered Eumenes Antigonus' position as royal general in Asia (D.S. 18.57.3–4; 58.1; Plu. *Eum.* 13.1). By accepting the title and the alliance Eumenes broke his agreement with Antigonus. This commander would not make the mistake of trusting Eumenes again.[2] While the sources list Antigonus and Eumenes as 'friends' (D.S. 18.41.6–7; Plu. *Eum.* 10.5), this was a formal political relationship of two powerful individuals that likely dates from the reign of Philip II.[3] Its limits were clearly shown, when prior to the defeat that led to Eumenes being besieged in Nora, Antigonus had offered a 100-talent reward to anyone who would murder his erstwhile friend (Plu. *Eum.* 8.11);[4] and after the latter's release from Nora and his alliance with Polyperchon, Antigonus had again demanded that Eumenes' forces kill him (D.S. 18.63.1–2). Of course, in the final analysis, after Eumenes was surrendered, Antigonus did have him executed (D.S. 19.44.2–4; Plu. *Eum.* 18.6; 19.1; Nepos *Eum.* 12.4).

Plutarch's evidence, however, strongly suggests that victory apparently might not have brought a different result, just different executioners.[5] The veracity of Plutarch's account, however, has been called into question. Christoph Schäfer (2002, 158) contends that this allegation of a pre-battle conspiracy against Eumenes is without foundation. For Schäfer, Eumenes' officers were basically loyal, and Plutarch's contention is an attempt to maintain the parallelism of his comparison of Eumenes with Sertorius.[6] Plutarch did wish to demonstrate that 'they were strangers, aliens, and exiles, ... continually in command of all sorts of peoples', but that in contrast, 'Sertorius ... held a command which was given him by all his confederates because of his reputation, and ... Eumenes that many contended with him for the leadership' (*Eum.* 20[1].2–3). While it is true that Plutarch does select his evidence from multiple sources often to highlight such comparisons and contrasts, yet, there is no reason that with certain caveats Plutarch's evidence cannot be accepted. While the disloyalty of certain of his troops and commanders was a central theme in Plutarch's *Life of Eumenes*, as witnessed by the emphasis it is given in his *Comparison of Eumenes and Sertorius*,[7] this theme of disloyalty is a common one in the sources.[8] Apparently on three separate occasions in the last year of his life Eumenes was forced to elicit an oath of loyalty from his army (Just. 14.3.3–9; Nep. *Eum.* 10.2; cf. Plu. *Eum.* 17.8–9). Yet, when, as they say, the chips were down, the troops insisted that Eumenes be in overall command (D.S. 19.24.5–6; Plu. *Eum.* 14.2,7–9). This preference for the Cardian accentuated the almost continuous rivalry over the chief command.[9] This competition made perceived plots not a function of paranoia, but of prudence. On two occasions Eumenes had recourse to the 'Alexander Tent'.[10] Here, the conclave of officers would be held in a pavilion, as if in the presence of Alexander, with the commanders first offering incense and doing obeisance before a replica of Alexander's throne.[11] Symbolically this practice placed everyone on an equal footing in the mystical presence of their dead king. Nor was this the only device that Eumenes used to secure the support of forces ostensibly under his command. In the late summer or early fall of 316, Eumenes had attempted through a forged letter to augment his authority by claiming that Cassander was dead and that Polyperchon had crossed to Asia and was already in Cappadocia and heading east (D.S. 19.23.2–3; Polyaen. 4.8.3). On occasion Eumenes, as royal general in Asia, also used his access to the royal treasuries to influence many of his fellow commanders (D.S. 19.15.5). That Eumenes was driven to these extremes by the rivalry over the chief command suggests that the danger was real. It is also abundantly clear that Eumenes often had his orders ignored or disobeyed. After the Battle of Paraetacene, Eumenes had wished to return to the battlefield and claim victory (D.S. 19.31.3–4). His troops, however, wished to return to camp and it was Antigonus who returned to the field of conflict and claimed the victory (D.S. 19.31.4–5).[12] Prior to the battle of Gabene, Eumenes' troops had scattered into separate camps in some cases a six-day march apart (D.S. 19.37.1; Plu. *Eum.* 15.4–5; Polyaen. 4.6.13). The principal explanation for the separate camps was a resurgence of insubordination (Plu. *Eum.* 15.3; Nep. *Eum.* 8.1–4).[13] Even during this latter battle Peucestas withdrew before the advance of Demetrius (D.S. 19.42.4; cf. 19.40.1). While it could be argued that his retreat was reasonable given that the opposing cavalry force was superior in numbers, his later refusal to rejoin the conflict when so ordered by Eumenes cannot be explained as anything other than insubordination (D.S. 19.43.2–3).[14] Despite Peucestas' action Eumenes still managed to hold back Antigonus' cavalry before retiring behind his own right wing (D.S. 19.42.5–7). Plutarch's evidence of a plot certainly fits in with the circumstances of Eumenes' command.

There are, however, certain aspects of this passage regarding the plot in Plutarch that are questionable. Plutarch's claim (*Eum.* 16.1) that 'most of the satraps and generals' were part of the conspiracy, for example, would appear to be an exaggeration. This is a point noted by Brian Bosworth (1992, 70), who suggests that the relationships in this coalition were far more complex than Plutarch implies. In fact, the only names that are mentioned with respect to the conspiracy specifically are those of Antigenes and Teutamus (Plu. *Eum.* 16.2), although it is very likely that Peucestas, the satrap of Persis, would be involved as well.[15] He had been in charge of the collective forces from the upper satrapies and had earlier contested with Eumenes over the chief command (D.S. 19.14.5).[16] Even though Antigenes and Peucestas were rivals, during Eumenes' sickness prior to the Battle of Paraetacene they had shared the duties of command apparently amicably (D.S. 19.24.6).

Most of the leaders from these eastern provinces, however, had little to fear from Eumenes, and much to dread from Antigonus and especially from his ally Pithon, who had earlier attempted to gain power over the upper satrapies (D.S. 19.14.1–3), but had been foiled in this attempt by the coalition led by Peucestas.[17] It was the threat from Pithon that had been the catalyst for the union of the forces of the commanders from these eastern provinces. In a sense Eumenes should have been grateful to Pithon for this force was already in place when he arrived on the scene in late spring of 316 (for the date, see Anson 2004, 162). After the battle on the Coprates River later that summer (D.S. 19.18.3–7) and Antigonus' retreat into Media (D.S. 19.19.1), Eumenes and the forces that he had brought east with him wished to return to the west. It was at the insistence of those from the upper satrapies that Eumenes and the other commanders had remained

(D.S. 19.21.1–2). It is very likely that Eumenes after a decisive victory over Antigonus would have returned to Asia Minor, leaving the satraps and their personal forces intact in the Upper Satrapies. Eumenes had only moved east in flight from Antigonus in hopes of finding allies, not to acquire any territories (D.S. 18.73.2).

The one consistent location of Eumenes' post-Alexander ambitions from the moment Perdiccas assigned him the satrapy of Cappadocia and Paphlagonia was Asia Minor. Here, Eumenes had gained the support of the local nobility by granting remission of taxes, and bestowing gifts and honors (Plu. *Eum.* 4.3). Connecting with the indigenous elites had been one of the keys to Alexander's success in avoiding insurgencies. The great Conqueror most often found ways to accommodate local leaders without compromising his overall authority. One result of Eumenes' close ties with the Cappadocian and Paphlagonian nobles was that in 321, he was able to raise a force of 6300 Cappadocian and Paphlagonian cavalrymen (Plu. *Eum.* 4.2–3),[18] and many of these troops rejoined him after he was released from Nora (D.S. 18.53.7; Plu. *Eum.* 12.6).[19] Eumenes' wife and children remained in Cappadocia throughout his campaigns and his body was sent there after his death (Nep. *Eum.* 13.4; cf. D.S. 19.44.2; Plu. *Eum.* 19.2).

It is very possible that Eumenes was placed in charge of Asia Minor when Perdiccas moved south against Ptolemy and Egypt in 320, because that was to be his charge, if Perdiccas succeeded, as he had planned, in moving to Macedonia and claiming the throne (see Anson 2004, 85–93). Eumenes would then have become something akin to what he later became, royal general in Asia. The Cardian had been pushing for Perdiccas to seize the throne; his reasons were unlikely to be altruistic (see Anson 2004, 86–87). While Eumenes is often depicted in the sources as acting only in the interests of Alexander's family and heirs,[20] it is clear that such loyalty, when it arose, was entirely based on self-interest (see Anson 2004, 1–2, 9, 45–46). Being a non Macedonian, at least, perhaps, in his mind, and certainly in that of the Macedonian aristocrats,[21] made him an unlikely candidate for the regency. However, if the king was in Macedonia, being general for Asia was a real possibility. Especially since, given his Cardian birth, the new king would likely not see him as a threat. Eumenes had used his origins earlier to assuage the concerns of the native Macedonian aristocrats about his ambitions.[22]

It was the knowledge of Perdiccas' 'plans' that precipitated the First Diadoch War (see Anson 2004, 86–99). In the summer of 321, Alexander's body, after long preparations, was to journey from Babylon to the Macedonian city of Aegae, to be buried there as required by Macedonian custom. Perdiccas planned to divorce his wife and marry Alexander's sister Cleopatra,[23] and then with his new wife accompany the dead king to Macedonia (D.S. 18.23.3; 25.3,6), where he would conduct the funeral rites traditionally performed by the new king (Errington 1976, 142–43; Anson 2004, 91–93). To arrive in Macedonia conveying the dead king, in the company of Alexander's half-brother and young son, 'the kings', as Cleopatra's husband, and likely to be met by Alexander's mother, Olympias (Arr. *Post Alex.* 1.21; cf. Just. 13.6.4), would have made Perdiccas king. His maturity and prestige would have stood in stark contrast to the so-called kings, one, an infant, the other, mentally disabled.[24] After the plan was discovered and Ptolemy in

Egypt and Antipater in Macedonia prepared to prevent its fulfillment, Perdiccas put this scheme in abeyance and launched an attack on Egypt. When he and the bulk of his forces went south, he left Eumenes in charge of all of Asia Minor (D.S. 18.29.2). When Antipater crossed to Asia, he offered Eumenes control of this same area in unfulfilled hopes of getting him to change his allegiance (Plu. *Eum.* 5.6).

Eumenes' later alliance with Polyperchon would have given the Cardian what he had hoped to achieve under Perdiccas.[25] The new regent had offered Eumenes an alliance and given him in the name of the kings the title of royal general with supreme authority in Asia (D.S. 18.58.1). The difficulty was that Polyperchon faced a war in Greece and his rival there, the former regent's son Cassander, was in alliance with Eumenes' old nemesis Antigonus, the current royal general in Asia (D.S. 18.54.3). Eumenes moved what forces he had accumulated in the months since his release from Nora to Cilicia to acquire the argyraspids, Alexander's old infantry guard (Anson 1988, 131–33), who had been ordered by the regent and hence the 'kings', to accept the Cardian's authority,[26] and then to Phoenicia, to build a fleet to aid his new ally (D.S. 18.63.6).

Another issue concerning Plutarch's claim is that the plot is revealed to Eumenes by Eudamus, the master of the elephants, and Phaedimus, an otherwise unknown individual, motivated to do so because Eumenes owed them money (Plu. *Eum.* 16.3–4; cf. Plu. *Eum.* 13.12; D.S. 19.24.2–3). The motivation, given that they were preparing for a major battle and that their positions and very lives were at stake, does appear weak. It is very doubtful that these commanders would have jeopardized their own survival in this manner, when the success of the conspiracy might have acquired for those involved the wealth of Asia, and for those loyal to Eumenes, death. They had likely given Eumenes money because they supported him.[27] Eumenes, when informed of the plot, contemplated flight back to Cappadocia with those whose loyalty was clear, but in the end he decided to see the battle through, since, in the words of Plutarch, 'his fortunes were so often changeable' (Plu. *Eum.* 16.4–6).

Much of this coloring in all probability comes from Plutarch himself; his source for much of this account is surely Duris of Samos, an author noted for dramatizing and augmenting the basic facts (Landucci Gattinoni 1997, 119). As is well known, Plutarch used many sources in writing his *Lives*, selecting those who, he believed, would most illuminate the character of the individual. Moreover, he was writing parallel lives and was interested in maintaining a comparison, which might include emphasizing those elements in the available sources that supported this purpose. This last point is made most strongly by Brian Bosworth (1992, 56–73).

While there may be questionable aspects of Plutarch's testimony, his outline of the plot should be accepted. Given the rivalry that began with Eumenes' alliance with the argyraspids and intensified with the subsequent one with the satraps, it certainly fits into the context. Moreover, when one looks at Eumenes' dispositions of his forces at Paraetacene and Gabene, it would appear that he was conscious that betrayal might occur at any time. Eumenes was very careful to surround himself with troops whose loyalty he could depend on. At Paraetacene,[28] Eumenes commanded the cavalry on the right flank. 2900 elite cavalrymen, who, with the exception of 1100 under the command of Peucestas and Tlepolemus, the satrap of Carmania, were all personally selected by and presumably loyal to Eumenes himself, including his 900 'companions', his personal cavalry bodyguard (D.S. 19.28.3–4), as noted by Bosworth (1992, 131–32). While the description of the Battle of Gabene is not as full as that of the preceding clash at Paraetacene, it is clear that Eumenes once again commanded the elite cavalry units as he had previously.[29]

If his forces were victorious, then he would immediately negotiate with the beaten troops, offering them employment under his command. If defeated, he would be in a position to flee back to the west, either hoping to frighten Antigonus' allies with that commander's vastly increased power, or to seek refuge with Polyperchon. Unknown to Eumenes was that at this time his Macedonian ally had been driven from Macedonia by Cassander (see Anson 2004, 173–74).

During the course of the battle, Peucestas withdrew, according to Diodorus (19.42.4) and Plutarch (*Eum.* 16.5), this withdrawal was the result of cowardice, but the conclusion is unlikely. Brian Bosworth (2002, 154) has suggested that Peucestas and others as part of the conspiracy 'rather than risk defeat and the loss of their contingents ... would retreat and leave Eumenes to be overwhelmed by Antigonus and his cavalry'. Relying on a victory of the argyraspids over the phalanx of Antigonus, they would be in a position to 'negotiate with Antigonus from a position of strength' (Bosworth 2002, 154). It was also possible that both Eumenes and Antigonus would be eliminated. After all, Peucestas did have a reputation for bravery.[30] As Bosworth suggests, the satrap of Persis likely hoped for the defeat and possible death of Eumenes, with the anticipated victory by the coalition forces. Such a situation would have opened the way for Peucestas to assume the leadership role. He was playing a dangerous game, but his attempt to gain the support of the other satraps and commanders for his overall command had failed. If Eumenes won a complete victory, then Peucestas, given the plot, might be executed, or, at the least, lose his province. As it was for Eumenes and the other contenders for power, so it was for Peucestas, the gamble was seen as well worth it.[31]

While Eumenes' cavalry was defeated by Antigonus' heavy cavalry, the Cardian's infantry, led by the argyraspids, swept all before it. But, as at Paraetacene, again there was no clear victor. While Antigonus had lost far more troops, 5000 infantry to only 300 of Eumenes' men,[32] he had succeeded in capturing Eumenes' camp. In the course of the fighting, given the dryness of the soil, a cloud of dust had arisen which obscured the battlefield. When Antigonus observed these conditions, he sent part of his cavalry to capture Eumenes' camp. These troops rode around the enemy's left flank unnoticed, and easily defeated Eumenes' camp guards.[33] The camp, while fortified, had been hastily constructed as a result of the initial wide dispersal of Eumenes' forces before the battle (D.S. 19.39.1).

Eumenes attempted to retrieve the situation, trying to collect all of his remaining cavalry and renew the fight, but Peucestas refused to join him and only retreated further (D.S. 19.43.2–3). Since night was approaching, Eumenes was forced to withdraw. The battle had ended like the first. No decisive victory. Eumenes was now presented with a delicate situation. His plans had centered on there being either a decisive victory or an equally crushing defeat, but a stalemate could result in a subsequent battle, where Eumenes' infantry still might carry the day. That evening Eumenes and all of the satraps and commanders took counsel together. Most, likely led by Peucestas, wished to retreat into the upper satrapies as rapidly as possible, but Eumenes declared that they should stay and renew the battle. He pointed out that the phalanx had been victorious inflicting heavy losses on the enemy, and that Eumenes' cavalry numbers had not been significantly reduced (D.S. 19.43.5–8).

It is likely that Eumenes would have prevailed in this discussion. In the middle of winter where would this army go? They had originally entered the region of Gabene as the only viable area in the region for the maintenance of a large army (D.S. 19.26.1–2). If the satraps divided their forces, then Antigonus would be able to pick them off one at a time. But, the decision was taken from the council's hands. Antigonus possessed the camp. For the argyraspids, many of whom had served almost two decades in Asia, their belongings included their children, wives, and relatives, not to mention the wealth accumulated in years of campaigning and pillaging. The argyraspids independently opened negotiations with Antigonus to retrieve their lost families and possessions.[34] Antigonus' price was the surrender of all the elephants and their overall commander, Eumenes. Apparently unbeknownst to Antigenes he was also part of this surrender package, for shortly afterwards he was executed with utmost cruelty by Antigonus (D.S. 19.44.1). While he may have intrigued against Eumenes, he was apparently no friend of Antigonus.

While protests were issued by most of the army, the argyraspids delivered Eumenes to his enemy. With his surrender most of the satraps fled, others, like the bulk of Eumenes' troops, joined Antigonus, some commanders were captured and executed. Among these were Antigenes and Eudamus (D.S. 19.44.1). Peucestas, his plan to become the leader in eastern Asia a failure, surrendered to Antigonus. The war in the 'Upper Satrapies' was over. In what might be called poetic justice the argyraspids, the best fighting unit, perhaps, in the world, were now dispersed. 1000 of the most troublesome were given to Sibyrtius, the satrap of Arachosia,[35] who was commanded by Antigonus to see to their destruction; the rest were divided up and sent to various remote garrisons (Polyaen. 4.6.15; D.S. 19.48.3).[36] Eumenes himself was put to death in January of 315 (see Anson 2004, 189–90).

Eumenes, despite the threat of betrayal, had remained at Gabene. A victory had the potential to make him the greatest power in Asia. As overall commander a victory would gain him even greater support among the rank-and-file, but more importantly, a decisive victory would gain for him control of the majority of Antigonus' forces. In this age it had become customary for beaten armies to enlist with the victor.[37] These troops would have no ties to the other commanders in Eumenes' force. Except for two brilliant moves by Antigonus, both battles would have been defeats for that commander.[38] As it was, both were setbacks that were redeemed. In the second, it was the traitorous activity of the argyraspids that snatched defeat, if not from the jaws of victory, at least from the staleness of a draw. The 'fickleness of fortune' (D.S. 18.59.4–5), so prominent a theme in the surviving accounts of Eumenes' career, or more precisely his gamble for power, had now run its course.

Bibliography

Anson, E. M. (1977) The Siege of Nora: A Source Conflict, *Greek, Roman and Byzantine Studies* 18, 251–56.

Anson, E. M. (1988) Hypaspists and Argyraspids after 323, *Ancient History Bulletin* 2, 131–33.

Anson, E. M. (2003) The Dating of Perdiccas' Death and the Assembly at Triparadeisus, *Greek Roman and Byzantine Studies* 43, 373–90.

Anson, E. M. (2004) *Eumenes of Cardia: A Greek among Macedonian.* Brill Academic Publishers. Leiden and Boston.

Anson, E. M. (2006) Dating the Deaths of Eumenes and Olympias, *Ancient History Bulletin* 20, 1–8.

Billows, R. A. (1997) *Antigonos the One-Eyed and the Creation of the Hellenistic State.* Berkeley and London.

Boiy, T. (2007) *Between High and Low: A Chronology of the Early Hellenistic Period.* Frankfurt.

Bosworth, A. B. (1992) History and Artifice. In P. A. Stadter (ed.) *Plutarch and the Historical Tradition*, 54–89, London and New York.

Bosworth, A. B. (2002) *The Legacy of Alexander: Politics, Warfare, and Propaganda under the Successors.* Oxford.

Devine, A. M. (1985a) Diodorus' Account of the Battle of Paraitacene, *The Ancient World* 12, 75–86.

Devine, A. M. (1985b) Diodorus' Account of the Battle of Gabiene, *The Ancient World* 12, 87–96.

Errington, R. M. (1976) Alexander in the Hellenistic World. In E. Badian (ed.) *Alexandre le Grand: image et réalité: 7 exposés suivis de discussions / par A. B. Bosworth ... [et al.], avec la participation de Denis van Berchem ... [et al.]; entretiens préparés par E. Badian, présidés par Denis van Berchem, Vanduvres-Genève, 25–30 aout 1975, Entretiens sur l'Antiquité classique*, vol. 22, Fondation Hardt, 137–79, Geneva.

Goukowsky, P. (ed.) (1978) *Diodore de Sicile, bibliothèque historique, Livre XVIII.* Paris.

Hornblower, J. (1981) *Hieronymus of Cardia.* Oxford.

Landucci Gattinoni, F. (1997) *Duride di Samo.* Rome.

Schäfer, C. (2002) *Eumenes von Kardia und der Kampf um die Macht im Alexanderreich.*

Notes

1 For the date, see Anson 2003, 373–90.

2 While our sources present Antigonus as of divided mind with respect to the disposition of Eumenes (D.S. 19.44.2; Plu. *Eum.* 18.3–6; Nepos *Eum.* 10.3–11.2; 12.1–3), this was likely only a ruse to assuage those of his companions, in particular his son Demetrius, who wished to save the Cardian (Plu. *Eum.* 18.6). It is clear in the sources that the majority of Antigonus' advisors were adamant that Eumenes should be put to death (D.S. 19.44.2; Plu. *Eum.* 18.6; Nep. *Eum.* 10.4). Billows 1990, 104 n. 29 suggests that Hieronymus may here be attempting to ameliorate Antigonus' guilt in the death of Eumenes. However, since in the final analysis it is Antigonus who has him executed, this delay would not do much to soften the charge, and Billow's claim is, therefore, unlikely.

3 In many cases a 'friendship' is simply another name for a political alliance. These relationships were then multi-faceted and often predicated on self-interest. In the case of this particular 'friendship',

Eumenes and Antigonus had not been in direct contact since Alexander had left Antigonus in Phrygia in 333. They formally renewed their relationship in 319 at the beginning of the siege of Nora (D.S. 18.41.6; Plu. *Eum.* 10.5). On these political 'friendships', see Anson 2004, 47–48.

4 Justin (14.1.11) reports that Eumenes claimed to have fabricated the letters to test his soldiers' loyalty.

5 Plutarch (*Eum.* 16.4–6) records that Eumenes made up his will and destroyed all his papers.

6 This analysis owes much to Bosworth 1992, 58–71.

7 Eumenes was plotted against by many, and 'in consequence of his victories ... [was] in peril at the hands of those who envied him' (Plu. *Eum.* 20[1].3–4).

8 D.S. 18.60.1,3–4; 62.7; 19.13.1; Nep. *Eum.* 1.2–3; 7.1–2; Polyaen. 4.8.2–3. It is generally believed that the thematic emphasis originated with Eumenes' fellow Cardian and subsequent historian, Hieronymus (see for example, Hornblower 1981, 9).

9 D.S. 18.61.2; 19.15.1–2; 21.1–2; 23.1; 24.1; Plu. *Eum.* 13.4,10; 14.5–6. Eumenes throughout his career suffered from the envy of the Macedonian aristocratic class. While the Macedonian soldiers were unaffected by his Cardian origin, these aristocrats saw Eumenes as their inferior due to his birth and previous position as secretary (see Anson 2004, 55–56, 103, 251–53).

10 D.S. 18.60.5–61;19.15.3; Plu. *Eum.* 13.4–8; Polyaen. 4.8.2; Nep. *Eum.* 7.2–3.

11 It is very doubtful that these were Alexander's actual regalia (so Goukowsky 1978, 163). R. M. Errington (1976, 140–41) rightly holds that they were manufactured for the occasion.

12 In fact, this battle was a defeat for Antigonus. He was forced to retire into Media, while Eumenes occupied the original objective of both commanders, Gabene (D.S. 19.34.7).

13 Diodorus (19.39.1) only reports that the troops were camped in widely scattered villages, but Polyaenus (4.6.11) states that Eumenes had stationed forces 'everywhere' along the road leading from Media, Antigonus' location, into Gabene. The defense of the road leading to Gabene might be a valid explanation for the dispersal of his camp, given that supplies should not have been the problem. Earlier Diodorus (19.34.7) reported that Gabene 'was unplundered and capable of supplying everything in abundance for the army'. However, Polyaenus uses the rather amorphous '*dunamis*' to describe the forces dispersed along the '1000 stades' of road. *Dunamis* could be taken to mean the entire army or detached contingents, with the latter likely being the correct translation. Why would Eumenes spread his entire army over more than 100 miles of road, when a small force located at a distance could alert the entire army of any enemy approach, and such a wide separation of forces would create problems assembling the different units for battle? The likely explanation is that he did not. The dispersal of his forces was due, as reported by Plutarch and Nepos, to the rivalry among the commanders.

14 Brian Bosworth (2002, 150–51) has suggested that some of the unrest in the ranks of the generals and satraps could be the result of news of activities back in Macedonia, in particular, the successful return of Cassander. This information would be especially disconcerting, but unlikely to have been known at this time. Cassander's successful invasion occurred in the late summer of 316, and the battle of Gabene in the winter of 316 (for the chronology, see Anson 2006, 8–9).

15 However, Peucestas and Antigenes had different agendas. They had clashed with respect to the overall command (D.S. 19.15.1), and it is possible that Peucestas had usurped control of Susiane, Antigenes' assigned satrapy (D.S. 18.39.6; Arr. *Post Alex.* 1.35), in the latter's absence. After the regent Perdiccas' death, Antigenes had been assigned the task of bringing part of the treasure from Susa to Cyinda in Cilicia (Arr. *Post Alex.* 1.38), where Eumenes found him with the argyraspids in the summer of 318 (D.S. 18.59.3).

16 In the initial meeting of Eumenes and the satraps of the upper provinces, Peucestas demanded that he be given over-all command (D.S. 19.15.1). Later in Persis, he had attempted again to acquire chief command by lavishly entertaining the troops (D.S. 19.21.1–3).

17 Pithon had been appointed satrap of Media at Triparadeisus (D.S. 18.39.6), but had tried to assert his authority over all the provinces east of Babylonia.

18 A Paphlagonian had killed Craterus (Arr. *Post Alex.* 1.27).

19 Plutarch (*Eum.* 11.7–9) makes it clear that most of those who had entered Nora with Eumenes were cavalrymen, who likely were those he had raised in his province earlier.

20 D.S. 18.53.7; 57.4; 58.2–4; 19.44. 2; Plu. *Eum.* 1.4; 3.14; Nep. *Eum.* 6.5,13; 13.3.

21 On the nature of the prejudice that Eumenes faced, see Anson 2004, 233–58.

22 After Alexander's death, when a riot had occurred pitting the Macedonian and Greek infantry against the cavalry and the Asiatic forces, Eumenes had portrayed himself as a neutral, 'it was not business of his, since he was a stranger, to meddle in disputes of Macedonians' (Plu. *Eum.* 3.1).

23 In the summer of 321 Perdiccas had married Nicaea, the daughter of the commander in Macedonia, Antipater (Arr. *Post Alex.* 1.21; D.S. 18.23.1; Just 13.6.6).

24 At the time of Alexander's death there were only three surviving male members of the once numerous royal Argead clan and none of them was competent to govern on his own. The three were Alexander's half-brother, Arrhidaeus, who was mentally deficient, Heracles, a three or four-year old son, the result of an informal liaison with the daughter of a prominent Persian, and a soon-to-be-born son by Alexander's Sogdian wife Roxane. Alexander's father Philip and Alexander himself had culled the ranks of their clan to the point of near extinction. After some initial turmoil a dual monarchy was established of Arrhidaeus, who now would reign as Philip III, and the Conqueror's and Roxane's infant son, Alexander IV. Since neither 'king' was able to rule on his own, a regency was created under Perdiccas, Alexander's former second-in-command. See Anson 2004, 59–60.

25 Antipater had died in the summer of 319 (see Anson 2004, 3), having appointed Polyperchon as his successor rather than his son Cassander (D.S. 18.48.4).

26 D.S. 18.59.1–3; Plu. *Eum.* 13.3–4; cf. D.S. 18.58.1.

27 This whole episode is curious. Eumenes had given this same Eudamus 200 talents less than nine months earlier (D.S. 19.15.5), and at the same time had paid the argyraspids six-months salary. He had likely taken additional funds with him from the treasury in Susa. Why he would need cash at this time is unknown.

28 Devine 1985, 75–86; Bosworth 2002, 98–141; Anson 2004, 147–82.

29 While the specific units are not listed, Eumenes is in command of the heavy cavalry ('the best horsemen') (D.S. 19.40.2). On the Battle of Gabene in general, see Devine 1985, 87–96; Bosworth 2002, 141–59; Billows 1997, 99–103; Anson 2004, 182–90.

30 During a siege in India Peucestas had risked his life to save Alexander, covering him with his body and shield (Arr. *An.* 6.10.2).

31 Eumenes had earlier charged Sibyrtius, the satrap of Arachosia, with conspiring with Antigonus and sent a cavalry contingent into Arachosia that seized the satrap's baggage, forcing Sibyrtius to flee (D.S. 19.23.4). It is also clear that Peucestas had not entered into a secret alliance with Antigonus. Despite Peucestas' obvious desire for power, earlier, when Eumenes needed additional troops, he asked Peucestas to summon an additional 10000 archers from Persia. At first, Peucestas ignored this request, still angry over not receiving the chief command, but Diodorus (19.17.5–7) comments that it was 'his fear of Antigonus' that ultimately convinced him to summon these forces.

32 D.S. 19.43.1; Polyaen. 4.6.13; Just. 14.3.5. Devine (1985b, 92) believes that the figure for Antigonus' losses is too high and that for the argyraspids too low. He, however, presents little argumentation to support his position. It should be noted that after the battle Eumenes argued that they should renew the action as soon as possible because the phalanx of the enemy had been destroyed (D.S. 19.43.6). Polyaenus (4.6.13) and Nepos (*Eum.* 10.2) refer to the battle as a victory for Eumenes that was turned into defeat by the treachery of the argyraspids.

33 D.S. 19.42.3; Polyaen. 4.6.13; Plu. *Eum.* 16.10–11; Just. 14.3.3.

34 D.S. 19.43.8; Plu. *Eum.* 17.1–2; Just. 14.3–10. Plutarch (*Eum.* 17.1) states that it was Teutamus who approached Antigonus. Given that Antigenes is later executed by Antigonus, it is very possible that he did not approve or, perhaps, even know of this action.

35 Today this is the region from Kandahar, Afghanistan to the Indus.

36 Diodorus (19.48.4) clearly quoting Hieronymus, declares that those 1000 argyraspids sent to Sibyrtius were those most responsible for Eumenes' betrayal; Antigenes, the commander of the argyraspids, was put into a pit and burned alive (D.S. 19.44.1). Teutamus now disappears from the historical record.

37 When Eumenes defeated Neoptolemus in 320, that commander's forces joined Eumenes (D.S. 18.29.5–6;

Plu. *Eum.* 5.5–6); after Antigonus' defeat of Eumenes in 319, the latter's forces joined Antigonus (D.S. 18.40.8–41.1; Just. 14.2.3); after Antigonus' defeat of Alcetas in 319, the beaten commander's forces joined Antigonus (D.S. 18.45.4). On the mercenary characteristics of most of the veterans serving in Asia after Alexander's death, see Anson 2004, 118–19, 253–57.

38 At the Battle of Paraetacene Antigonus faced total defeat, but he observed that, as Eumenes' victorious forces pursued the retreating enemy, a gap opened in the line between the phalanx and the cavalry on Eumenes' left. Antigonus charged into the break and forced Eumenes to recall his victorious forces. The result was that Antigonus was able to reassemble his forces and compel a stalemate (D.S. 19.30.7–31.2).

ALEXANDER'S ARGYRASPIDS: TOUGH OLD FIGHTERS OR ANTIGONID MYTH?

Elizabeth Baynham

On April 1st 2003, *The Australian,* one of the flagship newspapers of Rupert Murdoch's Antipodean media stable, featured a front page photograph of two ageing Iraqi soldiers, one 59, the other, 62, veterans of the Iraq/Iran conflict in the 1980s, who were grimly taking arms again, but this time against the Coalition invasion. Given the paper's date (April Fools' Day), it was clear from the caption (*Who do you think you are kidding, Mr Bush?*) that the accompanying short article was meant to be amusing. However, the photograph itself was genuine; the work of a British free-lance journalist, Mr Stuart Clarke, who was in Iraq at the time.

Moreover, the image has a certain poignancy, suggesting that only a society placed in an extreme position obliges its older citizens (as well as women and children on occasion) to defend it. Men in their 60s and 70s undertook military service in Germany during both World War I and II; so too, in Soviet Russia. In a much loved British television series of the 1970s the inept but well meaning veterans of *Dad's Army* kept the fictitious Walmington-on-Sea in the south of England safe from Mr Hitler. Such an affectionate and gentle parody was perhaps largely possible because Britain had been fortunate enough to escape invasion, although apparently there were concerns at the BBC prior to general broadcasting that the British public might consider the comedy 'disrespectful' to the Home Guard. In fact, the show was a great hit (in general, see McCann 2002).

However, in Ovid's *Amores* (1.9.4) the Roman poet draws an extended analogy between the pursuit of a lover and fighting a battle, and he sneeringly declares *turpe senex miles* ('an old soldier is a disgusting thing'). Within this context, the repellent old warrior is thus linked with an old man's desire for sex; both are physically unattractive and the capacity to perform is reduced in each. Although Ovid's tone is humorous, the portrayal of an older soldier is often used to evoke pathos, rather than necessarily imply cowardice on the part of the aged warrior, or scorn from an audience, as Tim G. Parkin (2003, 242–43) has noted. Pathetic sentiment about older soldiers is echoed elsewhere by Aeschylus (*A.* 72–82), Livy (6. 23.4–7) and Tacitus (*Ann.* 1.17–18; 1.34–35; 3.43; see Parkin 2003, 414, n. 14). We shall return to the 'pitiable' aspect of old soldiers at a later point in this discussion.

Of course depressing comments about the physical and mental deterioration that often accompanies old age occur frequently throughout Greco-Roman literature, in all areas of human activity not just in relation to military capacity. As a general rule ancient armies comprised citizen militias, mostly young men at the peak of their physical strength. Given both the punishing demands of military service and the inevitable presence of youth in any kind of ideal bodily concept or physical engagement - an obsession which is just as prevalent in our own society as it was in Greco-Roman culture - it is not surprising that war also was - and still is - considered a task for the young. Although definitions of 'non-combatants' in the ancient world may vary according to context and culture, there is a strong, prevalent theme among our ancient writers from Homer to Caesar that women, children and old men remained at home while young men went to war (Parkin 2003, 242 with n. 7, 412–13).

Yet in 1640 the great Spanish artist Diego Velázquez depicted Mars as a weary, ageing warrior, sitting upright upon a dishevelled bed, his chin resting thoughtfully, if in a melancholy fashion, upon his hand. With his face deeply shadowed by his helmet, he gazes out at the viewer, his armour and weapons lying at his feet. His robust body nevertheless shows signs of deterioration in its sagging skin, protruding collar bones and heavy pouches under the eyelids. It is a powerful and brooding image of the god, and its association with maturity is at once evocative and confronting: war has been around a long time.[1]

There is a particularly striking group of war-hardened veterans from the era of the Diadochi. According to Diodorus Siculus (19.41.2) and Plutarch (*Eum.* 16.4) (who are almost certainly drawing on Hieronymus of Cardia), one of the most formidable and highly prized infantry units in the Hellenistic world, the so-called Silver Shields (or Argyraspids) consisted of some 3,000 men of whom the youngest were 60 (D.S. 19.41.2; Plu. *Eum.* 16.4), with some even in their 70s. These men participated in the battles of Paraetacene and Gabiene over 317/16. They were veterans whose record of service could be as long as 40 years. The origins and identity of the Argyraspids are problematic, but the most likely view of their formation (on the evidence of Curt. 8.5.4 and Just. 12.7.4–5)[2] was that they were originally a select group of hypaspists in Alexander's army who took their distinctive insignia of silver decorations on their shields in 326, during the king's campaign in India. The vivid paintings of the recently discovered, late fourth century Macedonian tomb at Agios Athanasios, show two guards, almost certainly hypaspists, of near life size, who stand on either side of the door to the tomb, beneath the painted frieze of a banqueting scene. They are wearing the distinctive Macedonian *kausia,* or flat topped cap, *krēpides* (military boots) and leaning on their *sarissai* in an attitude of mourning (Tsimbidou-Avloniti 2005; also 2002, 91–98). The opulence of their clothing suggests that the hypaspists had some kind of rich parade ground dress; and we might expect that the Argyraspids would use expensive and showy insignia which marked them out as an elite unit. Alexander's desire to impress local Indian rulers, who were themselves great exhibitionists of their wealth (Curt. 8.9.23–27), might have also been another factor in allowing the Argyraspids to show themselves off (Curt. 8.5.4; see Yardley and Heckel 1997, 236).

As we know, in addition to undertaking other types of special military activity, the

Argyraspids participated in an elite phalanx, whose main weapon was the *sarissa* – a five metre pike, tipped with a 55cm iron blade and balanced by a butt spike, which weighed about 7 kg. The sarissa was most likely constructed in two parts and joined by a collar in the middle, which made disassembling the pike for transport easier (see Heckel, 2006, 58–60), and the elite infantryman's weapons would have been carried by baggage animals or slaves. Nevertheless a phalangite would have faced taxing marches, in often harsh and testing conditions. The final campaigns of the Silver Shields took place in what is now modern Iraq and Iran where summer temperatures can reach 50 degrees Celsius. Examples of natural phenomenona responding to the extreme heat are mentioned in our sources; barley explodes out of the ground in the region around Babylon (Thphr. *HP* 8.11.7; *Ign.* fr. 44; cf. Plu. *Alex.* 35.7), while lizards are fried alive if they tried to cross a street in Susa at midday (Str. 15.3.10 C731; Bosworth 2002, 115, with n. 71). More plausible information is also reported about the same area: according to Plutarch (*Alex.* 35.7), the local inhabitants slept on inflated animal skins filled with cool water during the hot season. Even if certain details about Babylon's climate are exaggerated, it is clear that active military service in these regions would have been demanding, as recent medical studies on the effect of heat stress upon the Coalition troops stationed in Southern Iraq have demonstrated (see Grainge and Heber, 2005, 101–04).

The Silver Shields were also capable of exploiting their ages by using taunts deliberately aimed at unsettling their opponents, as a well known vignette from Diodorus' account of Gabiene illustrates. Just before the final battle between the forces of Eumenes and Antigonus, one of Alexander's veterans rode his horse along the Antigonid phalanx shouting that Antigonus' troops were 'sinning against their fathers, the men who conquered the world with Philip and Alexander' (Plu. *Eum.* 16.4; see Bosworth 2002, 151–52). Diodorus' (D.S. 19.41.2) and Plutarch's remarks on the Argyraspids' ages occur within this passage, and again, we shall revisit its content shortly.

This essay will explore the following theme: the historicity of the Argyraspids' ages, in connection with some observations about the prevalence and depiction of the older soldier in Greco-Roman literature. Our sources' claims about the Argyraspids' ages may seem fanciful, given the high mortality rate in the ancient world and the apparently unlikely factor of many men (3,000; cf. D.S. 18.58.1) in the one cohort surviving the multiple campaigns from the reigns of Philip II (359–336) and Alexander (336–323). The chances of developing septicaemia from wounds or complications resulting from trauma like compound fractures would have been high. Even if soldiers recovered from physical hurt, they would have also been exposed to the debilitating effects of injuries as well as parasites, infections, dental problems, deteriorating eyesight, hearing, and chronic illness, especially inflammatory or degenerative diseases that are often associated with ageing, like arthritis, cardiovascular disease, osteoporosis, neurological disorders, and cancer. Yet apparently the Argyraspids were not only still capable of fighting – *but fighting extraordinarily well.*

Accepting the truth of the claims about the seniority of the Argyraspids is not a new difficulty; faced with such a story many scholars are understandably sceptical and dismiss it out of hand. Over fifty years ago R. H. Simpson (1959, 376) called the information 'foolish assertion', arguing that it could not have originated with Hieronymus – who 'was an eye-witness' - and agreeing with Tarn (1948, 123–24) that the story must have come from the Alexander Romance. It is also worth sharing the recent (2010), eloquent, if acerbic comments of an anonymous referee: '... are we to take seriously the idea that 60- and 70-year-olds could, without even a leavening of younger men (their own sons, perhaps), remain invincible in the bruising field of Makedonian phalanx warfare? It seems a lot easier to disbelieve Hieronymus of Kardia than to believe *that*'.

Interestingly, such a view actually raises a common problem in the study of ancient history; often it is all too easy to dismiss difficult evidence as fanciful, propagandist, or the garbled compilations of an incompetent derivative writer, without further testing or exploration. Pace Tarn and Simpson, it seems appropriate to assume that Hieronymus is responsible for the story. Earlier scholarship argued that our extant sources may have drawn on several different traditions apart from Hieronymus, and more recently scholars like Franca Landucci Gattinoni (1997) (and others) have made a strong case for the influence of Duris of Samos upon the various traditions. However, as Anson (2004 3 with n. 15) has observed, even though Hieronymus' history survives in only 18 fragments, and there is much that we do not know about the work, the 'burden of proof' falls upon those who try to claim a particular passage is not from Hieronymus. His dominance of our extant tradition is pretty much universally conceded and he is deemed to have been at the basis of nearly every source, from Diodorus to the Heidelberg Epitome (see Wheatley, this volume). I am not suggesting that we should accept everything Hieronymus (or any other ancient historian) says at face value. Excellent scholarship from Jane Hornblower (1981) to Joseph Roisman (2010, 135–48) has pointed out that apart from his literary aspirations, Hieronymus clearly had other agendas, such as promoting an 'elitist' perspective.

Yet although Hieronymus' history has been preserved only through the work of later writers, he is considered one of the most reliable sources in antiquity. He was an eye-witness to many of the events he describes and very long lived himself – one of the few centenarians whom we hear of from the ancient world. Significantly, Hieronymus was involved in the battles in which the Silver Shields played a critical part. He also worked for both sides – he was a friend and possible relative of Eumenes (D.S. 19.44.3; cf. Hornblower 1981, 8; Anson 2004, 5 with n. 29) and a companion and consultant for Antigonus, his son Demetrius and grandson, Antigonus Gonatas. In view of Hieronymus' later association with Eumenes' great opponent, it is also true that it would be in the historian's interest to make Antigonus' victory all the more impressive by aggrandizing the skill and ferocity of the soldiers he faced. This might seem paradoxical; after all, on one level where was the challenge in Antigonus' phalanx facing a feeble and doddery line of old soldiers? But in both the critical battles against Antigonus' forces the Argyraspids are described as getting the better of their opponents;

at Paraetacene they are responsible for the victory of Eumenes' phalanx (D.S. 19.30.5), whereas at Gabiene, they prevailed right up until the desertion of Peucestas, satrap of Persia and cavalry commander, and the capture of their camp; at which point, cut off from their cavalry support they formed a square and retreated (D.S. 19.42.4; 43). That is precisely Hieronymus' point; he has to convince us that there was nothing absurd or comical about the Argyraspids – they were no *Dad's Army*. However, if Hieronymus' claim about the Silver Shields is demonstrably exaggerated or false, then the worth of his information elsewhere would also be questionable.

It is one of those ironies of history that the Argyraspids' long continuity of service was maintained because of the death of Alexander. Their career is not easily traced, and the details of their movements are uncertain and often controversial. However, almost certainly they were among the 10,000 or so veterans who were discharged at Opis (Arr. *An.* 7.12.1; cf. D.S. 17.109.1; 18.4.1; Just. 12.12.7). These men were meant to be sent home in retirement, and they were on their way to Macedonia at the time of the king's death but had not travelled much further than Cyinda in Cilicia. Most of them never did get home. Heckel (1997, 237, 276) has suggested that they could have accompanied Perdiccas when he invaded Egypt in 321 – and presumably they survived or avoided both the crocodiles and swollen Nile waters that claimed so many Macedonian lives in the disastrous river crossing (cf. also Anson, 2004, 78 with n. 3). The Argyraspids were back in Cilicia after having escorted part of the treasury from Susa to Cyinda (Arr. *Post Alex.* 1.38), when Polyperchon ordered them to serve with Eumenes (D.S. 18.58) and their commander Antigenes (Arr. *Post Alex.* 1.35) decided to support Eumenes' commission rather than side with Antigonus, in order to protect and expand his satrapy (D.S. 18.62.5–7; Bosworth 1992, 66; Anson 2004, 147–50). The Argyraspids had remained in the East more or less because of circumstances, although Arrian (*Post Alex.* 1.35,38) also emphasises that they were truculent and difficult men to command; Justin (14.2.7) explicitly states that they had little respect for any of their leaders after Alexander, and considered it an indignity to serve other rulers.

Anson (2004, 148) rightly highlights the Argyraspids' autonomous nature as a 'curious blend of Macedonian custom and mercenary characteristics', but interestingly, rebelliousness, independent and mutinous behaviour is associated elsewhere with older soldiers in Greco-Roman literature, as we shall see shortly. However, it is also clear that veterans could act as experienced advisors and wise mentors, like the character of Nestor in Homer's *Iliad.* According to Justin (11.6.4–5), when Alexander was selecting his troops for his Asian campaign, he deliberately selected Philip's veterans, *ut non tamen milites quam magistros militiae lectos putares* (cf. Ps.Callisth. A. 1 25, 3–5: Tarn 1948, 124). Justin has exaggerated certain details (Heckel 1997, 113); nevertheless, at the siege of Halicarnassus in 334, Philip's veterans do more at a moment of crisis than mere counselling. They sharply rebuke their younger comrades at the same time as actively engage in the battle (D.S. 17.27.1–3; cf. Curt. 8.1.36). We have already noted the anecdote where a single Argyraspid effectively disturbed Antigonus' phalanx with his 'short pithy sound bite' (Bosworth 2002, 152). Antigonus' men were not only reminded of the achievements of the generation that had marched with Philip and Alexander, but were deeply ashamed of facing them under arms. The motif of shame in relation to younger men either fighting against or with older ones occurs in other parallels in Greco-Roman literature. One of Alexander's Companions, Erigyius described by Curtius (7.4.33) as *gravis quidem aetate, sed et animi et corporis robore nulli iuvenum postferendus* ('certainly burdened with age, but neither in spirit nor in bodily strength inferior to younger men') dramatically strips off his helmet displaying his white hair, prior to a Homeric style duel with the rebel Bactrian leader, Satibarzanes. In a famous poem by Tyrtaeus (*Elegy* 10) the poet describes a grey haired Spartan hoplite who has been killed in the front line, and has fallen clutching his bloodied genitals. Such an emotionally powerful image is aimed at shaming - and enraging - younger colleagues. In each episode shame is used to intimidate, unnerve or inspire; and if the thought of a grizzled old Spartan still engaging in hoplite warfare seems incongruous, we need only recall a photograph published in John Ma's recent study on the Lion of Chaeronea; namely the skull of a Theban hoplite (Gamma 16) who had previously lost some of his front teeth, possibly in a an earlier engagement or very rough training. Forensic technology calculated his age to have been 50 or over (Ma 2008, 80 with n. 104; see plate 4c).[3]

What was so formidable about the Argyraspids? Justin (14.2.6) describes them as 'invincible'. Diodorus (19.41.2), who was possibly paraphrasing Hieronymus' own words, claims: 'they were irresistible (*anupostatoi*) because of their expertise (*empeiria*) and their physical strength, which had been gained through continuous battles'. In Plutarch's *Life of Eumenes* 16.4, the Argyraspids are described as *athlētai polemōn*, 'athletes of war'. One meaning of *athlos/on* is that of a labour or contest undertaken for a prize – and booty is often given as a motivation for veterans. But *athlētai polemōn* does not seem to be a particularly common expression; it appears several times in Plato in relation to the Guardians of the Republic (cf. *R.* 403e, 404a, 416d, 422b, 521d, 543b) and Polybius (1.6.6), who also uses the image of an athlete to highlight the Romans' many battles against the Samnites and the Celts as 'training in the art of war'. However, another significant example of a connection between older men and martial prowess occurs in Dionysius of Halicarnassus (10.44.3–4). He mentions the episode of the tribune Lucius Sicinius Dentatus (Siccius in Dionysius) and his force of 800 veterans (athletes of many wars), who went to stop the Aequians plundering Tusculum in the mid 5th century BC; Dionysius comments that this contingent was at that time far superior to the rest of the army 'both in experience and courage'. The consul Romilius refers to Sicinius' '40 year' of service in his attempt to shame the tough old campaigner into undertaking what is likely to be a suicide mission; Romilius wanted to get rid of such an annoying champion of the plebeians as Sicinius was in favour of land redistribution. Veterans could be troublesome, if not a force for social and political change, for the elite classes in an ancient society. The parallel with the Argyraspids is striking.

Moreover, Caesar's legions offer additional information about the political and social impacts of long-serving Roman soldiers and veterans (Keppie 1997, 89–102).[4] For example, the 'Alaudae', the V Gallica, a legion raised by Caesar in Gaul in 52 (Suet. *Jul.* 24;

Plin. *Nat.* 11.121), served with distinction in Gaul (52–50), and then fought with Caesar in every campaign of the civil war (49–45). After this the Alaudae played a crucial part in the political and military manoeuvres in the immediate aftermath of the death of Caesar in 44 (e.g. Cic. *Phil.* 1.20; 5.12; 13.3; 37; Nic.Dam. *Vit.Caes.* 115–30), as Mark Antony struggled to establish a power-base in Italy. This legion was led by Antony to crush the assassins of Caesar at Philippi (42), it also campaigned for some years with Antony in the east (App. *BC* 5.3), and finally it formed part of Antony's land-force at Actium (31), when he was crushed by Caesar Octavian. The legion, the 'Alaudae', maintained its identity during the early Roman Empire until it was wiped out in AD 86. Although the maturity of the soldiers was given as a factor by an ancient source (D.C. fr. 100) in at least one mutiny, this element has been generally overlooked by modern scholars seeking explanations for such actions (Keaveney 2007; de Blois 2007, 164–79).[5] Older soldiers also feature prominently in the great mutiny in Pannonia in AD 14 (Tac. *Ann.* 18.1).

We have already examined some episodes in our sources where the veteran soldier is used for pointed literary effect. But historically, albeit anecdotally, individual examples of aged soldiers who continue to take an active military role are surprisingly common. The Spartan king Agesilaus was 84 when he died in Egypt while offering mercenary service (Plu. *Ages.* 40). The Athenian general Phocion was continually elected *stratēgos* for 45 years and was still active at the age of 80 (Plu. *Phoc.* 24). The focus of this volume, the Diadochi, particularly those dynasts who succeeded in carving out the early Hellenistic kingdoms – Antigonus, Ptolemy, Lysimachus, Seleucus and Cassander, died as old men – and three – or four, counting Demetrius, died violently. Only two – Cassander and Ptolemy appear to have died in their beds – and only one, Ptolemy, in extreme old age. Antigonus 'the One-Eyed' was 81 years old (Billows 1990, 183), when he took the field on the plain of Ipsus (301) against the grand coalition organised by his rival, Seleucus. According to Justin (17.1.10–11), both Seleucus and Lysimachus were in their mid 70s when they fought their last battle at Corupedion. That the octogenarian Antigonus still possessed the energy required to take the battlefield (and according to Plu. *Demetr.* 19.4, his excessive weight hampered him more than his age), just like the famed Silver Shields of this investigation, directly supports one of the underlying premises of this paper: namely that older men have played a part in war – and probably more often – and more effectively – than is usually appreciated.

Antigonus, the Argyraspids, Tyrtaeus' old dying Spartan, Curtius' white haired Erigyius, the Athenian general Phocion, Lucius Sicinius Dentatus, and the Alaudae are not isolated figures. Their counterparts can be found throughout the annals of war; from the 70–olds of Hitler's *Volkssturm* (see Ryan 1966, 382–83), to the over 50 and 60 year old Americans who have died in contemporary wars in Iraq and Afghanistan.[6] Veteran soldiers can be found in the ranks alongside and often leading their junior comrades; their motivation for doing so is another area for investigation, but beyond the parameters of this discussion.

Finally, although we can concede that there are probably literary elements in relation to the role of veterans in ancient historiography, and that there are also some propagandist aspects in Hieronymus' narrative, this does not mean that he is not telling the literal truth about the ages of the Silver Shields; that the youngest of them were 'about sixty' (D.S. 19.41.2: cf. Plu. *Eum.* 16.7 'not a man younger than sixty'). But what is less clear is exactly how many remained from Alexander's original veteran corps of hypaspists who first took their distinctive decorations in India. It does seem hard to believe that there would have been the 3,000 that Diodorus claims (18.58.1; cf. 19.28.1). One wonders whether the Argryapids' ranks – like those of other hypaspists – had been supplemented by new recruits in order to keep their number constant, much in the same way as the famous 10,000 Immortals of the Persian army. There is some evidence that might support this: Arrian (*An.* 7.6) describes the integration of Persians into elite Macedonian units like the *agēma* and the Companion cavalry. Whether the Argyraspids were expected to absorb new recruits, or whether outsiders would have been perceived as compromising their 'corporate identity' (so to speak) is another matter: however, Anson (2004, 187 n. 118) has plausibly suggested that while many of the officers could have been in their sixties – or older, they would not necessarily have been the front line troops and over time replacements would have filled in the ranks of the dead, injured or ill. So in other words, while the unit itself was old, probably many individual soldiers would have been much younger men.

Yet even if Diodorus has conflated the number of the Argyraspids with more recently recruited hypaspists, or if Hieronymus himself exaggerated the figures, there must have still been enough of these aged soldiers to have been remarkable: their brilliant reputation was based on their record of invincibility. So we could well ask: in the late 4th century, is it so hard to accept that a significant percentage of one army unit could be over the age of 60? Paradigms on life expectancy in the ancient world can be difficult if not misleading – as Tim Parkin has shown – and it is difficult to apply expectations about a general population to a military context, but probably more people in antiquity reached the age of 60 and beyond, than is popularly thought (Parkin 2003, 46–56; cf. Kebric 1988, 298–99).

The late N. G. L. Hammond had no difficulty accepting the historicity of the Argyraspids' advanced ages. He cited the robust strength and physical capacity of 60 and 70 year old Sarakatsani shepherds who traditionally lived in the mountainous regions of the Pindus ranges (Hammond 1984, 52–53, with n. 9). To this evidence, we could add the example of Cliff Young, a former potato farmer from Victoria, Australia who won the first Westfield Sydney to Melbourne Ultra Marathon (875 kilometres) in 1983 at the age of 61. He claimed to have trained for the gruelling endurance event by running after sheep on his farm in Beech Forest, south eastern Victoria, in country consisting of low rolling hills and shallow valleys (see Young 1995).

The living conditions of the Argyraspids – such as their access to an optimum diet, water supply and shelter – would be other factors likely to affect their longevity (Engels 1978, 17–22). Although living conditions would have varied considerably – one might immediately think of the monsoonal rains of the Hydaspes campaign – or the other extreme, the Gedrosia crossing – on the whole, I think we can assume that their conditions must have been generally more favourable than not. The Argyraspids were an elite force and treated as such. Provided that they escaped injury or illness, these men would have received the best of everything – booty, food, slaves, women and money.[7] They had also benefited from the leadership of good generals (leaving out Perdiccas' debacle), and we should not discount their own morale and pride in their identity and image. Their concern over their baggage train which had fallen into Antigonus' hands, and which included not only their wives and children but also their collective nest eggs for their retirement, was the main reason for betraying Eumenes and their commander Antigenes to the enemy (D.S. 19.43.7; Plu. *Eum.* 17). Our sources condemn them for their treachery, and Diodorus (19.48.3–4; cf. Plu. *Eum.* 19.2) exploits the literary neatness of their dispersal afterwards to remote and troublesome areas in the eastern areas of the empire, where their chances of surviving for very long were low, as a fitting punishment for their crime. However we should not be critical of their behaviour; one wonders what might have happened at Gaugamela, if Alexander (at least according to Arrian) had not given up his pursuit of Darius when both the left wing of the Macedonian army (commanded by Parmenion) and the baggage train came under pressure from the Persians (Arr. *An.* 3.14.4–15.2). Alexander returned to their defense, and to consolidate his victory; in this instance, the baggage train was also a crucial prize, containing high status Persian prisoners including Darius' mother and family (Curt. 4.13.35).[8]

If we accept that many of the Argyraspids were indeed as old as Hieronymus says they were, the reasons for their longevity and their success might be also worth investigation. Again, while such a topic is beyond this essay, the key must surely lie in their experience – as Diodorus (19.43.1), via Hieronymus, suggests (see Hammond 1984, 53; 1980, 53–63). At Gabiene, the Argyraspids not only destroyed Antigonus' phalanx, but did not themselves sustain a single casualty. The very nature of phalanx warfare could well serve as a protection for its most skilled practitioners; what was required was not so much speed or strength alone, but rather superb timing, discipline, co-ordination (particularly in relation to effectively rotating men in and out of the front ranks), and energy conservation. It would have also been important to prevent the loss of muscle mass and bone density which often occurs as humans age and hormone levels subside, although both of these factors are affected by gender, genetics, physiological history, time and circumstances. However sustained physical activity, especially weight bearing exercise like walking, or carrying burdens of any kind, would have undoubtedly contributed to maintaining strong bones as well as cardiovascular health.

Diet and an active lifestyle could well have played a significant role. For a short time after Alexander's death most of the Argyraspids probably enjoyed a hiatus away from active service, and, human nature being what it is, it is perhaps dubious that during their rest periods in Susa and Cyinda that they regularly put themselves through the ancient equivalent of boot camp in order to maintain peak fitness; Alexander's stay in Babylon towards the end of 331 had demonstrated the morale sapping delights of city life only too well (Curt. 5.1.36–39).[9] However, thanks to Perdiccas, Polyperchon and Eumenes the veterans were forced on the move again from 321/20 and again from 319/18. No doubt the long marches restored their endurance.

To conclude; the Argyraspids were an accident of history but like the Diadochi, they have been overshadowed by the achievements of Alexander. Further research into these tough old fighters' amazing durability might illuminate some issues in the debate about the contribution of older people for us today, especially as my generation – the much vaunted and over publicised 'Baby Boomers' – reaches the ages of Alexander's Silver Shields.[10]

Bibliography

Anson, E. M. (1981) Alexander's Hypaspists and the Argyraspids, *Historia* 30, 117–20.

Anson, E. M. (2004) *Eumenes of Cardia. A Greek Among Macedonians*. Leiden.

Berve, H. (1926) *Das Alexanderreich auf prosopographischer Grundlage*. 2 vols. Munich.

Billows, R. (1990) *Antigonos the One Eyed and the Creation of the Hellenistic State.* Berkeley.

Bosworth, A. B. (2002) *The Legacy of Alexander*. Oxford.

Bosworth, A. B. (1992) History and Artifice in Plutarch's Eumenes. In P. A. Stadter (ed.) *Plutarch and the Historical Tradition*, 56–89, London.

De Blois, L. (2007) Army and General in the Late Roman Republic. In P. Erdkamp (ed.) *A Companion to the Roman Army*, 164–79, Oxford.

Engels, D. W. (1978) *Alexander the Great and the Logistics of the Macedonian Army*. Berkeley and Los Angeles.

Grainge, C. and H. Heber (2005) The Role of the Physician in Modern Military Operations: 12 Months Experience in Southern Iraq, *J R Army Med Corps* 151, 101–04 http://www.ramcjournal.com/2005/jun05/grainge.pdf.

Hammond, N. G. L. (1980) Training in the Use of a Sarissa and its Effect in Battle, 359–333 BC, *Antichthon* 14, 53–63.

Hammond, N. G. L. (1984) Alexander's Veterans after his Death, *Greek, Roman and Byzantine Studies* 25, 51–61.

Heckel, W. (1992) *The Marshals of Alexander's Empire.* London.

Heckel, W. (2006) *Who's Who in the Age of Alexander*. London.

Heckel, W. and C. Hook (2006) *Macedonian Warrior: Alexander's Elite Infantryman*. Oxford.

Hornblower, J. (1981) *Hieronymus of Cardia*. Oxford.

Jiménez-Blanco, M. D. (ed.) (2009) *The Prado Guide*. Madrid.

Keaveney, A. (2007) *The Army in the Roman Revolution*. London.

Kebric, R. B. (1988) Old Age, the Ancient Military, and Alexander's Army: Positive Examples for a Graying America, *The Gerontologist* 28, 298–302.

Keppie, L. (1997) The Changing Face of the Roman Legions (49 BC–AD 69), *Papers of the British School at Rome* 65, 89–102.

Landucci Gattinoni, F. (1997) *Duride di Samo*. Rome.

Lock, R. A. (1977) The Origins of the Argyraspids, *Historia* 26, 373–78.

Ma, J. (2008) Chaironeia 338: Topographies of Commemoration, *Journal of Hellenic Studies* 128, 72–91.

McCann, G. (2002) *Dad's Army: The Story of a Classic Television Show*. London.

Parkin, T. G. (1992) *Demography and Roman Society*. Baltimore and London.
Parkin, T. G. (2003) *Old Age in the Roman World*. Baltimore and London.
Roisman, J. (2010) Hieronymus of Cardia: Causation and Bias from Alexander to his Successors. In E. Carney and D. Ogden (eds) *Philip II and Alexander the Great: Father and Son, Lives and Afterlives*, 135–48, New York.
Roisman, J. (2012) *Alexander's Veterans and the Early Wars of the Successors*. Austin.
Ryan, C. (1966) *The Last Battle*. New York.
Schäffer, C. (2002) *Eumenes von Kardia*. Frankfurt.
Simpson, R. H. (1959) Abbreviations of Hieronymus in Diodorus, *American Journal of Philology* 80, 370–79.
Tarn, W. W. (1948) *Alexander the Great. Sources and Studies*. Vol. II. Cambridge.
Tsimbidou-Avloniti, M. (2002) Excavating a Painted Macedonian Tomb near Thessaloniki. An Astonishing Discovery. In M. Stamatopolou and M. Yeroulanou (eds) *Excavating Classical Greece*, 91–98, Oxford.
Tsimbidou-Avloniti, M. (2005) *Macedonian Tombs at Phoinikai and Agios Athanasios in Thessaloniki*. Athens.
Yardley, J. and W. Heckel (1997) *Justin Epitome of the Philippic History of Pompeius Trogus*. Oxford.
Young, C. (1995) *Cliffy's Book*. Dargo.

Notes

1 *Mars*, oil on canvas, 181 × 99 cm. See A. Pancorbo in Jimenez-Blanco (2009), fig. 77, 107. Velázquez was himself an old man at the time that he painted this imaginative interpretation.

2 There is some debate about the origins and constitution of the Argyraspids, but they seem to have had connections with Alexander's hypaspists; see Berve 1926, I, 128; Lock 1977, 373–78; *contra*, Anson 1981, 117–20 and, more recently, 2004, 143, n. 89. See also Heckel 1992, 307; Yardley and Heckel 1997, 237–38. It is also worth mentioning that two fine biographies of Eumenes have enriched the discussion about these elite troops: Schäffer 2002, but especially Anson 2004.

3 On the difficulties in general of using skeletal evidence for determining a person's age at death, see Parkin 1992, 50–58.

4 See also Parkin 2003, 414, n. 14 for inscriptional references to examples of some very long serving soldiers in the Roman army.

5 I am grateful to Dr Jane Bellemore for the references to the Alaudae.

6 Some 19 older soldiers (over 50) had died as of 2007 (cf. manyeyes.alphaworks.ibm.com). I thank Professor Lawrence Tritle for the information.

7 I am grateful to Dr Pat Wheatley for this observation.

8 The sources vary considerably on Parmenion's messages, his actions and Alexander's response cf. Plu. *Alex*. 32.3–4; 33.7; Curt. 4.16.2–4; D.S. 17.60.6–8.

9 Professor Edward Anson pointed out that the Argyraspids' *esprit de corps* and their reputation would have been enough incentive for maintaining their fitness and integrity.

10 Unfortunately Professor Roisman's important new study on Alexander's veterans (2012) appeared too late for me to use. I am grateful to Professor A. B. Bosworth for his comments on this paper; also to Professors Waldemar Heckel, Lawrence Tritle, and Drs Jane Bellemore and Patrick Wheatley for their contributions. I should also like to thank Professors Edward Anson and Victor Alonso Troncoso for their careful critiques which have so enriched the discussion, and Victor Alonso Troncoso for the opportunity to present a paper at the Diadochi conference at the University of La Coruna in September, 2010, and both the University and graduate students for help and generous *hostelería*.

AGORA XVI 107 AND THE ROYAL TITLE OF DEMETRIUS POLIORCETES

Paschalis Paschidis

The decree: date, context and possible content

Agora XVI 107 is the earliest preserved Attic decree after the 'liberation' of Athens by Demetrius Poliorcetes in the summer of 307. As is often the case with Attic decrees, it has received attention mostly on account of its implications for the Attic calendar – a subject which need not concern us here.[1] Admittedly, only insignificant traces of the decree itself have been preserved: apart from the preamble, only c. 30 letters in five lines of the motivation clause survive. These traces, however, may serve as a starting point for our investigation.

Previous publications and personal inspection of the stone allow for the following text:[2]

307/6, *pryt.* I — *stoichedon* 27

['Επὶ Ἀναξικράτους ἄρχ]οντος ἐπὶ [τ]-
[ῆς ..... 10 ..... πρώτης] πρυ[τ]ανẹί[α]-
[ς ἧι Λυσίας Νοθίππου Δ]ιο[μ]ẹι<u>εὺ</u>[ς ἐ]-
[γραμμάτευεν· Ἑκατομ]β̣α[ιῶ]νος ἐ̣[νδ]-
[εκάτει, ἑνδεκάτει τῆς] πρυταν[εία]-
[ς· ἐκκλησία κυρία· τῶν] <u>π</u>ρ̣οέδρω̣[ν ἐπ]-
[εψήφιζεν ———---]· *vacat*
[———---]· *v* ἔδοξε̣[ν τῶ]
[ι δήμωι· ...... 12 ......]οστράτ[ου .]-
[.... 7 ... εἶπεν· ἐπει]δ̣ὴ Ἀνδρόν[ικο]-
[ς .... 17 ....]ΣΥΠΟΔΗ̣[...]
[........ 16 ....]<u>δ</u>ου ἐπὶ τη̣[...]
[........ 16 ....]<u>ο</u>υ̣ κ̣ατὰ τὰ̣ [...]
[........ 16 ....]<u>Ο</u>Ν̣Υ̣[...]<u>ΗΝ</u>[...]
[————————---]

The inscribed surface was already much worn when the stone was discovered. I do not record minor differences from previous editions in dotted letters. The underlined letters are those read by only one of the previous editors; given that neither my autopsy nor the expert eye of Stephen Tracy confirm these letters, some of them at least should be considered doubtful. L. 2: Ἐρεχθεΐδος or Κεκροπίδος are the only options. L. 3: [Δ]ιο[μ]ει[εὺς] Pritchett / Meritt; Walbank's reading of the second *epsilon* and the *ypsilon* were not confirmed by the autopsy. L. 4, *in fine*: [ἐνδ]- Pritchett / Meritt; I confirm Walbank's reading of a partial *epsilon*. L. 6: Pritchett / Meritt mark as visible the

Fig. 1. Agora XVI 107 (inv. no. I 5884). Copyright: American School of Classical Studies at Athens: Agora Excavations.

first letter of προέδρων; neither Walbank's reading nor my autopsy confirm this. L. 10: Ἀνδρο[. . . .] Pritchett / Meritt, Ἀνδροṿ[. . .] Tracy, Ἀνδροσ̣[. . .] Woodhead, based on Walbank's readings; the autopsy verified Tracy's reading (in fact, the *nu* is well preserved). L. 11: ΣΥΠΟΔ[. . . .] Pritchett / Meritt, ΣΥΠΟΔΗ̣[. . .] Woodhead, based on Walbank; indeed, a vertical stroke is – barely – discernible on the right side of the last visible *stoichos*. L. 12: ου ἐπὶ τ[. . . .] Pritchett / Meritt, δ̣ου ἐπὶ τη̣[. . .]

Woodhead / Walbank; I was able to verify the final *eta* of Walbank's reading, but not the initial *delta*, which I consider rather doubtful. L. 13: [---]ATA[. . . . .] Pritcett / Meritt, [---]KATA[. . . . .] Tracy, ο̣υ̣ κ̣ατὰ τ̣ὰ̣ [. . .] Woodhead / Walbank, which the autopsy verified, with the exception of the first letter. Στ. 14: neither Pritchett / Meritt nor Tracy report traces of letters; Walbank reads [---]ONY[. . .]HN; I was able to verify only the sequence NY, perhaps also a faint trace of the *nu* in the end.

The decree was enacted on the 11th day of the first prytany of 307/6, in the immediate aftermath of the 'liberation'. Here is a brief outline of the events:[3] Dionysius – Cassander's phrourarch at Mounychia – and Demetrius of Phalerum – *de facto* ruler of Athens implanted by Cassander – had attempted to thwart Poliorcetes' surprise attack on the Piraeus, but were forced to retreat, Dionysius at Mounychia, Demetrius in the civic centre. The very next day, Poliorcetes advanced towards the city, negotiated the safe departure of the philosopher, then conquered and 'freed' Megara,[4] and finally returned to the Piraeus, where he besieged, conquered and razed the fort of Mounychia. He then formally declared the freedom of Athens and signed an alliance with the Athenians, after which he received, on Stratocles' proposal, a long series of extraordinary honours from his grateful new allies.

These events form one of the very few episodes in early Hellenistic history which can be dated with a great deal of precision. According to Plutarch, the first attack on the Piraeus occurred on Thargelion 26 (Plu. *Demetr.* 8.5), i.e. more than a month before the end of the Attic year 308/7. This is confirmed by the *Parian Chronicle*, which puts the capture of the Piraeus in 308/7 and the razing of Mounychia in 307/6 (*FGH* 239 B 20–21). Philochorus dates the capture of Megara in the very beginning of 307/6 (*FGH* 328 F 66). Finally, Diodorus (20.46.3) notes that the final assault on Mounychia lasted merely two days. In other words, four sources confirm that Demetrius concluded the conquest of Athens, declared its freedom and received honours from the Athenians within the very first days of 307/6, presumably during the first week of the year. This is also confirmed by the Attic calendar of 307/6. The new allocation of demes to the tribes (now twelve, after the addition of two new tribes in honour of Poliorcetes and his father) seems to have been finalized only during the fifth prytany (Pritchett and Meritt 1940, 10; Woodhead, *Agora* XVI p. 168); nevertheless, it is certainly no accident that the Council's secretary in our decree is Lysias son of Nothippus from Diomeia – the deme of Stratocles! – a deme which was now assigned to the new tribe Demetrias (now tribe II). Whether the secretary cycle had been abolished from the beginning of Demetrius of Phalerum's ten-year rule, as is more likely,[5] or sometime during his rule, the appointment of a secretary from Demetrias, a tribe named after the Liberator of the city, means that a new cycle was inaugurated in 307/6, on Stratocles' instigation. In other words, the calendar of 307/6 was designed with the administrative changes in mind, already before the year had begun, when Demetrius' initial success made clear what the outcome would be. In any case, the reorganisation of the Attic prytany calendar had been decided upon *before* the enactment of the decree under consideration, which is its first attestation.[6] The inevitable conclusion is that our decree is securely dated after the 'liberation' of Athens by Poliorcetes, and, almost certainly, after the honours voted on Stratocles' proposal, even if only by a few days.

The preserved letters of l. 11 allow us, I believe, to understand the content of the decree. For the sequence of letters ΣΥΠΟΔΗ to make sense, we must assume that the first letter, *sigma*, belongs to the ending of a word and then inevitably recognize the preposition ὑπό,[7] which is used in Attic decrees almost exclusively to denote the grammatical agent.[8] Furthermore, the absence of the article after the preposition obliges us to envisage the sequence ὑπὸ + personal name. Given the historical context, the obvious candidate with a name beginning with *Dē-* is no other than Demetrius Poliorcetes. I therefore propose to supplement in lines 11–12 the phrase [κατασταθεὶ]ς *vel* [καθεστηκὼ]ς *vel sim.* ὑπὸ Δη̣[μητ]|[ρίου]. Since the name of the honorand is certainly Andronicus (Tracy 1995, 146), there is a good candidate for the identification of the honorand, as well: Andronicus from Olynthus, a high-ranking official of Antigonus Monophthalmus and adviser of Demetrius in the battle of Gaza.[9] Therefore, ll. 10–12 may be restored as follows:

[. . . . 7 . . . εἶπεν· ἐπει]δ̣ὴ Ἀνδρόν̣[ικο]-
[ς Ὀλύνθιος (?) καθεστηκὼ]ς (*vel sim.*) ὑπὸ Δη̣[μητ]-
[ρίου . . . . . . 12 . . . . . .]δ̣ου ἐπὶ τη̣[. . .]

The construct ἐπὶ + genitive or accusative in l. 12 makes clear that ll. 12 ff. record Andronicus' exact mission and/or role in the siege of Athens,[10] but I can find no plausible supplement.[11]

Antigonus and Demetrius: *basileis* in 307? Ptolemy I: *basileus* in 308?

If the restoration of Poliorcetes' name is correct, the certain absence of the royal title seems to contradict Plutarch.[12] As is well known, Plutarch reports that the Athenians, 'first from all the other peoples, proclaimed Demetrius and Antigonus kings, although both had up to that time refrained from taking up that title' (Plu. *Demetr.* 10.3).

An obvious solution would be to assume that our decree was enacted a few days before Stratocles' decree. Diodorus (20.45.5) reports that, after the departure of Demetrius of Phalerum and before the razing of Mounychia, 'honours were voted for those who were responsible for the city's autonomy'; these honours were apparently distinct from those proposed by Stratocles, which Diodorus himself mentions in a following paragraph (20.46.2) and must have preceded them. There are, however, two difficulties with this assumption: a) as we saw, the fact that the secretary belongs to the new tribe Demetrias favours a date *after* Stratocles' decree for *Agora* XVI 107; b) the capture of the Piraeus is securely dated to 308/7, in fact almost a whole month before the end of the year, given the surprise nature of Demetrius' initial attack. Dating our decree after the capture of the Piraeus but before Stratocles' decree would mean that the Athenians waited for more than a month before honouring those who participated in the first part of the military operations, but did not wait a few more days in order to honour them along with the other honorands. It is a theoretically possible but implausible and unnecessarily complicated scenario.

Another solution would be to assume that Plutarch is exaggerating. We know, for example, of at least one occasion, albeit in a very different context, where one of the Successors (Demetrius again!) is reportedly called a king well before 306;[13] we also know – if our literary sources are not back-projecting later developments – that it was not deemed inappropriate to invest a Successor with regal attributes, to offer him gifts befitting a king, to claim that he possessed royal stature, or that he ruled over an area *as* a king, again before the official assumption of the royal title.[14] Can we not suppose that, here as well, Plutarch merely exaggerates, carried away by the lavishness of the rest of the honours bestowed upon Demetrius by the Athenians? I think not: Plutarch clearly reports something more official than a casual exclamation of a thankful citizen in the Athenian *agora*; he clearly includes the royal title in the honours the Athenians *voted on* (Plu. *Demetr.* 10.2) and his choice of a verb (*anagoreuō*) must mean that he has in mind a formal declaration or recognition of the royal title. One cannot be formally declared (or recognised as) a king and be addressed without the royal title in the very city which so declared him.[15]

The only remaining option is to disregard Plutarch's claim.[16] In what follows, I hope to show that there are good reasons for doing so anyway, because a) Plutarch's account of the honours voted in 307 is substantially flawed; b) no other literary source corroborates him; c) no epigraphic source where Antigonus and/or Demetrius are called kings can be plausibly dated to before 306; d) epigraphic sources (from Athens and elsewhere) dated between the summer of 307 and the summer of 306 do not call Antigonus and/or Demetrius a king and, e) most importantly, Plutarch's information is very unlikely *per se*.

It has long been observed that Plutarch's account of the honours voted by the Athenians for Antigonus and Demetrius is problematic in many respects.[17] To begin with, Plutarch's account fails to mention some of the honours mentioned by Diodorus and/or other sources: the golden statues of Antigonus and Demetrius on a chariot which were set up in the agora, the 200 talents-worth golden crowns, the annual games, the procession and sacrifices in honour of the two Macedonians and the building of two sacred triremes bearing their name.[18] Moreover, on a number of honours reported by more than one source, Plutarch's account is proved to be flawed:

1. The liberators of Athens were declared *Sōtēres*, not *Theoi Sōtēres* (*Demetr.* 10.4) and, if there ever were annual priests of their cult, they certainly did not replace the eponymous archons, as Plutarch claims.[19]
2. It is rather doubtful that ambassadors to Demetrius were now called *theōroi* (*Demetr.* 11.1; cf. *Mor.* 338a).[20]
3. The erection of an altar of Demetrius Kataibates (*Demetr.* 11.1; cf. *Mor.* 338a) belongs to 304 and not to 307 (Habicht 1970, 48–50).
4. The month *Mounuchiōn* was not renamed *Dēmētriōn*, and the festival of Dionysia was not renamed *Dēmētria* (*Demetr.* 12.2); the *Dēmētria* were merely celebrated alongside the Dionysia, probably after 294.[21]
5. Dromocleides' decree to ask Demetrius for an oracle about how best to restore dedications to the temple of Apollo at Delphi (*Demetr.* 13.2) undoubtedly belongs to the late 290's (Habicht 1979, 34–44).

There is a clear pattern in these errors: Plutarch merely juxtaposes a series of honours for Demetrius with no chronological order (and thus not necessarily connected with the events of 307), misinterpreting a number of them and clearly focussing on honours which could be –and were– considered *risqué* from a religious or moral point of view. Plutarch's account apparently draws, in his usual uncritical and haphazard way, mostly on sources hostile to Stratocles and the Antigonids, hence its emphasis on honours that have attracted criticism in those sources.[22]

No other source (literary or epigraphic) corroborates Plutarch;[23] in fact, there are several which disprove him. There is at least one decree (*IG* II^2 466), certainly attributable to 307/6, which mentions Antigonus and Demetrius without the royal title.[24] Another decree useful for present purposes is *SEG* 31 (1981) 80 (*IG* II^2 561), a honorific decree for two or three bodyguards of a king Alexander (most probably IV): Antigonus and Demetrius certainly do not carry the royal title (ll. 11–12), while Alexander does (ll. 7–8); hence, the decree is usually dated to early 306.[25] Conversely, I know no decree of the period 306–301 which mentions Demetrius and/or Antigonus without the royal title;[26] in fact, Demetrius can be referred to merely by his title, without his name ever being mentioned (see e.g. *IG* II^2 486 [Osborne 1981, n° D46] ll. 11–12).

The only epigraphic evidence which has been adduced to support Plutarch's claim is *IG* II^2 3424, an epigram devoted by a number of citizens to the Saviours of the city Antigonus and Demetrius in which, according to Adolf Wilhelm's – as usual – bold but brilliant restorations, the two Successors are termed 'leaders of Greece and kings of Asia'.[27] Wilhelm's text, however, hardly corroborates Plutarch. First of all, there is no reason to date the epigram to 307 (as Wilhelm 1937, 207 tentatively suggests and Müller 1973, 58 takes for granted) and not to 306, when a number of Greek cities must have congratulated the newly declared kings (e.g. *IvO* 45, 304, 305 [*IByzantion* 4–6]). Secondly, recent studies on the term 'king of Asia' from Alexander the Great to Mithridates VI of Pontus make clear that this was a term pertaining to the discourse of power rather than to official nomenclature;[28] as Ritter (1965, 52) had already noted, it had 'keine staatsrechtliche Bedeutung'. In other words, this epigram (a poetic text commissioned by individual citizens, not an official state document) cannot be used as corroborating evidence for what Plutarch clearly describes as a formal declaration of kingship.

Finally, and most importantly, not even Plutarch himself takes his Athenian story seriously when, *later in the same work*, he recounts the actual assumption of the royal title by Antigonus and Demetrius: 'After this [sc. the staged hailing of Antigonus as a king by Aristodemus], the crowd proclaimed Antigonus and Demetrius kings *for the first time*' (*Demetr.* 18.1).

The conclusion is – to my mind – obligatory: Plutarch is proved yet again to be very haphazard with his choice of dates; the Athenians did not proclaim Demetrius and Antigonus kings in 307, but merely recognized their royal title in 306, along with the rest of the Greek world. It was a semblance of a Macedonian Assembly which proclaimed Antigonus and Demetrius kings for the first time, in accordance with the *mos Macedonum*.[29]

Before we proceed to a possible explanation of Plutarch's error, we need to examine in detail a well-documented hypothesis put forward some years ago by Brian Bosworth: namely, that a semi-formal use of the royal title by officials or subjects of the Successors, and particularly of Ptolemy I, was in use well before 306.[30] Apart from his dating of *PKöln* 6.247 (see next section), his case relies mostly on the following pieces of evidence:

1. According to the manuscripts of Plu. *Demetr.* 17.6, Aristodemus exclaimed to Antigonus in 306: 'Hail king Antigonus, we have been victorious over *king* Ptolemy'. The royal title before Ptolemy's name has been deleted by most modern editors of Plutarch as a gloss; Bosworth, however, claims that this *lectio difficilior* should be retained and that it corroborates the reading of most manuscripts of Diodorus (20.27.1), where, in the very beginning of the exposition of the events of 309, Ptolemy is termed Πτολεμαῖος ὁ τῆς Αἰγύπτου βασιλεύων.
2. *IIasos* 2–3 is an epigraphic dossier on the relations between Iasus and Ptolemy I.[31] *IIasos* 2 records a sworn contract between the Iasians and soldiers occupying the citadels and a sworn treaty of alliance between the Iasians and Ptolemy. Both agreements were brokered by Polemaeus, Antigonus' nephew, who had just switched sides, joining Ptolemy; therefore, both agreements are usually dated to the winter of 309/8, since by early 308 Polemaeus had left for the Greek mainland, fallen out of grace with Ptolemy, and had taken his own life. Next in the dossier are engraved letters by two Ptolemaic officials (*IIasos* 3), Aristobulus and Asclepiodotus, which pertain, as the *communis opinio* goes, to the reaffirmation of the alliance and the renegotiation of its terms. In these letters (ll. 8, 15, 25), and in contrast with the first document, Ptolemy carries the royal title. Bosworth claims that these letters should not be dated as late as *paullo post* 304, because a) the Iasians cannot have waited so long after the death of Polemaeus in 308 in order to reaffirm their privileges; and b) Ptolemy cannot have had the naval power to retain Carian strongholds so soon after his defeat at Salamis, which is why references to Ptolemaic strongholds in Caria appear only much later, in the 280's, an improbable date for the letters, since Aristobulus already held a high position in the Ptolemaic hierarchy by 311. Bosworth's conclusion is that Aristobulus' letter should be dated shortly after the Iasian decree and that '[w]e now have a documentary example of the informal use of the regal title before Ptolemy officially adopted the royal diadem and royal nomenclature'.
3. Similar is the case with *SEG* 17 (1960) 639, a decree attesting good relations between Aspendus in Pamphylia and king Ptolemy (see Bosworth 2000, 233 n. 116, with the essential bibliography, to which add Grainger 2009, 79–82). According to Bosworth, there is no evidence for Ptolemaic operations in Pamphylia after 304, while there is evidence from 309/8 for the presence of Ptolemy in nearby Lycia and for Ptolemaic operations in the vicinity of Pamphylia, led by officers mentioned in the Aspendian decree;[32] accordingly, Bosworth dates the decree to 308, same as the dossier from Iasus.

I would argue that these arguments are not compelling. First of all, deleting the royal title before Ptolemy's name in the account of Antigonus' royal proclamation makes perfect sense. Naming Ptolemy a king in that context is rhetorically inconceivable: Aristodemus' goal and the purpose of the whole episode were to publicly proclaim that Antigonus, victorious over the worthless Ptolemy, was now rightfully a king. This is the very essence of the elaborate staging of this first royal proclamation of the 'Year of the Kings' and conceding the royal title to Ptolemy – *even if* Ptolemy had been called a king earlier – would simply ruin Aristodemus' and Antigonus' argument.[33] The sarcasm that Bosworth's theory implies – a worthy king imposing a devastating victory over a king who has been proven unworthy of the title – would be too subtle a rhetorical device in these circumstances. This was not a time for innuendos and hidden ironies; this was a time to incite the assembled Macedonian army to declare Antigonus formally as their rightful king. The message had to be clear, concise and solemn: Antigonus imposed a smashing and glorious victory over Ptolemy; *ergo*, Antigonus has earned his right to be declared a king.

As for the epigraphic evidence from Iasus and Aspendus, one should, to begin with, restate the commonplace cautionary remark: our knowledge of the very complex military operations of that period in western and southwestern Asia Minor is so limited, that arguments *e silentio* are particularly unsafe.[34] While it is true, for example, that there is no certain evidence for Ptolemaic overlordship in parts of Pamphylia or for Ptolemaic operations near Aspendus in the decade or so after 304, it is also true that there is no evidence for operations in the area by any other Successor either. In fact, it has been suggested that Ptolemy I may well have held his vital possessions at Phaselis and Coracesium, at the two extremes of the Bay of Antalya, simply because no one ventured to wrest them away from him (Grainger 2009, 79–80). Moreover, a closer look at the Aspendian decree makes a date c. 308 quite unnecessary. The decree honours the mercenaries led by Philocles and Leonides who 'arrived' (l. 5: *paragenomenoi*) at Aspendus and proved helpful to king Ptolemy and to the city. The contingent in question is neither a permanent Ptolemaic garrison nor a Ptolemaic contingent residing somewhere in the vicinity; it is merely a mercenary force led, and presumably paid for, by two Ptolemaic officers. There is simply no reason to assume that Ptolemy, his generals or his army were in the immediate vicinity at the time of the events alluded to by the decree and, thus, no reason to associate the decree with known events of the *grande histoire* of the Successors.

Giovannini's detailed examination of the dossier from Iasus has shown that our understanding of these important texts has been burdened with a number of misconceptions. The one crucial to the argument under consideration is the meaning of *IIasos* 3, ll. 1–4. According to the prevailing view, the ambassadors asked Aristobulus (acting on behalf of Ptolemy) to reaffirm the freedom and autonomy of the city, then Aristobulus asked for guarantees – presumably an oath of allegiance taken by the ambassadors – after which he reaffirmed Iasus' free and autonomous status and modified the earlier treaty with the new clauses on the money paid by the Iasians for the protection of their territory by Ptolemaic forces (*suntaxis*) and on the portuary taxes. Giovannini convincingly argues that all this is impossible from a procedural point of view. The earlier treaty had been sealed by an oath delivered by the body politic of Iasus and Ptolemy himself; thus, neither Aristobulus nor the ambassadors had the legal competence to reaffirm, renegotiate or modify the treaty without a new oath being delivered by the same two contracting parties, the Iasian assembly and Ptolemy himself. What is described in ll. 1–4 is a different affair: the ambassadors first formally presented the city's status as a free, autonomous and allied city; Aristobulus required assurances (*pistin*); the ambassadors complied, presumably presenting Aristobulus with a copy of the older treaty (cf. *Labraunda* III 1,3); Aristobulus accepted the validity of the treaty (*epechōrēthē*); then, and only then, did the ambassadors move on with their actual demands, the proper designation of the *suntaxis* and the right to keep portuary taxes and other revenues; Aristobulus readily conceded the second demand, but referred the first to the king. The new agreement was sealed by a new oath, by which Aristobulus (not Ptolemy, nor Aristobulus in the name of Ptolemy) swore to maintain Iasus' free and autonomous status, to concede portuary taxes and other revenues to the Iasians, and to receive by the Iasians whatever *suntaxis* the king ordered; the Iasians would presumably take a new oath to seal the agreement.

In other words, the agreement between Iasus and Aristobulus was technically not directly dependent on the earlier treaty between Iasus and Ptolemy; therefore, the difficulty Bosworth sees in the traditional dating of Aristobulus' letter after 304 vanishes: the Iasians did not wait for several years for the reaffirmation or renegotiation of the treaty; the treaty between Iasus and Ptolemy remained valid and unchanged and the requests to Aristobulus were a different matter, at least from a procedural point of view. In fact, a similar argument can be put forward for the upper limit of what Bosworth sees as too long a time-span between the treaty and the letter of Aristobulus if we date the latter after 304. The adventures of Polemaeus are more or less irrelevant to the treaty, to its validity and to the relations between Iasus and Ptolemy in general. As Giovannini 2004, 77–78 convincingly shows, Polemaeus is not a contracting party in any of the two treaties recorded in the Iasian decree, since he is not mentioned among those taking the oath either in the agreement between the Iasians and the soldiers occupying the citadels, or in the peace- and alliance-treaty concluded between the Iasians and Ptolemy. Polemaeus was simply the intermediary who had instigated the negotiations, which had already been concluded by the time of the agreement (see *IIasos* 2, l. 18: 'as has already been agreed upon'). In other words, Polemaeus had become immaterial to the whole affair and his adventures and subsequent death cannot be used as a binding *terminus ante quem* for the decree. Thus, there is no difficulty in dating *IIasos* 2 even several months after the beginning of 309/8,[35] and Aristobulus' letter in *IIasos* 3 shortly after 304. The epigraphic dossier of Iasus, as was usual in such 'archives on stone', consisted of several documents, not necessarily interdependent, pertaining to the relationship of the city with a monarch.[36]

Apart from considerations of military history and the possible dating of crucial pieces of evidence, however, there is a more fundamental problem with Bosworth's assumption. The very idea of an 'informal use of the regal title before Ptolemy officially adopted the royal diadem and royal nomenclature' is hard to fathom. When a letter by a Ptolemaic official or a civic decree calls Ptolemy a king, this is hardly an informal usage of the title. How can members of a Successor's administrative structure, or his subjects and allies, nonchalantly use the royal title for someone who has not yet been formally declared a king? Speaking of a Successor as if he were a king and *de facto* treating him as such, is one thing; calling him a king in official civic and royal documents, however, is quite a different matter. One is either formally a king or he is not; when he is called a king in an official document, he must be one, in the very formal sense of the word.

Some scholars tend to deny the importance of the official proclamation of the royal title by the Successors; in Michel Austin's important and influential collection of translated primary sources on the Hellenistic period (2006, 94–95), one reads that the assumption was of little practical significance, since the future kings already signed treaties and founded cities in their name, received divine or heroic honours and could be called king by their Greek and Oriental subjects alike. If the official assumption of the royal title was of so little consequence, however, one wonders why the Successors waited for more than four years after the murder of the rightful king before they travelled this new path.

This brings me back to my starting point and to what I see as the major obstacle in accepting Plutarch's account of the events of 307 in Athens; a proclamation of Antigonus and Demetrius as kings by the Athenians makes no sense institutionally and, more importantly, is incomprehensible politically. The preparation for the assumption of the royal title was a long and carefully designed process (Müller 1973, 45–77; Gruen 1985, 273–74; Wheatley 2001, 148–56). In that process, the occasional use of words, insignia and ceremonies associated with kingship played an important part, especially in the crucial parameter of recognising one Successor's superiority over the others. Nevertheless, an event such as the one Plutarch recounts would be severely detrimental to the Successors' final goal. A strong weapon in the antagonism of prospective kings was legitimacy; all detailed sources on the careful staging of the official proclamations in 306–304 make clear that *plēthos*, *ochlos*, *populus* or *stratos*, i.e. assembled armed forces of the Successors acting *in lieu* of an Assembly of Macedonians, played a part in the formal proclamation of the royal title, in proper Macedonian custom.[37] In other words, the Successors went to great lengths in order to invest what was, in fact, a self-proclamation with the façade of institutional legitimacy.[38] It would accordingly be rather imprudent for a Successor to risk the displeasure of his army and the propagandist scorn of his antagonists with the official proclamation of the royal title by a political body as institutionally irrelevant as the Athenians.

The recognition of the royal title by the world of the cities

Rejecting Plutarch's account, however, obliges us to explain it; in order to do so, we need to turn our attention to Rhodes, and, especially, *PKöln* 6.247 (see Lehmann 1988, with text and commentary), a fragment of a late-second or early-first-century Rhodian historiographical work which mentions the assumption of the royal title by the Successors.

A final digression on chronology is, unfortunately, in order here. The whole passage has been taken to imply that the assumption of the royal title by Ptolemy followed very closely that of Antigonus and, thus, should be dated not to the spring of 304 (a date supported by a combination of Egyptian demotic texts, the *Ptolemaic Canon* and the *Marmor Parium*),[39] but in 306, when the literary tradition seems to date Ptolemy's proclamation.[40] There are, however, several strong arguments against such a date: 1) The documentary sources supporting 304 are by definition more reliable than later historiographical accounts; the fact that the latter seem to date Ptolemy's assumption of the royal title already in 306 is simply due to their need to recount all relevant developments (the assumption of the royal title by the other Diadochi) in the same place. 2) The Egyptian sources can only be explained by the rather desperate assumption that Ptolemy waited for more than a year after assuming the royal title in order to assume the pharaonic title. 3) It is hardly plausible that the recently defeated Ptolemy assumed the royal title in the autumn of 306. 4) Finally, it should be stressed that *PKöln* 6.247 cannot be used as a decisive piece of evidence in matters of chronology. This is not a dry historical narrative respecting chronology;[41] it is a highly polemic text not recounting events but interpreting troubled times and exalting Rhodes' position in those times retrospectively,[42] and is thus of very dubious credibility as far as chronology is concerned (so also Billows 1990, 351–52).

An even earlier date for the contextual date of the Rhodian text (in the eve of Ptolemy's campaign in 308) is – expectedly – advocated by Bosworth (2000, 236–38). He points out that the text does not record the assumption of the royal title by Ptolemy, but merely 'the decision of his friends to dignify him with the regal title';[43] which he dates, yet again, to 308. First of all, however, the narrative has to be situated after the *official* assumption of the royal title by Antigonus (col. I, l. 18–21: 'Antigonus son of Philippus was the first to proclaim himself a king');[44] dating *that* event in 308 is simply impossible. If the contextual date of the text is 306, Bosworth himself admits that Ptolemy was then still too weak and the Rhodians had no reason to recognize him as a king. In other words, 308 is an impossible and 306 an improbable contextual date for the events recounted in the Rhodian text. On the contrary, in 304 it made perfect sense for the Rhodians to accept Ptolemy's title: Ptolemy had offered substantial help to the Rhodians during the siege by Poliorcetes, and was lavishly honoured accordingly (cf. Gruen 1985, 253 and D.S. 20.93.2–4, with Paschidis 2008, 357–58).

The core message the Rhodian text aims to convey is that 'his [sc. Ptolemy's] friends dignified him with the royal title, and among them were the Rhodians'.[45] The Rhodians feature prominently among the king's friends who immediately recognized his royal title – in fact they are presented as playing an essential part in the whole affair from the very beginning – just as the Athenians were (supposedly) the first people to proclaim Antigonus and Demetrius kings.[46] The bond between Rhodes and Ptolemy I, as presented in the Rhodian text, closely resembles the one between Athens and Demetrius as presented by Plutarch. In both cases we are dealing with strong *poleis*, whose alliance is important to the Successors in terms of geography, politics, military power and ideology. The cities – or, to be precise, the supporters of the particular kings within the ruling elite of the cities – had every reason to emphasize the fact that they were key supporters of the (new) kings. The recognition of the royal title by the cities, in its turn, was a powerful ideological weapon in the kings' arsenal. The first step towards their kingship's legitimacy undoubtedly was its acceptance by the Macedonians; its acceptance by their allies was a crucial second step. If I may paraphrase Plutarch (*Demetr.* 8.3), the explicit goal of Demetrius' mission in the summer of 307 was to earn the *eunoia* of Athens, a beacon tower for the whole *oikoumenē*, which would spread the glory of Antigonus and Demetrius 'to all people'.[47] This is an exact parallel with the disputed passage where the supposed royal title is declared by the Athenians, 'first from all the other peoples' (Plu. *Demetr.* 10.3).[48] The term *oikoumenē* used by Plutarch in *Demetr.* 8.3 is equally interesting: the Rhodian text also uses it, again for Antigonus, but in the negative sense ('convinced... that he could lead over the entire oikoumene');[49] a curious incomplete note on kingship in the *Suda* also uses it, again in the negative sense ('but those who had no merit in becoming kings of almost the entire oikoumene...');[50] finally, Duris, one of Plutarch's sources, uses it for Demetrius (the king was portrayed in a wall painting in Athens as 'riding over the oikoumene').[51] This oikoumene was the real prize in the Wars of the Successors, at least for Antigonus.[52] In the Rhodian text and in the entry of *Suda*, Antigonus' aspirations are portrayed as illegitimate and harmful for the Greeks:[53] '... the Rhodians considered Antigonus' growth oppressive (*bareian*)'.[54] The same word (*barus*) is used by Plutarch for Demetrius, obviously reflecting an Athenian source hostile to Antigonus, Demetrius and their Athenian supporters: 'now that Demetrius had appeared so great and glorious in his benefactions, they rendered him obnoxious and oppressive (*barun*) by the excessiveness of the honours they bestowed upon him'.[55]

In all these texts, apart from the striking similarities in the choice of crucial and ideologically charged words, one can discern the same pattern: for the supporters of a particular Successor, their great ally is a powerful, legitimate and beneficial ruler, the only one worthy of the royal title and the one who will better take care of their interests. Accordingly, they emphasize both to audiences within the city and to the rest of the Greek world that they are among the ruler's most important allies, and the first who rushed to acknowledge his new title. Their goal is twofold: to audiences outside the city gates, particularly to the new royal courts, they attempt to enhance their city's status as an important and necessary ally of the king; to local audiences, they attempt to enhance their own political status, as supporters of a powerful and worthy ruler, supporters well-placed to promote the city's interest at the ruler's court. The political adversaries of these supporters, within and without, paint the reverse picture – either because they did not support that ruler or because they supported another. They brand the supporters of the 'wrong' Successor as petty flatterers and the 'wrong' Successor as an immoderate and loathsome pretender to Alexander's legacy, who is oppressive and detrimental to the interests of their cities. This whole battle of words may well be fought in the field of local literary production, but clearly reflects ideological motives emanating from the courts of the Diadochi: if Antigonus and Demetrius are worthy kings, the rest of the Successors are worthless, and vice versa.[56] Although in official communication between them the kings readily accepted the new reality of a plurality of kings, in the field of ideology the game of the 'worthy king' remained a zero sum game. And, although the antagonism of the Successors obviously predates 304, this rhetorical battle clearly makes much better sense after the assumption of the royal title by *all* the Successors and not before. The conclusion for the passage under consideration is obvious: in his account of how the Athenians, 'first from all other peoples', proclaimed Antigonus and Demetrius kings, Plutarch draws from material pertaining not to the historical narrative for 307, but to the political struggle in Athens – and elsewhere – after 304.[57]

The new reality that the assumption of the royal title by the Successors of Alexander created, especially for the ruling elites of the Greek *poleis*, was very much a matter of discourse. Words mattered in that context, and words denoting power were powerful words – and were treated as such.

Bibliography

Anson, E. M. (2004) *Eumenes of Cardia: A Greek among Macedonians.* Boston and Leiden.

Austin, M. M. (2006) *The Hellenistic World from Alexander to the Roman Conquest. A Selection of Ancient Sources in Translation.* 2nd ed. Cambridge and New York.

Bagnall, R. S. (1976) *The Administration of the Ptolemaic Possessions outside Egypt.* Leiden.

Bielman, A. (1994) *Retour à la liberté. Libération et sauvetage des prisonniers en Grèce ancienne.* Athens and Paris.

Billows, R. A. (1990) *Antigonos the One-Eyed and the Creation of the Hellenistic State.* Berkeley, Los Angeles, London.

Bosworth, A. B. (2000) Ptolemy and the Will of Alexander. In A. B. Bosworth and E. J. Baynham (eds) *Alexander the Great in Fact and Fiction*, 207–41, Oxford.

Bosworth, A. B. (2002) *The Legacy of Alexander. Politics, Warfare, and Propaganda under the Successors.* Oxford.

Brogan, T. M. (2003) Liberation Honors: Athenian Monuments from Antigonid Victories in their Immediate and Broader Contexts. In O. Palagia and S. V. Tracy (eds) *The Macedonians in Athens, 322–229 BC. Proceedings of an International Conference held at the University of Athens, May 24–26, 2001*, 194–205, Exeter.

Buraselis, K. (1982) *Das hellenistische Makedonien und die Ägäis. Forschungen zur Politik des Kassandros und der drei ersten Antigoniden (Antigonos Monophthalmos, Demetrios Poliorketes und Antigonos Gonatas) im Ägäischen Meer und in Westkleinasien.* Munich.

Caroli, C. A. (2007) *Ptolemaios I. Soter. Herrscher zweier Kulturen.* Konstanz.

Davies, J. K. (1971) *Athenian Propertied Families, 600–300 BC.* Oxford.

Dreyer, B. (1998) The *Hiereus* of the *Soteres*: Plut. *Dem.* 10.4, 46.2, *Greek, Roman and Byzantine Studies* 39, 23–38.

Ferguson, W. S. (1911) *Hellenistic Athens. An Historical Essay.* London.

Flacelière, R. and E. Chambry (1977) *Plutarque, Vies, tome XIII, Démétrios – Antoine.* Paris.

Giovannini, A. (2004) Le traité entre Iasos et Ptolémée Ier (IK 28,1, 2–3) et les relations entre les cités grecques d'Asie mineure et les souverains hellénistiques, *Epigraphica Anatolica* 37, 69–85.

Giovannini, A. (2007) *Les relations entre états dans la Grèce antique, du temps d'Homère à l'intervention romaine (ca. 700–200 av. J.-C.).* Stuttgart.

Grainger, J. D. (2009) *The Cities of Pamphylia.* Oxford.

Gruen, E. S. (1985) The Coronation of the Diadochoi. In J. W. Eadie and J. Ober (eds) *The Craft of the Ancient Historian. Essays in Honor of Chester G. Starr*, 253–71, Lanham, MD.

Habicht, C. (1970) *Gottmenschentum und griechische Städte.* 2nd ed. Munich.

Habicht, C. (1979) *Untersuchungen zur Geschichte Athens im 3. Jahrhundert v. Chr.* Munich.

Hatzopoulos, M. B. (1996) *Macedonian Institutions under the Kings. I. A Historical and Epigraphic Study. II. Epigraphic Appendix*. Athens.

Hauben, H. (1987) On the Ptolemaic Iasos Inscription IGSK 28.1, 2–3, *Epigraphica Anatolica* 10, 3–5.

Hauben, H. (2010) Rhodes, the League of the Islanders, and the Cult of Ptolemy I Soter. In A. Tamis, C. J. Mackie and S. G. Byrne (eds.) *Φιλαθήναιος. Studies in Honour of Michael J. Osborne*, 103–21, Athens.

Hazzard, R. A. (1992) Did Ptolemy I Get his Surname from the Rhodians in 304? *Zeitschrift für Papyrologie und Epigraphik* 93, 52–56.

Hazzard, R. A. (2000) *Imagination of a Monarchy: Studies in Ptolemaic Propaganda*. Toronto.

Heckel, W. (1992) *The Marshals of Alexander's Empire*. London and New York.

Henry, A. S. (1972) *The Prescripts of Athenian Decrees*. Leiden.

Hölbl, G. (2001) *A History of the Ptolemaic Empire*. London and New York.

Huß, W. (2001) *Ägypten in hellenistischer Zeit, 332-30 v. Chr.* Munich.

Johnson, C. (2000) Ptolemy I's Epiklesis Σωτήρ: Origin and Definition, *Ancient History Bulletin* 14, 102–06.

Juhel, P. (2009) {Ὁ ἐπὶ + substantif au génitif}, titre des fonctionnaires de l'administration hellénistique en général et des hauts fonctionnaires royaux de la Macédoine antigonide en particulier, *Tyche* 24, 59–76.

Kolde, A. (2003) *Politique et religion chez Isyllos d'Epidaure*. Basel.

Kotsidu, H. (2000) *Τιμὴ καὶ δόξα. Ehrungen für hellenistische Herrscher im griechischen Mutterland und in Kleinasien unter besonderer Berücksichtigung der archäologischen Denkmäler*. Berlin.

Koumanoudes, S. N. and S. G. Miller (1971) I.G. II^2 1477 and 3046 Rediscovered, *Hesperia* 40, 448–58.

Lehmann, G. A. (1988) Das neue kölner Historiker-Fragment (*P.Köln* Nr. 247) und die χρονικὴ σύνταξις des Zenon von Rhodos (*FGrHist* 523), *Zeitschrift für Papyrologie und Epigraphik* 72, 1–17.

Lewis, D. M. (1988) The Last Inventories of the Treasurers of Athena. In D. Knoepfler (ed.) *Comptes et inventaires dans la cité grecque. Actes du colloque international d'épigraphie tenu à Neuchâtel du 23 au 26 septembre 1986 en l'honneur de Jacques Tréheux*, 297–308, Geneva.

Lund, H. (1992) *Lysimachus. A Study in Early Hellenistic Kingship*. London and New York.

Manni, E. (1953) *Plutarchi. Vita Demetri Poliorcetis*. Florence.

Marasco, G. (1981) Introduzione alla biografia plutarchea di Demetrio, *Sileno* 7, 35–70.

Marek, C. (2006) *Die Inschriften von Kaunos*. Munich.

Mastrocinque, A. (1979) *La Caria e la Ionia meridionale in epoca ellenistica (323–188 a.C.)*. Rome.

Mauersberger, A. (1961) *Polybios-Lexikon*. I 2. Berlin.

Meritt, B. D. (1961) *The Athenian Year*. Berkeley.

Mikalson, J. D. (1998) *Religion in Hellenistic Athens*. Berkeley, Los Angeles, London.

Mooren, L. (1998) Kings and Courtiers. Political Decision-Making in the Hellenistic States. In W. Schuller (ed.) *Politische Theorie und Praxis im Altertum*, 123–33, Darmstadt.

Muccioli, F. (2004) 'Il re dell'Asia': ideologia e propaganda da Alessandro Magno a Mitridate VI. In L. Criscuolo, G. Geraci and C. Salvaterra (eds) *Simblos IV. Scritti di storia antica*, 105–58, Bologna.

Müller, O. (1973) *Antigonos Monophthalmos und 'Das Jahr der Könige'*. Bonn.

Osborne, M. J. (1981) *Naturalization in Athens*. I. Brussels.

O'Sullivan, L. (2009) *The Regime of Demetrius of Phalerum in Athens, 317–307 BCE. A Philosopher in Politics*. Leiden and Boston.

Paschidis, P. (2008) *Between City and King. Prosopographical Studies on the Intermediaries between the Cities of the Greek Mainland and the Aegean and the Royal Courts in the Hellenistic Period (322–190 BC)*. Athens.

Pritchett, W. K. and B. D. Meritt (1940) *The Chronology of Hellenistic Athens*. Cambridge, MA.

Ritter, H.-W. (1965) *Diadem und Königsherrschaft. Untersuchungen zu Zeremonien und Rechtsgrundlagen des Herrschaftsantritts bei den Persen, bei Alexander dem Großen und im Hellenismus*. Munich.

Samuel, A. E. (1962) *Ptolemaic Chronology*. Munich.

Schettino, M. T. (1998) *Introduzione al Polieno*. Pisa.

Tataki, A. B. (1998) *Macedonians Abroad. A Contribution to the Prosopography of Ancient Macedonia*. Athens.

Tracy, S. V. (1995) *Athenian Democracy in Transition. Attic Letter-Cutters of 340 to 290 BC*. Berkeley.

Tracy, S. V. (2000) Athenian Politicians and Inscriptions of the Years 307 to 302, *Hesperia* 69, 227–33.

Walbank, M. B. (1985) Greek Inscriptions from the Athenian Agora, *Hesperia* 54, 309–25.

Weber, G. (1993) *Dichtung und höfische Gesselschaft. Die Rezeption von Zeitgeschichte am Hof der ersten drei Ptolemäer*. Stuttgart.

Wheatley, P. (2001) The Antigonid Campaign in Cyprus, 306 BC, *Ancient Society* 31, 133–56.

Wiemer, H.-U. (2001) *Rhodische Traditionen in der hellenistischen Historiographie*. Frankfurt.

Wiemer, H.-U. (2002) *Krieg, Handel und Piraterie. Untersuchungen zur Geschichte des hellenistischen Rhodos*. Berlin.

Wilhelm, A. (1937) Ein Gedicht zu Ehren der Könige Antigonos und Demetrios, *Archaiologike Ephemeris*, 203–207 (= *Inschriftenkunden* II 181–85).

Notes

1 Publication: Pritchett and Meritt 1940, 7–8 (whence *SEG* 21 [1965] 334; Henry 1972, 59); *Agora* XVI no. 107, with readings by M. B. Walbank. Discussion: for ll. 1–6, see Meritt 1961, 177–78 and Woodhead, *Agora* XVI p. 167–69, 177–78; on the cutter and l. 10, see Tracy 1995, 146. A brief note on the proposer of the decree (ll. 9–10): Walbank 1985, 318 n. 25, followed *verbatim* by Woodhead, *Agora* XVI no. 107 (Tracy 2000, 229 n. 21 and 230 apparently concurs, without comments), suggested the identification of the proposer with Πυθόδωρος Νικοστράτου Ἀχαρνεύς, an offspring of a rich Athenian family of the 4th century. Nothing, however, connects this family (see Davies 1971, 481–84) with the regime of 307–301, and the traces of the name that survive are compatible with a large number of Athenian names. Even if we limit ourselves to the name Νικόστρατος (and not any of the 24 other names ending in -όστρατος and attested in Attica) and to 8-letter demotics, there are at least 6 demes where this very common name is attested. In an unpublished communication (delivered at the 2000 Symposium whose acts were published as *Ἀττικαὶ ἐπιγραφαί. Πρακτικὰ συμποσίου εἰς μνήμην Adolf Wilhelm (1864–1950)*, Athens 2004), J. D. Morgan advanced an even bolder suggestion, namely that the proposer of the decree was no other than Δημήτριος Φανοστράτου Φαληρεύς, which would be another proof that Diodorus gets his dates wrong. As we shall see, however, the dating of the events by literary and epigraphic sources is quite secure, and on the eleventh day of 307/6, the philosopher was definitely at Thebes, safely away from Athens.

2 I have had the opportunity to study the stone twice at the storage room of the Stoa of Attalus, once in March 2003 and once in June 2010; I am grateful to the staff of the American School of Classical Studies at Athens (especially Sylvie Dumont, Jan Jordan and Craig Mauzy) and the First Ephorate of Classical and Prehistoric Antiquities for permissions and help during both visits.

3 Main sources: D.S. 20.45.1–46.1,3; Plu. *Demetr.* 8.1–10.2; secondary sources are indicated below.

4 D.S. 20.46.3 places the conquest of Megara after the conquest of the Piraeus, which seems, indeed, more reasonable, but the more detailed account of Plutarch (*Demetr.* 8–10), in combination with Philoch. *FGH* 328 F 66, puts the conquest of Megara before the final capture of the Piraeus; Diodorus may have tried to rationalize the order of events.

5 Secretaries are mentioned neither in the two certain decrees of 317/6–308/7 (*IG* II^2 450b and 453) nor in the two decrees which Tracy 1995, 36 n. 2 believes may belong to this period (*IG* II^2 592 and 727). This makes it highly probable that the secretary cycle was abolished from the outset of the philosopher's rule. Tracy's suggestion (1995, 37 n. 6) that the irregularity of the secretary cycle in the years 303/2–302/1 can be explained by assuming that secretaries from tribes III-VIII had served under Demetrius of Phalerum is not plausible: in order to accommodate for six secretaries serving in the ten years of Demetrius' rule, one would need to make a second unsubstantiated assumption, namely that the secretary cycle was only abolished in 312/11 (cf. O'Sullivan 2009, 120–22, with earlier literature). I have elsewhere provided a different explanation for the irregularities in the secretary cycle of 303/2–302/1 (Paschidis 2008, 90–103).

6 Cf. Pritchett and Meritt 1940, 8, 10–11, 21 and Tracy 1995, 37 n. 6. The secretary of 318/17 came from Aegeis, then tribe II (*IG* II^2 448; *melius* Osborne 1981, 101–05, D38; cf. Meritt 1961, 231). If the cycle had been designed simply to continue where it had stopped, 307/6 should have a secretary from Pandionis (tribe III), while Diomeia formerly belonged to Aigeis (tribe II).

7 The other possible options would be words beginning with ὑποδη-, all of them rare and obscure or unattested epigraphically or very hard to envisage in an Attic honorific decree: some form of the verbs ὑποδηῶμαι or ὑποδηλῶ, the noun ὑπόδημα or one of its compounds, or very obscure words such as ὑποδημόσιον, ὑποδημιουργός, ὑποδήμιος, etc.; the two verbs are, if I am not mistaken, epigraphically unattested, and hard to envisage in a public document, while ὑπόδημα and its compounds cannot belong to a civic decree.

8 For instance, a search in the post-Euclidean Attic decrees in the *IG* (*IG* II^2 1–1319) yields only five exceptions (*IG* II^2 1076, l. 19; 1079, l. 9; 1286, l. 2; 1304, ll. 20 and 30; 1308, l. 13).

9 See Billows 1990, 367–68 no. 9; Heckel 1992, 341–42 no 6.4; Tataki 1998, 129 no. 5, with sources, earlier literature and discussion. Whether we identify this Andronicus with Andronicus son of Agerrus in Alexander's army (an identification which I consider very unsafe) or not is irrelevant for present purposes. The last mention of Andronicus from Olynthus is in D.S. 19.86.1–2; the Antigonid officer, then serving as phrourarch of Tyre during the city's siege by Ptolemy, is praised for his loyalty towards Antigonus and Demetrius; he was taken prisoner by Ptolemy, who treated him benignly as a *philos*. This last remark, as Billows aptly remarks, need not mean that Andronicus switched camps: the whole episode is used by Diodorus merely as an illustration of Ptolemy's *philanthropia* and Andronicus may well have returned to Antigonus' and Demetrius' staff afterwards.

10 There are many parallels in Attic decrees of καθεστηκὼς or κατασταθεὶς with a king or a royal official as the participle's agent – *IG* II^2 1285, with Wilhelm's restorations in *SEG* 3 (1922) 123 ([στρατηγὸς δὲ ἐπ'] Ἀντιμάχου ἄ[ρχοντος κατασταθεὶς ὑπὸ Ἀντιγόνου]); *Agora* XVI 122, ll. 6–8 (κ[ατασταθεὶς ὑπὸ το]ῦ βασιλέως Δημητρίου πρόεδρος ἐν τῶι κοινῶι συνεδρίωι); *IRhamn* 8 ([κ]ατασταθεὶς στρατηγὸς ὑπό τε τοῦ βασιλέως Ἀντιγόνου) – often accompanied by a clause with ἐπὶ + genitive or accusative: *IG* II^2 469, ll. 2–4: κατασταθεὶ[ς ἐπὶ τὴν] | [τ]οῦ Εὐρίπου φυλακὴν ὑπὸ Πολεμα[ίου]; *IRhamn* 17, ll. 5–6: κατασταθεὶς μετὰ τοῦ πατρὸς Ἀπολλωνίου ὑπὸ το[ῦ] | [βα]σιλέ[ως Ἀν]τ[ιγ]όνου ἐπὶ τὴν φυλακὴν τοῦ φρουρίου; *IG* II^2 650, ll. 9–10: [καθεστηκ]ὼς ὑπὸ τοῦ βασιλέως | Πτολ[εμαίου ἐπὶ τῶν ἀ]φράκτων; *IG* II^2 1225, ll. 8–9: καθεστηκὼς ὑπὸ τ|[ο]ῦ βασιλέως στρατηγὸς ἐπὶ τοῦ Πε<ι>ραιέως. Καθεστηκὼς is preferable to κατασταθεὶς since it allows the restoration of the ethnic in l. 11. I restore the ethnic rather than a patronym because, when the name of the honorand is not complete (name, patronym, ethnic) or plain in the motivation clause of an Attic decree, the combination name + ethnic (see e.g. *IG* II^2 360; 373; 408; 493) is far more common than name + patronym (a construction of which I know no certain examples, at least from the early Hellenistic period). The use of the ethnic *Olynthios* long after the destruction of Olynthus is, of course, in no way problematic (see Tataki 1998, 129–45). Apart from καθεστηκὼς or κατασταθείς, there are obviously other participles which can be associated with a position in

the royal administration: among those most often encountered in epigraphy, one may single out τεταγμένος, ἀποσταλείς, ἐξαποσταλείς, καταλειφθείς. Τεταγμένος is by far the most common, but it is almost exclusively associated with permanent appointments, rather than with particular missions or temporary appointments, as is most probably the case here; ἀποσταλείς, on the contrary, would be a valid alternative (cf., e.g. *Agora* XVI 208, ll. 14–15: οἱ ἀποσταλέντες ὑπὸ τῶν Λαμιέων ἐπὶ τὰς δίκας). On the construct ἐπὶ + substantive in the genitive as an administrative label in the Macedonian army and administration, see Juhel 2009 with an abundance of examples. Mauersberger 1961, col. 876–908, s.v. ἐπί, especially col. 880–81 ('Machtbereich') collects and discusses the uses of ἐπὶ in that sense in Polybius.

11 I had initially thought of [καθεστηκὼ]ς ὑπὸ Δη[μητ]|[ρίου ἡγεμὼν τῆς ἐφό]δου ἐπὶ τὴ[ν Μο]|[υνιχίαν], a supplement that would fit the lacuna perfectly; actually we may have a mention of the attack on Mounychia and the expulsion of Cassander's guard in a decree enacted some months later (*IG* II² 466a; cf. below). It is true that the word ἔφοδος is almost never used in the military sense of 'attack' (esp. 'sudden attack') in Attic epigraphy (with one interesting exception, *IG* II² 2788, l. 24: κατὰ τὴν Περσῶν ἔφοδον, which is echoed in Plb. 2.35.7: τὴν Περσῶν ἔφοδον ἐπὶ τὴν Ἑλλάδα), but it is often used in this sense in inscriptions from other areas (see e.g. Bielman 1994, no. 51 [*IG* XII 3, 171/1286], l. 16; *Lindos* II 2 D 6; *ISmyrna* 573 [*OGIS* 229; *SVA* III 492], l. 3; *OGIS* 654, l. 4); moreover, the sense of 'sudden attack' would be very appropriate for the events of 307 (cf. Plu. *Demetr.* 8.5). There is, however, a major difficulty: although the phrase ἡγεμὼν τῆς ἐφόδου is not inconceivable in Greek (Heliod. *Aethiop.* 1.33.1), the objective genitive after *hēgemōn* almost always denotes a territory, a state division, or a military unit, not a military mission. It should be noted, finally, that the reading of the *delta* in the beginning of the visible part of l. 12 is rather doubtful (see the apparatus). The sequence KATATA in l. 13 may belong either to a form of the verb κατατάσσω or to a phrase with κατὰ + article (τὰ or τάς), a construct which is almost invariably attested in Attic epigraphy with the meaning 'in accordance with' (as in the phrases κατὰ τὰ γεγραμμένα, κατὰ τὰς συνθήκας, etc.) with the interesting exception of the honorific decree for Artemidorus of Perinthus (*Agora* XVI 172), a high-ranking officer of Lysimachus, in which κατὰ has a temporal sense (κατὰ τὰς πρεσβείας ταύτας).

12 The title cannot be restored after Demetrius' name, for the text would then be both awkward and unrestorable: ὑπὸ Δη[μητ]|[ρίου τοῦ βασιλέως .]δου ἐπὶ τη[- - -].

13 D.S. 19.97.3: the Nabataeans, under siege, call Demetrius a king. Bosworth 2000, 237 n. 132 is certainly correct in denying the plausibility of Müller's assumption (1973, 49) that Hieronymus (certainly Diodorus' source here) simply translates an Arabian term carelessly.

14 On this aspect of 'das Streben nach Legitimität' for the Successors, see Müller 1973, 45–77 and Bosworth 2000, 228–41 (on whose theories on the royal title, however, see below). Antigonus receives royal honours and rules as if he were a king over Asia in 316: D.S. 19.48.1. 'Royal gifts' presented to Antigonus by Seleucus, again in 316: D.S. 19.55.2. Seleucus rules over the barbarians '*as* a king' before 306: Plu. *Demetr.* 18.3. Seleucus possesses 'royal stature' in 306: D.S. 19.92.5. Polyaenus' summary statement that, already after the battle of Gabiene, Antigonus 'was declared king over the whole of Asia' (*Strat.* 4.6.13) is clearly an exaggeration, absent in parallel and more authoritative accounts. Polyaenus or his anecdotal source simply aim to strengthen the effect of the stratagem described (see, already, Müller 1973, 46–47); alternatively, Polyaenus may be betraying here his proud pro-Macedonian and pro-Antigonid attitude (cf. Schettino 1998, 230). On the informal use of the term 'king of Asia', see n. 28, below.

15 One could object that occasionally the royal title is lacking even after 306: see for example *Syll*³ 349 (*IByzantion* 4), where the royal title is lacking in ll. 1, 2, 5 but may be plausibly restored in l. 8, and *Syll*³ 352 (*IEphesos* 1448), where the title is lacking in l. 9, because it appears in the previous phrase in l. 8. However, the two phenomena are of a totally different order. In these cases, the occasional lack of the royal title is easily explained by its presence elsewhere in the text. In our decree, the one part of the document where the royal title would be expected is the one where it is lacking: 'designated by king Demetrius' would be the appropriate phrasing had Demetrius been recognised as a king a couple of days before.

16 Despite the evident difficulties that Plutarch's account poses, his claim has usually been left

unchallenged: Müller 1973, 58; Austin 2006, 43 n. 6 and Bosworth 2000, 235 n. 126 accept it unreservedly (Bosworth, in fact, claims that Plutarch is technically incorrect, since Antigonus had been proclaimed king since 316 [D.S. 19.48.1; cf. n. 14, above]); Ferguson 1911, 107–08 accepts it in his text but remains sceptical in a note (107 n. 4); Manni 1953 *ad loc.* and in p. xxii rejects Plutarch's account summarily; Ritter 1965, 79–80 only uses the passage in order to explain the reference to the *plēthos* in Plutarch's later account of the actual assumption of the title; Flacelière and Chambry 1977, 194 correctly point out that Plutarch's account is contradicted a few paragraphs later in Plu. *Demetr.* 18.1; in most major modern accounts of the period, Plutarch's assertion is usually left out, without comment.

17 Plu. *Demetr.* 10.2–11.1; 12.1–2; 13.1–3; the other main literary sources are D.S. 20.46.1–2 and Philoch. *FGH* 328 F 48, 165, 166. Literary, epigraphic and archaeological sources are conveniently gathered by Kotsidu 2000, 33–54 no. 9–12; see also the detailed discussion of Habicht 1970, 44–55 and Mikalson 1998, 79–103 with earlier literature.

18 D.S. 20.46.2 (statues, games, procession, sacrifices); Philoch. *FGH* 328 F 165; *Suda*, s.v. Πάραλοι (triremes); for the statues, cf. Brogan 2003, 195; for the crowns, cf. Koumanoudes and Miller 1971, 455–56, who argue that the crowns recorded in *SEG* 38 (1988) 143 B II, l. 19–21 belong to 307/6; *contra* Lewis 1988, 304.

19 For the cult, see the inscriptions gathered by Kotsidu 2000, 38–45, Habicht 1970, 44–48 and Mikalson 1998, 80, 83–85. Dreyer 1998 attempts to salvage part of Plutarch's credibility, supposing that his reference is to the ἀναγραφεῖς of 294/3–292/1; even if this assumption is accepted, Plutarch's account still would have nothing to do with the events of 307.

20 D.S. 20.46.4 expressly mentions *ambassadors* to Demetrius in the autumn of 307. Plutarch's error here probably echoes criticism in his sources for two events unrelated to 307: Stratocles' (supposed?) decree in 303 on accepting royal decisions as if they were divine decrees (Plu. *Demetr.* 24.9) and Dromocleides' decree in c. 291 on asking Demetrius for an oracle (Plu. *Demetr.* 13.1–2).

21 Philoch. *FGH* 328 F 166 apparently corroborates Plutarch on the renaming of *Mounuchiōn*, but this fragment is far from secure, since it derives from *Scholia* in Pindar, and, more importantly, there is abundant evidence for *Mounuchiōn* in 307–301. On the celebration of the *Dēmētria* alongside the Dionysia, see *SEG* 45 (1995) 101, l. 42.

22 Müller 1973, 55–57 argues that Plutarch also draws on Hieronymus, especially for the crucial passage of 10.3, but Marasco 1981, 58–64 convincingly shows that the sources on Poliorcetes and Athens are mostly Athenian, namely Philochorus (for the annalistic details), and fervently anti-Macedonian writers, especially Philippides and Demochares (the latter probably through Duris).

23 Müller 1973, 58 resorts to hypothesizing: 'Es darf wohl auch damit gerechnet werden, daß Antigonos und Demetrios in verschiedenen Weiheinschriften, die ihnen zu Ehren in Athen aufgestellt wurden, im Jahre 307/6 mit dem Königstitel genannt wurden'.

24 *IG* II^2 466 is a honorific decree for Tenos and its ambassadors, who came to Athens to congratulate the city and/or Demetrius on the successful outcome of recent events (the expulsion of Cassander's guard is mentioned in ll. 13–14). Antigonus and Demetrius are mentioned in l. 7 and Demetrius again in ll. 12–13 and the royal title is not attested in either case.

25 The long discussion on the identity of the king (Alexander III or IV), and the number, names and identities of the honorands need not concern us here; see Paschidis 2008, 83–84, with earlier literature. On the date of the decree, see e.g. Billows 1990, 395. An interesting parallel is the famous decree of the *koinon* of the Islanders on the inauguration of the *Dēmētria* (*IG* XI 4, 1036). As Buraselis 1982, 67–75, has pointed out, the decree must be dated to 307 and not to 306 and the altar mentioned in ll. 45–46 must be an altar [τῶν Σωτήρω]ν and not [τῶν βασιλέω]ν, independently of the fact that in ll. 3–4 Demetrius does not have a royal title (cf. Paschidis 2008, 425 n. 2). *IG* XII 6, 20 and 21 have also been dated to 307 because of the lack of the royal title for Antigonus and Demetrius, but an independent confirmation of the dating is here impossible.

26 Even in *IG* II^2 498 (*Syll*^{3} 342), where Demetrius is not expressly called a king in ll. 16–17, the title is present in the plural βασιλεῦσι in l. 14.

27 *IG* II^2 3424, l. 5: ['Ελλάδος ἡγεμόνες βασιλεῖς τ'] Ἀσίας.

28 Muccioli 2004 successfully traces the term from the age of Alexander, where it appears to be a powerful tool of propaganda aiming to denote both continuity and a clean break from the Achaemenid past,

down to the age of Mithridates, when it had long become a necessary *topos*, an integral part of the *imitatio Alexandri*.

29 Gruen 1985, 256–57 makes much of the novel character of Demetrius' accession to the throne, which he interprets as a protocol-breaking decision by Antigonus, who sent his son the diadem and proclaimed him a king in a letter (Plu. *Demetr.* 18.1). The beginning of Plutarch's passage, however, makes clear that this was not an arbitrary decision by Antigonus: the assembled Macedonians had already proclaimed as kings both father *and* son and Antigonus' letter, of an informative rather than constitutional nature, followed.

30 Bosworth 2000, 228–36. I should perhaps stress that I unreservedly agree with Bosworth's main argument in that paper, namely that the *Liber de Morte*, the fictional account of Alexander's last days and testament, is best understood in the context of the Third Diadochi War and probably emanates from Ptolemy's court. Nevertheless, Ptolemy having aspirations for the throne in 308 (which is certain) and Ptolemy actually being called a king by subjects and officials in 308 are two different matters.

31 New text (and French translation) in Giovannini 2004, who is apparently unaware of Bosworth's study. Cf. Giovannini 2007, 267–71 no. T13, 108 and 400.

32 Ptolemy in Lycia: D.S. 20.27.1. Philocles at nearby Caunus: Polyaen. *Strat.* 3.16; cf. D.S. 20.27.2 (the connection between the two different accounts is certain: see Bosworth 2000, 234 n. 12 with earlier literature and Marek 2006, 97). Leonides in Rough Cilicia: D.S. 20.19.4; *Suda*, s.v. Δημήτριος.

33 Denying the royal title to an enemy was a standard ideological weapon in the official discourse of the Successors and the *poleis* alike. In Athenian official documents, Cassander is consistently referred to without his royal title (see Osborne 1981, D43 [*IG* II^2 467; *Syll*^{3} 327]; *IG* II^2 469 [*Syll*^{3} 328; *IG* II^2 470]; *SEG* 30 [1980] 325 and 36 [1986] 165) until after Ipsus, when Athens became Cassander's ally (*IG* II^2 641 [*Syll*^{3} 362]). In the third epiphany of Athena in the *Lindian Chronicle* (*Lindos* II 2 D 95–115 [*FGH* 532 D 3]), the text speaks of a letter to *king* Ptolemy (l. 101), while denying the royal title to Poliorcetes (l. 95). For Poliorcetes' attitude toward the other kings, see Plu. *Demetr.* 18.4 and below, n. 56.

34 Until the recent publication of an important new text (*IKaunos* 4), for example, who would have thought that Antigonus Gonatas, as early as 270/69 (rather than 269/8), that is, only a few years after he had secured the throne, ventured a naval expedition with concrete successes in a part of the Asian coast which, according to the *communis opinio*, had been under Ptolemaic control practically throughout the third century (see Marek 2006, 96–98)?

35 A passage of the oath taken by the soldiers (*IIasos* 2, l. 37–39) has also been seen as pointing to a date in the winter of 309/8: the soldiers swear 'not to accept a soldier by anyone during the four days after the departure of the embassy to Ptolemy, nor later, without the consent of the Iasians'. This has been taken to imply (e.g. by W. Blümel, the editor of *IIasos* and Hauben 1987, followed by Bosworth 2000, 230–31 n. 106) that the soldiers were waiting for instructions and/or reinforcements by Ptolemy and/or his forces, who must have been somewhere in the vicinity. Giovannini 2004, 75 again convincingly argues that the explanation for this part of the oath must be simpler: the Iasians merely wished to assure that the soldiers occupying the citadels would not increase the number of the beneficiaries of the treaty with irrelevant outsiders. If the presence of Polemaeus or Ptolemy and his forces in the vicinity of Iasus are not implied by the Iasian decree, as the *communis opinio* held, nothing obliges us to date the decree precisely to the winter of 309/8. It could very well, e.g., be dated several months later (cf. Mastrocinque 1979, 28–32). I cannot, however, agree with Giovannini 2004, 78–79, who dates the decree as late as 305. The Swiss scholar sees a confirmation of such a date in the layout of the inscribed documents on the stone: a line is left blank between the letter of Aristobulus and the letter of Asclepiodotus, while there is no space between the Iasian decree and the letter of Aristobulus. This detail leads Giovannini to assume that the decree recording the treaties and Aristobulus' letter should be close in time, indeed part of the same affair, although he insists that, technically, the treaty between Iasus and Ptolemy (decree) and the treaty between Iasus and Aristobulus (first letter) are two distinct diplomatic procedures. He assumes, therefore, that after the conclusion of the treaty between Iasus and Ptolemy, which should be dated to only months before the assumption of the royal title by Ptolemy, the Iasians addressed the general responsible for the area with two further demands; Aristobulus' reply was drafted after the assumption of the royal title (which Giovannini dates to 305,

but corrects his error in Giovannini 2007, 270 n. 4), which had just occurred. All this is too much of a coincidence to be credible, and I am afraid that Giovannini sees too much in a blank line: the fact that Asclepiodotus' letter (which Giovannini himself admits must be dated much later) is inscribed on the same stone, and by the same cutter, proves that this is a regular case of an epigraphic dossier on a particular issue, a dossier the engraving design of which is by definition unitary, regardless of the precise dating of its constituent parts.

36 The following letter by Asclepiodotus strengthens this assumption: Asclepiodotus is asked by the Iasians to take the same oath as Aristobulus had done and the normal explanation is that he was his successor (Bagnall 1976, 89–91, followed by Giovannini). The Iasians, in this case, need to reaffirm their privileges accorded to them by his predecessor several years earlier.

37 Plu. *Demetr.* 17.2–18.1; App. *Syr.* 54; Just. 15.2.10–11; the exceptions are the shortened versions of D.S. 20.53.2 and the *Heidelberg Epitome* (*FGH* 155 F 1). On the role of a proper or simulated Macedonian assembly in the assumption of the royal title, see Hatzopoulos 1996, I, 276–79, 303–12.

38 Nep. *Eum.* 13.2–3 is an interesting passage on the legitimacy of the new kings (despite the mess it makes of chronology, with the Successors claiming the throne immediately after Eumenes' death!); given that the ultimate source of practically the entire literary tradition on Eumenes is almost certainly Hieronymus (Anson 2004, 1–33), this passage may echo displeasure in the middle ranks of the Macedonian army with the prospect of the assumption of the royal title by leading Successors.

39 See, for example, Samuel 1962, 4–11; Ritter 1965, 95–99; Müller 1973, 94–100 and Caroli 2007, 129–31, 175–78, with the sources and further literature.

40 So already Lehmann 1988, 6–10; cf. Weber 1993, 56; Hölbl 2001, 20; Mooren 1998, 123; Huß 2001, 184–85; Wiemer 2001, 236 n. 165; 2002, 83; Hauben 2010, 106–08 among others.

41 In fact, fr. a, which joins col. I, deals with earlier events and so does col. III; see Lehmann 1988, 5 and Wiemer 2001, 233.

42 Cf. Wiemer 2001, 230–31, who convincingly argues that D.S. 20.81–82 (where Rhodes is presented as a naval power minding its own business, behaving with the utmost rationality, possessing the finest institutions, desiring only peace and having excellent relations with all Successors, especially Ptolemy I) is clearly a part of the Rhodian self-image of the second century, retrospectively projected to the glorious past of the resistance against the Besieger – a focal point for later Rhodian historiography.

43 It is true that the text does not refer to the official assumption of the title by Ptolemy *expressis verbis*. In col. II, ll. 6–7, the reference to the official proclamation may be negative: the sense seems to be that the Rhodians should *not* proclaim Ptolemy a king before he has the chance to communicate with them; in col. II, ll. 18–19, there is simply a mention of 'the outward dignity of a king' (τὴν βασιλικὴν ἔσχε πρόστασιν). At best, however, the contextual date is in the immediate eve of the official assumption, otherwise the whole text does not make sense; cf. below.

44 [Ἀντίγονος] ὁ Φιλίππου προσ[ηγόρε]υσεν ἑαυτὸν βασι[λέα πρ]ῶ̣τος. Bosworth 2000, 236 translates: 'entitled (had entitled?) himself king first', obviously implying that the Rhodian text does not refer to the official assumption of kingship by Antigonus, but προσαγορεύω may very well be used in a formal sense (cf. Plb. 12.15.8; Plu. *Aem.* 8.3 and *Pomp.* 8.2; Str. 12.1.2 C534).

45 *PKöln* 6.247, col. II, ll. 28–31: [---] ο̣ἱ δ̣ὲ φίλ̣ο̣ι κα{ι}τ̣ηξί|[ου]ν̣ αὐτὸν τῆς βασιλικῆς | [ἐπι]κ̣λήσεως, ἐν ο̣ἷς κα̣ὶ Ῥό|[διο]ι.

46 Another interesting Rhodian claim is that the Rhodians were the first who called Ptolemy a Soter (Paus. 1.8.6). This claim may well be false, too: see Hazzard 1992 (cf. Hazzard 2000, 6 n. 16); *contra* Johnson 2000; Kolde 2003, 392–94; Hauben 2010, 104–14 with further bibliography. Apart from my remarks in Paschidis 2008, 357 n. 3, I should point out that the distinction between a local and an imperial cult of Ptolemy I as Saviour, on which Hauben 2010 insists, actually strengthens Hazzard's point about the absence of the title in official Rhodian documents rather than refuting it: if there existed such a local cult already by 304, it should be reflected in local texts of the period (cf. Caroli 2007, 193–97).

47 Ἀντίγονος... ἐπιβάθραν... ἔφη καλὴν καὶ ἀσάλευτον εἶναι τὴν εὔνοιαν, τὰς δ' Ἀθήνας, ὥσπερ σκοπὴν τῆς οἰκουμένης, ταχὺ τῇ δόξῃ διαπυρσεύσειν εἰς ἅπαντας ἀνθρώπους τὰς πράξεις. The fact that the source of the anecdote is obviously Athenocentric is irrelevant to my point.

48 Πρῶτοι μὲν γὰρ ἀνθρώπων ἁπάντων...

49 *PKöln* 6.247, col. I, ll. 21–25: πεπεισμένος (...) [αὐ]τὸς δ' ἡγήσεσθαι | [τῆς οἰκο]υμένης ἁπάσης.

50 *Suda*, s.v. βασιλεία: τοὺς δὲ μηδὲν προσήκοντας βασιλεῖς γενέσθαι σχεδὸν ἁπάσης τῆς οἰκουμένης...

51 Duris *FGH* 76 F 14: ἐπὶ τῆς οἰκουμένης ὀχούμενος.

52 See D.S. 19.56.2, where Seleucus accuses Antigonus of seeking πᾶσαν τὴν Μακεδόνων βασιλείαν, or 18.50.1, where Antigonus is portrayed as going after τὴν τῶν ὅλων ἡγεμονίαν. For the controversy over whether the rest of the Successors also aspired to the totality of the kingdom or only to their respective spear-won territories, see Gruen 1985; Lund 1992, 51–52; Bosworth 2002, 246–47, with earlier literature.

53 Fr. a of *PKöln* 6.247, which may belong to col. I, apparently deals with the machinations of Antigonus and the assassination of leading Macedonians, as far back as 319 (see Lehmann 1988, 3–4).

54 *PKöln* 6.247, col. II, ll. 30–34: ἐν οἷς καὶ Ῥό|[διο]ι, τὴν μὲν αὔξ[η]σ[ιν] | [τὴ]ν Ἀντιγόνου προ[σδε|χό]μενοι βαρεῖαν ἐσ[ο|μέ]νη[ν].

55 Plu. *Demetr.* 10.2: οὕτως λαμπρὸν ἐν ταῖς εὐεργεσίαις καὶ μέγαν φανέντα τὸν Δημήτριον ἐπαχθῆ καὶ βαρὺν ἐποίησαν τῶν τιμῶν ταῖς ἀμετρίαις ἃς ἐψηφίσαντο.

56 Cf. Plu. *Demetr.* 25.7: Ἐκεῖνος δὲ (sc. Demetrius) χλευάζων καὶ γελῶν τοὺς ἄλλον τινὰ πλὴν τοῦ πατρὸς καὶ αὐτοῦ βασιλέα προσαγορεύοντας, ἡδέως ἤκουε τῶν παρὰ πότον ἐπιχύσεις λαμβανόντων Δημητρίου βασιλέως, Σελεύκου δ' ἐλεφαντάρχου, Πτολεμαίου δὲ ναυάρχου, Λυσιμάχου δὲ γαζοφύλακος, Ἀγαθοκλέους δὲ τοῦ Σικελιώτου νησιάρχου. Gruen 1985, 259–60 is probably correct to date the anecdote in the 290s, but this is irrelevant to my argument.

57 As we saw in the second section, above, Plutarch's sources had painted a picture for the honours of 307 which clearly included strokes belonging to later periods of Demetrius' rule, especially after 304.

ADEIMANTUS OF LAMPSACUS AND THE DEVELOPMENT OF THE EARLY HELLENISTIC *PHILOS*

Shane Wallace

The Hellenistic period is replete with examples of individuals who, in the service of a king, acted as links between him and the cities under him (Savalli-Lestrade 1998 and Paschidis 2008). These individuals are frequently called 'friends' (*philoi*). The term was not defined until the late Hellenistic period, but in the late fourth and early third centuries it denotes an individual whose high-standing in the royal administration was based on his personal bonds with the king. There are no set criteria for what constitutes a *philos*, but for the purposes of this paper I follow Paschidis (2008, 25 n. 4), who uses *philos* 'to include all the occupants of the higher positions of royal administrations, whether our sources call them *expressis verbis* φίλοι or not'. *Philoi* were also often described as flatterers (*kolakes*) and their relationship with the king was presented as one of hollow sycophancy. This image, however, is deliberately pejorative. Such *kolakes* were frequently powerful and important individuals who served royal power and received gain because of it. Their relationship with the king was predominantly personal, and criticised because of this, but ultimately based on their ability and usefulness (Herman 1980–1981).

Some *philoi* are particularly well known and their individual importance as ties between city and king can be traced. Callicrates of Samos, a Ptolemaic admiral of the mid-third century, is one such case and Peter Bing (2002–2003) has recently explored the multifarious ways in which he bridged the gap between city and king by integrating old Greece with the new Hellenistic world.[1] However, Callicrates' example is unusual. In the vast majority of cases very little detail is known of the roles these *philoi* played in facilitating contact between city and king. This is particularly true for the formative early Hellenistic period, when contemporary literary sources are almost non-existent. Important and high-ranking individuals such as Nicomedes of Cos and Sostratus of Cnidus are known through the preservation of numerous civic decrees in their honour (see last section below), but since these decrees rarely offer detailed accounts of their actions we remain ignorant of the various roles they assumed in their dealings with the Greek cities and the ways in which the cities integrated them into their political and cultural life. In this regard the example of Adeimantus of Lampsacus is exceptional. A courtier of Demetrius Poliorcetes in the late fourth and early third centuries, Adeimantus is an early Hellenistic *philos* about whom a relatively large and diverse number of literary and epigraphic sources are preserved (Robert 1946; Billows 1990, App. 3 no. 1). These sources detail the tension between and intersection of his multiple identities as royal *philos* and civic official and they elucidate the ways in which Adeimantus moved between civic and royal office, acting always as a nexus between Demetrius and the Greek cities under his control.

Both Louis Robert (1946) and Franca Landucci Gattinoni (2000) have stressed Adeimantus' closeness to Demetrius and concluded that he was one of the king's most high-ranking and trusted associates. In this paper I develop their work by focusing on Adeimantus' closeness to and engagement with the Greek cities under Demetrius. First, I analyse the literary evidence for his career and explore what this tells us about the means by which Adeimantus as royal *philos* interacted with Athens. Secondly, I turn to the epigraphic evidence and outline the duality of Adeimantus' roles as *philos* of Demetrius and *proedros* (president) of his and his father's Hellenic League of 302/1. Dwelling on Adeimantus' letter to Demetrius from Delphi (*CID* IV 11), I offer a new interpretation of both its contents and historical context. Thirdly, I examine Adeimantus' career as a case-study for the wider phenomenon of the royal *philos* in the early Hellenistic period. His example is exceptional because the evidence for his career offers a uniquely detailed view of the sophisticated methods of interaction that existed between city and king in the late fourth century.

The Literary Evidence: Adeimantus at Athens

> Among the flatterers (*kolakes*), then, of king Demetrius, those associated with Adeimantus of Lampsacus erected a temple (*naos*) and set up statues (*agalmata*) at Thria, naming them from Aphrodite Phila; they also called the place Philaion after Phila, the wife of Demetrius, as Dionysius the son of Tryphon says in the tenth book of his *Onomastikon*.
>
> Ath. 6.255c

Athenaeus refers to a section from the tenth book of the work *On Names* by Dionysius, son (or student) of Tryphon, a Greek grammarian of the first century AD. Adeimantus is described as a flatterer who consecrated at the Athenian deme of Thria, near Eleusis, divine statues and a temple called the Philaion in honour of Demetrius' wife Phila, here Phila-Aphrodite.[2]

Although Adeimantus is called a *kolax*, his high-rank and closeness to Demetrius are revealed through the nature of his flatteries: the erection of a temple, the Philaion, and the dedication of cult statues to Phila-Aphrodite both imply a close, personal connection to the entire royal family and emphasises Adeimantus' standing within the royal court.[3] Further, the consecration on Athenian land of a temple and cult statues to a queen, even if part of a personal rather than public cult, intimates a degree of influence over the city and a strong association with it.

Paschalis Paschidis (2008, 366 n. 6, citing Habicht 1970, 43–44) has recently questioned Dionysius' testimony by arguing that, since temples were rarely erected for rulers, a *naos* for a queen would be strange. But temples for queens were erected: Harpalus allegedly erected a shrine (*hieron*), precinct (*temenos*), temple (*naos*), and altar (*bōmos*) for his courtesan Pythionike-Aphrodite (Theopomp.Hist. *FGH* 115 F 253), a *temenos* for queen Phila stood on Samos shortly after 306 (*IG* 12 (6) 1, 150, ll. 23–24), Callicrates of Samos erected a *naos* for Arsinoe-Cypris in Egypt in the late 270s or early 260s (see below), as did Epichares in Rhamnous in 268 (see below), while Ptolemy Philadelphus dedicated shrines (*hiera*) and temples (*naoi*) to his courtesan Bilistiche-Aphrodite in Alexandria some time before 246 (Plu. *Mor.* 753e; Ogden 2008). An important piece of evidence allows us to propose a date for Adeimantus' temple to Phila-Aphrodite. In a fragment of a play by the comic poet Alexis (Ath. 6.254a) a character offers a toast to king Antigonus, his son Demetrius, and Phila-Aphrodite in honour of a victory, probably that of Salamis in early 306 (Arnott 1996, 309–10; Habicht 2006, 426 n. 31). The passage should be dated to 306 or shortly thereafter and reveals the institution of a cult to Phila-Aphrodite at this time. Further, it suggests that Adeimantus' temple to Phila-Aphrodite most likely dates to 307–305.[4]

An as yet fully unpublished inscription from Rhamnous in honour of one Adeimantus, probably but not certainly to be identified with our Lampsacian, is of importance here.[5] The editor, Basileos Petrakos, has published two non-consecutive sentences without line numbers or breaks:

> Adeimantus was [appoint]ed ([καταστ]αθεὶς) general of the [countryside] by king Demetrius [for two] years.
> When war was pres[sing from all sides he overs]aw the collection [of grain].
>
> Petrakos 1993, 7 (*SEG* XLIII 27)[6]

The general of the countryside (στρατηγὸς ἐπὶ τὴν χώραν) was an Athenian military office of considerable importance. Demetrius' appointment ([καταστ]αθεὶς) of Adeimantus to this office, without election, and his specification that it was for two years undermined Athens' democratic rotation of offices, more so if Adeimantus had not previously been awarded Athenian citizenship. However, since Petrakos has dated Adeimantus' term of office to the years 306/5 and 305/4,[7] when Demetrius was fighting at Salamis, Egypt, and Rhodes, we should understand Adeimantus' appointment in the context of the Four Years War (307–304), during which time Athens was defending itself from the repeated incursions of Cassander (Habicht 2006, 92–94). By making Adeimantus an Athenian general, Demetrius ensured that royal power was directly involved in the defence of Greece and Athens during these dangerous years. Moreover, by designating control to Adeimantus in his absence, Demetrius revealed Adeimantus' pre-eminence within the Antigonid circle at this time. His appointment certainly undermined the civic rotation of offices, but it also reveals the care with which Demetrius sought to structure royal power within the legal parameters of civic office. Adeimantus did not have to be made an Athenian *stratēgos*,[8] but his designation as such can be seen to reflect the synergistic integration of royal power and civic authority.

Adeimantus' years as *stratēgos* (306/5–305/4), as dated by Petrakos, correlate to the probable years of the cult of Phila-Aphrodite and provide a plausible context for his erection of a *naos* to the queen at Thria, near Eleusis. A point of concern, however, is that as general of the countryside Adeimantus was honoured and presumably based at Rhamnous, not Eleusis. By the mid-third century – from at least 268/7 onwards – two generals for the countryside were appointed: the general of the countryside (στρατηγὸς ἐπὶ τὴν χώραν), based at Eleusis, and the general of the coast (στρατηγὸς ἐπὶ τὴν παραλίαν), based at Rhamnous (Oliver 2007, 164–67). Although there is no solid evidence for such as division in the late fourth century, Graham Oliver (2007, 165) has suggested that the appointment of an unknown Athenian as general of the countryside with control over Sounion, Rhamnous, and the rest of the coast hints at some form of regionalised division in the final years of the fourth century (*IG* 2^2 1260, ll. 21–23). Another unpublished inscription from Rhamnous honours Cephisophon of Conthyle, Adeimantus' successor as general of the countryside in 304/3 (Petrakos 1993, 7; 1999, 33). The erection in Rhamnous of the honorary inscriptions for both Adeimantus and Cephisophon would seem to suggest that both held regionalised generalships of the coast. However, it is also possible that Adeimantus was general at Eleusis one year and at Rhamnous the other year, as was later the case with Aristeides of Lamptrai in 268/7 and 267/6.[9] Adeimantus' case was in every way unique. As he was appointed directly by the king for two consecutive years, it would be illogical to assume that the remit of his authority was strictly limited to coastal Attica, particularly since the heaviest fighting of the Four Years War took place in the area around Eleusis (Paus. 1.26.3), specifically Phyle and Panacton (Plu. *Demetr.* 23.2), Oropus (*ISE* 8; *SEG* XXXVI 165, ll. 19–22; Paschidis 2008, 90–93), and perhaps Salamis (Polyaen. 4.11.1; Paus. 1.35.2). In light of this, and since strictly regionalised divisions were not apparent in the late fourth century, it is also possible that Adeimantus held authority simultaneously over both the countryside at Eleusis and the coast at Rhamnous.

Thria, the location of the Philaion, was situated very near Eleusis with both demes being closely connected in the late fourth century, even sharing an agora (*IG* 2^2 2500). If we can posit Adeimantus' presence at Eleusis for some period of the two years of his generalship in 306/5–305/4, the probable years of the cult of Phila-Aphrodite, then it could well have been at this time and in this capacity that he consecrated at Thria the *naos* and *agalmata* to Phila-Aphrodite.[10]

Two early Hellenistic examples support this argument. First, a series of epigrams by Posidippus relates to the temple (*naos* or *hieron*) of Arsinoe-Cypris (i.e. Aphrodite) erected by the Ptolemaic admiral Callicrates of Samos on Cape Zephyrion, east of Alexandria, in the late 270s or early 260s.[11] Secondly, a recent emendation to the text of *IRhamn* 3, in honour of Epichares, Athenian general of the coast in 268/7, reveals that he had erected a *hieron* to the same Arsinoe in the area of Rhamnous.[12] In both cases an individual, whether royal admiral or civic general, consecrates a temple to a queen. Both temples are located in the countryside and both reflect the focus of each dedicant's office. Callicrates' temple to Arsinoe makes her the patron of the Ptolemaic navy he commands (Robert 1966, 201–02; Bing 2002–2003, 264–66), while Epichares' temple to Arsinoe at Rhamnous, the epicentre of his generalship, symbolises the importance of Ptolemaic naval support in aiding his and Athens' defence of Rhamnous during the

Chremonidean War – Ptolemaic military support is explicitly praised within Epichares' honorary decree (*IRhamn* 3, ll. 21–25).[13] The erection of temples to Arsinoe reveals not only the dedicant's personal affiliation with royal power but also the importance of that power's support in the attainment, maintenance, and completion of the dedicant's office.

Adeimantus' temple to Phila-Aphrodite draws a similar connection between royal patronage and civic office. Located at Thria, near Eleusis, the epicentre of the regional generalship of the countryside, it marks a strong statement on Demetrius' royal patronage of Adeimantus' civic position as Athenian *stratēgos*, while similarly revealing Adeimantus' prominent position within Athenian political life. If consecrated during his generalship in 306/5–305/4, the temple also displays the importance of Demetrius' continuing patronage of Athens and its freedom at a time when the city was threatened by strong external forces: in Adeimantus' case, Phila's brother Cassander during the Four Years War; in Epichares', Antigonus Gonatas during the Chremonidean War. Dedicated to Phila-Aphrodite, the temple ultimately displays Adeimantus' closeness to the royal court and his personal connection with the king and his family. By consecrating a temple to Phila, Demetrius' queen, wife, and mother of his son Antigonus Gonatas, rather than to his mistresses Lamia and Leaina, as the Athenians were later to do (see below), Adeimantus was drawing upon the legitimacy and authority of the royal family, perhaps even the developing dynasty, as a means of enforcing his standing in both Athens and the Antigonid circle during Demetrius' absence from Greece.

Adeimantus was also himself the recipient of cult honours in Athens. A passage of Demochares' *Histories*, preserved in Athenaeus, records that the Athenians erected temples to Leaina-Aphrodite and Lamia-Aphrodite, as well as altars, hero-shrines, and libations to Demetrius' flatterers Bourichus, Adeimantus, and Oxythemis, in whose honour paeans were sung. Such honours were not pleasing to Demetrius who considered that the Athenians had debased themselves in comparison with their ancestors.

> Demochares, at any rate, a relative of the orator Demosthenes, tells a story in the twentieth book of his *Histories* of the flattering conduct (*kolakeiai*) of the Athenians towards Demetrius Poliorcetes, and says that it was not to his liking. He writes as follows: 'Some of these things, it is plain, annoyed him, but other acts were downright disgraceful and humiliating, such as temples to Leaina-Aphrodite and Lamia-Aphrodite, and altars (*bōmoi*), shrines (*hērōa*), and libations (*spondai*) to Bourichus, Adeimantus, and Oxythemis, his flatterers (*kolakes*). To every one of these, paeans were chanted, so that even Demetrius himself was amazed at these actions, and declared that not a single Athenian of his time had shown himself great and fine in soul'.
>
> Ath. 6.253a = Democh. *FGH* 75 F 1

Demochares, nephew of Demosthenes, played a leading role in the democratic regime of 307–304 until his opposition to Demetrius' increasingly tyrannical actions led to his exile in 304/3. A first-hand witness who would have been personally acquainted with both Demetrius and Adeimantus, Demochares' account is important but not without bias. His focus is neither Demetrius nor his courtiers, but Athens, which acts as the sycophantic flatterer of Demetrius' sycophantic flatterers.[14] By emphasising Athens' debasement and Demetrius' disgust, Demochares presents himself as the lone voice of reason and piety.

The heroic honours offered to Bourichus, Adeimantus, and Oxythemis reveal them to have been more than just royal flatterers. In the late fourth and third centuries cities offered honours to individuals in thanks for or in pursuance of benefactions (Habicht 1970, 236–42; Gauthier 1985, 46–49, 62–65). The exemplary semi-divine nature of Athens' honours to three of Demetrius' *philoi* implies that their action was of exceptional significance to the city.[15] Their heroic honours manifest their ability to perform heroic benefactions, an ability dependent on their position as royal *philoi*. Bourichus, Adeimantus, and Oxythemis appear as conduits of civic concerns and royal power and they draw upon their position as royal *philoi* to act as civic *euergetai*. Establishing a date and context for the heroic honours is difficult. Mikalson (1998, 88) suggests that they were passed by the *ekklesia* in 302/1, but we do not know for certain their year nor whether they were public or private. Demochares' account implies that all three individuals received the same honours from the Athenians, suggesting that they were honoured together for a single action worthy of heroisation. All were present in and active on behalf of Athens between 304–301 and Habicht (1970, 55–58, 255–56) has argued convincingly that their honours date from 302/1.[16] If so, then these honours may have been voted by Athens and connected with the Hellenic League of 302/1, of which Athens was a leading member (see next section below).

Despite the apparently negative and sycophantic image of Adeimantus presented within the accounts of Dionysius and Demochares, it is clear that he maintained an exceptionally high standing with Demetrius Poliorcetes and the city of Athens. His status as *philos* of the king led to his appointment as Athenian *stratēgos*, in which role he may have consecrated the Philaion to Phila-Aphrodite. There were numerous interconnected layers to Adeimantus' career. With the assumption of the royal title by Antigonus and Demetrius, he held an intimate position within the court, while as civic *stratēgos* he was integrated into the Athenian political and military establishment. His dedication of the Philaion and his heroic honours reveal his standing as civic benefactor and display also his religious integration into the civic landscape. As *proedros* of the Hellenic League, Adeimantus would continue to operate as a nexus of civic and royal concerns.

The Epigraphic Evidence: Adeimantus and the Hellenic League

In the spring of 304, after his unsuccessful siege of Rhodes, Demetrius returned to Greece. He forced Cassander to withdraw past Thermopylae before, in late 304 or early 303 (see Paschidis 2008, 90–95), invading the Peloponnese in a whirlwind campaign that removed Cassander's troops from almost the entire peninsula. In order to formalise the power structure between himself and his new Greek allies, Demetrius called a meeting of representatives from each city and founded at the Isthmian games of spring 302 a league of Greek states in the image of the long defunct Corinthian League of Philip and

Alexander. Plutarch, in his *Life of Demetrius*, refers to the foundation of Antigonus' and Demetrius' Hellenic League: 'at the Isthmus of Corinth, where a general assembly (*koinon synedrion*) was held and throngs of people came together, Demetrius was proclaimed commander-in-chief (*hēgemōn*) of the Greeks' (Plu. *Demetr.* 25.3).

A substantial portion of the League charter is preserved from Epidaurus and offers a detailed picture of its administrative organisation.[17] Although the League (*symmachia*) operated differently during times of peace and war, its basic structure remained unchanged. At the top were the kings (*basileis*) Antigonus and Demetrius – contrary to Plutarch the charter does not refer to them as *hēgemōnes*. Both kings held equal authority but in practice Demetrius ruled in Greece and so exercised direct royal control over the League. The central administrative body, the *koinon synedrion*, consisted of *synedroi* (representatives) elected and sent by member states. The *synedrion* debated motions and passed *dogmata*, which were then binding over member states; *synedroi* were un-accountable at home for decisions taken in the *synedrion*. Overseeing the *synedrion* was the board of *proedroi* (presidents) who decided on what motions it was to debate and for how long it was to sit. In peacetime five were chosen by lot from among the *synedroi* and were accountable to it for their actions; in wartime the kings were permitted to appoint any number of *proedroi* themselves.[18] Acting in conjunction with the *proedroi* and maintaining similar powers was the *stratēgos*, Demetrius' direct representative who maintained royal interests and presumably held military control over League troops during the king's absence. In peacetime the League met at the Panhellenic Games; in wartime the location, frequency, and duration of meetings were decided by the royal *proedroi* and the king or, in his absence, his *stratēgos*.

Consisting of kings, *stratēgos*, *proedroi*, *synedroi*, and the individual *poleis*, *ethnē*, and alliances they represented, the League was a mix of interests and influences over which constantly shifting degrees of control, concession, and interaction had to be exercised. This was achieved not only by the king but also by his *philoi* and partisans within the allied cities and his *stratēgos* and *proedroi* within the League. Adeimantus provides one case study for this process.

> [Since Adeimantus acted] in [earlier times saying and] doing whatever good [he could for the] Athenian *dēmos*, and now, having been ap[pointed (κ[ατασταθεὶς]) by] king Demetrius as *proedros* [in the] *koinon synedrion*, continues to act in the best interests of the kings, [the *dēmos* of] the Athenians, and the other [allies, he] called together [all] the Greeks [to] the *koinon synedrion* [at the Isthmus with] the Athenians and the other allies, [and acting as *proedros*] he proposed a motion on these matters [---]. It was resolved by the *synedroi*, that if ever [someone attacks an ally] all the [allies] are to help [with] arms... etc.
>
> *Ath.Agora* XVI 122, ll. 3–17

Adeimantus is honoured with a gold crown (ll. 25–26) for acting in Athens' interests while *proedros* of the League. The mention of the *koinon synedrion* and Demetrius' selection of Adeimantus as *proedros* dates the decree between spring 302 and autumn 301, but since no dating formulae are preserved it is impossible to suggest a precise context. Martin (1996) argued that it refers to events after Demetrius' departure for Asia in autumn 302,[19] but it perhaps more likely refers to the foundation of the League at the Isthmus in spring 302, in which case it shows that Adeimantus was entrusted by Demetrius with the unique role of convening and establishing the League itself. As with his earlier position as general of the countryside, Adeimantus is once again appointed (κ[ατασταθεὶς]) to an office by Demetrius. As *proedros*, Adeimantus called a (the founding?) meeting of the League and proposed a *dogma* of some apparent interest to Athens – perhaps a resolution inaugurating the League – which was then passed by the *synedroi*.[20]

The decree displays the authority that was invested in the position of *proedros* and was employed by Adeimantus to Athens' advantage. The League charter habitually refers to the *proedroi* operating as a board. It tells us that *proedroi* could call meetings, choose their location, frequency and duration, and decide on what was to be debated; they could introduce motions, lead the debate, discipline members, and ensure order; they validated and drafted *dogmata* before forwarding them to the secretaries while keeping copies themselves (*SV* 446, ll. 67–87). The Athens decree, however, shows that Adeimantus could employ by himself the full range of a *proedros*' powers. He called a meeting of the *synedrion*, which he would then have chaired, proposed a motion for debate, validated and drafted the resulting decision before then issuing it as a League *dogma*. The Athens decree reveals the control that could be exercised over the League by a royally-appointed *proedros*, emphasised more so because Adeimantus does not appear to have had his power curtailed by four other *proedroi*. That Adeimantus had the ability to act with such impunity reveals the degree of trust Demetrius had in him and the influence that he as an individual had over both the League and its member states.

Adeimantus also appears as *proedros* in his fragmentary letter to Demetrius, preserved at Delphi. The text survives on one face of a rectangular block – frag. A – that originally formed part of a monumental pillar at least three metres high and dating to the 170s.[21] This pillar, of which five blocks survive, was likely dedicated to king Perseus and surmounted by a bronze statue of him. On it was inscribed a catalogue of texts recording the history of Delphic-Antigonid relations. That Adeimantus' letter was the uppermost inscribed text suggests that it was the earliest noteworthy document pertaining to Antigonid relations with the Delphic Amphictyony. In 1994 a second inscribed block from this pillar – frag. B – was found which recorded a treaty between Demetrius and Aetolia from 289 (*ed. pr.* Lefèvre 1998b, with commentary, photo and French translation). However, the first fifteen highly fragmentary lines of this inscription do not relate to the treaty and appear instead to be the last lines of either Adeimantus' letter to Demetrius or the king's reply. Fragments A and B (ll. 1–15) were recently published by Francois Lefèvre as *CID* IV 11. It is cautionary to remember that the text as we have it is a second century re-inscription, with revisions, perhaps, of a document from the late fourth century (Lefèvre 2002, 81 n. 109).

> Adeimantus to king Demetrius, greetings. I have sent to you, just as you wished, the decree (ψήφισμα) which the Amphictyones made la[st ye]ar, having proposed it (προθέντες) at the Isthmia and validated (ἐπικυρώσα[ντες]) it in Delphi. [Similarly], I enclose the letters from your friends, in order that you may follow the things [resolv]ed ([δεδογμέν]ον) by each of them. The letters have been inscribed on a stele and erected according to the *dogma* which we passed in the s[*ynedrion*] and the things.... [privileges] from the Amphictyones...
>
> (*CID* IV 11, fr. A)

The letter dates from 302/1 and records matters relating to the Hellenic League, as is revealed by terms such as Isthmia, *synedrion*, and *dogma*. However, a precise context has not been provided for it, nor an explanation of its contents given.

The Amphictyonic Council has just met in Delphi and validated a decree (ψήφισμα). Since the Council met twice a year, spring at Thermopylae and autumn at Delphi, our meeting must be the autumn meeting of either 302/1 or 301/0. As the Hellenic League was defunct by Antigonus' and Demetrius' defeat at Ipsus in late 301, our meeting is almost certainly that of autumn 302/1. This is revealed by the proposal of the Amphictyonic decree at the Isthmia 'last year', which must refer to the founding meeting of the Hellenic League at the Isthmian Games the previous calendar year, in spring 303/2 (Robert 1946, 20, 25–27). A more precise date is possible. The Pythian Games took place in the third year of an Olympic cycle. Since Olympic one began in summer 304/3 then Olympic three began in summer 302/1, with the Pythian Games scheduled for Delphi in autumn 302/1.[22] The Amphictyonic meeting at Delphi in autumn 302/1 was also, therefore, the occasion of the Pythian Games. This synchronism, originally spotted by Luigi Moretti (1975, 4), has gone ignored and its significance has not yet been explored.[23]

The charter of the Hellenic League records that during peacetime the *synedrion* was to meet at the Panhellenic games (*SV* 446, ll. 66–67), a routine probably also convenient during wartime. If so, then the Pythian Games of autumn 302 were also the occasion for a second meeting of the Hellenic League, which means that Adeimantus' presence there and his liaisons with the Amphictyonic Council have implications for our understanding of the function of the League and the interaction of its various parts. Taking advantage of their presence together and using the occasion to show their support for Demetrius and the League, the Amphictyonic Council proposed a decree (ψήφισμα) at the Isthmian games in spring 302. Since their meeting at the Isthmia was extraordinary, the Council only ratified this decree at their next scheduled meeting at the Pythian Games in Delphi, when the *synedrion* of the Hellenic League was also scheduled to meet. That Demetrius expressed an interest in the outcome of the Amphictyonic decree and Adeimantus saw fit to forward it to him reveals that the decree was of some concern to both Demetrius and the League itself. Robert's suggestion (1946, 26–27) that it referred to the acceptance of Demetrius' hegemony and the authority of the League is plausible, though a connection with Aetolia cannot be ruled out since fr. B mentions the Aetolians (*CID* IV 11 fr. B, l.13).

Since Adeimantus' letter dates to during or shortly after the Pythian Games of autumn 302 and is connected with meetings of the Amphictyonic and Hellenic Leagues, it is almost certain that Adeimantus was present in Delphi in his official capacity as *proedros* of the Hellenic League.[24] In this capacity he engaged with the Amphictyonic Council, one of the supra-*polis* bodies that made up the Hellenic League, and liaised with king, *synedrion*, and League members. He concerned himself with the resolutions of individual member-states and kept the king informed of them, thus ensuring that royal interests were represented.

Adeimantus also dispatched to Demetrius 'the letters from your friends' (τὰς παρὰ τῶν φίλων ἐπιστολάς) in order that he could follow the things resolved ([δεδογμέν]ον) by his *philoi*. The restoration [δεδογμέν]ον (Jacquemin *et al.* 1995, 131; Lefèvre 2002, 79), if correct, connects the *philoi* with League officials and suggests that their letters are League *dogmata*, passed by the *synedrion* but drawn up, published, and dispatched to the king by his *philoi-proedroi*, albeit via Adeimantus. That these letters are recent and most likely relate to the meeting of the Hellenic League at the Pythian Games is revealed by the fact that they are to be inscribed and published on a *stele* in accordance with the *dogma* passed by the *synedrion* at the Isthmian Games, the founding meeting of the Hellenic League, and forwarded by Adeimantus to Demetrius with the validated Amphictyonic decree. I would suggest that the *epistolai* are in fact *dogmata* of the Hellenic League, passed at a League meeting during the recent Pythian Games, and that the *philoi* are League officials, probably the wartime *proedroi* appointed by Demetrius.[25] The *philoi* are therefore Adeimantus' fellow *proedroi*; they may even be Bourichus and Oxythemis, whom together with Adeimantus received heroic honours in Athens (see above first section). It remains speculative, but these honours may have resulted from actions on Athens' behalf taken by them together in their official capacity as League *proedroi*. Whoever they are, Adeimantus' fellow *proedroi* were not mentioned in the Athenian decree – if the decree refers to the foundation of the League in spring 302 then the other *proedroi* may not yet have been selected. In the Delphic letter, however, Adeimantus' fellow *proedroi* are shown to have overseen the resolution of League *dogmata* and ensured their publication on stone in accordance with League procedure. These *dogmata* were then collected by Adeimantus and sent, along with the Amphictyonic decree, to Demetrius.[26]

Franca Landucci Gattinoni (2000, 222–23) argued that Adeimantus held the office of *proedros* to the detriment of his fellow *proedroi* since they are not mentioned in either the Athenian decree or Delphic letter. However, on my reading, the Delphic letter shows Adeimantus interacting with the other wartime *proedroi* and when he writes of 'the *dogma* which we passed in the *synedrion*' he reveals the collective of authority of all *proedroi* in validating *dogmata*. Nonetheless, Adeimantus remains pre-eminent. He collects the *dogmata* from his fellow *proedroi* and forwards them to the king. He alone monopolises the lines of communication with Demetrius.

Philos and *Proedros*

As *proedros*, Adeimantus served a vitally important role in creating and maintaining Demetrius' authority in Greece. When the king departed for Asia in summer 302, control of the League and the defence of Greece were apparently entrusted to Adeimantus, the first man in Antigonid Greece after the king.[27] As with his appointment as Athenian *stratēgos*, Adeimantus' actions as *proedros* emphasise the extent of royal control over the League as well as the care with which Demetrius sought to justify this control within accountable, legal parameters. The League consisted of disparate parts welded into a whole. To the essentially bipartite structure of kings and *synedrion* was added the *stratēgos*, *proedroi*, and *synedroi*, as well as the *poleis*, *ethnē*, and alliances that they represented. Adeimantus was the human glue that held it all together, one of John Davies' 'human hinges of Hellenism' (2002, 11–12). He was present with Demetrius at the League's foundation at the Isthmia and later re-appears at Athens and Delphi as *proedros*. He liaises with the Amphictyonic Council, forwards its decisions to Demetrius, and acts as a physical bridge between the Amphictyonic and the Hellenic Leagues. He copied both Amphictyonic decrees and League *dogmata* to Demetrius and took an active part in publishing these *dogmata* on stone, presumably in the Panhellenic sanctuaries.

Adeimantus was also honoured at Eretria with citizenship and a bronze statue for his goodwill towards the Greeks and Eretrians (*IG* 12 (9) 198; *IEretr.Decr*. XIII). The decree lacks dating formulae but its mention of 'the Greeks' denotes the Hellenic League and dates it between summer 302 and autumn 301.[28] It is perhaps connected with Demetrius' actions in early summer 302 when he circumvented Cassander' position at Thermopylae by sailing from Chalcis and landing behind him (D.S. 20.110.1–2). An Eretrian decree mentions citizen troops serving on Demetrius' ships, perhaps as part of League forces (*IG* 12 (9) 210; *IEretr.Decr*. XIV). As at Delphi, we can again imagine Adeimantus acting in his official role as *proedros*, liaising with Eretria, overseeing the League in action, and ensuring the safety of Eretrian citizens and League troops. His success and importance are revealed through the high standard of honours awarded him. Adeimantus manifests the League in action, and at Delphi, Eretria, and Athens we see him using his position as *proedros* to offer a closer, more personal, connection between king and city.

Adeimantus' authority did not stem solely from his position as *proedros*. To the Greek cities he was first and foremost a royal *philos*; his position as *proedros* was a manifestation of this status and it was from his relationship with Demetrius that he ultimately drew his authority. Adeimantus owed his positions as *stratēgos* at Athens and *proedros* of the League to his status as *philos* of Demetrius, and in both cases he is said to have been appointed directly (κατασταθεὶς) by the king. The situation is reflected in that of the brothers Hippodamus and Hippostratus of Miletus, each of whom, as *philos* of king Lysimachus, was appointed (κατασταθεὶς) *stratēgos* of the Ionian cities.[29] Again, personal connections with the king lead to one's appointment to office.

As an individual, Adeimantus was not unique, either in the early Hellenistic period or in the Antigonid court. Other high ranking *philoi* are known but the evidence for them does not allow the depth of analysis that it does for Adeimantus. Nicomedes of Cos, for example, was a high-ranking courtier of Antigonus Monophthalmus closely involved with the king's diplomatic relations, specifically embassies between the king and the cites under his control (Billows 1990, App. 3 no. 82; Paschidis 2008, 361–65). He is known through twenty-six honorary decrees passed by cities of the Aegean and western Asia Minor.[30] However, these decrees are all fragmentary and none of them preserves specific details of the means by which he facilitated relations between king and city. Perhaps the only early Hellenistic *philos* about whom a diversity of sources exists comparable to those pertaining to Adeimantus is Sostratus of Cnidus, a high-ranking Ptolemaic courtier of the early third century.[31] He dedicated either the Pharos lighthouse or the statue of Zeus atop it (Bing 1998), was honoured at Delos by the Nesiotic (*IG* 11 (4) 1038) and Delian Leagues (*IG* 11 (4) 563), Caunus (*IG* 11 (4) 1130), and by one Etearchus of Cyrene (*IG* 11 (4) 1190). He was honoured at Delphi (*FD* III 1 299; *CID* IV 26) where he also dedicated a statue to Arsinoe (Amandry 1940–1941, 63–65 no. 3). Further, he acted as Ptolemaic ambassador to negotiate with Demetrius and Athens in early 287 (*SEG* XXVIII 60, ll. 32–36) and later with Antigonus Gonatas (S.E. *M.* 1.276). However, Sostratus' role as an agent of interaction between city and king remains largely unknown, because, as with Nicomedes, the decrees in his honour rarely preserve specific details regarding his relations with and actions on behalf of the Greek cities. We simply do not know the ways in which he integrated civic and royal concerns, the offices or positions he assumed in his dealings with the Greek cities, or the means by which he struck the delicate balance between royal control and civic authority.

The evidence for Adeimantus allows us to explore in unique depth not only the means by which royal *philoi* integrated civic and royal concerns but also the multiplicity of roles they could assume in negotiating the tension between the intersection of royal power and civic authority. To the Greek cities Adeimantus was first and foremost a royal *philos*, from which all others positions stemmed. To many he was also *proedros* of the Hellenic League and he switched between both roles when needed. In the Delphic letter he recounts actions undertaken in his professional capacity as *proedros* but he writes to Demetrius in his personal capacity as *philos*. He also maintained personal connections with individual cities, thus embedding himself more deeply within the *polis* structure. At Athens, his selection by Demetrius as *stratēgos* afforded him military influence while his own heroisation and his consecration of a temple to Phila-Aphrodite integrated him into the city's cultic landscape. Further, as recipient of a copy of Theophrastus' will, he was also part of the city's socio-cultural life (D.L. 5.57).[32] His celebrity throughout the Hellenic world cannot be underestimated. When Strabo (13.1.19) lists the most famous sons of Lampsacus – 'Charon the historian, Adeimantus, Anaximenes the rhetor, and Metrodorus the friend of Epicurus' –, Adeimantus alone appears without description; three centuries after his lifetime he remained by himself 'un homme bien connu' (Robert 1946, 31–32). Adeimantus' career displays the fluidity of the status of royal *philos* and the numerous ways in which the Greek cities integrated and authorised such *philoi* and the royal power they personified. His specific example reveals the depth and sophistication of king-city relations from as early as the late fourth century and as such provides a uniquely informative case-study for the development of the early Hellenistic *philos*.[33]

Abbreviations

BD Bagnall, R. S. and P. Derow (2004) *Historical Sources in Translation: The Hellenistic Period*. London.

ProsPtol Peremans, W. and E. van't Dack (eds) (1968) *Prosopographia Ptolemaica. VI. La cour, les relations internationales et les possessions extérieures, la vie culturelle*. Leuven.

SV Schmitt, H. H. (1969) *Die Staatsverträge des Altertums*. II. Munich.

Bibliography

Amandry P. (1940–1941) Dédicaces delphiques, *Bulletin de correspondance hellénique* 64/65, 60–75.

Arnott, W. G. (1996) *Alexis: The Fragments. A Commentary*. Cambridge.

Asmonti, L. (2004) Il retore e il gabelliere. Il ruolo di Democare di Leuconoe nella trasmissione dell'ideale democratico, *Acme* 57, 25–42.

Austin, C., and G. Bastianini (2002) *Posidippi Pellaei quae supersunt omnia*. Milan.

Bickerman, E. (1963) Sur un passage d'Hypéride (*Epitaphios*, col. VIII), *Athenaeum* 41, 70–85.

Billows, R. A. (1990) *Antigonos the One-Eyed and the Creation of the Hellenistic State*. Berkeley.

Bing, P. (1998) Between Literature and the Monuments, In M. Annette Harder, R. F. Regtuit and G. C. Wakker (eds) *Genre in Hellenistic Poetry*, 21–43. Groningen.

Bing, P. (2002–2003) Posidippus and the Admiral: Kallikrates of Samos in the Milan Epigrams, *Greek, Roman, and Byzantine Studies* 43, 243–66.

Carney, E. (2000) The Initiation of Cult for Royal Macedonian Women, *Classical Philology* 95, 21–43.

Clinton, K. (2008) *Eleusis. The Inscriptions on Stone. Documents of the Sanctuary of the Two Goddesses and Public Documents of the Deme. II. Commentary*. Athens.

Daux, G. (1936) *Delphes au IIe et au Ier siècle*. Paris.

Daux, G. (1953–1954) Adeimantos de Lampsaque et le renouvellement de la ligue de Corinthe par Démétrios Poliorcète, *Αρχαιολογική Εφημερίς* 92/93, 245–54.

Davies, J. K. (2002) The Interpretation of Hellenistic Sovereignties. In D. Ogden (ed.) *The Hellenistic World: New Perspectives*, 1–21, London.

De Sanctis, G. (1941) Un decreto del sinedrio di Corinto, *Rivista di filologia e di istruzione classica* 69, 194–97.

Ferguson, W. S. (1911) *Hellenistic Athens: An Historical Essay*. New York.

Gauthier, P. (1985) *Les cités grecques et leurs bienfaiteurs (IVe–Ier siècle avant J.-C.). Contribution à l'histoire des institutions*. Paris.

Gorman, R. J. and V. B. Gorman (2000) The Tyrants around Thoas and Damasenor (Plut. *Q.G.* 32.298c–d), *Classical Quarterly* 50, 526–30.

Habicht, C. (1970) *Gottmenschentum und griechische Städte*. 2nd edn. Munich.

Habicht, C. (2006) *Athènes hellénistique: Histoire de la cite d'Alexandre le Grand à Marc Antoine*. 2nd edn. Paris (trans. from German).

Hauben, H. (1970) *Callicrates of Samos. A Contribution to the Study of the Ptolemaic Admiralty*. Leuven.

Herman, G. (1980–1981) The 'friends' of the Early Hellenistic Rulers: Servants or Officials?, *Talanta* 12/13, 103–49.

Jacquemin, A., D. Laroche and F. Lefèvre (1995) Delphes, le roi Persée et les Romains, *Bulletin de correspondance hellénique* 119, 125–36.

Knoepfler, D. (2001) *Eretria fouilles et recherches* XI. *Décrets érétrians de proxénie et de citoyenneté*. Lausanne.

Landucci Gattinoni, F. (2000) Il ruolo di Adimanto di Lampsaco nella *basileía* d Demetrio Poliorcete, *Papyrologica Lupensia* 9, 211–25.

Lefèvre, F. (1998a) *L'Amphictyonie Pyléo-Delphique: Histoire et Institutions*. Paris.

Lefèvre, F. (1998b) Traité de paix entre Démétrios Poliorcète et la confédération étolienne (fin 289?), *Bulletin de correspondance hellénique* 122, 109–41.

Lefèvre, F. (2002) *Corpus des inscriptions de Delphes*. IV. *Documents Amphictyoniques*. Paris.

Marasco, G. (1984) *Democare di Leuconoe: Politica e cultura in Atene fra IV e III sec. A.C.* Florence.

Martin, T. R. (1996) Adeimantos of Lampsakos and Demetrios Poliorketes' Fraudulent Peace of 302 BC. In R. W. Wallace and E. M. Harris (eds.) *Transitions to Empire. Essays in Honour of Ernst Badian*, 179–90, Oklahoma.

Mikalson, J. (1998) *Religion in Hellenistic Athens*. Berkeley.

Mooren, L. (1975) *The Aulic Titulature in Ptolemaic Egypt: Introduction and Prosopography*. Brussels.

Moretti, L. (1967–75) *Iscrizioni storiche ellenistiche*. 2 vols. Florence.

Müller, S. (2009) *Das hellenistische Königspaar in der medialen Repräsentation: Pyolemaios II. und Arsinoe II*. Berlin.

Ogden, D. (2008) Bilistiche and the Prominence of Courtesans in the Ptolemai Tradition. In P. McKechnie and P. Guillaume (eds) *Ptolemy Philadelphus and his World*, 353–85, Leiden.

Oliver, G. J. (2001) Regions and Micro-Regions: Grain for Rhamnous. In Z. Archibald, J. Davies, V. Gabrielsen and G. J. Oliver (eds) *Hellenistic Economies*, 137–55, London.

Oliver, G. J. (2007) *War, Food, and Politics in Early Hellenistic Athens*. Oxford.

Osborne, M. (2009) The Archons of Athens, 300/299–228/7, *Zeitschrift für Papyrologie und Epigraphik* 171, 83–99.

Paschidis, P. (2008) *Between City and King: Prosopographical Studies on the Intermediaries between the Cities of the Greek Mainland and the Aegean and the Royal Courts in the Hellenistic Period (322–190 BC)*. Athens.

Petrakos, B. (1993) Anaskaphes: Rhamnous, *Τὸ Ἔργον τῆς Ἀρχαιολογικῆς Ἑταιρείας* 40, 1–9.

Petrakos, B. (1999) *Ὁ Δήμος τὸυ Ραμνοῦντος* I: *Τοπογραφία*. Athens.

Petrakos, B. (2003) Anaskaphes: Rhamnous, *Τὸ Ἔργον τῆς Ἀρχαιολογικῆς Ἑταιρείας* 50, 13–16.

Robert, L. (1946) Adeimantos et la Ligue de Corinthe. Sur une inscription de Delphes, *Hellenica* 2, 15–33.

Robert, L. (1966) Sur un décret d'Ilion et sur un papyrus concernant des cultes royaux. In A. E. Samuel (ed.) *Essays in Honour of C. Bradford Welles*, 175–211, New Haven.

Roussel, P. (1923) Le renouvellement de la ligue de Corinthe en 302, *Revue archéologique*, 117–40.

Sánchez, P. (2001) *L'Amphictyonie des Pyles et de Delphes. Recherches sur son rôle historique, des origines au IIe siècle de notre ère*. Stuttgart.

Savalli-Lestrade, I. (1998) *Les Philoi Royaux dans l'Asie Hellénistique*. Geneva.

Shearl, T. L. (1978) *Kallias of Sphettos and the Revolt of Athens in 286 BC*. Princeton.

Sonnabend, H. (1996) *Die Freundschaften der Gelehrten und die zwischenstaatliche Politik im klassischen und hellenistischen Griechenland*. Hildesheim.

Steinhauer, G. (2009) A propos du décret de Rhamnonte en l'honneur d'Épichares. In A. Themos and N. Papazarkadas (eds) *Ἀττικαὶ Ἐπιγραφαί. Μελέτες πρὸς τιμὴν τοῦ Christian Habicht*, 193–200, Athens.

Wehrli, C. (1968) *Antigone et Démétrios*. Geneva.

Notes

1 On Callicrates, see *ProsPtol* 14607; Hauben 1970; Mooren 1975, 58–60, no. 10; Paschidis 2008, 393–96. Translations of literary sources are from the Loeb Classical Library.

2 Athenaeus says οἱ περὶ Ἀδείμαντον … νεὼν κατασκευασάμενοι καὶ ἀγάλματα ἱδρυσάμενοι, but this most likely refers to Adeimantus since οἱ περί τινα can, from at least the Roman period, be used periphrastically to refer to the τίνα (Gorman and Gorman 2000). A mid-third century example is *IEryth.* 31, ll. 21–22: οἱ περὶ Θαρσύνοντα καὶ Πυθῆν και Βοτ|τᾶν.

3 A *temenos* of Phila, another Philaion perhaps, existed on Samos post-306 (*IG* 12 (6) 1 150; Robert 1946, 30; cf. Paschidis 2008, 388 n. 4).

4 Ferguson 1911, 114–15 n. 7; Carney 2000, 31–32. Robert 1946, 31 n. 4 dated the cult and temple post-306, Martin 1996, 182, post-307 or around 304, and Arnott 1996, 309–11, 326–28, to 305.

5 The identification is accepted by Oliver 2007, 167–68, and Paschidis 2008, 89 n. 2, 112 n. 4, 451 n. 1. Knoepfler 2001, 220 n. 752 and Habicht 2006, 427 n. 38 feel that he is an Athenian officer.

6 See also Petrakos 1999, 32–33 (*SEG* XLIX 4). On the importance of grain collection at Rhamnous, see *IRhamn* 3 with Oliver 2001.

7 Habicht 2006, 427 n. 38 suggests an alternate date of 294/3–293/2, co-terminus with Olympiodorus' double archonship, on which see Habicht 2006, 106–08 (analysis); Osborne 2009, 85 (sources).

8 His appointment is probably an exception rather than the rule at this early time (Paschidis 2008, 112–13 n. 4). Other Antigonid officers are attested at Athens in 306/5: Polycleitus Athenaeus and Heraclei[..]s Erythraeus (*IG* 2^2 1492b, ll. 104–7, 115–17; Billows 1990, App. 3 no. 48 and 102; Paschidis 2008, 88–89).

9 Petrakos 2003, 15–16; Clinton 2008, 245: yet a third unpublished inscription from Rhamnous.

10 The Philaion may simply have been the sanctuary of Aphrodite at Daphni assimilated with queen Phila (Robert 1946, 30 n. 3; Paschidis 2008, 366 n. 6).

11 Posidipp.Epigr. 39,116,119 (Austin and Bastianini 2002). On this cult, see most recently Bing 2002–2003; Müller 2009, 215–16, 238–42, 266–80.

12 *IRhamn.* 3, ll. 15–16. Petrakos read τὸ ἱερὸν | τῆς [Νεμέσεω]ς κατασκευάσας; Steinhauer (2009) suggests τὸ ἱερὸν | τῆς [Ἀ]ρσ[ι]ν[ό]ης κατασκευάσας.

13 On Ptolemaic presence in Attica during the Chremonidean War, see Oliver 2007, 153–58.

14 'Beau thème pour un historien moralisateur ou rhéteur' (Robert 1946, 29 n. 4). On Democh. *FGH* 75 F 1 see Marasco 1984, 191–98; Asmonti 2004, 36–38.

15 Habicht 1970, 57–58. Adeimantus also received citizenship and a bronze statue from Eretria for certain unknown benefactions (*IEretr.Decr.* XIII; see below third section). On Athens' earlier heroic honours for Hephaestion, see Arr. *An.* 7.14.7; Hyp. *Epit.* 8.17–24; Bickerman 1963; Habicht 1970, 28–36.

16 *Bourichus*: D.S. 20.52.4; Billows 1990, App. 3 no. 26. *Oxythemis*: *IG* 2^2 558; Billows 1990, App. 3 no. 86. *Adeimantus*: *Ath.Agora* XVI 122; Billows 1990, App. 3 no. 1. Knoepfler 2001, 227–29 prefers the less likely 294–288.

17 *IG* 4^2 1 68; *SV* 446 (edition and commentary); *ISE* 44 (edition, Italian translation, commentary); *BD* 8 (English translation).

18 *SV* 446, ll. 76–77,91; Roussel 1923, 132–34; Robert 1946, 24; Landucci Gattinoni 2000, 222–23.

19 De Sanctis 1941 suggested that it refers to the defence of Elateia.

20 I thank Victor Alonso for his insightful comments here.

21 Daux 1936, 351 n. 2 (*ed. pr.*); Robert 1946 (fourth century date and context); Daux 1953–1954, 245–54 (new edition; photo of squeeze); *ISE* 72 (commentary; Italian translation); Jacquemin, Laroche, Lefèvre

1995 (new edition; commentary; French translation; focus on pillar and re-inscription in 170s); Lefèvre 1998a, 97–100, 351 (focus on Dephic Amphiktiony); Sánchez 2001, 270–74 (follows text of Jacquemin 1995 and analysis of Robert 1946).

22 On Amphictyonic meetings and the dating of the Pythian Games, see Lefèvre 1998a, 197–204.

23 Robert 1946, 27–28 recognised that 302/1 was a Pythian year but he did not draw the connection.

24 Lefèvre 1998a, 97–98; 2002, 82–83 suggests that Adeimantus was Demetrius' *hieromnemos*.

25 Robert 1946, 20; Wehrli 1968, 123, and Moretti 1975, 4 saw the *philoi* as Demetrius' partisans and officers, and the letters as congratulations on his proclamation as *hēgēmōn*. Savalli-Lestrade 1998, 276 n. 90 calls the *philoi* 'agents royaux, tels les stratèges et les πρόεδροι de la Ligue, nommés par les rois pendant toute la durée de la guerre'. She ascribes this view to Robert (1946, 22), but he had only identified Adeimantus as *proedros*.

26 An example of the League's provision that *proedroi* keep copies of *dogmata*, *SV* 446, ll. 80–1: τοὺς προέδρους…[τὰ] δόξαν[τα μεταδιδόναι] | τοῖς γραμματεῦσι, καὶ αὐτοὺς ε[ὔσημα ἀν]τίγροφα [ἔχοντ]ας.

27 Robert 1946, 29; Wehrli 1968, 123–24; Moretti 1967, 118; Knoepfler 2001, 226.

28 Robert 1946, 22; Moretti 1967, 19; Knoepfler 2001, 227–29.

29 *ISmyrna* 557 (Smyrna); *SIG* 368 (Miletus); *SEG* LVI 999 (Cos); *SEG* XXXV 926 (Chios).

30 Preserved on two opistographic stelae at Cos: *ICos* ED 71a-g, 162, 203; *IC* 18–19, 221. Paschidis 2008, 361–2 n. 3 provides a useful catalogue of the decrees.

31 *ProsPtol* 16555; Mooren 1975, 56–57, no. 8; Shear 1978, 23–25; Sonnabend 1996, 237–43, 251–53.

32 The will was brought by his son Androsthenes, indicating the family's integration into Athenian cultural life. Knoepfler 2001, 227–29 (cf. Paschidis 2008, 140) suggests that due to his connection with Theophrastus Adeimantus may have had a hand in Demetrius' decision to allow the return of the exiled oligarchs in 292/1 (D.H. *Din*. 3,9).

33 I would like to thank in particular the editors Victor Alonso Troncoso and Edward Anson. Earlier versions of this paper were presented at a Hellenistic Personalities workshop in Edinburgh and at the Irish Institute of Hellenic Studies in Athens. Andrew Erskine and Ioanna Kralli read drafts of this paper and I am grateful to them for their comments.

IRANIANS IN THE DIADOCHI PERIOD

Marek Jan Olbrycht

Introduction

In the scholarship,[1] the Diadochi are thought to be the only Macedonian commanders who fought for power after Alexander's death.[2] Missing from the lists of the Diadochi are usually even such Macedonian potentates as Peucestas and Peithon, whose role was of paramount importance for Iran.[3] As Diadochi, Iranians are never even spoken of. This is partly due to the fact that the classical sources lay emphasis on selected figures of Macedonians or Greeks from Alexander's entourage, while Iranians usually appear in the background. It is the main problem for the historian of the Diadochi epoch. For fresh evidence the scholar must turn to other source categories. The enduring mystery of Iranian culture has been compounded by the archaeological materials accumulated in recent decades.[4] Precious historical information is found in Babylonian sources (recorded from a Babylonian domestic perspective, see Stolper 2006; Boiy 2007) and in numismatic evidence (Houghton and Lorber 2002; Bopearachchi 2005).

In Achaemenid and post-Achaemenid times there were several Iranian peoples of significance, including Persians, Medes, Bactrians, Parthians, Sogdians and Arachosians in the areas of what today are Iran, Afghanistan, and Central Asia (Uzbekistan, Turkmenistan, and Tajikistan). In his seminal treatise *Geographika* Eratosthenes of Cyrene, drawing notably from the authors from the time of Alexander and the Diadochi, uses the name 'Ariane' as an ethnic designation for peoples on the Iranian plateau and in the adjacent regions of Afghanistan and Central Asia (in Str. 15.2.1–9; 2.1.22–33). He perceives 'the term Ariane as of a single ethnical group' (Str. 2.1.31), a phrase clearly implying a kind of community. Moreover, Eratosthenes highlights that the peoples of Ariane 'were speaking approximately the same language, with but slight variations' (in Str. 15.2.8). His definition of 'Ariane' is given in two versions: one embraces the lands between the Caspian Gates (near modern Tehran) and the Indus valley; the other, all the Iranian plataeu countries (including Persis and Media) and the Central Asian lands of Bactria as well as Sogdiana. The latter, more comprehensive approach defines exactly the extension of the lands of high-density Iranian habitation in Western and Central Asia in the post-Achaemenid period. Eratosthenes' usage of the notion 'Ariane' derives from Old Iranian **Āryana-* (Avestan *Airiiana-*). The closely related term *Ariya* was used by Achaemenid rulers, including Darius I and Xerxes, as defining their Iranian ('supra-

Persian') identity; the notion occurs in the phrases like *ariya*, *ariya ciça*, 'Arya, of Arya origin', and *pārsa*, *pārsahyā*, *puça ariya*, *ariyaciça*, 'a Persian, son of a Persian, Arya, of Arya origin' (Bailey 1987). The term 'Iranian' may also be understood as relating to cultural and religious traditions developed by Iranian-speaking peoples living in Western and Central Asia. An integral part of Iranian history formed Zoroastrianism with its local differentiation. Iranian cultural, religious and political influences affected some countries predominantly inhabited by ethnically non-Iranian peoples, including parts of Anatolia and Transcaucasia; this is why pursuing the Iranians' role in the Diadochi period leads inevitably to the part played by the Iranians satraps and dynasts ruling in Armenia, Cappadocia and Pontus.

I am dealing with states in transition and changing political processes in extended geographical spaces. Thus, this chapter neither claims to give a full picture of the period, nor in fact to analyze all essential aspects. What it will give are some new insights into the available evidence and recent discoveries. Most importantly, it shall demonstrate the validity of an Iranian perspective, challenging some widely accepted views on the Diadochi period in Iran and Central Asia. Macedonians or Greeks in the lands of Iranian habitation, however mighty, were a minority, and had to recognize the aspirations of native population to a large extent. Let us try to give Iranians credit where it is due.

Alexander's Iranian Policy

Alexander's Successors had to choose between either continuing or breaking with the great conqueror's policy. Therefore, Alexander's objectives in pursuing a pro-Iranian policy, assiduously implemented after 330, will be briefly considered first.[5] Alexander's adoption of Iranian regalia, garments, customs, and institutions was initiated in Parthia in 330. These reforms, followed by other novelties in Central Asia (329–327), in India (327–325), in Persis, at Susa, and at Opis (324), demonstrate that Alexander had formulated a comprehensive pro-Iranian monarchic program.

Alexander's policies in Asia should be seen as two distinct areas: local and imperial. In respective lands Alexander fell back on local traditions, as was the case in Lydia, Egypt, and Babylonia. That said, such traditions had little bearing on the imperial sphere in which Alexander followed the Achaemenid model, adopted a number of Iranian traditions, and began to create an élite composed mostly of Macedonians and Iranians.

The dual nature of Alexander's policy as conqueror and as ruler, seeking support among inhabitants of the Iranian Plateau and Central Asia, is reflected in his two-fold perception by Iranians. There was in Iran staunch opposition to Alexander and to his successors (Wolski 1969), invoking purely Iranian traditions in politics and culture. From that spirit arose the Arsacid dynasty (247 BC–AD 224) (Olbrycht 1998). Still, there was a political orientation in Iran which sought compromise with Alexander and supported his efforts to build a new empire with Iranians as a co-ruling nation with Macedonians. These were people like Atropates, Oxyartes, Mazaeus, and Phrataphernes. The Iranians predominated in Alexander's frontline army in the last years of his reign (Olbrycht 2004) and their elite units were appropriated by the Diadochi. In addition, there were satrapal military contingents from Iran and Central Asia which were composed mainly of Iranians, since Macedonians were few there, and Greeks proved to be *en masse* politically unreliable. After Alexander's sudden death the Diadochi engaged in an all-out struggle for power.

Satraps in Iran and Central Asia after Alexander

On the Iranian plateau and in Central Asia, a decisive role in the period between Alexander and Seleucus was played by satraps.[6] At the end of Alexander's reign, Iranian satraps controlled Media, Parthia-Hyrcania, Paropamisadae, Babylonia (Stamenes/Ditamenes) and Susiana (Oropius). While it is true that near the end of his reign Alexander reduced the number of Iranian satraps, with rebellious Greeks in the Upper Satrapies the importance grew of Iranian satrapal contingents, regardless of satraps' ethnic background. Iranian, Macedonian or Asiatic Greek governors were more than before dependent on local armies and thus on Iranians.

One of the most powerful Iranian satraps was Oxyartes, Alexander's father-in-law, who ruled over the Paropamisadae and parts of Bactria (Arr. *An.* 6.15.3; Curt. 9.8.10). Another Iranian potentate was Phrataphernes, the satrap of Hyrcania and Parthia, who had belonged in the category of the most loyal governors of Alexander. Here also belongs Atropates, the powerful satrap of Media, faithful to Alexander; at Susa, his daughter married Perdiccas. Atropates won genuine independence in 323 and was confirmed as satrap of Lesser Media, called henceforth Atropatene (Old Persian **Ātropātakāna*), now known as Azarbaijan.

Even when he selected Macedonians or Asiatic Greeks for satraps in the regions east of the Euphrates, Alexander required them fully to accept local Iranian customs and Iranian political aspirations in accordance with the king's policy. A key case in point is that of Persis (in 324–323), where Alexander chose a trusted candidate for the office of satrap: he was the Macedonian Peucestas, a Hypaspist officer in the king's personal guard (Wiesehöfer 1994, 45–49). Ostentatiously supported by the king, Peucestas quickly won recognition among the Persians for holding their traditions above Macedonian ones: he learned to speak Persian, wore Persian dress, 'and in all matters followed Persian ways' (D.S. 19.14.5; cf. Arr. *An.* 6.30.3; 7.6.3).

For eastern Iran, the figure of Stasanor, the satrap of Areia from 329, with Drangiana added later, reassigned to Bactria-Sogdiana at Triparadisus, calls for a word of comment. Stasanor secured the attachment of the native population by his skillful and moderate politics (D.S. 19.48.1). The question suggests itself, why did Alexander name satrap a Cypriot Greek, and not a Macedonian? It seems that he must have considered the Greek's familiarity with the Persian culture, perhaps language, too. Cyprus seems to be strongly Persianized in the Achaemenid period (see Zournatzi 2008). Stasanor was replaced in Areia-Drangiana by Stasander, again a Cypriot Greek (D.S. 18.39.6).

As with Stasanor, Tlepolemus in Carmania (since 325) knew how to ingratiate himself with Iranians, hence his successful career in Alexander's time and in the troubled circumstances of the Diadochi period (D.S. 19.48.1).

By and large it is clear that in 323–311 most satraps of the Upper Satrapies conducted policies which aimed at gaining the support of native Iranian populations. Eastern Iran and Central Asia remained between 323 and Seleucus' invasion (c. 307–305) virtually independent, with the satraps ruling there as local dynasts.

Those Iranian satraps and dynasts who entertained the intention of creating fully independent kingdoms must have reckoned with the possibility that some Macedonian protagonists would attempt to crush such aspirations. In this connection, an object lesson was Perdiccas' expedition in Cappadocia, a country that had escaped conquest by Alexander. Its Iranian ruler Ariarathes openly resisted Macedonians threat and, although he amassed a huge army, he was defeated by Perdiccas (Arr. *Post Alex.* 1.11; D.S. 18.16.2; Plu. *Eum.* 3.6). This was an instructive demonstration of power, commanding respect and dampening aspirations among anti-Macedonian Iranian dynasts and élites. It is to be noted that the Iranians were then divided and fought both in Ariarathes' and Perdiccas' armies. Nor were the Macedonians united, belonging to different factions.

While scrutinizing the Iranians' role in the Diadochi epoch, one must not forget those peoples who had not been touched by Macedonian conquests or remained under Macedonian control just for a short time. In India, Macedonian rule was quickly thrown off (Schober 1981, 90–93). Armenia remained under the rule of Iranian satraps from the Orontes' clan, a fact of paramount significance for the political constellation in the Near East (Schottky 1989). Iranian dynasties were established in Cappadocia (Ariarathids) and Pontus (Mithradatids). There remains another important area – Chorasmia and the steppe peoples between Sogdiana and the Caspian Sea, including Dahae, a significant factor in post-Achaemenid Central Asia (Olbrycht 1996; 1998, 27–60).

The Upper Satrapies at the Babylon Conference

At Babylon, commanders of the Macedonian and Iranian troops (the latter were numerically about ten times stronger – see Olbrycht 2004, 196–201) decided about a new arrangement of the empire left by Alexander (Schober 1981, 3–26). Perdiccas, securing his preeminence, was acknowledged as chiliarch and king's regent. His new appointments concerned notably the western regions of Alexander's empire (Bosworth 2002, 50–58). For the Upper Satrapies, critically important is Diodorus' report (18.3.2) that Perdiccas decided 'not to disturb the remaining satrapies of Asia but to permit them to remain under the same rulers'. In other words, Alexander's arrangement in Iran and Central Asia was basically to be continued. Thus, Oxyartes was confirmed in Paropamisadae and parts of Bactria, likewise Phrataphernes in Parthia-Hyrcania, Tlepolemus in Carmania, Peucestas in Persis, Sibyrtius in Arachosia-Gedrosia, Stasanor in Areia-Drangiana, and Philippus in Bactria-Sogdiana. Two Iranian lands – Media and Susiana – witnessed changes. The rich satrapy of Greater Media was awarded to Peithon

(D.S. 18.3.1), formerly one of Alexander's Bodyguards. Lesser Media (unconquered by Macedonians) remained under Atropates' suzerainty. In Susiana, Coenus replaced Oropius, who was charged with revolt and stripped of his power (Dexipp. *FGH* 100 F 8.6; Just. 13.4.14). It appears that in Alexander's last year Archon succeeded Stamenes/ Ditamenes as satrap in Babylonia (Curt. 8.3.17; cf. Heckel 2006, 43). Greater Media, Babylonia and adjacent Susiana, with highways running between Central Asia, Iran and the Levant, belonged to the strategically most sensitive satrapies.

Peithon's Iranian-Macedonian Army versus Rebelling Greeks

At Babylon, Peithon got a dangerous task to be performed – he had to cope with a Greek rebellion in the Upper Satrapies (Schober 1981, 27–37; Holt 1988, 87–91). Peithon's strong, Iranian-dominated army easily subdued the rebels (December 323, see Bosworth 2002, 61). Perdiccas gave Peithon 3,800 Macedonians. The satraps in Iran were instructed by Perdiccas' letters to contribute 18,000 horse and foot (D.S. 18.7.3), apparently all of them Iranian.[7] Diodorus (18.7.4) speaks of Peithon's intrigues to cooperate with the rebels and to 'win the Greeks over, and after making his army great through alliance with them, to work in his own interest and become the ruler of the Upper Satrapies'. Such designs were against Perdiccas' orders to kill the rebels and to distribute the spoils (D.S. 18.7.5). The military pressure of Peithon's forces, notably his Iranian cavalry, largely outnumbering the rebels' horse (8,000 Iranian and 800 Macedonian cavalry versus 3,000 Greek horse), led to a quick victory. The British scholar W. W. Tarn (1930, 71) rightly notes: 'A mere demonstration of his [sc. Peithon's] cavalry strength sufficed to make the Greeks surrender without fighting, though it is fair to add that treachery was also at work'. Now Diodorus (18.7.8–9) points to the Macedonians who - remembering Perdiccas' orders - 'shot the Greeks all down with javelins and seized their possessions for plunder'. It is obvious that not only Macedonians, but also the prevailing Iranian troops, mostly light infantry and cavalry traditionally fighting with javelins, must have been essential in the bloody operation carried out contrary to Peithon's designs. Apparently, most satraps and the Iranian local élites shared with Perdiccas the same political interest for he seemed to be guarantor of the continuity of Alexander's pro-Iranian policy. Indeed, he relinquished a broad scope of autonomy to the eastern satraps (D.S. 18.3.2). Moreover, Perdiccas must have been perceived in Iran as the most powerful and rightful successor of Alexander, belonging to the closest collaborators of the former monarch in his pro-Iranian policy and being the king's second-in-command in 323. Alexander is said to have handed Perdiccas his signet ring and to have entrusted him with his Iranian wife Roxane with her child.[8]

Triparadisus – Peithon's, Peucestas', and Oxyartes' Predominance in the East

Peithon had played an essential part in the assassination of Perdiccas (320) and for a brief time he shared the regency with Arrhidaeus. At Triparadisus (a place in Syria, with a

Greek-Iranian name), Peithon and Arrhidaeus resigned the office of *epimeleia*. Antipater was elected as guardian of the kings with full power (*epimelētēs autokratōr* – D.S. 18.39.2) and distributed the satrapies anew (D.S. 18.36.6–7; 18.39.2–3; Schober 1981, 41–42). Peithon was confirmed as satrap of Greater Media, like Peucestas in Persis, Tlepolemus in Carmania, Sibyrtius in Arachosia-Gedrosia, and Oxyartes in Paropamisadae. Among new satraps there was Seleucus in Babylonia, as well as Antigenes in Susiana and Amphimachus in Mesopotamia. Some changes were undertaken for eastern Iran and Central Asia: Phrataphernes is not named and his satrapy appeared as governed by a certain Philippus - it is possible that as belonging to Perdiccas' faction (Bosworth 2002, 105) the Parthian was removed from his satrapy by Peithon; Stasanor was moved from Areia-Drangiana to Bactria-Sogdiana, while Stasander assumed control of Areia-Drangiana. It was probably at Triparadisus that Peithon received the office of 'commander of the Upper Satrapies' - *stratēgos tōn anō satrapeiōn* (D.S. 19.14.1; but see Anson 2004, 160–61).

Peithon tried to enlarge his Median dominium, invaded Parthia and installed his brother Eudamus as satrap of the area (D.S. 19.14.1–3). Alarmed by these actions, the satraps of the lands of Iranian habitation formed a coalition which comprised Peucestas (with the strongest army numbering 14,000), Tlepolemus, Sibyrtius, Oxyartes (represented by his commander Androbazus), and Stasander. From India came Eudamus. Peithon's troops were defeated and driven out of Parthia (317) (D.S. 19.14.2–8; see Schober 1981, 79 n. 1). Upon his failure Peithon withdrew to Babylonia and made an alliance with Seleucus (D.S. 19.14.3). Peithon's politics and the formation of the satrapal coalition in the Upper Satrapies lavishly illustrate essential aspects of the political situation in the whole Iranian area. First, Macedonians fought against Macedonians (like Peithon against a Macedonian *stratēgos* in Parthia), Iranians (from Media) against Iranians (from other satrapies). What mattered were the interests of satraps and of their respective realms. Second, it was the struggling satraps who determined the political situation in Iran and in Central Asia. No one could rule there without their approval and they ruled mainly thanks to the support of Iranians. Third, the creation of a satrapal coalition indicates that there existed a sense of political community in the Upper Satrapies that relied on a recognition of the autonomy of Iranian lands as a whole. Apparently Peithon was perceived as a usurper imposed by the potentates ignoring the political agenda of the eastern satraps. Many centrifugal forces stood in the way of unification, but in face of the danger posed by potentates like Peithon, claiming to rule over the entire area east of Babylonia, most satraps united their armies. They viewed the West with concern, awaiting an invasion by one or more of the struggling protagonists.

Eumenes and Antigonus in Iran

In his politics towards Asian populations, notably in highly Iranized Cappadocia, Eumenes put into effect a number of concepts borrowed from Alexander's pro-Iranian policy and, realizing that the Macedonian soldiers' loyalty was shaky, he decided to recruit the natives of Cappadocia (322). Thus, he 'raised a force of cavalry as a counterpoise (*antitagma*) to them by offering the natives of the country who were able to serve as horsemen immunity from contributions and tributes (...)' (Plu. *Eum.* 4.2–4). Eumenes' cavalry *antitagma* (more than 6,300 men) emulated in a way the Iranian infantry *antitagma* created by Alexander to counterbalance the Macedonian phalanx after the mutiny at Opis (Olbrycht 2008). Eumenes' élite cavalry army was able to crush select Macedonian formations. His greatest victory was in the battle 'near Cappadocia', in which Craterus and Neoptolemus fell, and the Macedonian phalanx pitifully surrendered (D.S. 18.30–32; 18.37.1; Plu. *Eum.* 7–8; Nep. *Eum.* 4.3).

In the initial stage of the Iranian campaign of Antigonus, one of the best commanders of his time, was the battle at the Coprates river. Eumenes' forces, including Persian bowmen and cavalry, routed Antigonus' advanced troops (D.S. 19.17.4–7; 19.18.2–7; Plu. *Eum.* 14.2; Bosworth 2002, 116–17; Anson 2004, 168–70).

Peucestas versus Eumenes - Feast in Persepolis

The most powerful satrap in Iran, Peucestas, had significant allies outside his satrapy. Among his friends was Sibyrtius, the satrap of Arachosia (D.S. 19.23.4; Heckel 2006, 248–49). Another close friend and ally was Orontes, the Iranian satrap of Armenia (D.S. 19.23.3; Polyaen. 4.8.3; Schottky 1989, 84–91). Thus, Peucestas created an alliance uniting lands with considerable ressources and manpower. It was apparently part of a large network of satraps-dynasts. To that network Media Atropatene should be added, forming strategically a link between Armenia and Cappadocia in the west as well as the satrapies of Iran proper in the east.

Shortly before the military confrontation between the satraps' coalition and Antigonus' army, Peucestas organized a feast in Persepolis to show his own resplendence and to gain the chief command (D.S. 19.22.2–3; 19.23.1; Plu. *Eum.* 13). The feast was celebrated probably just next to the high terrace with Achaemenid royal palaces (Fig. 1). The participants were grouped in four concentric circles around the place of sacrifice with altars for the gods, for Philip and Alexander. Much of the ceremony (resembling the famous Macedonian-Iranian feast at Opis) was in accordance with Persian tradition (Wiesehöfer 1994, 53–54; 2007, 38–39), mixed with evocations to Alexander and Philip. For Iranians, such prayers honoured the dead kings' souls (Iranian *fravashis*). In this fashion, Peucestas showed himself as a genuine successor of both Persian/Iranian and Macedonian traditions, appealing to both ethnic groups gathered at Persepolis.

That the essential factor in the hot rivalry between Eumenes and Peucestas were now the satraps and their Iranian forces is proved by the fact that the former schemed against the satrap of Persis: Eumenes fabricated a letter, ascribed to Orontes, the satrap of Armenia, to lower the position of Peucestas and to announce rumors about the successes of his own protectors - Olympias, Alexander IV, and Polyperchon (D.S. 19.23.2–3; cf. Anson 2004, 172–73). Significantly, the letter was in the 'Syrian characters',

Fig. 1. Persepolis (Iran). View of the southern part of the high terrace with the ruins of royal palaces as seen from the Mountain of Mercy (Kuh-e Rahmat). Photo: M. J. Olbrycht.

i.e. Aramaic, language known to Iranians, but not Macedonians. Eumenes proved a ruthless manipulator: he brought Sibyrtius to trial and forced him to flee. Furthermore, he exacted from satraps and stratēgoi hostages and money to prevent their deserting him. At the end, Eumenes assumed command but that he did not reckon with Iranians' aspirations proved fatal (D.S. 19.23.4–24.1–3). In fact, he intimidated many commanders and satraps including Peucestas. Is it, therefore, any wonder that at a time of trial Peucestas deserted Eumenes?

The Satraps of Iran in the Conflict between Eumenes and Antigonus

The confrontation between Antigonus and the coalition led by Eumenes engaged Iranians on both sides (Schober 1981, 79–90; Bosworth 2002, 98–168; Anson 2004, 147–90). Peucestas bore a grudge for not having received the generalship (D.S. 19.17.5), but he refused alliance with Antigonus. His remarkable stance implies that he was a staunch defender of his Persian realm's interests.

The battle in Paraetacene demonstrates the all-important role of cavalry in the Iranian theatre of war. Unlike with Peucestas and Eumenes, Antigonus' chief strike force was cavalry, notably Tarentines and Peithon's Iranian horsemen. Peithon commanded a strong cavalry division (totaling 6,900) including 2,500 Medes and Parthians as lancers and famed horse-archers. Iranian mounted archers, one of the most effective military formations of the ancient world, had appeared in Alexander's army in India and in southern Iran (327–324), exclusively in combination with picked Macedonian units.[9] Peithon's cavalry was ordered to avoid a frontal engagement and to confine themselves to wheeling tactics (D.S. 19.29.2). The Iranian cavalry struck the enemy with repeated showers of missiles – both javelins and arrows (D.S. 19.30.1–3). Now Antigonus' right wing charged and routed enemy troops, forcing Eumenes to stop his advance in the center. Antigonus' phalanx lost, but his cavalry, notably due to Peithon's tactics that neutralized the elephants and best enemy's horse, carried the day (D.S. 19.30.4–10).

With a new recruitment in Media Antigonus had expanded his cavalry. The key role was to be played by Peithon with a massive cavalry division, including about 5,000 Iranians.[10] In Gabiene, Peithon turned Antigonus' phalanx' defeat into a great victory. In a bold charge Peithon's cavalry captured baggage park of Eumenes. Moreover, the satrap of Media attacked Eumenes' phalanx and forced the Silver Shields to withdraw (D.S. 19.39.6–44). The result still hung in the balance, but Peucestas deserted Eumenes preferring not to bleed his contingent. Other satraps intended to withdraw to continue the war elsewhere (D.S. 19.43.6; cf Plu. *Eum.* 16.1). As rightly stated by A. B. Bosworth (2002, 157), 'anything rather than continue under Eumenes' leadership'. The Silver Shields handed Eumenes over to Antigonus in exchange for their families and baggage-park. Contrary to a widespread opinion, the military role of the Silver Shields was of secondary importance for the final result - they managed to beat the phalanx of Antigonus but, in spite of that success, the victory had gone to Antigonus and Peithon. Eumenes lacked his cavalry *antitagma*, lost in Anatolia. But more importantly, his position was undermined by political factors – the satraps of Iran withdrew their forced support for the protagonist.

The Elimination of Peithon and Peucestas

After his triumph in Gabiene and the execution of Eumenes, Antigonus planned to neutralize the chief threat to his power in Iran, i.e., to eliminate satraps representing Iranian political aspirations. As such Iranian-backed potentates were active on both sides, Antigonus struck both at his ally Peithon and his recent enemy Peucestas. Although Peithon, on a charge of rebellion was executed (D.S. 19.46.1–4), Antigonus must have concluded that he needed to make some deal with Iranians, since he appointed the Mede Orontobates satrap of Media. However, the new governor was merely a puppet, supervised by the *stratēgos* Hippocrates with mercenaries (D.S. 19.46.5). There was an outcry in Media. A strange, although actually logical coalition was formed in western Iran, uniting supporters of both Eumenes and Peithon like Meleagrus, Menoitas, and the Mede Ocranes (D.S. 19.47.1–4). Its composition proves that there existed a real political interest uniting parts of native élites, some Macedonians and most of the satraps having hold in the Upper Satrapies, accelerated by Antigonus' pressure. The struggle was over the dominion in Media, but it was much the same in Persis. The defeated Persians were forced to give 'royal' honours to the victorious Antigonus (D.S. 19.48.1). Peucestas was removed,[11] for Antigonus perceived that he was enjoying great favor among the Persians. Thespius, a Persian leader acting against Antigonus, was executed (D.S. 19.48.5). Antigonus' politics clearly alienated western Iranians in Persia and Media (D.S. 19.92.4).

Antigonus' Failure in Iran

At Persepolis, Antigonus redistributed the eastern satrapies. Persis received Asclepiodorus, who was given 'a sufficient number of soldiers' to enforce his disputed authority (D.S. 19.48.5). This was no lasting solution for stable government, but rather temporary occupation for a country in turmoil. Asclepiodorus makes no later appearance in the sources. In 312 Evagrus/Evagoras is mentioned as the satrap of Persis (D.S. 19.92.4).[12] Sibyrtius was sent back to Arachosia but he would not play any role in the subsequent events (cf. Bosworth 2002, 163–65). In Areia, Stasander, probably killed in war, was replaced by Evitus, and the latter, after his quick demise, by Evagoras (D.S. 19.48.2). In a pro-Iranian gesture, Antigonus appointed Aspeisas satrap of Susiana (D.S. 19.55.1; Billows 1990, 376–77). After the brutal pacifications in Media and Persis, no one took such flourishes seriously any more. Based on an occupation force, western Iran was supervised by Antigonus' appointee Nicanor, with the title of *stratēgos* of the Upper Satrapies (Billows 1990, 409–10).

The One-Eyed was not able to dislodge the hostile satraps in eastern Iran and Afghanistan and had to accept the status quo there. Thus, Oxyartes remained beyond Antigonus' sphere of influence 'for he could not be removed without a long campaign and a strong army' (D.S. 19.48.2). The same applies to Tlepolemus in Carmania and Stasanor in Bactria; Antigonus was not able 'to remove them by sending a message since they had conducted themselves well towards the indigenous inhabitants (*enchōrioi*) and had many supporters (*polloi synagōnistai*)' (D.S. 19.48.1). This is an essential insight into the real political situation in the Upper Satrapies. Certainly, the relations between Greeks or Macedonians and Iranians, e.g. Bactrians, were not free of tensions. Onesicritus (*FGH* 134 F 5) reports the custom according to which old and sick peoples were thrown out alive as prey to dogs, but Alexander broke up this habit. A similar restriction, introduced by Stasanor, caused discontent amongst the Bactrians (Porph. *Abst.* 4.21).

Proclaimed at Persepolis by Antigonus, the new order for the satrapies of Iran sounded grotesque and no stability was in sight. In confrontation with weak Seleucus (311), Nicanor proved helpless, for many Iranians, conscripted into his army, deserted him remembering Antigonus' repressions (D.S. 19.92.2–4). One of the main reasons for the military and political successes of Seleucus was his ability to find common ground with the native populations in Babylonia and Iran. The One-Eyed showed real interest in the Iranian lands. However, he forgot that one can win battles with bayonets, but one cannot sit on them.

Seleucus' Rise to Power

The early history of the Seleucids has inevitably tended to be studied from the Mediterranean and, more recently, Babylonian perspectives.[13] In both approaches, the role of Iran is underestimated and deserves greater recognition. When entering Babylon in 312/311, Seleucus led about 1,000 soldiers given to him by Ptolemy. Seleucus' companions were disheartened by their small numbers in relation to the forces they would face (D.S. 19.90.1–2). Next year, Seleucus marched against Nicanor's force (numbering 17,000 soldiers), with a tiny army of 3,400. Compared with other Diadochi, Seleucus' initial position seemed extremely modest and desperate. Surprisingly, Seleucus not only defeated his powerful enemies (Antigonus, Demetrius and Nicanor), attacking him from the west and east, but he also managed to create a strong state with a formidable military potential. What were actually the decisive factors which contributed to Seleucus' epochal achievements?

Seleucus knew the prevailing spirit in western Iran and appreciated the region's potential which could be used as long as Iranians' aspirations were respected. All he needed was to accept the model presented by Peucestas in Persis. Seleucus did just that, and not only did he dominate almost all lands on the Iranian plateau, but he also built an empire including Central Asia, Mesopotamia and the Levant. In western Iran, Seleucus skilfully used resentments against Antigonus and employed politics based on gaining the local populations by securing them some privileges and autonomy. Diodorus (19.92.5) clearly implies this, emphasizing that Seleucus demonstrated his magnanimity (*philantrōpia*) and easily won over Susiana, Media and 'some of the adjacent lands'. Similarly, Seleucus' position in Babylonia was strong for he 'had showed himself generous to all' and gained 'support (*eunoia*) of the common people' during his satrapal rule (320–315) (D.S. 19.91.2).

After a surprising victory over Nicanor on the Tigris, Seleucus subjugated Susiana, Media, Persis, and probably Parthia. During this period, between 310 and 308, Babylonia was repeatedly devastated by Demetrius' and Antigonus' invading armies (Wheatley 2002), its economic potential being largely damaged. The Babylonians do not appear as soldiers in the armies of the Diadochi period (Schober 1981, 125, 137; Walbank 1988, 110–12). By and large, Seleucus could enlist in Babylonia and western Iran no more than several thousand Greeks and Macedonians in his field army. By contrast, the potential of Persis under Peucestas exceeded 20,000 soldiers. The manpower of the Cossaeans can be estimated at 10,000 soldiers at least,[14] of Media at 5,000 horse (like in Gabiene). Taking into account these rather lowered numbers, it can be safely assumed that Seleucus could recruit at least 35,000 western Iranians, including superior cavalry, excellent light infantry (archers and slingers), and *pantodapoi* (phalanx soldiers). It was the western Iranians who made up the core of Seleucus' troops and enabled him to dislodge Antigonus' and Demetrius' armies from Babylonia – one of the most unexpected victories of the period.

In Bactria, Seleucus met strong resistance (Just. 15.4.12; Oros. 3.23.44; Schober

1981, 149–50). Seleucus' chief asset in his policies in Afghanistan and Transoxiana was his Iranian wife Apama, daughter of famous Spitamenes, who certainly helped her husband to develop good relations with the Bactrian and Sogdian aristocracy. However, Seleucus' skilful policy, so effective in Babylonia and western Iran, proved largely a failure in Bactria-Sogdiana. The Bactrian Greeks and parts of the native Iranian élites had tended obviously to establish their own independent realm (Holt 1999). Seleucus' military threat forced the Bactrians to capitulate, but the feelings of autonomy and independence remained vivid: in about 60 years after Seleucus' anabasis, the inhabitants of Bactria founded their own kingdom. It is conceivable that being in the neighbourhood of the independent Indian state under such great rulers as Chandragupta and Asoka exerted a strong influence upon the political developments in Bactria, also in terms of its reluctance to accept Seleucid suzerainty (Wolski 1969).

After a war on the Indian empire of Chandragupta, Seleucus appeared in Cappadocia, his army being for the most part Iranian, supported by a huge number of Indian elephants and a typical Achaemenid formation – the scythed chariots (D.S. 20.113.4; Billows 1990, 181–85). Seleucus' cavalry (12,000, including the formidable Central Asian mounted archers), in fact, decided the confrontation of Ipsus. Antigonus fell in battle, killed by javelins hurled by Iranian cavalrymen of Seleucus (details in Olbrycht 2005).

Seleucus as King

While naming the crowned Macedonian Successors, Plutarch (*Demetr.* 18.3) notes: 'Lysimachus began to wear a diadem, and Seleucus also in his interviews with the Greeks; with the Barbarians he had before this dealt as king'. This much dabated account implies that Seleucus had called himself 'king' and used a diadem before the proclamations of the 'year of the kings'. Plutarch points to the circumstance that Seleucus' royal concept depended on the respective audience. His legitimation efforts must be seen in a broader context. Until Antigonus' proclamation in 306, none of the Diadochi dared to usurp the Macedonian royal title of *basileus* – 'king'. Seleucus assumed that title after gaining the Upper Satrapies, i.e. in about 305/304 (D.S. 20.53.4; Bosworth 2002, 246–47). In taking the royal Macedonian title of *basileus*, Seleucus' intention was to challenge Antigonus and Demetrius and to demonstrate his royal status to other Macedonian potentates. In Iranian eyes, the Macedonian title had no significance – in the Upper Satrapies, the royal dignity must have been related to the Iranian traditions. Initially Seleucus possibly avoided the Iranian royal title of *khshayathiya* (Old Persian *xšāyaθiya*) in favour of the more modest 'lord', as indicated by the Naqsh-e Rostam inscription (see below). But with time Seleucus' status elevated. Taking this into account one can assume that, as implied in Plutarch, Seleucus used the Iranian royal title vis-à-vis Iranians after the subjugation of western Iran, c. 310. Seleucus possibly claimed connections to the Achaemenids through his wife Apama (Tarn 1929), although her genuine relation to the Persian dynasty remains unclear. Plutarch (*Demetr.* 18.3) implies that Seleucus, like later other Diadochi, used a diadem which clearly belongs to Achaemenid tradition (Olbrycht 2004, 282–93).

In the Diadochi period, Macedonian and Asiatic protagonists sought for new forms of rulership and kingship, suitable to their claims. It is to be noted that some Iranian dynasts assumed the royal title perhaps even before 306, but their proclamations may have been related to the Iranian concept of kingship. These were Ardoates (Orontes?) in Armenia (D.S. 31.19.5 with Schottky 1989, 94–96) and Atropates in Lesser Media (Str. 11.13.1 with Schottky 1989, 43–53).

In his politics vis-à-vis Iranians, Seleucus did make mistakes. Characteristic was his attitude toward the temple of Anahita/Aine in Ecbatana. As had previously Antigonus Monophtalmus, followed later by Antiochus III, Seleucus robbed the temple as he was chronically short of money (Plb. 10.27). Such acts could not win him much sympathy among Medes and other Iranians.

It is striking that Seleucus I and Antiochus I did not show any special attachment to Alexander III except for a few proclamations clearly addressed to a Macedonian audience. Thus, e.g., among numerous early Seleucid foundations no city was named after Alexander (Olbrycht 2004, 211–22). True, Appian (Syr. 57, 295–298) ascribes to Seleucus 59 new foundations, including two cities named Alexandria in honour of Alexander - Alexandreschate and Alexandropolis in India[15]. Actually, both cities were established by Alexander himself and thus Appian's claim is groundless.

The Upper Satrapies under Seleucus I and Antiochus I

In talking about the Diadochi period in Iran, one must not overlook Seleucus' Iranian wife Apama, married to Seleucus at Susa in 324.[16] Despite Seleucus' marriage to Stratonice (299), Antiochus remained the successor to the throne. Apame herself did not sever links with her former homeland, as shown in a decree of Miletus in her honour (299/98: *Didyma* 480), proposed by Demodamas: 'Queen Apama has previously displayed all goodwill and zeal for those Milesians who served in the army with king Seleucus'. One of these Milesians was surely Demodamas who conducted military operations in Sogdiana (Plin. *Nat.* 6.49), where Apama came from, and reached beyond the Iaxartes/ Syr-darya. Another Apama's activity was her 'no ordinary devotion' concerning the construction of the temple of Apollo at Didyma.

The young Antiochus I, grandson of Spitamenes, was particularly fit to be ruler in the Upper Satrapies (Capdetrey 2007, 79–84). As co-regent, he had royal coinage issued in the mints located in Seleucia on the Tigris, Ecbatana, Ai Khanom, and probably Bactra (Houghton and Lorber 2002, 117–63; Bopearachchi 2005, 349–69). Local imitations of early Seleucid coins of the Alexandrine patterns and of Antiochus I's issues were the country's first own mass coinages in Bactria. Unlike under Seleucus, Antiochus' colonizing efforts concentrated not on western Iran, but further to the east, in eastern Iran and Central Asia. It is worth digressing briefly to consider the Iranian lands at the time of the early Seleucids.

The richest country of the eastern part of the Seleucid empire was Bactria called the 'ornament of Ariana as a whole' (Apollod.Artem. *FGH* 779 F 7a). The Seleucid colonizing efforts focused on the Oxus/Amu-darya valley, where Seleucus and Antiochus refounded or established a number of cities and strongholds including Ai Khanom (Holt 1999, 27–28; Capdetrey 2007, 80–81; Lerner 2010).

A number of archaeological objects dating from the early Hellenistic period were found at the northern Bactrian fortress of Kampyr-tepa, established near a crossing point on the Amu-darya, perhaps by Alexander, and rebuilt by the early Seleucids. Layers from the Diadochi and Seleucid era rise seven meters high, an amazing phenomenon (Rtweladse 2009) (Fig. 2).

One more place in Bactria is worth looking at as it is extremely important for the Diadochi period: the sanctuary at Takht-e Sangin (also called the temple of the Oxus), in present-day Tajikistan. Years-long excavations revealed a temple built in the late 4th and early 3rd centuries and a large number of relics of arts and crafts (Litvinskii 2010; 2010a). The temple was devoted to the river god of the Oxus – Vakhsh (*Old Iranian *Vaxšu-*) and to Fire. Theophoric names containing an element Vakhsh (*Vaxšu-*) were common in Bactria. The father of Roxane, Alexander's wife, was named Oxyartes, i.e. Vakhshurta (or Vakhshurti) (see Rapin and Grenet 1983, 374–78; Schmitt 2002). It seems that Oxyartes himself might have erected the temple on the Oxus (among sculptured figures discovered in the Oxus temple, some depict Bactrian nobles – perhaps a gift sponsored by Oxyartes' powerful clan). In my view, another probable founder was Apama: if she is known to have supported a Greek sanctuary at Didyma, could she not just as well have supported an Iranian temple in her homeland?

One of the most recent archaeological discoveries in northern Bactria is the fortress of Kurganzol in the Baisuntau mountains (southern Uzbekistan) (Sverchkov 2008, 123–91; Swertschkow 2009), located on extremely high ground, controlling access to a vast valley (Fig. 3). In my opinion it was built in the Diadochi/early Seleucid period, perhaps in connection with Demodamas' campaigns.

The reign of Seleucus and Antiochus coincides with military actions by commanders Demodamas and Patrocles in the Upper Satrapies. Their operations were aimed at pacifying Central Asia and repulsing nomads. Demodamas set up altars to Apollo of Didyma near those already constructed by 'Cyrus, Semiramis, and Alexander' on the Iaxartes/Syr-darya (Plin. *Nat.* 6.49; see Olbrycht 1996; 1998, 44). Another objective was to reconnoiter the Caspian region, which was growing in significance for the Seleucids (Plin. *Nat.* 6.58; cf. Str. 11.6.1; 11.7.3; 11.11.5). As a sign of such interest, two parts of the Caspian Sea were named Seleucis and Antiochis (Plin. *Nat.* 2.167). The exploration of the Caspian Sea and the Transcaspian region were part of Seleucid designs to strengthen their position in the whole Caspian region and northern Iran.

Unlike in Bactria, Seleucid rule in Sogdiana was ephemeral, mainly due to the pressure of nomadic tribes including the Dahae (Rapin 2007).

Antiochus I invested huge resources in Margiana and Areia, called by Strabo 'the most powerful districts in this part of Asia' (11.10.1). A few words would be in order

Fig. 2. Kampyr-tepa (Uzbekistan). Fortress on the former course of the Oxus/Amu-darya. Photo: M. J. Olbrycht.

Fig. 3. Kurganzol (Uzbekistan). Fortress in the Baisuntau mountains. Photo: M. J. Olbrycht.

about the city of Antiochia in Margiana, i.e., Merv, since it is reasonably well explored archaeologically (Olbrycht 2004, 211–22). The origins of Merv as an urban center reach back to the the 6th century BC. In Merv, Alexander the Great established a colony (c. 328) protected by six forts. In the Diadochi period, Alexandria in Margiana was destroyed and hastily rebuilt as Seleucia in its place. Antiochus I reestablished the city henceforth called Antiochia. According to Strabo (11.10.2), 'admiring its [Margiana's] fertility, Antiochus Soter enclosed a circuit of fifteen hundred stadia with a wall [literally, a rampart about 250 km long] and founded a city Antiochia'. The city proper, now known as Gyaur-kala (380 hectares), was engirdled with walls measuring almost eight km in length. Gyaur-kala's walls, now still preserved to a height of 7 m, were up to 6.6 m thick at the base (Fig. 4). At an early stage, the Seleucid wall had a shooting gallery and a *proteichisma* (Zavyalov 2007, 67).

Antiochus I's enormous investment projects in Margiana were nearly matched in Areia, which also had grand fortifications built in it. While describing *Ariana regio*, Pliny (*Nat.* 6.93) names its cities: Artacoana, Alexandria, a city founded by Alexander, 'and the much more beautiful as well as older city of Artacabene, the fortifications of which were renewed by Antiochus, (which) covers an area of 30 stadia' (cf. Str. 11.10.1).

A special position in the Seleucid empire gained Media, 'the most notable principality in Asia, both in the extent of its territory and the number and excellence of the men and also the horses it produces' (Plb. 10.27.3). Its metropolises, Ecbatana and Rhagae, are said to have been established by Seleucus (Plin. *Nat.* 6.43; Str. 11.13.6), meaning a limited influx of colonists from the West. Both cities retained their predominantly Iranian character.

In Greater Media, there was an ancient holy place called Bisotun or Bagastana (Fig. 5), next to the Khorasan highway, connecting Babylonia and Central Asia as well as India. There is abundant evidence for the sanctuary being used in post-Alexander times. Greeks and Macedonians appear to 'have added their prayers to Zoroastrian ones' (Boyce and Grenet 1991, 91–93).

Lesser Media (Atropatene) played an important part in the Iranian revival in the post-Alexander's period. The country includes Iran's largest lake, Urmia, which Medes identified with legendary lake Chaechasta. In the *Avesta*, the lake was said to lie in eastern Iranian territory. A new, fictitious placement in Atropatene resulted from the increasing importance of that land in Iranian religious life under Atropates and his descendants. On the whole, Atropatene became a bastion of Iranian culture, politically independent in the post-Achaemenid period (Boyce and Grenet 1991, 69–86).

As far as Persis is concerned, the country's political situation under Seleucid rule remains shadowy. Archaeological materials point to the continuity of native Iranian traditions (Boucharlat 2006; Callieri 2007). At some point, probably under Seleucus I, Persians rebelled against Seleucid authority (Polyaen. 7.39). It is possible that authority over (parts of?) Persis was delegated by the Seleucids to native rulers called *frataraka*s. The *frataraka* coins show them as devout Zoroastrians. Persis became fully independent only at the beginning of the 2nd century (Wiesehöfer 1994; 2007). From the so-called

Fig. 4. Merv (Gyaur-kala) (Turkmenistan). Section of the city walls (south-west corner) of Antiochia excavated by Zavyalov. Photo: M. J. Olbrycht.

Fig. 5. Bisotun (Iran). General view of the holy mountain. Photo: M. J. Olbrycht.

Frataraka-temple area at Persepolis we know several stone slabs with Greek inscriptions naming Zeus Megistus (Fig. 6), Athena Basileia, Apollo, Artemis and Helius (Wiesehöfer 1994, 72–73). It seems that the inscriptions were employed in a syncretistic manner (like later on in Commagene) to designate both Macedonian-Greek and Iranian gods (Ahuramazda, Mithra, Anahita). They were cut probably under Peucestas or Seleucus I.

Aramaic in Iran

The above described episode of Eumenes fabricating a letter in 'Syrian' proves the importance of Aramaic writing in the Diadochi epoch. Aramaic was used as the chancery language through the Achaemenid empire, but the practice was continued under Alexander as well as in the Diadochi and Seleucid periods. Recently, a corpus of Aramaic documents from Bactria has been discovered (now in the Khalili Collection) dated to the reigns of Artaxerxes III, Darius III, and Alexander (Shaked 2004). Another significant example is a number of inscriptions issued by Asoka found in Pakistan and Afghanistan, dated to the mid 3rd century, written in Aramao-Iranian, a regional form intermediary between Imperial Aramaic (of the Achaemenid period) and Pahlavi script, or in Aramao-Indian (Humbach 1998).

In this connection, an inscription (in Aramaic script, but early Middle-Persian language), discovered in 1923 on Darius I's tomb at Naqsh-e Rostam (Herzfeld 1938, 12, pl. IV), from the Diadochi period is important. The inscription remains highly debatable, its text being differently reconstructed, interpreted and dated.[17] In the text, two names of Persian kings – Darius (Dārayavauš) and Artaxerxes (Artaxšasa<Artaxšaçā/Rtaxšaça) – are attested. W. Henning (1958, 24), who personally inspected the site in 1950, saw the name *slwk* – Seleucus. This reading, refuted by some specialists, should be retained. The name *slwk* (in line 4) is followed by the letters *ḥw* (...), which can probably be augmented to *ḥwt'y*, meaning *xwadāy* 'lord' in Middle Persian and other Middle Iranian languages. In all likelihood the inscription was cut on the order of Seleucus I, trying to show his attachment to the rightful Achaemenid kings of Persis.

Scholars recalling the use of Aramaic in Iran in the post-Achaemenid period often disregard the coins issued in the name of Vakhshuvar discovered in the Oxus hoard (Henning 1958, 24; Holt 1988, 97–98). On all these specimens appear legends in the Aramaic alphabet, including the names Vakhshuvar (*wḥšwwr*) and Vakhsh (*wḥšw*). The name Vakhshuvar is also preserved on a signet-ring in the Oxus hoard (Holt 1988, 97 n. 43). Some scholars identify the Vakhshuvar of coins with the satrap Oxyartes, father-in-law of Alexander.

That Aramaic was used by the Seleucid administration as one of the official languages along with Greek, is testified to by an official bilingual text in Greek and Aramaic inscribed on a distance marker from Tall-i Takht at Pasargadae (Persis, Fig. 7), dated to the early 3rd century (Bivar 1978; Sherwin-White and Kuhrt 1993, 50).

To the 3rd century seem to belong the earliest known Chorasmian inscriptions on silver bowls discovered in nomadic graves at Isakovka near Omsk (Southern Urals).

Fig. 6. Slab from Persepolis with a Greek inscription Dios Megistou. National Museum of Iran, Tehran (With kind permission of the National Museum at Tehran). Photo: National Museum of Iran.

Fig. 7. Stone distance marker from Pasargadai with a bilingual Greek-Aramaic inscription (face B). National Museum of Iran, Tehran (With kind permission of the National Museum at Tehran). Photo: M. J. Olbrycht.

Under unclear circumstances (gifts or booty) the inscribed vessels went from Chorasmia to the nomads (Livshits 2003). Thus, one can see that the use of Aramaic in post-Achaemenid times was quite widespread in the lands of Iranian habitation. During the 3rd–2nd centuries, several Iranian countries, including Parthia, Chorasmia, Sogdiana, and Persis adopted the Aramaic alphabet for their own languages (Skjærvø 1995; Graf 2000), a fact implying that Iranian culture was vibrant.

Conclusions

Looking at the history of Iran and Central Asia in the Diadochi period, it should be borne in mind that Macedonians and Greeks in the Upper Satrapies made up a small minority within the mass of native Iranian population. We do not know a lot of Iranian personal names from the Diadochi period and each prosopographical study, based notably on Greek inscriptions would demonstrate a prevailance of Macedonians and Greeks. But such an approach can often be misleading. For Seleucus' army in 310–301 we do not know a single Iranian name, but the evidence clearly implies that it was composed mainly of Iranians, a fact of paramount importance for Seleucus' politics. The history of the Iranian lands in Western and Central Asia should not be looked at merely through the lens of Greek- or Macedonian-oriented sources.

The legitimacy of rule is ultimately a matter of acceptance by those over whom it is exercised, a fact defining Diadochi efforts to legitimate their positions in their respective realms (Wheatley 2009, 60–66; Müller 2011a). As noted in the Suda (s.v. *Basileia*), the key to kingship in the post-Alexander period was not descent or legitimacy but military and political competence. This statement, commonly cited by modern scholars, points merely to one of the essential conditions, for military victories often remained without lasting effects in the sphere of rule's acceptance and effectiveness. Antigonus provides an instructive example – although victorious in western Iran against Eumenes and the satraps of the East, he was not able to stabilize his rule there for he ignored the prominent role of the indigenous population. The primary condition in maintaining a rule system in the lands of Iranian habitation was to meet the subjects' expectations and aspirations to an extent securing acceptance by the natives.

Political-military support from Iranians was decisive in elevating to power in western and central Asia Seleucus and his wife Apama, and in the making of the Macedonian-Iranian empire of the early Seleucids (Olbrycht 2005). After Ipsus, Seleucus' policy tied him up mostly in the west (Syria, Anatolia). In the Upper Satrapies, active politics were implemented by Antiochus I, who, however, after 281 became fully involved in conflicts in the Levant. The Upper Satrapies, especially eastern Iran and Bactria, increasingly receded in importance for the Seleucids, with local satraps and populations tending towards autonomy. This caused an understandable rise of independence movements.

Within a single generation after the death of Antiochus I in 261, separatisms in the Upper Satrapies, fueled by Iranian and Greek aspirations for independence, came into full force, producing the Graeco-Bactrian kingdom and the Parthian state (c. 240–238).

By 140, the Arsacid Parthians subjugated countries from parts of Bactria to Babylonia, putting the final seal on the revival of Iranian political and cultural traditions.[18]

Bibliography

Anson, E. M. (2004) *Eumenes of Cardia: A Greek among Macedonians*. Boston and Leiden.

Bailey, H. W. (1987) Arya, *Encyclopedia Iranica* 2, 681–83.

Billows, R. A. (1990) *Antigonos the One-Eyed and the Creation of the Hellenistic State*. Berkeley.

Bivar, A. D. H. (1978) The Aramaic Summary. In D. Stronach, Pasargadae, 161–62, Oxford.

Boiy, T. (2007) *Between High and Low. A Chronology of the Early Hellenistic Period*. Frankfurt am Main.

Bopearachchi, O. (2005) La politique monétaire de la Bactriane sous les Séleucides. In V. Chankowski and F. Duyrat (eds) *Le roi et l'économie*, 349–69, Paris.

Bosworth, A. B. (1980) Alexander and the Iranians, *Journal of Hellenic Studies* 100, 1–21.

Bosworth, A. B. (2002) *The Legacy of Alexander: Politics, Warfare, and Propaganda under the Successors*. Oxford.

Boucharlat, R. (2006) Le destin des résidences et sites perses d'Iran dans la seconde moitié du IVe siècle avant J.-C. In P. Briant and F. Joannès (eds) *La transition entre l'empire achéménide et les royaumes hellénistiques*, 443–70, Paris.

Boyce, M., and F. Grenet (1991) *A History of Zoroastrianism. III: Zoroastrianism under Macedonian and Roman Rule*. Leiden.

Briant, P. (1994) Sources gréco-hellénistiques, institutions perses et institutions macédoniennes: continuités, changements et bricolages, *Achaemenid History* 8, 283–310.

Callieri, P. (2007) L'archéologie du Fars à l'époque achéménide: quatre leçons au Collège de France. Paris.

Capdetrey, L. (2007) *Le pouvoir séleucide. Territoire, administration, finances d'un royaume hellénistique*. Rennes.

Frye, R. N. (1982) The 'Aramaic' Inscription on the Tomb of Darius, *Iranica Antiqua* 17, 85–90.

Graf, D. F. (2000) Aramaic on the Periphery of the Achaemenid Realm, *Archäologische Mitteilungen aus Iran* 32, 75–92.

Hammond, N. G. L. (1996) Alexander's Non-European Troops and Ptolemy I's Use of Such Troops, *Bulletin of the American Society of Papyrologists* 33, 99–109.

Heckel, W. (2006) *Who's Who in the Age of Alexander the Great*. Malden, MA.

Henning, W. (1958) Mitteliranisch, *Handbuch der Orientalistik* 1. Abt., 4. Bd. (Iranistik), 20–130, Leiden and Cologne.

Herzfeld, E. (1938) *Altpersische Inschriften*. Berlin.

Holt, F. L. (1988) *Alexander the Great and Bactria. The Formation of a Greek Frontier in Central Asia*. Leiden.

Holt, F. L. (1999) *Thundering Zeus: The Making of Hellenistic Bactria*. Berkeley.

Houghton, A. and C. Lorber (2002) *Seleucid Coins: A Comprehensive Catalogue*. 2 vols. New York.

Humbach, H. (1998) Epigraphy. I. Old Persian and Middle Iranian Epigraphy, *Encyclopaedia* Iranica 8, 378–488.

Landucci Gattinoni, F. (2005) La tradizione su Seleuco in Diodoro XVIII–XX. In C. Bearzot and F. Landucci Gattinoni (eds) *Diodoro e l'altra Grecia: Macedonia, Occidente, Ellenismo nella Biblioteca storica*, 155–81, Milan.

Landucci Gattinoni, F. (2008) *Diodoro Siculo: Biblioteca storica: libro XVIII: commento storico. Storia. Ricerche*. Milan.

Lerner, J. D. (2010) Revising the Chronologies of the Hellenistic Colonies of Samarkand-Marakanda (Afrasiab II–III) and Aï Khanoum (northeastern Afghanistan). In Olbrycht, M. J. (ed.) *Orientis Splendor. Studies in Memory of Józef Wolski* (= *Anabasis. Studia Classica et Orientalia* 1), 58–79, Rzeszow.

Litvinskii, B. A. (2010a) Problems of the History and Culture of Baktria in Light of Archaeological Excavations in Central Asia. In Olbrycht, M. J. (ed.) *Orientis Splendor. Studies in Memory of Józef Wolski* (= *Anabasis. Studia Classica et Orientalia* 1), 23–48, Rzeszow.

Litvinskii, B. A. (2010b) *Khram Oksa v Baktrii*. III. Moscow.

Livshits, V. A. (2003) Three Silver Bowls from the Isakovka Burial-Ground No. 1 with Khwarezmian and Parthian Inscriptions, *Ancient Civilizations from Scythia to Sibiria* 9, 147–72.

Mehl, A. (1986) *Seleucus Nikator und sein Reich*. Leuven.

Müller, S. (2011a) Herrschafstlegitimation in den frühhellenistischen Dynastien. In D. Lambach (ed.) *Politische Herrschaft jenseits des Staates*, 151–76, Wiesbaden.

Müller, S. (2011b) Die frühen Perserkönige im kulturellen Gedächtnis der Makedonen und in der Propaganda Alexanders des Gr., *Gymnasium* 118, 105–33.

Olbrycht, M. J. (1996) Die Beziehungen der Steppennomaden Mittelasiens zu den hellenistischen Staaten (bis zum Ende des 3. Jahrhunderts vor Chr.). In B. Funck (ed.) *Hellenismus. Beiträge zur Erforschung von Akkulturation und politischer Ordnung in den Staaten des hellenistischen Zeitalters*, 147–69, Tübingen.

Olbrycht, M. J. (1998) *Parthia et ulteriores gentes. Die politischen Beziehungen zwischen dem arsakidischen Iran und den Nomaden der eurasischen Steppen*. Munich.

Olbrycht, M. J. (2004) *Alexander the Great and the Iranian World*. Rzeszow (in Polish).

Olbrycht, M. J. (2005) Creating an Empire: Iran and Middle Asia in the Policy of Seleucus I. In V. P. Nikonorov (ed.) *Central Asia from the Achaemenids to the Timurids*, 231–35, Saint Petersburg.

Olbrycht, M. J. (2008) Curtius Rufus, the Macedonian Mutiny at Opis and Alexander's Iranian Policy in 324 BC. In J. Pigon (ed.) *The Children of Herodotus. Greek and Roman Historiography and Related Genres*, 231–52, Newcastle.

Olbrycht, M. J. (ed.) (2010a) *Orientis Splendor. Studies in Memory of Józef Wolski* (= *Anabasis. Studia Classica et Orientalia* 1). Rzeszow.

Olbrycht, M. J. (2010b) Macedonia and Persia. In J. Roisman and I. Worthington (eds) *Blackwell Companion to Ancient Macedonia*, 342–69, Malden, MA.

Rapin, C. (2007) Nomads and the Shaping of Central Asia: From the Early Iron Age to the Kushan Period. In J. Cribb and G. Herrmann (eds) *After Alexander: Central Asia before Islam*, 29–72, Oxford and New York.

Rapin, C. and F. Grenet (1983) Inscriptions économiques de la trésorerie hellénistique d'Aï Khanoum. L'onomastique iranienne à Aï Khanoum, *Bulletin de correspondance hellénique* 107, 315–81.

Rtweladse, E. V. (2009) Kampyr-Tepe-Pandocheion - Alexandria Oxiana. In S. Hansen, A. Wieczorek and M. Tellenbach (eds) *Alexander der Grosse und die Öffnung der Welt. Asiens Kulturen im Wandel*, 169–75, Mannheim.

Schmitt, R. (2002) Oxyartes, *Encyclopedia Iranica*, online edition, 2002.

Schober, L. (1981) *Untersuchungen zur Geschichte Babyloniens und der Oberen Satrapien von 323–303 v. Chr*. Frankfurt am Main.

Schottky, M. (1989) *Media Atropatene und Gross-Armenien in hellenistischer Zeit*. Bonn.
Shaked, S. (2004) *Le satrape de Bactriane et son gouverneur: documents araméens du IV siècle av. n. è.* (Persika 5). Paris.
Sherwin-White, S. and A. Kuhrt (1993) *From Samarkhand to Sardis. A New Approach to the Seleucid Empire*. London.
Skjærvø, P. O. (1995) Aramaic in Iran, *Aram* 7, 283–318.
Stolper, M.-W. (2006) Iranica in post-Achaemenid Babylonian Texts. In P. Briant and F. Joannès (eds) *La transition entre l'empire achéménide et les royaumes hellénistiques*, 223–60, Paris.
Sverchkov, L. M. (2008) The Kurganzol Fortress, *Ancient Civilizations from Scythia to Siberia*, 14, 123–91.
Swertschkow, L. M. (2009) Die Grabungen im Fort Kurgansol im Süden Usbekistans – neue Daten zur Geschichte Zentralasiens am Ende des 4. Jhs. v. Chr. In S. Hansen, A. Wieczorek and M. Tellenbach (eds) *Alexander der Grosse und die Öffnung der Welt. Asiens Kulturen im Wandel*, 145–53, Mannheim.
Tarn, W. W. (1929) Queen Ptolemais and Apama, *The Classical Quarterly* 23, 138–41.
Tarn, W. W. (1930) *Hellenistic Naval and Military Developments*. Cambridge.
Tuplin, C. (2008) The Seleucids and Their Achaemenid Predecessors: A Persian Inheritance? In S. M. Darbandi and A. Zournatzi (eds) *Ancient Greece and Ancient Iran: Cross-Cultural Encounters. 1st International Conference (Athens, 11-13 November 2006)*, 109–36, Athens.
Walbank, F. W. (1988) Review of A. Kuhrt and S. Sherwin-White (eds) *Hellenism in the East*, London 1987, *Liverpool Classical Monthly* 13, 108–12.
Wheatley, P. V. (2002) Antigonus Monophtalmus in Babylonia, 310–308 BC, *Journal of Near Eastern Studies* 61, 39–47.
Wheatley, P. V. (2009) The Diadochi, or Successors to Alexander. In W. Heckel and L. A. Tritle (eds) *Alexander the Great. A New History*, 53–68, Malden, MA.
Wiesehöfer, J. (1994) *Die «dunklen Jahrhunderte» der Persis. Untersuchungen zu Geschichte und Kultur von Fārs in frühhellenistischer Zeit (330 - 140 v. Chr.)*. Munich.
Wiesehöfer, J. (2007) Fars under Seleucid and Parthian Rule. In V. S. Curtis and S. Stewart (eds) *The Age of the Parthians*, 37–49, London and New York.
Wolski, J. (1969) Die Widerstandbewegung gegen die Makedonenherrschaft im Orient, *Klio* 51, 207–15.
Wolski, J. (1999) *The Seleucids. The Decline and Fall of Their Empire*. Kraków.
Zavyalov, V. A. (2007) The Fortifications of the City of Gyaur Kala, Merv. In J. Cribb and G. Herrmann (eds) *After Alexander: Central Asia before Islam*, 313–29, Oxford and New York.
Zournatzi, A. (2008) Cultural Interconnections in the Achaemenid West: A Few Reflections on the Testimony of the Cypriot Archaeological Record. In S. M. Darbandi and A. Zournatzi (eds) *Ancient Greece and Ancient Iran: Cross-Cultural Encounters. 1st International Conference (Athens, 11-13 November 2006)*, 239–55, Athens.

Notes

1 All dates are BC unless otherwise specified. The translations of the sources are drawn from the Loeb Classical Library with some modifications. The hotly disputed chronology of the Diadochi remains beyond the scope of this study. For recent treatments, see Boiy 2007 and Wheatley 2009.

2 See *OCD* s.v. *Diadochi*. Curiously enough, in common usage the term Diadochi/Successors is not related to the both half-Iranian sons of Alexander III, i.e. to Alexander IV and Heracles.

3 For political events in Iran and Central Asia in the Diadochi period, see Schober 1981; Wolski 1999; Mehl 1986; 2000; Sherwin-White and Kuhrt 1993; Wiesehöfer 1996; 2007; Olbrycht 1996; 1998, 41–50; 2005; Bosworth 2002; Anson 2004; Boiy 2007; Capdetrey 2007.

4 For new archaeological discoveries of Achaemenid and post-Achaemenid monuments in Iran and Central Asia, see Cribb and Herrmann 2007; Darbandi and Zournatzi 2008; Hansen and Wieczorek and Tellenbach 2010; Olbrycht 2010a; Litvinskii 2010b. On Iranian cultural traditions in the Diadochi period, see Boyce and Grenet 1991 (best outline); Boucharlat 2006; Callieri 2007; Litvinskii 2010a; 2010b. For an (rather sceptical) overview of possible Seleucid links to the Achaemenids, see Tuplin 2008.

5 For details, see Olbrycht 2004 (cf. the reviews in *Sehepunkte* 5, 2005, no. 7/8 [15.07.2005]; *Bryn Mawr Classical Review* 2006.03.41); 2008; 2010b. Cf. also Bosworth 1980; Briant 1994; Müller 2011b.

6 Fot the detailed references to the satraps' fates, see Olbrycht 2004; Heckel 2006.

7 Hammond 1996, 101 rightly remarks: 'The only troops which the satraps commanded at the time were those who had been recruited locally'. It is to be noted that in 324 Alexander had made the satraps discharge all Greek mercenaries (D.S. 17.106.3).

8 Curt. 10.5.4; cf. 10.6.4–5; Just. 12.15.12; D.S. 17.117.3; 18.2.4; *LM* 112, 118. Cf. Heckel 2006, 198.

9 Arr. *An.* 4.28.8; 5.12.2; 5.20.3; 5.22.5; 6.5.5; 6.6.1; 6.21.3; 6.22.1.

10 D.S. 19.40.1 gives for Antigonus' army 9,000 cavalry, besides the additional troops recently recruited in Media. The manpower of Media was significant - Issus (333) saw a force of 10,000 Median cavalry (Curt. 3.2.4; 3.9.5). Thus it can be safely estimated that after the Paraetacene battle Peithon was able to double his Iranian cavalry troops up to about 5,000.

11 Peucestas was kept in Antigonus' entourage in Asia Minor, see Heckel 2006, 205; Billows 1990, 417–18.

12 Some scholars identify him with the satrap of Areia/Drangiana, appointed by Antigonus at Persepolis (D.S. 19.48.2; Mehl 1986, 109; Billows 1990, 384–85).

13 On the beginnings of Seleucus's state and his career, see Schober 1981, 94–193; Mehl 1986, 104–93; Sherwin-White and Kuhrt 1993, 7–39; Wolski 1999, 19–27; Olbrycht 2005; Landucci Gattinoni 2005; 2008; Capdetrey 2007, 25–50.

14 The Cossaeans were capable of mobilizing a force up to about 13,000 archers (Nearch. *FGH* 133 F 1c. 40.6 and F 1g).

15 On the former, Curt. 7.6.26; Iust. 12.5; Arr. *An.* 4.4.1; Marm.Par. *FGH* 239 B 7; the city was renamed Antiochia in Scythia (St.Byz. s.v. *Antiocheia*). For Alexandropolis, Isid.Char. *Stathm.* 19; Ptol. *Geog.* 6.20.4. See Olbrycht 2004, 244–50.

16 Mehl 1986, 17–19. Apama is often regarded as the only Diadochi wife not immediately left by her husband after 323. But one should point to Amestris, the wife of Craterus. Another case is Artonis who remained the wife of Eumenes, for the latter's body was sent from Iran to her (Plu. *Eum.* 19.2).

17 See the differing opinions in Frye 1982, 86–87; Boyce and Grenet 1991, 118–20; Wiesehöfer 1994, 90–91.

18 This paper was written with the financial support of the Humboldt-Foundation (research stay in Münster, 2010), and National Science Center, Krakow (grant NN108205640). I would like to thank friends and colleagues who have discussed the material with me and supported my research. They include Peter Funke, Sabine Müller (Germany), Daryoosh Akbarzadeh (Iran), Eduard Rtveladze, and Jangar Ilyasov (Uzbekistan). Thanks are also due to Victor Alonso and Ed Anson for their comments and suggestions.

NULLIS UMQUAM NISI DOMESTICIS REGIBUS. CAPPADOCIA, PONTUS AND THE RESISTANCE TO THE DIADOCHI IN ASIA MINOR

Luis Ballesteros Pastor

In the unique speech of Mithridates recorded by Justin (38.7.2), the Pontic king proudly tells that all the countries under his rule had been subdued neither by the mighty Alexander, nor by his Successors and the other kings who came after them: 'Not one of the peoples subject to him had experienced foreign domination, he said; never had they been ruled by kings not of their own race – whether they looked at Cappadocia or Paphlagonia, or else Pontus or Bithynia, and likewise Greater and Lesser Armenia. None of these peoples had even been reached by the famous Alexander, who subdued the whole of Asia, nor by anyone who succeeded or preceded him'.[1] This claim seems to have constituted a key element in Eupator's propaganda in order to extol the glories of his empire, and it would therefore be necessary to determine to what extent this statement is true and what of exaggeration is present in the king's words. Thus, we should resolve whether the independence of these regions was a real fact or it was merely a *topos* developed by late-Hellenistic traditions.

Actually, we must admit that Alexander did not enter the lands which would comprise the domain of the Mithridatids, because the Macedonian conqueror marched southwards from Phrygia to Cilicia without entering Paphlagonia or crossing the Halys.[2] However, Alexander did not give up establishing his dominion over the southern shore of the Euxinus and eastern Anatolia. It is probable that during the king's wintering at Gordium the coastal cities sent him embassies to manifest their submission, with the exception of Sinope, where important pro-Persian elements might be still active.[3] We also know that Alexander assigned Calas the satrapy of Hellespontine Phrygia along with Paphlagonia, and appointed Sabictas as satrap of Cappadocia (Arr. *An.* 2.4.2; Curt. 3.4.1). The Macedonian took other measures such as the restoration of democracy to Amisus which was also exempt from tribute, as a sign of appreciation to this ancient Athenian colony.[4] Nonetheless, as we will see, those decisions did not represent an effective rule, but rather an ephemeral attempt to control a strategic area. In fact, we hear nothing more about Sabictas (Debord 1999, 99).

After Alexander's death, Asia Minor became a stage for the struggles which arose among the Diadochi. But after various vicissitudes, several non-Macedonian dynasties would be settled in Bithynia, Cappadocia and what would later be called the kingdom of Pontus. The dynasts who ruled over those countries had their own armies and resources, and therefore the Diadochi could not ignore these leaders: on the contrary, Alexander's Successors had to attract them or to subdue them to their power (Kobes 1996, 119; Anson 2004, 70–73). In fact, it is remarkable the important number of troops gathered by Ariarathes and Eumenes in their Cappadocian campaigns (Bosworth 2002, 17; Schäefer 2002, 64–65; Anson 2004, 81).

For our approach we will mainly focus on the kingdoms of Cappadocia and Pontus, for several reasons: Persian satraps had ruled these regions, their territories had been assigned to Eumenes, and in both realms would later be settled dynasties with Achaemenid roots. To study these kingdoms we have to face many problems. First, this region has barely been excavated for the period we are studying. Second, the literary sources are scarce, scattered and sometimes contradictory: the mythical character of the accounts about the foundation of these kingdoms reflects a series of confused genealogies.[5] Finally, the toponyms used by the ancient historians can be misleading, as seen for example when the term 'Cilicia' is applied to the lands between the Taurus and the Halys, following the Herodotean perspective. The survival of those place names throughout time appears at least in Strabo, Nepos and Trogus. We think that this confusion is what has raised the debate about Alexander's route, as Curtius and Arrian alluded to a passage through Cappadocia, while Hieronymus of Cardia denied it. The answer is simple: Curtius and Arrian refer to the Cappadocia of their time, while Hieronymus probably followed the so-called 'Herodotean map'.[6]

Cappadocia had been a territory of particular interest for the Persians, who probably colonized that region. Before the arrival of the Macedonians in Asia, Paphlagonia and Cappadocia had been rebellious areas, which played a key role in the so-called 'Great Satraps Revolt' (Debord 1999, 105–15). The study of the administrative organization of this country within the Achaemenid Empire is problematic. Strabo (12.1.4) informs about two Achaemenid satrapies east of the Halys: Pontic Cappadocia, and Cappadocia on the Taurus or Greater Cappadocia. But this statement is not reflected in other sources, and it is therefore considered that this division would have existed, in any case, only after the end of the 'Satraps Revolt'.[7] But despite its brevity, this situation would have legitimized the further development in this area of two different royal houses: that of the Mithridatids to the north and in the south that of the Ariarathids. If we admit Strabo's notice, when Alexander entered Asia there may have been two Persian governors east of the Halys. Debord (1999, 109) proposes that Ariarathes would have been the satrap of southern Cappadocia, while Mithrobuzanes would have ruled on the maritime area. After the latter's death in the Battle on the Granicus, Ariarathes would have seized the entire country, arousing within the Macedonians a sense of danger that needed a solution.[8] In fact, Alexander was planning in 323 a campaign to subdue this region (D.S. 18.3.1).

Upon Alexander's death, Paphlagonia, Cappadocia and the lands along the southern Euxinus as far as Trapezus were assigned to Eumenes. It was a territory to conquer, what demonstrates that Alexander's attempt to hold that region had not become a permanent Macedonian rule.[9] In support of Eumenes came Perdiccas, who defeated Ariarathes.

The Persian satrap was pursued to his city and crucified.[10] Although the location of this place is not specified in our sources, it was probably Gaziura, in the Lycus valley. Strabo (12.3.15) describes this site as an ancient royal capital, and there are coins with the legend 'Ariorath' in Aramaic bearing the image of the god Baal worshipped in this city (Hornblower 1981, 242; Debord 1999, 108–09). After this disaster, the Cappadocian nobles fled to Armenia, from where they would go back later to resume their domains.[11]

The rivalries between the Diadochi had arisen early, and that region became one of the stages in the fight that broke out: in the settlement at Triparadeisus it was decided to appoint Nicanor as satrap of Cappadocia to replace Eumenes.[12] Later, Antigonus sent there new forces under the command of Menander to prevent a resurgence of the Cardian's power.[13] After Eumenes' defeat in Gabiene, Cassander aimed to seize Cappadocia.[14] But the powerful Monophthalmus would not give up that satrapy: while Asclepiodorus, Cassander's general, was besieging Amisus, Antigonus sent his nephew Ptolemaius to liberate this city, thus gaining control of that country.[15] After Ipsus most of Asia Minor was given to Lysimachus, although we know nothing about his rule east of Amastris, and Appian (*Syr.* 55) suggests that Cappadocia passes directly from Cassander to Seleucus.[16] The latter sent there Amyntas as a *stratēgos*, but this governor was beaten by Ariarathes II, the son of Perdiccas' rival, with the support of Ardoates, ruler of Armenia.[17] Nevertheless, the Seleucids remained ruling over lands north of the Taurus which would later belong to the Ariarathid dynasty.[18]

There were also in Asia Minor other active pockets of resistance to Macedonian power, which would eventually lead to the emergence of new kingdoms. In Bithynia, Calas had been defeated at the hands of Bas. Zipoetes, son of the latter, was able to maintain his power in Bithynia against the ambitions of Antigonus and Lysimachus, consolidating a dynasty that lasted for two centuries.[19] But the political map of northern Anatolia had been altered by another fact: Mithridates, a Persian nobleman, had taken refuge in Paphlagonia, constituting a modest principality that would become the important kingdom of Pontus. Little is known about the first of the Mithridatids. The narratives concerning him include mythic elements which foreshadow the future greatness of his dynasty. Mithridates belonged to the family of the Persian dynasts who had ruled Cius in Mysia, and he was probably a nephew of the last one, who was crucified by Antigonus under the suspicion of conspiring with Cassander (D.S. 20.111.4). Mithridates had joined Eumenes' forces which fought at Gabiene (D.S. 19.40.2). After the Cardian's defeat, the Persian noble was handed over to the victorious Antigonus, and entered his service, while engaging in a close friendship with the young Demetrius.[20] But probably during the siege of Tyre, Demetrius warned his friend that Antigonus was planning to kill him. The One-eyed had dreamt that he was sowing gold-dust in a fair field. A golden spike sprang up, but when he came back after a while, the golden crop had disappeared. In his dream Antigonus heard voices telling that Mithridates had reaped the crop and fled to the Euxinus. After knowing that, Demetrius promised his father not to utter a word about the dream, and therefore he wrote his friend a warning on the sand: 'Fly, Mithridates'. The Persian escaped along with six horsemen, and became strong in Cimiata, a remote place in the mountains of Paphlagonia. From there he expanded his domains, resulting in a kingdom which several generations later would become large and powerful.[21]

As we see in this legendary account, the tradition includes Mithridates I Ctistes among the great founders of empires. First, we face a man of high birth who had shown a special military aptitude from his childhood (D.S. 19.40.2) and is a good comrade of the young Demetrius. The Macedonian feels a sincere affection towards his friend, to the point of revealing him a secret entrusted by his father. Premonitory dreams reflect supernatural intervention, which foreshadows the greatness of the future kingdom. It seems as if Mithridates were destined to reap the harvest of glory sown by the Macedonians. As many other heroes, he has to endure several dangers which are a proof of his exceptional aptitudes. The flight path is shown also in Antigonus' dream: it is the Black Sea, which appears as a God-appointed destination.[22]

From a more realistic perspective, it should be considered that Mithridates Ctistes had his own troops which made possible the formation of this small principality. In fact, the so-called 'Founder of Pontus' extended his possessions from a stronghold in inner Paphlagonia, and his son reached the coast by the conquest of Amastris (Memn. *FGH* 434 F 1 9.4). Nevertheless, contrary to common opinion, it is very possible that these first dominions of the Pontic dynasty did not extend beyond the Halys.[23]

It is difficult to trace the primary sources for the passages of Diodorus and Appian concerning the first ruler of Pontus. As in Cappadocia, the Mithridatic kingdom held some traditions regarding its early history, about which we have certain echoes recorded in the classical sources. We consider that Appian took the legend of Mithridates the Founder from Pompeius Trogus. There are remarkable similarities between the puzzling *Epitome* written by Justin from Trogus' work and the Alexandrian's biography of Eupator, although we can not here develop this theme at length.[24] It is evident that Appian had thought to compose a book on the Roman province of Bithynia and Pontus, but when this author found in Trogus a complete account on Mithridates VI he decided to write a biography of this king.[25] The story of premonitions, dangers and escapes of Mithridates Ctistes is similar to other passages in the *Philippic Histories*.[26] Trogus expressed a particular interest in the *origines gentium* and accordingly he records the beginnings of the Bithynian, Cappadocian and Armenian dynasties, among many others. However, we do not know the sources used by the Gallic author for his account on Mithridates I: of course one of them could be Hieronymus, who was also interested in the origins of peoples and kingdoms. However, it has been pointed out that the tale about the dream is clearly an account *post eventum*, which would indicate a later source.[27] Along with this, we must stress that Appian refers to Mithridates' imprisonment by Antigonus, while according to Diodorus the Persian noble runs away immediately after Demetrius' warning. Appian just mentions Hieronymus regarding Alexander's route, but this does not allow us to consider that the whole passage on Mithridates Ctistes in the *Mithridateios* would have been taken from the Cardian's work. It is clear that Appian echoes in this book a Cappadocian perspective which would not fit completely with Hyeronimus' account.[28]

Both the Mithridatid and Ariarathid dynasties claimed to derive from an old Persian lineage: the Pontics were presumed to be descendants either from one of the Seven Persians who murdered Gaumata, or from Cyrus and Darius. The Cappadocians pretended to come from Atossa, who was a sister of Cambyses, the father of Cyrus the Great. Anaphas (Otanes), a great-grandson of Atossa and her husband Pharnaces, was one of the Seven who killed the Magus, and was granted with the satrapy of Cappadocia as a domain exempt from tribute.[29]

It has been supposed that a rivalry arose between these royal houses in order to exalt their respective genealogies, trying to date them back as early as possible.[30] Thus, the Cappadocian would at first sight be an older lineage, but we should remember that king Mithridates VIII of Bosphorus (great-great-grandson of Eupator) solemnly declared to be a descendant of Achaemenes (Tac. *An.* 12.18.2), that is, directly going back to the founder of the Persian royal line. Likewise, both dynasties seem to claim that their respective dominions had been transferred by Darius the Great. But there may have been further versions about the origin of these kingdoms: Polybius (fr. 54) recounts an anecdote according to which an Achaemenid king (perhaps Artaxerxes) was saved from a lion by a Persian noble; they climbed to the top of a high mountain in Cappadocia and the ruler bestowed on his savior all as his eyes reached.[31] It is well known that hunting, and particularly the lion, was a key element in the legitimation of the royal power in both Persia and Macedonia (Briant 1991; Palagia 2000). As we have seen, the Ariarathids were alleged to descend from Otanes. Herodotus (3.83–84) tells that this noble was the only Persian who did not pay obedience to anyone else because of his important role in the plot against Gaumata, and this privilege was transmitted to his descendants. Perhaps the Cappadocian kings, claiming to belong to Otanes' line, would have developed some propaganda about an ancestral independence of this territory in regard with the Achaemenid rule. However, it does not fit whith the historical evidence which shows that the satraps of Cappadocia had been under the authority of the Great Kings of Persia (Briant 1996, 145–6).

It is also quite probable that, at some time in the second century BC, both Mithridatids and Ariarathids would have pretended to come from the abovementioned Pharnaces, who can be found in the tradition of both realms. But despite this, Cappadocians and Pontics must have had their own legends of foundation, since Pompeius Trogus (*Prol.* 34, 37) treated separately the origins of these two dynasties, and in fact we know some details in the accounts of their beginnings that differentiate one realm from another. With regard to Pontus, it has been noticed that Mithridates Ctistes is described flying in the company of six associates, what recalls the story of Darius and the conspiracy of the 'Seven Persians'. The presence of seven noble founders is also recorded in Arrian's account about the origin of the Parthians: so we are very likely facing an Iranian-rooted tradition that pointed to a resurgence of the Achaemenid glory.[32] The 'Cappadocian Chronicle' of Diodorus presents a different view about the origins of the Ariarathid kingdom, mentioning two brothers who shared power: Ariarathes I and Orophernes. While the former governed the realm, the latter helped the Persians fighting against the Egyptians. This kind of diarchy is recurrent in some Hellenistic accounts about the foundation of peoples and empires: to the well-known tale of Romulus and Remus, it should be added those legends regarding the founders of Scythians, Amazons, and even the Parthians. Besides Diodorus, Arrian, Apollonius of Rhodes and Justin collect myths of foundation which have these same traits.[33]

It is not easy, however, to interpret this part of the 'Cappadocian Chronicle': it is worth noting that the names of those dynasts match the future Ariarathes V and his brother Orophernes, who ruled jointly for some time in mid-second century BC (cf. Breglia Pulci Doria 1978, 122, on the interpretation of this coincidence). In any case, the Diodorean account presents Ariarathes I under the heroic aureole of the founders, and this also may be related with the longevity that Lucian attributed to him. At the same time, alluding to these Cappadocian dynasts as 'kings', and giving the total number of rulers within the dynasty, would indicate that the Sicilian consulted sources which were actually written after the time of the Diadochi, once the Ariarathid rulers had assumed the royal title (an anachronism noted by McGing 1986a, 13). Our conclusion from all these accounts is that, according to Panitschek (1987), the tradition concerning the lineage of these dynasties would have been modified throughout time. As we see, Iranian culture was present in the Pontic and Cappadocian ruling houses. Despite the process of Hellenization which takes place in both kingdoms, their sovereigns never renounced their ancestral identity: they continued to bear Iranian names, although their portraits on the coins became Hellenized, without beard and wearing diadems (in general, see Michels 2009, 183–246).

Pontus could be regarded as a kingdom closer to the Hellenic world when compared to Cappadocia.[34] The true situation, however, would have been not so simple: the Greek colonies on the coast were a major factor of Hellenization, but in fact the presence of Persian traditions was intense in Pontus. Together with the scarcity of archaeological evidence, the main obstacle we have to assess the importance of Iranian culture in this kingdom is the work of Strabo, who is considered an undisputed authority regarding his native country. Proud of his Greek roots, this writer probably hated being considered a 'Cappadocian', due to the depictive connotation that it had within the Graeco-Roman world. Thus, while Josephus calls him 'Strabo the Cappadocian', our author speaks of the Cappadocians in the third person, as if he did not belong to this people.[35] The Iranian branch of the geographer's genealogy is represented in his work only by the mention of Moaphernes, whereas there is a wider account about his Greek ancestors.[36] Strabo's Pontus lacks magi and other facets of Iranian civilization. If to this biased perspective we add the enthusiasm of many Greeks towards Eupator and the king's image on the coins, evoking Alexander's portrait, it is easy to understand how our perception of Mithridatic Pontus can be disconcerting.[37]

The Persian features in Eupator's kingdom have been analyzed by B. McGing, who highlights aspects such as onomastics, the satraps, the enunchs, and the worship of Iranian deities.[38] To this should be added the use of tiara (Plu. *Pomp.* 42.3), or the existence in the kingdom of magi, whom we only have indirect references. As we have told, Appian collects traces of Iranian traditions within the reign of Mithridates: to the foundation myth reminiscent of Darius, we could add the use of Persian punishments as putting golden shackles on the prince Mithridates, or pouring molten gold into the mouth of Manius Aquillius.[39] The sacrifices to Zeus Stratius performed by the king (App. *Mithr.* 66, 70), although not identical with the rituals to Ahura-Mazda, had certain analogies with Persian cults (Olshausen 1990, 1901–03; Ballesteros Pastor 2003). Mithridates' own behaviour presents some features associated with Achaemenid rulers, such as being able to drink wine in abundance.[40] In the Pontic kingdom there were sanctuaries for Anaitis, the Persian Artemis. As we have seen, in Gaziura Baal was worshiped, and the palace of Cabeira had a zoological garden, characteristic of the Achaemenid royal sites (Str. 12.3.30).[41]

This survival of Achaemenid traditions is found also among Mithridates' successors. Pharnaces II proclaimed himself as 'Great King of Kings' and bore no royal Greek epithet. This ruler decreed the emasculation of the young Amisenians, using another kind of Persian punishment.[42] One of his sons was named Darius (Hoben 1969, 34–39), and there is a bust of Dynamis (Podossinov 2002, 32), Pharnaces'daughter, in which she appears wearing a Phrygian cap. Finally, as we have regarded, the pride of belonging to the Achaemenid line reached at least until Mithridates VIII.

There are significant discrepancies in establishing the time when these Anatolian dynasts adopted the title of king. Numismatic evidence contradicts the literary sources that, in turn, provide different versions which are difficult to reconcile. The era on the Bithynian coins began in 297/6, probably coinciding with the successes of Zipoites against Lysimachus' forces. However, the first known royal coinage was issued by Nicomedes I, who came to the throne in 280.[43] Mithridates Eupator adopted the Bithynian era, but this does not mean that the Pontics would have assumed the kingship at the same time as the neighbouring dynasty. It has been deduced from Synkellos that Mithridates I took the title of king towards 280, but this can not be confirmed with any other evidence, and the meaning of the Chronographer's dates about Pontus is a matter of discussion. In fact, the first royal Pontic coin we have is dated after the time of the Founder.[44] With regard to Cappadocia, Diodorus (31.19.9) gives for the Ariarathid dynasty 170 or 160 years, which would go back to the assumption of the royal dignity in the time of Ariaramnes, in the first half of the III century BC. By contrast, Strabo (12.1.2) tells that Ariarathes III, son of that sovereign, was the first Cappadocian ruler who bore the title of king. Strabo's passage about the two districts of Achaemenid Cappadocia (12.1.4) refers to a different position of the Macedonians regarding the change of both satrapies into kingdoms. In one case, it would have been against the will of the Macedonians, meanwhile in the other they would have welcomed it. The order in Strabo's sentence suggests that the reticent attitude would be referred to the Mithridatids, but we can not know how was shown that Macedonian opposition to the new dynasty.[45] In any case, it was after the rulers of these three countries had been proclaimed as kings when their respective dynasties began to establish matrimonial ties with the Macedonian royal houses.[46]

In short, Alexander's Successors sought to keep under their power the territories extending from southern Euxinus into Anatolia. Different armies of the Diadochi walked that region which became a stage for their glories and miseries. However, the Macedonians had finally to acknowledge the power of the Persian dynasties with whom, some generations later, they would end up mixing their bloodlines. Therefore, we have to qualify the opinion attributed to Mithridates, denying the Macedonian presence in his domains. In Justin's speech the Pontic King of Kings states that these countries had always been ruled by native sovereigns: therefore, the Iranians seem to be presented as legitimate rulers although it is not entirely clear in this passage.[47] Perhaps Eupator combined different traditions in order to exalt the glory of his empire: Otanes' privileges, Calas' defeat, the successful flight of Mithridates Ctistes, the failure of the Seleucids in their aim to conquer the whole Cappadocia, and the independence of the Caucasian peoples.[48] Centuries after Alexander's conquests, the heirs of those Persians who had fought the Macedonians in Anatolia had maintained their power, their traditions and many of their identity, which was not completely removed by the Hellenic influence. Thus, the Achaemenid glorious past resurfaces as a reference, and, from the second century BC on, becomes an element of pride against Rome, which, after the conquest of Greece and Macedonia, is calling on the doorstep of Asia.

Bibliography

Anson, E. M. (2004) *Eumenes of Cardia. A Greek among Macedonians.* Leiden.

Archibald, Z. H. (1998) *The Odryssian Kingdom of Thrace. Orpheus Unmasked.* Oxford.

Archibald, Z. H. (2007) Contacts between the Ptolemaic Egypt and the Black Sea in the Early Hellenistic Age. In V. Gabrielsen and J. Lund (eds) *The Black Sea in Antiquity. Regional and Interregional Economic Exchanges*, 253–71, Aarhus.

Atkinson, J. E. (1980) *A Commentary on Q. Curtius Rufus'* Historiae Alexandri Magni. *Books 3 and 4.* Amsterdam.

Atkinson, J. E. (1994) *A Commentary on Q. Curtius Rufus'* Historiae Alexandri Magni *Books 5–7.2.* Amsterdam.

Avram, A. (2003) Antiochos II Théos, Ptolémée II Philadelphe et la Mer Noire, *Comptes Rendus de l'Académie d'Inscriptions et Belles Lettres* 147, 1181–1213.

Ballesteros Pastor, L. (1996) *Mitrídates Eupátor, rey del Ponto.* Granada.

Ballesteros Pastor, L. (2003) El culto de Mitrídates a Zeus Estratio. In M. Garrido-Hory and A. Gonzalès (eds) *Histoire, espaces et marges de l'Antiquité. Hommages à Monique Clavel-Lévêque*, vol. 2, 209–22, Besançon.

Ballesteros Pastor, L. (2006) El discurso de Mitrídates en el *Epítome de las Historias Filípicas de Pompeyo Trogo* (Iust. XXXVIII 4–7): un estudio sobre las fuentes, *Mediterraneo Antico* 9, 581–96.

Ballesteros Pastor, L. (2002–2007) Del Reino Mitridátida al Reino del Ponto: orígenes de un término geográfico y un concepto político, *Orbis Terrarum* 9, 3–10.

Ballesteros Pastor, L. (2008) Cappadocia and Pontus, Client Kingdoms of the Roman Republic. From the Peace of Apamea to the Beginning of the Mithridatic Wars (188–89 BC). In A. Coskun (ed.) *Freundschaft und Gefolgschaft in den auswärtigen Beziehungen der Römer (2. Jhr. v. Chr.–1 Jhr. n. Chr.)*, 45–63, Frankfurt.

Ballesteros Pastor, L. (2009a) Bears and Bees in Themiskyra: A Sanctuary for Artemis in the Land of the Amazons? In B. Poulsen and T. Fischer-Hansen (eds) *From Artemis to Diana. The Goddess of Man and Beast*, 333–40, Copenhagen.

Ballesteros Pastor, L. (2009b) Troy, between Mithridates and Rome. In J. M. Højte (ed.) *Mithridates VI and the Pontic Kingdom*, 217–31, Aarhus.

Ballesteros Pastor, L. (2009c) Pompeyo Trogo, Justino y las críticas a Roma: a propósito del discurso etolio (Iust. XXVIII, 2), *Mediterraneo Antico* 12, 381–92.

Barat, C. (2009) Sinope et ses rélations avec la péninsule Anatolienne: réseaux, échanges des biens et des hommes. In H. Bru, H. Kirbihler and S. Lebreton (eds) *L'Asie Mineure dans l'Antiquité. Échanges, populations et territoires*, 351–75, Rennes.

Billows, R. A. (1990) *Antigonos the One-Eyed and the Creation of the Hellenistic State*. Berkeley.

Bohak, G. (2005) Ethnic Portraits in Graeco-Roman Literature. In E. S. Gruen (ed.) *Cultural Borrowings and Ethnic Appropriations in Antiquity*, 207–37, Stuttgart.

Bompaire, J. (2003) *Lucian. Ouvres*. II. Paris.

Bosworth, A. B. (1980) *A Historical Commentary on Arrian's History of Alexander*. Vol. I: *Commentary on Books I–III*. Oxford.

Bosworth, A. B. (1997) The Emasculation of the Calchedonians: A Forgotten Episode of the Ionian War, *Chiron* 27, 297–313.

Bosworth, A. B. (2002) *The Legacy of Alexander. Politics, Warfare, and Propaganda under the Successors*. Oxford.

Bosworth, A. B. and P. V. Wheatley (1998) On the Origins of the Pontic House, *Journal of Hellenic Studies* 118, 155–64.

Breglia Pulci Doria, L. (1978) Diodoro e Ariarate V. Conflitti dinastici, tradizione e propaganda politica nella Cappadocia del II secolo a.C., *La Parola del Passato* 33, 104–29.

Briant, P. (1991) Chasses royales macedoniennes et chasses royales perses: le thème de la chasse au lion sur *la chasse de Vergina*, *Dialogues d'Histoire Ancienne* 17, 211–55.

Briant, P. (1996) *Histoire de l'Empire Perse. De Cyrus à Alexandre*. Paris.

Burstein, S. M. (1976) *Outpost of Hellenism: The Emergence of Heraclea on the Black Sea*. Berkeley and Los Angeles.

Burstein, S. M. (1980) The Aftermath of the Peace of Apamea. Rome and the Pontic War, *American Journal of Ancient History* 5, 1–12.

Callataÿ, F. de (1999) *L'Histoire des Guerres Mithridatiques vue par les monnaies*. Louvain-la-Neuve.

Callataÿ, F. de *The First Royal Coinages of Pontos (from Mithridates III to Mithridates V)*. In J. M. Højte (ed.) *Mithridates VI and the Pontic Kingdom*, 63–94, Aarhus.

Campanille, M. D. (1996) Città d'Asia Minore tra Mitridate e Roma. In B. Virgilio (ed.) *Studi Ellenistici* 8, 145–73, Pisa and Rome.

Cohen, G. M. (1995) *The Hellenistic Settlements in Europe, the Islands, and Asia Minor*. Berkeley.

Debord, P. (1999) *L'Asie Mineure au IVe siècle (412–323 a.C.). Pouvoirs et jeux politiques*. Bordeaux.

Dundes, A. (1990) The Hero Pattern and the Life of Jesus. In R. A. Segal (ed.) *In Quest of the Hero*, 179–223, Princeton.

Eddy, S. K. (1961) *The King is Dead. Studies in the Near Eastern Resistance to Hellenism*. Lincoln.

Facella, M. (2006) *La dinastia degli Orontidi nella Commagene ellenistico-romana*. Pisa.

Fleischer, R. (2009) The Rock-tombs of the Pontic Kings in Amaseia (Amasya). In J. M. Højte (ed.) *Mithridates VI and the Pontic Kingdom*, 109–119, Aarhus.

Frye, R. N. (1964) The Charisma of Kingship in Ancient Iran, *Iranica Antiqua* 4, 36–54.

Gabelko, O. L. (2009) *The Dynastic History of the Hellenistic Monarchies of Asia Minor according to the* Chronography *of George Synkellos.* In J. M. Højte (ed.) *Mithridates VI and the Pontic Kingdom*, 47–61, Aarhus.
García Moreno, L. A. (1993) Nacimiento, infancia y primeras aventuras de Mitrídates Eupátor, rey del Ponto, *Polis* 5, 91–109.
García Sánchez, M. (2009) *El Gran Rey de Persia. Formas de representación de la alteridad persa en el imaginario griego.* Barcelona.
Goukowsky, P. (2001) *Appien. Histoire Romaine. Livre XII. La Guerre de Mithridate*. Paris.
Grainger, J. D. (1997) *A Seleukid Prosopography and Gazetteer*. Leiden.
Harmon, M. (1913) *Lucian.* I. Cambridge, MA.
Heckel, W. (2006) *Who's Who in the Age of Alexander the Great: Prosopography of Alexander's Empire.* Malden, MA.
Heckel, W. (2007) Nicanor, Son of Balacrus, *Greek, Roman and Byzantine Studies* 47, 401–12.
Henke, M. (2005) *Kappadokien in hellenistischer Zeit*. Diss. Münster.
Herman, G. (2006) Iranian Epic Motifs in Josephus'Antiquities (XVIII, 314–370), *Journal of Jewish Studies* 57, 245–68.
Hind, J. (1994) The Bosporan Kingdom, *The Cambridge Ancient History*. Vol.VI: *The Fourth Century BC*, 2nd edn, 416–511, Cambridge.
Hoben, W. (1969) *Untersuchungen zur Stellung kleinasiatischen Dynasten in den Machtkämpfen der ausgehenden Römischen Republik*. Diss. Mainz.
Højte, J. M. (ed.) (2009a) *Mithridates VI and the Pontic Kingdom.* Aarhus.
Højte, J. M. (2009b) The Death and Burial of Mithridates VI. In J. M. Højte (ed.) *Mithridates VI and the Pontic Kingdom*, 121–30, Aarhus.
Hornblower, J. (1981) *Hieronymus of Cardia.* Oxford.
Klinkott, H. (2000) *Die Satrapienregister der Alexander- und Diadochenzeit.* Stuttgart.
Kobes, J. (1996) *'Kleine Könige'. Untersuchungen zu den Lokaldynasten im hellenistischen Kleinasien (323–188 v. Chr.).* St. Katharinen.
Landucci Gattinoni, F. (1992) *Lisimaco di Tracia. Un sovrano nella prospettiva del primo ellenismo.* Milano.
Landucci Gattinoni, F. (2005) Per un commento storico del libro XVIII di Diodoro: riflessioni preliminari. In D. Ambaglio (ed.) *Syngraphé. Atti del convegno 'Epitomati ed epitomatori: il crocevia di Diodoro Siculo'*, 175–90, Como.
Lebreton, S. (2011) Mazaca: un site a 'tous égards naturellement impropre à l'habitat', *Res Antiquae* 8, 1–33.
Leschhorn, W. (1993) *Antike Ären. Zeitrechnung, Politik und Geschichte im Schwarzmeerraum und in Kleinasien nördlich des Tauros.* Stuttgart.
Lund, H. S. (1992) *Lysimachus: A Study in Early Hellenistic Kingship*. New York.
Marek, C. (1993) *Stadt, Ära und Territorium in Pontus-Bithynia und Nord-Galatien.* Tübingen.
Martin, P. M. (2001) La tradition de la double royauté dans la Rome des origines. In V. Fromentin and S. Gotteland (eds) *Origines Gentium*, 241–62, Bordeaux.
Mastrocinque, A. (2005) I magi e l'educazione del principe. In V. Alonso Troncoso (ed.) *ΔΙΑΔΟΧΟΣ ΤΗΣ ΒΑΣΙΛΕΙΑΣ. La figura del sucesor en la realeza helenística*, 177–84, Madrid.
McGing, B. C. (1986a) *The Foreign Policy of Mithridates VI Eupator, King of Pontus.* Leiden.
McGing, B. C. (1986b) The Kings of Pontus: Some Problems of Identity and Date, *Rheinisches Museum für Philologie* 129, 248–59.

McGing, B. C. (1998) On the Fringes. Culture, History and the Kingdom of Pontus (Russian, with English summary), *Vestnik Drevnej Istorii*, 97–112.

Meyer, E. (1925) *Die Grenzen der hellenistischen Staaten in Kleinasien*. Zurich and Leipzig.

Michels, C. (2009) *Kulturtransfer und monarchischer 'Philhellenismus'. Bithynien, Pontos und Kappadokien in hellenistischer Zeit.* Göttingen.

Muccioli, F. (2004) 'Il re dell'Asia' : Ideologia e propaganda da Alessandro Magno a Mitridate VI, *Simblos* 4, 105–58.

Olshausen, E. (1978) Pontos, *RE* Supl. 15, 396–442.

Olshausen, E. (1990) Götter, Heroen und ihre Kulte in Pontos. Ein erster Bericht, *Aufstieg und Niedergang der Römischen Welt* II 18.3, 1865–1906.

Palagia, O. (2000) The Royal Hunt of Alexander the Great. In A. B. Bosworth and E. J. Baynham (eds) *Alexander the Great in Fact and Fiction*, 167–206, Oxford.

Panichi, S. (2005) Cappadocia through Strabo's Eyes. In D. Dueck, H. Lindsay and S. Pothecary (eds) *Strabo's Cultural Geography. The Making of a* Kolossourgia, 200–15, Cambridge.

Panitschek, P. (1987) Zu den genealogischen Konstruktionen der Dynastien von Pontos und Kappadokien, *Rivista Storica dell'Antichità* 17/18, 73–95.

Petrović, Z. (2009) Mithridates II and Antiochos Hierax, *Klio* 91, 378–83.

Podossinov, A. V. (2002) Am Rande der griechischen Oikumene. In J. Fornasier and B. Böttger (eds) *Das Bosporanische Reich*, 21–38, Mainz.

Portanova, J. J. (1988) *The Associates of Mithridates VI of Pontus*. Diss. Columbia University, Ann Arbor.

Poulsen, B. (1991) The Dioscuri and Ruler Ideology, *Symbolae Osloensis* 66, 119–46.

Primo, A. (2006) Il termine ultimo delle *Storie* di Ieronimo di Cardia, *Athenaeum* 94, 719–22.

Primo, A. (2008) Seleuco e Mitridate Ktístes in un episodio di Demetrio il Giovane. In B. Virgilio (ed.) *Studi Ellenistici* 20, 409–25, Pisa and Rome.

Reinach, T. (1886) Essai sur la numismatique des rois de Cappadoce, *Revue Numismatique* s. 3.4, 301–35, 452–83.

Reinach, T. (1890) *Mithridate Eupator, roi de Pont*. Paris.

Schäfer, C. (2002) *Eumenes von Kardia und der Kampf um die Macht im Alexanderreich.* Frankfurt.

Sofou, A. (2005) Strabo and the Historical Geography of Cappadocia, *Mediterraneo Antico* 8, 739–66.

Syme, R. (1995) *Anatolica. Studies in Strabo*. Oxford.

Thornton, J. (1998) *Misos Rhomaion* o *phobos Mithridatou*? Echi storiografici di un dibattito diplomatico, *Mediterraneo Antico* 1, 271–309.

Torres Guerra, J. B. (2006) Apiano de Alejandría: traductor (BC IV 45 y V 191), *Emerita* 74, 17–28.

Van Wickevoort-Crommelin, B. R. (1993) *Die Universalgeschichte des Pompeius Trogus. Herculea Audacia Orbem Terrarum Adgressus*. Hagen.

Weber, G. (2000) *Kaiser, Träume und Visionen in Prinzipat und Spätantike.* Stuttgart.

Wiesehöfer, J. (2001) *Ancient Persia*. London.

Wolski, J. (1996) *L'Empire des Arsacides*. Leuven.

Yardley, J. C. (trans.) (1994) *Justin. Epitome of the Philippic History of Pompeius Trogus.* Atlanta.

Yardley, J. and W. Heckel (1997) *Justin.* Epitome *of the* Philippic History *of Pompeius Trogus*. Vol. I: *Books 11-12: Alexander the Great*. Oxford.

Notes

1 Trans. Yardley 1994, 242. Cf. Just. 37.3.2; Ballesteros Pastor 2006, 585–86. A commentary on this idea seems to be implicit in Josephus' speech of Herod Agrippa II (*BJ* 2.366–67). Appian (*Mith.* 8) tells that he does not know who ruled that region prior to the Macedonians, although in another passage (*Mith.* 83) this author states that Amisus had been under the Achaemenid rule: cf. McGing 1998, 97.

2 On Alexander's route, see Arr. *An.* 2.4.1–2; Plu. *Alex.* 18.5; App. *Mith.* 8; Bosworth 1980, 188–89; Hornblower 1981, 240; Briant 1996, 1051, 1070; Debord 1999, 144, 455–56, 463. Curtius 3.1.22–24, affirms that the Macedonians passed through Paphlagonia and Cappadocia, but we have no other notice about this. The allusion to Cappadocia may be a mistake due to the use of different toponyms: see below n. 6. The Anatolian lands of the Mithridatids beyond the Halys were not probably called 'Pontus' until the reign of Eupator: see Ballesteros Pastor 2002–2007.

3 See above n. 2. The Sinopeans sent envoys and probably troops to Darius: Arr. *An.* 3.24.4; Curt. 6.5.6–9; cf. 4.1.34. Following Arrian, Alexander captured these legates but treated them with clemency, because they did not belong to the Corinthian League and were still subjects of Darius. Bosworth 1980, 353, critizices this view because Sinope, as part of Paphlagonia, was under Macedonian authority. Arrian's phrase would indicate the importat Persian influence on Sinope: Reinach 1890, 28; Briant 1996, 719; Barat 2009, 355.

4 App. *Mith.* 8; 83. Hornblower 1981, 240, doubts this exemption of tribute, which may have been just a local tradition. Sabictas is wrongly called Abistamenes by Curtius. Briant 1996, 1051, proposes that the region assigned to him could have been just Cataonia. On Calas, see Arr. *An.* 2.4.2; Curt. 3.1.23; 4.5.13; Memn. *FGH* 434 F 1 12.4; Atkinson 1980, 97; Briant 1996, 718–19; Debord 1999, 158–59; Heckel 2006, 74–75, s.v. 'Calas'. Alexander's rule over Cappadocia and Paphlagonia was also recorded in Curt. 6.3.3; Plu. *Alex.* 18.5; cf. Memn. *FGH* 434 F 1 4.1. See further Briant 1996, 1051, 1070; Debord 1999, 144, 455–56, 463. In several ancient passages the Macedonian is called 'master of the whole Asia', but this concept is undoubtedly a *topos*: see Muccioli 2004; Ballesteros Pastor 2006, 586–87.

5 Reinach 1886, 311–12; Breglia Pulci Doria 1976, 111–12; Hornblower 1981, 241; Debord 1999, 90, 108–09. See below n. 29 and 31.

6 Curt. 3.1.24; Arr. *An.* 2.4.2; Hieronym.Hist. *FGH* 154 F 3 (*apud* App. *Mith.* 8); see above n. 2. On the 'Herodotean map', see Hdt. 1.72; cf. 5.49.6; Debord 1999, 87, 318. This extension of Cilicia appears implicitly in Just. 37.1.2. Nepos (*Dat.*1.1) mentions in Cilicia Leucosyrians, who were identified with the Cappadocians (see for instance Hdt. 5.49.6; Str. 12.3.5,9,12,25). Strabo places Mazaca in Cilicia, which was one of the districts (*stratēgiai*) of Ariarathid Cappadocia (12.2.7). For further references, see Sofou 2005, 743–48. Arrian's allusion to Galatia (*An.* 2.4.1) is an anachronism. Many place names recorded in the sources about the Diadochi have not been located yet, as is the case of Nora, the fortress where Eumenes was besieged: see Anson 2004, 130–31 n. 52, and Briant 1996, 1501.

7 Hornblower 1981, 240; Debord 1999, 109, 162–63; cf. Panichi 2005, 200 n. 3.

8 Debord 1999, 109–10; Michels 2009, 17. Our sources do not specify the area ruled by these satraps: for a different reconstruction, cf. Heckel 2006, 168, s.v. 'Mithrobuzanes'. Debord's hypothesis may be based on the aid sent to Darius by the Sinopeans (see above n. 3). Sofou 2005, 741–42, denies the two satrapies even for a short time. Ariarathes would have controlled the whole of Cappadocia in 322: D.S. 18.16.1–3; Arr. *Post.Alex.* 1.11; Just. 13.6.1–3; Plu. *Eum.* 3.4. Anson 2004, 66, points out that there were no hostilities between Antigonus and Ariarathes before Eumenes' arrival in Cappadocia.

9 D.S. 18.3.1; 31.19.4; Plu. *Eum.* 3.2; Arr. *Post.Alex.* 1.5; Just. 13.4.16; 13.6.14; App. *Mith.* 8; Nep. *Eum.* 2.2; 3.2; Curt. 10.10.3; Bosworth 2002, 58; Schäfer 2002, 62; Anson 2004, 71.

10 D.S. 18.16.1–3; 22.1; 31.19.4; App. *Mith.* 8; Just. 13.6.1; Plu. *Eum.* 3.12–13; Lucian. *Macr.* 13; Arr. *Post.Alex.* 1.11; Klinkott 2000, 107. Justin calls him king (*rex*), meanwhile Diodorus considers him as a 'ruler' (*dunastēs*): for the meaning of that term in this author, see Kobes 1996, 9–24. Hornblower 1981, 65, 329, states that Hieronymus probably inspired the accounts of Justin and Diodorus, and could have influenced Appian's. Diodorus (31.19.3–5) tells that Ariarathes died on the battlefield: Hornblower 1981, 47, attributes this version to a local Cappadocian source, recorded by Polybius. There are different traditions on Ariarathes' death: following Arrian, the satrap was hanged, while Lucian seems to indicate

that he was crucified: see Harmon 2003, 30 n. 36. This satrap was defeated in two different battles (Arr. *Post.Alex.* 1.11; Anson 2004, 73 with n. 92, 77). For a critical review of the sources of Diodorus' book XVIII, see Bosworth 2002, 24–28; Anson 2004, 11–25; Landucci Gattinoni 2005. On the meaning of this victory for Perdiccas' aspirations, see Bosworth 2002, 60–62.

11 D.S. 31.19.5. Perdiccas sent forces to Armenia, where there was a strong resistance: see Anson 2004, 79–81. On the date of the reconquest of Cappadocia and the identity of its protagonists, see Facella 2006, 169.

12 D.S. 18.39.6; Arr. *Post.Alex.* 1.37; cf. App. *Mith.* 8; Billows 1990, 409–10 n. 79; Klinkott 2000, 68–70; Heckel 2006, 118, s.v. 'Nicanor [12]'; Id. 2007, 408–09. Whether Nicanor actually seized this land or not is a matter of discussion: Anson 2004, 135–36 n. 68; cf. Heckel 2007, 408.

13 D.S. 18.59.1–2. We do not know how long Menander remained in that region. Heckel 2007, 408 n. 22, tells that this officer was not sent specifically to replace Nicanor, but he was the commander-in-chief of Antigonus' troops in Cappadocia: see Billows 1990, 409; Anson 2004, 147; Henke 2005, 49.

14 D.S. 19.57.1.The sources inform about a certain Asander, who received Lycia or Cilicia, although it is clear that Cassander had interests in that area: Bosworth 2002, 214 n. 19; Heckel 2006, 56–57, s.v. 'Asander [1]'.

15 D.S. 19.57.1,4; 19.60.2. Diodorus calls him Polemaius, who has been identified with the Ptolemaius mentioned by Nep. *Eum* 10.3: see Billows 1990, 426–28, s.v. 'Polemaios II'; cf. Heckel 2006, 234, 238, s.v. 'Ptolemy [2]' and 'Ptolemy [7]', for discussion. After the battle of Gaza (311), Cappadocia remained in Antigonus' hands.

16 The extent of the Anatolian territories under Lysimachus' rule has been debated. Lund 1992, 82, 226 n. 3, following Meyer 1925, 22, states that the Halys would have been the eastern limit of Antigonus' domains, but it is contradicted by Monophthalmus' rule over Amisus. See further Landucci Gattinoni 1992, 159–60.

17 D.S. 31.19.5; Breglia Pulci Doria 1976, 117; Henke 2005, 47. Trogus *Prol.* 17, alludes to a Seleucid general called Diodorus who was defeated in Cappadocia c. 281. Some authors (Burstein 1976, 145; McGing 1986a, 20; Primo 2006) hold that it was in Pontic Cappadocia, but Justin distinguishes between Cappadocia and Anatolic Pontus: Just. 37.1.2; 37.3.4; 38.7.2; Trog. *Prol.* 32, 34, 37, cf. Reinach 1890, 32 n. 1; Henke 2005, 48 n. 232; Ballesteros Pastor 2006, 595. Grainger 1997, 76, proposes for this struggle a later date, c. 260, but this is difficult to relate with Diodorus, who places it in the time when Seleucus and Antigonus were fighting. Facella 2006, 169, proposes that the correct reading of the Armenian king's name would be Orontes (III).

18 App. *Syr.* 54, alludes to a 'Seleucid Cappadocia': on its extension and the date of its annexation, see Sofou 2005, 747 n. 43. Pliny *NH* 5.33, records a conquest of Antigonus in the territory of the Arieneans, where he founded a city called Apamea: see Reinach 1890, 32; Cohen 1995, 375. Cataonia was acquired by the Ariarathids in a later date: perhaps this land was given as a dowry by Antiochus II when his daughter Stratonice married Ariarathes III: Str. 12.1.2; Henke 2005, 51–52; cf. for a different view Sofou 2005, 753.

19 Memn. *FGH* 434 F 1 12.4. However, Antigonus founded there a city which would be later called Nicaea (Cohen 1995, 398; Syme 1995, 22). Memnon's genealogy of the first Bithynian kings may be fictitious: two of them lived just 76 years. On the chronological problems of Memnon's work, cf. Avram 2003, 1184–85. On Calas, see Kobes 1996, 115; Heckel 2006, 74–75.

20 Regarding Mithridates' genealogy, see Bosworth and Wheatley 1998, 162; cf. McGing 1986b, 251–52; Billows 1990, 404 s.v. 'Mithridates'. His status at Antigonus' court is unknown: Kobes 1996, 96, affirms that he was a 'friend' (*philos*). McGing 1986b, 286, reasonably defends that he would have been sent as a pledge. We do not discard that Demetrius could have a homoerotic relationship with Mithridates: the Macedonian's homosexuality is described in Plu. *Dem.* 24.1–3.

21 Plu. *Demetr.* 4; *Mor.* 183a; App. *Mith.* 9,112; Tert. *Anim.*46; Lucian. *Macr.* 13; Goukowsky 2001, 132 n. 65; cf. Reinach 1890, 7. The date of this episode is discussed: we follow the hypothesis of Bosworth and Wheatley 1998, 162–64, who also noted that the anecdote of the dream is clearly *post eventum.* On Cimiata, see Str. 12.3.41; Marek 1993, 122–24; Bosworth and Wheatley 1998, 162–63. Billows 1990, 404–05 s.v. 'Mithridates', relates Polyaen. 7.29.2, with this noble's flight, but we should regard that the paragraph

preceding this episode in the *Stratagemata* deals about the Mithridates who murdered Datames. Lucian's version is difficult to translate: Bompaire 2003, 30 n. 35, remarks that the text could be interpreted either as a flight or as an exile, or may have been a confusion with Mithridates (II) of Cius, who was crucified by Antigonus (D.S. 20.111.4). Kobes 1996, 118, points out that the escape to the mountains would have been a consequence of the Macedonian presence in Paphlagonia. This author (1996, 120 with n. 37) tries to find in App. *Mith.* 9 a reference to Mithridates' conquest of a former Macedonian or indigenous settlement in that region. Primo 2008 has detected the analogy between this episode and the anecdote recorded by Libanius (*Or.* 9.80–82) about a warning which Demetrius writes on the sand to encourage Seleucus to escape from Babilonia because Antigonus wanted to kill him.

22 As Bosworth and Wheatley 1998, 163, deduced from Appian (*Mith.* 9), perhaps during some years Mithridates would have lived untroubled and in relative outlawry: this could be also related with another commonplace in the legend of heroic figures who had to fly to remote lands: Eddy 1961, 179; Dundes 1990, 191. On this *topos* in Eupator's life, see Just. 37.2.7–9; García Moreno 1993, 107–08.

23 Some scholars have supposed that Ctistes conquers Amasya and settles his court there, but this does not appear in any literary source. There are only five royal tombs in the necropolis at Amasya and we can not say to whom belonged each of the graves. For different approaches to this problem, see Burstein 1980, 11 n. 35; McGing 1986b, 250–51 n. 10; Fleischer 2009, 115–18; Højte 2009b, 127–28. On Ctistes' forces, see Kobes 1996, 119. Bosworth and Wheatley 1998, 164, think that Antigonus' death would have left without employment mercenaries who were recruited by Mithridates. This dynast could have joined Lysimachus, who was the master of Heraclea, and after Ipsus the Iranian noble would have been rewarded with some territories: see also Kobes 1996, 119; Michels 2009, 15. It seems that Mithridates I resisted the attack of Ptolemy II with the aid of Galatian mercenaries: Apollon.Aphr. *FGH* 740 F 14; Olshausen 1978, 403; Archibald 2007, 259.

24 On the relationship between Appian's *Mithridateios* and Justin's chapters on Eupator, see Ballesteros Pastor 2006, 583 n. 9; 2009b, 223–24; 2009c, 390. The former author used to translate from Latin sources: see Torres Guerra 2006. Obviously, Appian *Mith.* 9, is wrong when placing Cimiata in Cappadocia: Olshausen 1978, 402. In this same sense, Diodorus' notice about Ctistes' rule over 'Cappadocia and Paphlagonia' (20.111.4) could have been a mistake based on the later extension of the Pontic kingdom.

25 This work begins with the origins and rulers of Bithynia (App. *Mith.* 1–7) and concludes with the account of the wars of Pharnaces II against Rome (App. *Mith.* 120–21). Despite this, the *Mithridateios* may be considered as the only known biography written by Appian which even includes two obituaries (*Mith.* 112 and 118–19). Leaving aside the accounts on the Civil and Hannibalic Wars, the other known works of Appian deal about the history of regions of the Roman Empire. Justin knew the *Mithridateios* and Trogus' *Histories*, and he transcribed in the *Epitome* information which had not been copied by the Alexandrian, also making important modifications. Despite Justin's words about his accuracy (38.3.11), the famous speech of Mithridates (38.4–7) was not taken verbatim from Trogus: see Ballesteros Pastor 2009c, 390.

26 Just. 1.4; 18.8.17–20; 23.4.3–11; 37.2; 43.2; 44.4.1–13.

27 Bosworth and Wheatley 1998, 162. Plutarch *Demetr.* 4, does not mention expressly Hieronymus in his account of Antigonus' dream and records the total number of kings of the Pontic dynasty, which reveals that the Chaeronean consulted for this passage authors who wrote after the end of the Ariarathid line. A similar reflection could be done about Diodorus' 'Cappadocian Chronicle', which could not be wholly attributed to Polybius. Some scholars have supposed the existence of an official document of the Cappadocian court which was reflected in our sources: see Breglia Pulci Doria 1976, 128–29; Debord 1999, 102; Gabelko 2009, 52; Lebreton 2011, 21, 30. Hornblower 1981, 242, likewise admits that Lucian's use of the term 'king of Pontus' (*Macr.* 13) proves that this author does not follow literally the Cardian. This scholar (1981, 69, 74, 123), however, defends that the anecdote about the dream was taken from Hieronymus, who would have been the common source of Appian and Plutarch. As Bosworth and Weathley noted (1998, 163), Lucian mentions Hieronymus as his source on Mithridates' age, together with 'other writers'. See below n. 29.

28 Trog. *Prol.* 16 (Bithynia), 35 (Cappadocia), 42; Just. 42.2.8–10; 3.8–9 (Armenia). On Trogus' interest

in the *origines gentium*, see Van Wickevoort-Crommelin 1993, 95–100, 189–94. On this Cappadocian perspective, see Ballesteros Pastor 2009b, 223–24.

29 On the Pontics, see Plb. 5.43.2; D.S. 19.40.2; Flor. 1.40.1; Sall. *Hist.* fr. 2.85M *apud* Ampel. 30.5; Just. 38.7.1; App. *Mith.* 9,112,115; *De Vir.Ill.* 76.1; Luc. *Macr.* 13; Tac. *An.* 12.18.2. On the Cappadocians, see D.S. 31.19.1–4. It has been considered that there is confusion with Atossa, the daughter of Cyrus, and that Anaphas would have actually called Otanes: Reinach 1886, 310; Breglia Pulci Doria 1978, 113–14; Panitschek 1987, 74–75; Briant 1996, 146; Debord 1999, 310. Diodorus' genealogy of the Ariarathids contains evident contradictions, which have led a number of scholars to consider that it is a fictititous reconstruction: cf. Reinach 1886, 311–12; Breglia Pulci Doria 1978, 107, 111–17; Briant 1996, 116, 147; Debord 1999, 102–10; Henke 2006, 34. See above n. 27.

30 Breglia Pulci Doria 1978, 119–20; Panitschek 1987, 76; Henke 2006, 123.

31 Plb. fr. 54 Büttner-Wobst; Hornblower 1981, 240. Briant 1996, 116, 146–47, considers that this notice comes from Hieronymus and relates this fragment to Artaxerxes II. Panitschek 1987, 88, proposes that this noble would have been Camisares, the father of Datames, but we should also recall that Darius II was saved from the attack of two lions by Tiribazus (D.S. 15.10.3), the satrap of Western Armenia. This would give credit, at least partially, to Polybius' account. Lebreton 2011, 18, proposes that the mountain may be the Argeus, near Mazaca.

32 Frye 1964, 43 n. 2; Panitschek 1987, 86; Kobes 1996, 119; Weber 2000, 177–79.

33 It should be noted that one 'sibling' remains in the kingdom and the other goes to fight abroad, just like in the accounts on the Amazons (Just. 2.4.20; Oros. 1.15.4) and related with the Spartan realm. A diarchy of brothers or sisters appears also in legends foundation regarding the origin of Scythians, Amazons, Parthians and Romans: Just. 2.4.1–2; 42.2.1–3.1; Arr. *Parth.* 1.2; D.S. 2.43.3–4; Oros. 1.15.8–9; cf. Apoll.Rhod. 2.386–87; Martin 2001; Ballesteros Pastor 2009a, 338 n. 22 (we omit here other references to diarchy where there is no mention of ruling brothers). On the problems about the historicity of Tiridates, see Wolski 1996, 58–71; Wiesehöfer 2001, 131–32. We could also find references to presumed historical diarchies of brothers: Spartocus II and Pairisades in Bosporus (Hind 1994, 495), Cetriporis and Scostoces in Thracia (Just. 8.3.14; Oros. 3.12.22), although this latter example could come from a manipulated tradition: Archibald 1998, 232. Arrian's account has been related to the tale of the brothers Asineus and Anilaeus (I. *AI* 18.314–370; Hermann 2006). In general, see Poulsen 1991.

34 For example, Strabo (15.3.14) tells about Cappadocian magi, whereas he does not mention them in Pontus. The Cappadocian lords could have remained semi-independent: Str. 12.2.11; Just. 37.1.5; 38.5.9; cf. 38.2.8; Plb. 24.14.9; 31.7.1; Cic. *Att.* 6.13; Breglia Pulci Doria 1978, 123–24; Ballesteros Pastor 2008, 46 n. 4. Cappadocia lacked any Greek colony in its territory. See also D.S. 31.19.8, about the reign of Ariarathes V: 'Cappadocia, so long unknown to the Greeks'.

35 Str. 12.3.5; cf. 11.8.4. On Josephus, see: I. *AI* 13.286; 14.35,104,111,138; 15.9; *Ap.* 2.84. On the pejorative description of Cappadocians and Paphlagonians in Classical literature, see Bohak 2005, 201–14; Ballesteros Pastor 2002–2007, 7–8.

36 On Moaphernes, Strabo's maternal uncle, see Str. 11.2.18; 12.3.33. About his Greek relatives, see above all Str. 10.4.10; Portanova 1988, 349–50, 402–03, 698.

37 On the Greeks' attitude towards Eupator, see McGing 1986a, 101–08; Portanova 1988; Ballesteros Pastor 1996, 432–36; Thornton 1998. As noted by Syme 1995, 171, Strabo's account about Pontus is surprisingly inaccurate.

38 See above all McGing 1998. The Pontic *praefecti* mentioned in several sources may have actually been satraps: Fron. *Str.* 1.5.18; 11.20; Flor. *Epit.* 1.40.8; Just. 38.2.1; Gell. 15.1.4,6; *Vir.Ill.* 75; Oros. 6.5.2; Vell. 2.23.3; Liv. *Perioch.* 78, 81; cf. App. *Mith.* 41.

39 App. *Mith.* 9,21,64; Plin. *Nat.* 33.48; Ballesteros Pastor 2009b, 224, 228 n. 72. On the golden or silver chains and shackles in Persian tradition, see Atkinson 1994, 153; Yardley and Heckel 1997, 177. About the possible existence of magi in Pontus see Mastrocinque 2005, 178–79. The presence of these men might also be found in Justin's account on Eupator's education (37.2.4–5).

40 Plu. *Mor.* 624a; Nic.Dam. *FGH* 90 F 73 (*apud* Athen. 10.415e); Ael. *VH* 1.27; App. *Mith.* 66. In general, on the Achaemenids, see Briant 1996, 297–304; García Sánchez 2009, 348–50.

41 On these worships, see Str.11.8.4; 12.3.37; cf. 12.3.31; Olshausen 1990, 1870–71, 1877; Briant 1996,

509. Anaitis was also worshipped in Cappadocia: Briant 1996, 762. Pompeius conquered a 'country of Anaitis' in Armenia Minor, which may be a temple-state (D.C. 36.48.1, cf. 53.5).

42 App. *BC* 2.91; Hirt. *Bell.Alex.* 70, cf. 41; Bosworth 1997. On Pharnaces' title, see Hoben 1969, 15–16.

43 Leschhorn 1993, 83, 179–91, 484; Kobes 1996, 116; Michels 2009, 14–15, 158–59.

44 Syncellus 523.5; 593.7 Bonn, *FGH* 251 F 5a and 5b; Olshausen 1978, c. 403, with the remarks of McGing 1986a, 19 n. 39; Kobes 1996, 170; Primo 2006; Michels 2009, 15. For an alternative chronological framework, see also Gabelko 2009, 47–48. On the first royal Pontic coinage, see De Callataÿ 2009; Michels 2009, 183–90.

45 It has been supposed that Ariarathes' assumption of the royal title would have been connected with his marriage with the daughter of Antiochus II (D.S. 31.19.6; Porph. *FGH* 260 F 32.6; Just. 27.3.7; cf. Henke 2005, 22, 50–53; Michels 2009, 17). However, we do not know the exact date of this union, which took place after Antiochus' accession to the throne in c. 266/65 (see Henke 2005, 51). The Ariarathid line ended c. 98 BC (De Callataÿ 1999, 195). It might be supposed that Diodorus regarded Ariarathes IX as a member of this dynasty, because he was the nephew of Laodice, queen of Cappadocia. However, this king was considered as belonging to a foreign royal house (Just. 38.1.10–2.1; App. *Mith.* 15, cf. 13).

46 Mithridates II married Laodice, the sister of Seleucus Callinicus (Porph. *FGH* 260 F 32.8; Just. 38.5.3); Prusias I married Apame, the sister of Philip V of Macedon (Liv. 42.12.2; App. *Mac.* 11; *Mith.* 2). On Cappadocia, see above n. 45. For further references to the relationship of these dynasties with the Macedonian houses, see Michels 2009, 29–36; Petrović 2009. If the Pontic rulers proclaimed themselves as kings prior to their alliance with the Seleucids, it would have provoked some stress about which we have no evidence.

47 It is also quite probable that this tradition could have been manipulated by later writers. The redaction of this passage has to be dated in Julio-Claudian times (Ballesteros Pastor 2006, 595), and to this we should add the Cappadocian perspective and the pro-Armenian bias which can be found in Justin (see for instance, Just. 38.3.2; 40.1).

48 On Bithynia, Paphlagonia and the countries east of the Halys, see above n. 1–3. On Cappadocia, see further D.S. 18.16.1; Anson 2004, 65–66. The Iberians of Caucasus claimed to have kept free from Alexander's rule (Plu. *Pomp.* 34.5). Aitolians and Spartans also highlighted to have resisted the Macedonian dominion: Just. 28.3.12; 28.4.1; 32.1.3; Cic. *Tusc.* 5.42; Plu. *Mor.* 235b.

THE FEMALE ELEMENT OF THE POLITICAL SELF-FASHIONING OF THE DIADOCHI: PTOLEMY, SELEUCUS, LYSIMACHUS, AND THEIR IRANIAN WIVES

Sabine Müller

Introduction

At Hellenistic courts, a royal woman's status mainly depended on the following aspects: the political significance of her father, distinction of her descent, importance of her former husband in case she had been married before, and ability to give birth to a potential successor. In most cases, the wedding was motivated by either her father's or former husband's political influence while her dynastic prestige determined her position at the royal court. If she had borne the heir apparent, her maternity would influence her long-term standing in the empire.

Functioning as a part of the royal image and political self-fashioning, royal women were represented as important members of the royal house and complements to the king (Carney 2000, 245). Together, they guaranteed dynastic legitimacy, promised prosperity and political stability within the empire, and acted as benefactors (Carney 2010, 45–53). There were various strategies to make Hellenistic royal women visible. First of all, the adoption of the title *basilissa* and the royal diadem emphasized their dynastic importance (Müller 2009, 76). Then, they could be honoured and commemorated by eponymous city foundations named after them constructing a dynastic net on the map (Fraser 2009, 172–73; Carney 1988). In addition, royal women stepped out of the dark as dedicants, worshippers, benefactresses, and sponsors supporting the cultural and religious policy of the kings (Bringmann 1993, 7–24). Some royal Macedonian women were also given the chance to demonstrate their dynastic importance in the context of the battlefield (Carney 2004, 184–94). They could either be represented as military leaders like Arrhidaeus' wife Adea-Eurydice (Polyaen. 8.16; Athen. 13.557b, 560f; Arr. *Post.Alex.* 22–23) or Berenice II, the wife of Ptolemy III (Catul. 66.25–28; Hyg. *Astr.* 2.24.11–18), or exercising symbolic leadership like Arsinoe III, the wife of Ptolemy IV, who was said to have encouraged the troops at the battle of Raphia (Plb. 5.83.3–84.1; 87.6; cf. Müller 2007, 149), as well as administrative leadership like that exercised by Olympias (Athen. 13.560f; cf. Carney 2006, 72–73).[1] Alternatively, royal women could publicly sacrifice for the sake of military campaigns or act as dedicants of gifts in order to thank the gods for their support.

Royal women could also become visible in the economic field, where they were attested as landowners like the Seleucid queen Laodice III, who donated parts of her revenues acting as a royal charity lady;[2] or they could act as patronesses and protectresses of trade like the Ptolemaic queens Arsinoe II and Cleopatra II (Müller 2009, 57 n. 251). Thus, within a Greek cult in Egypt, Arsinoe II was honoured as Kypros Zephyritis caring especially for seafarers of the Ptolemaic fleet and sea traders as well as for their wives and fiancées they had left behind.[3] In this context, Arsinoe's deification proved to be an ideal way to proclaim that the Ptolemies whom the goddess represented, even the dead ones, were able to protect the inhabitants of their empire every time and everywhere.

In order to visualize royal women's images commemorating their public role, their portraits could be commissioned. Mostly, their iconography hinted at their public duties and was often complemented by the divine attributes of their patron deities.

However, most of these public images of Macedonian royal women are dated to times when their dynastic profiles were already institutionalized. Therefore, this paper's purpose is to examine the earliest stage of this development: the status and public visibility of the wives of the Successors Ptolemy, Seleucus, and Lysimachus.

In this context, it is important to note that at least Ptolemy and Seleucus were not free to choose their first known brides. Concurrently with Alexander, who married two Achaemenid princesses at Susa in 324 in order to demonstrate the continuity of Persian rule under the Macedonian usurper,[4] they were forced to take Iranian wives. As their treatment of these brides seems to be a crucial point in the history of the Successors' legitimization and political image that also sheds some light on their attitude towards Alexander, his Iranian policy, and political legacy, the paper will focus on the role of their Iranian women within their self-fashioning. The examples of Ptolemy, Seleucus, and Lysimachus provide three different treatments of the Iranian brides, revealing not only the difference of their regal image, career, and attitude towards the memory of Alexander as king of Asia and his Persian policy but also the specific challenges their realms posed to them.

Alexander and his Asian wives

In comparison to his father Philip II, who had taken seven wives (Athen. 13.557c-e; cf. Carney 2006, 22; Wirth 1985, 28–29), Alexander married on a less large scale at a relatively advanced age (Greenwalt 1988, 93–95). In 327, he took his first wife, the Bactrian noble Roxane, daughter of Oxyartes, one of the influential rebels of the Bactrian-Sogdian revolt that severely threatened the Macedonian conquest.[5] Despite the domination of the love theme in the ancient sources, the wedding was a less-than-ideal emergency solution to stop the rebellion after the failure of military repression.[6] As a token of the loyalty of her father (Holt 1988, 68), who negotiated the surrender of his allies (Arr. *An.* 4.21.6–10; Curt. 9.8.10), Roxane lost her symbolic aura as soon as the revolt came to an end. However, the romance theme may have stemmed from the official Macedonian propaganda that justified the marriage by depicting Alexander as the self-restraint philosopher king who was smitten by Roxane's youthful charms, but who did not abuse his victor's right to violate her (Arr. *An.* 4.19.5; Curt. 8.4.25; Plut. *Alex.* 47.7; *ME* 29). This probable official version focussed on Alexander's continence stressing his image of being *philosophos* by mastering his passions. As for the Bactrians and Sogdians, they might also have been shocked at the marriage as they regarded it as a symbol of the Macedonian occupation (Carney 2003, 245–46; Bosworth 1995, 131; Wirth 1993, 165 n. 470). Since also large numbers of the Macedonians obviously felt offended by the marriage thought to be a *mésalliance* (Curt. 8.4.30; 10.6.13–14; cf. Bosworth 1995, 132), Alexander wisely refrained from incorporating Roxane into his political self-fashioning (Briant 2010, 114; Müller 2008, 278–79; Carney 2003, 245; 2000, 107). Thus, he kept on being styled as the adventurous new epic hero and beardless youthful warrior king (Alonso 2010, 16–21), wandering around experiencing military adventures together with his comrades-in-arms (Hölscher 2009, 30–32).

Curtius' indication (8.4.26) that Alexander tried to style Roxane as his Briseis takes up a common motif in Roman rhetoric and was most probably irony on his part: the moralist mocks the former philosopher king who revealed his loss of morals and senses by marrying a dancing girl inferior in birth right on the spot (Baynham 1998, 192).

Being denied a public profile, Roxane remained a shadowy figure bearing the stigma of being an outsider at the Macedonian court. Only the Syrian satirist Lucian mentions a painting by the Greek artist Aetion that depicted Roxane and Alexander as a couple united in the bridal chamber (Luc. *Herod.* 5–6; *Im.* 7). However, the picture might either have been commissioned after 323 in the interests of the claims of Alexander IV, or alternatively, given Lucian's satirical tone, one may think that the *ekphrasis* was but one of his literary parodies, in this case ridiculing Aetion's actual picture *The Wedding of Semiramis and Ninus* (Plin. *Nat.* 35.78) and making fun of Alexander's greater passion for his best man Hephaestion (Stewart 2003, 41). It is debated, however, whether a Pompeian fresco was a copy of the painting showing Roxane represented as a Greek woman or even one embodying Aphrodite (Stewart 1993, 20, 186–90). But it is not certain that the fresco was a copy of Aetion's picture. In fact, there is no certainty about any copy originating from it (Bröker and Müller 2004, 5).

Roxane's status was diminished in 324, when Alexander married the daughters of the two last Persian great kings Artaxerxes III and Darius III (Briant 2010, 128; Heckel 2009, 242). Probably, he planned to integrate his Achaemenid wives into his political self-fashioning in order to mirror the new character of his Greco-Macedonian-Asian empire. However, as he had to consider that many Macedonians resented his Persian policy and objected to his wives as visible symbols of this debated new regal style, he was probably forced to cling to the strategy of denying his wives a political and public profile. Conceivably, he would have tried to make a change putting them in a public place if he had lived longer and thus been able to gain wide acceptance for his new policy, but it was not meant to be.

When Alexander died, Macedonian objections to his Asian policy were at its height and were voiced publicly (Curt. 10.6.13–14; Just. 13.2.5–6; cf. Olbrycht 2009, 234–36). He had died, perhaps, too soon to make the Macedonian majority accept his new Macedonian empire centred in Asia. On the other hand, he had lived long enough to turn any possible former ideas of a Macedonian empire centred in Europe into a questionable matter of debate.

Obviously, in order to cast off the memory of Alexander's autocratic regal style and his new concept of empire, most of the Macedonians repudiated their Iranian wives who had been forced on them by their ruler (Braund 2005, 24). It seems to have been an attempt to free themselves from the consequences of his unpopular policy as the successor of the Achaemenids.

However, already during Alexander's lifetime a range of different attitudes to Alexander's Asian policy occurred. For instance, he was supported by Peucestas (Arr. *An.* 6.30.2) and his confidant Hephaestion (Plu. *Alex.* 48.5).[7] While after his death hostility against the Iranian element of his empire including the Iranian wives seems to have dominated, not all of the leading generals shared this attitude. Aiming at power, they chose to pursue Alexander's political goals. This was the case with Perdiccas, who built his power on his acting as regent of Alexander's whole empire in his unborn son's and half-brother's interest. He especially devoted himself to the support of Roxane, defending her child's disputed legitimacy (Braund 2005, 22; Bosworth 2002, 9, 38; Carney 2000, 146). According to Plutarch (*Alex.* 77.6), Perdiccas even consented to the assassination of Roxane's Achaemenid rival Stateira to secure her child's interests (Rathmann 2005, 32, 43; Atkinson and Yardley 2009, 180–81). Probably, she also eliminated Alexander's second Achaemenid wife Parysatis as both could have made trouble for Roxane and her supporters, like Perdiccas, by claiming to be pregnant.[8]

Building and justifying his power in the empire of the dead Alexander in his role as protector for the former king's policy and family, Perdiccas' most prestigious symbols of Alexander's heritage were Roxane and her child. However, as they were highly unpopular with most of the Macedonians, it was necessary to elevate their status and increase their popularity. Presumably, as their influential position heavily depended on the rank of his protégés, Perdiccas and his supporters had to launch a propaganda campaign to make them more acceptable. Perhaps, Roxane's dedications of precious gifts to Athena Polias recorded in a very fragmentary later inventory of the joint deeds of the Treasurers of Athens (*IG* II^2 1492 a 45–57) also formed part of this image campaign.[9]

Traces of this attempt to enhance Roxane's standing can probably be found in the *Metz Epitome*, a breviary of Alexander's career, in which Perdiccas', as well as Roxane's, role was suspiciously highlighted. Therefore, it is plausible that the *Metz Epitome* derived ultimately from a pamphlet written in favour of Perdiccas (Rathmann 2005, 68–70; Merkelbach 1954, 54–55, 132, 164–92). In order to stress the legitimacy of her son, Alexander's relationship with Roxane is idealized and romanticized while his rival wives were left in the shadow. Stressing their close bond, the *Metz Epitome* is the only source to mention that she bore him a son on the Hydaspes in 326, who was either still-born or died in infancy (*ME* 70). As this claim presumably formed part of the image campaign, its authenticity may be doubtful. In addition, the final tender scenes depicting Roxane comforting her dying husband are exaggerations in the interests of the claims of her son (*ME* 101–102, 110, 112; cf. Heckel 2009, 242). Significantly, the *Metz Epitome* contains a striking deathbed scene in which Alexander entrusted his wife to Perdiccas giving him the order to marry her (*ME* 112, 118). Concurrently with the tradition that Perdiccas received Alexander's signet ring, indicating that he was to be his successor, the story illustrates his claims to step into Alexander's shoes with the king's approval. As a presumable piece of Perdiccas' contemporary propaganda, the anecdote has to be treated with great caution.

Obviously, the campaign in favour of Roxane did not prove to be that successful: Perdiccas and the other of Alexander's generals never attempted to marry his widow. On the contrary, Perdiccas preferred to court Macedonian women, wooing Nicaea, the daughter of Antipater, and Cleopatra, the full sister of Alexander, who gained importance as a legitimizing symbol of the Argead house.[10]

Thus, until her violent death at the hands of Glaucias, one of Cassander's henchmen, in 311,[11] for most of the time, Roxane remained a foreigner, marginalized by great parts of the Macedonians (Braund 2005, 27) although her father Oxyartes made a rather successful career as satrap of Parapamisadae, the only Iranian in the region among Macedonians, under Alexander's reign (Berve 1926, 293).

At least, Roxane gained a bit more prominence when Olympias and her supporter Polyperchon defended her and her son Alexander IV as a token of Alexander's heritage.

However, only posthumously, she became most prominent when she was erroneously represented as the daughter of Darius III in the Alexander Romance (Ps.Callisth. 2.20; cf. Müller 2012, 301–03). However, this confusion suited the storyline: after his conquest, Alexander reconciled with the dying Achaemenid king and united the two empires by marrying his daughter and fathering an heir (Stoneman 2008, 29). As the Greek Alexander Romance influenced the medieval Eastern and Western Alexander Romances, as well as Renaissance and Baroque art, Roxane turned out to be his most prominent wife.

Ptolemy and Artacama

During the mass ceremony at Susa, when around 92 marriages were forced onto the Macedonians,[12] Ptolemy married Artacama,[13] one of the daughters of Artabazus, the son of the famous satrap Pharnabazus and the Achaemenid Apama.[14] Artabazus, the former satrap of Hellespontic Phrygia, had briefly governed Bactria under Alexander (Arr. *An.* 3.29.1).

Since, as a variant, Plutarch (*Eum.* 1.7) calls Ptolemy's bride Apama, it is suggested that his presumable source Duris confused her with Seleucus' bride (Tarn 1929, 139–40;

Heckel 2009, 296 n. 136), while Arrian's source Ptolemy will have known his own wife's name (Tarn 1929, 140 n. 1). On the other hand, Apama may have been her alternative name as it probably meant 'youngest child' or 'nestling' (Shabazi 1987, 150). It may also have been her official name, intended to underline her prestigious descent from her grandmother Apama, the daughter of king Artaxerxes II (Brosius 1996, 185).

This being so, Ptolemy was honoured by being given an Achaemenid bride, in addition to the sister of Alexander's former lover Barsine (Curt. 10.6.11; Just. 11.10; Plu. *Alex.* 21.4). At least, Alexander might have thought that he honoured him, but as nothing is further heard of Artacama, it is widely assumed that he was wrong: probably, like many other Macedonian husbands, Ptolemy repudiated her soon after Alexander's death (Heckel 2009, 55–56; Mehl 1996, 823–24; Seibert 1967, 72). While Ptolemy fathered three children with his mistress, the Athenian *hetaira* Thais,[15] apparently acknowledging them (Müller 2009, 29; Seibert 1967, 72), no children seem to have sprung from his union with Artacama. Her memory faded so quickly that even her name became a matter of controversy. However, this fate was shared by other Iranian women who were forced to celebrate their wedding at Susa: for instance, Plutarch (*Eum* 1.7) calls the Iranian wife of Eumenes Barsine, while Arrian (*An.* 7.4.6) names her Artonis.

If Ptolemy repudiated Artacama, his reasons were quite complex. The suggestion that she 'would have been of no political value to him in Egypt' (Macurdy 1932, 77) is an understatement. Actually, she would have been a liability. Although Ptolemy might have 'hit the jackpot when he gained control of Egypt' (Burstein 2004, 36), he had to obtain the acceptance of the native population, mainly accessible through the Egyptian priests (Pfeiffer 2010, 103–04; Müller 2009, 172–75; Burstein 2004, 36–38). Priestly circles had been the centres of at least intellectual resistance to the Persian dominion, creating and circulating negative images of the Persians as evil elements of chaos, led by their ruthless tyrant king (Collins 2009, 195–96; Blasius and Schipper 2002, 285–86; Lloyd 1982). For instance, Egyptian priestly grievance found expression in the form of lurid tales about the Persian conqueror Cambyses II told to Herodotus on his visit to Egypt. According to this biased information, the king appeared as a tyrannical madman who violated sanctuaries, ridiculed the Egyptian religion, and murdered the holy Apis (Hdt. 3.10–16; 3.27–37; 3.64–66). When he allegedly charged his soldiers to burn the temple of Ammon at Siwah, they were punished by divine forces. Crossing the desert, they were buried in masses of sand raised by a sudden storm and never arrived at Siwah (Hdt. 3.17.1; 3.25.3–26.2).

Obviously knowing Herodotus' account very well (Müller 2011a, 118–20), Callisthenes, Aristobulus, and Ptolemy described Alexander's trip to Siwah as a divinely guided and protected mission without any cases of death or missing persons (Plu. *Alex.* 27.2–3; Str. 17.1.43; Arr. *An.* 3.3.3–6).

Since the image of the evil Persian conqueror filling Egypt with terror still prevailed in Alexander's days, the Macedonian invader was wisely advised to proclaim that he intended to liberate Egyptian from the Persian yoke (Curt. 4.7.1–3; D.S. 17.49.1–2).[16] Adopting this policy, Ptolemy tried to act in true Pharaonic style.[17] The famous Satrap

Stela (CGC 22182) shows that it was a successful strategy (Müller 2009, 300–01; Goedicke 1985). Set up in 311/10 by the priests of the temple of Buto in the western Nile Delta, the monument served to commemorate the restoration of temple property. Officially under the reign of Alexander IV, Ptolemy called *chaschadrapana* (satrap), is depicted as the real pharaoh. Highly praised for having restored the temple's holy books and cult statues stolen by the Persians (Klinkott 2007, 36–37), Ptolemy is also spoken of in high terms because he reinstalled the temple's rights once taken away by the Persian king Xerxes, who is portrayed as an impious rake.[18] His name is lacking a cartouche and written with the sign for a bound, decapitated foe with a knife sticking in his chest (Klinkott 2007, 37–41). In contrast, Ptolemy is compared to king Chababash, a Libyan or Nubian counter-king during the Persian dominion, who became a programmatic symbol of Egyptian native resistance (Klinkott 2007, 39; Burstein 2000, 151–52).

In any case, Ptolemy was well advised to win the favour of the Egyptian priests. For instance, the *Oracle of the Potter*, one of the so-called Egyptian apocalyptic prophecies in which native opposition found literary expression, a Greek translation from a Demotic text originally dating from the second century BC (Hoffmann 2000, 186; Huß 1994, 165), illustrates the dangers of being compared to the Persians. Emanating from priestly circles, the text depicts the Macedonian dominion as a period of misery and oppression leading to the collapse of the divine order. The Macedonians and Greeks are represented as demonic followers of the evil Typhon/Seth and called 'Girdle-Wearers' in the sense of uncouth military enemies (Austin 2006, 570; Hoffmann 2000, 186–87; Lloyd 1982, 51–53). While the author avoids naming Alexandria, the Ptolemaic residence is referred to as the evil 'city of foreigners':

> And the river [will rise not having sufficient] water, but only little, so that [the land] will be scorched, but against nature. In the [time] of the Typhonians [they will say]: 'Wretched Egypt, you [have been] wronged [by the terrible] ill-treatment inflicted on you'. The sun will grow dim as it cannot bear to witness the evils perpetrated in Egypt. The earth will not agree with the seeds (...) Fighting will break out in Egypt (...) There will be [war and slaughter] (...) For [this will happen] (...) and the Girdle-Wearers will destroy each other [as they are Typhonians ...] (...) and the city of foreigners which was founded will be destroyed.
>
> (Austin 2006, no. 326, 568–69)

Although Ptolemy did not seem to have voiced his objections to Alexander's Persian policy explicitly in his *History of Alexander*, he might not have favoured his new regal style. Hence, the general Egyptian resentment towards the Persians might have been comfortable for him. By keeping his distance from this part of Alexander's memory, he could please the conservative Macedonian factions (Böhme 2009, 177–80), as well as great parts of the Egyptian population and priests (Müller 2011, 108). This suited Ptolemy's dual role as Macedonian king and Egyptian pharaoh. In consequence, it would have been a political mistake to have a Persian wife at his side: Artacama would have been a contradiction to his political self-fashioning. Nevertheless, it is possible that he did not repudiate her but allowed her to spend her days quietly and undisturbed in his palace at Alexandria without any public appearance. At least, he also did not feel the need to marry an Egyptian wife.

Anyway, it is difficult to assess whether Ptolemy gave his wives a public profile. Probably, the prominence of Eurydice and especially Berenice arouse during the reign of Ptolemy II, who became the 'chief architect' of the Ptolemaic dynastic image. For instance, he created their specific dynastic 'trademark' by emphasizing the importance of royal duality of brother and sister (Müller 2009, 138).

Seleucus and Apama

An exception to the rule of repudiating or ignoring Alexander's imposed bride's was Apama, the Iranian wife of Seleucus (Arr. *An.* 7.4.6; Plu. *Demetr.* 31.5). She was the only bride from the marriages at Susa making a career as queen mother: her son Antiochus succeeded to the throne. Seleucus held her in honour and integrated her into his political self-fashioning. Especially after his adoption of the royal title and diadem, he must have profited from his decision to retain her. Lacking Argead blood, the traditional major factor of Macedonian royal legitimacy, the Successors had to display as many other status symbols as possible. Their wives formed part of their symbolic funds. While a royal descent was useful, Apama's Achaemenid descent probably proved to be of specific importance in Seleucus' east Iranian realm, making her a valuable token of legitimacy (Bielman Sánchez 2003, 45–46; Mehl 1986, 19).

However, his reasons why he retained her are uncertain. After Alexander's death, he could not have known about his future as the founder of the Seleucid Empire. Thus, although aristocratic marriages were a matter of policy (Seibert 1967, 72), it is possible that they developed feelings for each other. Later on, he profited from his decision to hold her in honour (Macurdy 1932, 77–78; Grainger 1997, 38 n. 3), although it is not quite clear to what extent (Mehl 1986, 19).

According to Arrian (*An.* 7.4.6; cf. *ME* 20), Apama was the daughter of the Bactrian noble Spitamenes (see Heckel 2009, 39, 239 n. 92), the leader of the great revolt against Alexander in Bactria and Sogdiana (Curt. 7.6.14–15; Arr. *An.* 4.3.6–7; 4.5.2–6.4), and, perhaps, of Iranian ancestry as her name may indicate (Heckel 2009, 264; Tarn 1929, 140). On the contrary, Strabo (15.8.15) calls her the daughter of Artabazus indicating that she was an Achaemenid, the sister of Ptolemy's Iranian wife. Strabo may simply have confused her with Artacama but he also might have been right as her name may recall her Achaemenid ancestry (Heckel 2009, 55; Brosius 1996, 185).[19] Plutarch (*Demetr.* 31.3) may also hint at this by simply calling her 'Apama the Persian'.

Presumably, Arrian's list of brides and bridegrooms was taken from Ptolemy (Heckel 2009, 296 n. 136). Thus, he was responsible for the report that Seleucus' wife and mother of his heir apparent was the offspring of one of Alexander's most bitter enemies, the dangerous rebel who resisted Alexander's invasion with determination until he died.

According to Arrian (*An.* 4.17.4), Spitamenes was betrayed by the Scythian Massagetae, who murdered him and sent his head to Alexander (cf. Str. 11.11.6). His source seems to have indicated that this was another example of stereotypical barbarian fickleness, causing the end of Spitamenes, who finally got what he deserved. In addition, the story is reminiscent of Herodotus' account of the death of the Persian king Cyrus II. Driven by insatiable despotism, he tried to conquer the realm of the Massagetae, died in battle and was punished by their queen Tomyris. Symbolically, she shoved his head into a wineskin filled with human blood in order to quench his thirst for blood (Hdt. 1.214.4–5).

Arrian himself might have been responsible for the Herodotean colouring as he wrote his *Anabasis* in the time of the Second Sophistic imitating his literary heroes, Herodotus and Xenophon (Whitmarsh 2005, 48; Bosworth 1972, 167). But the Herodotean motif might also have originated with Ptolemy and the other Alexander historiographers (Müller 2011, 129–30). Despite their personal experience in Asia, these authors tended to adopt the traditional literary motifs prevalent in the works of Herodotus, Xenophon, and Ctesias, all of whom were regarded as the ultimate authorities concerning Persia.

Hence, Spitamenes' violent end, comparable to the death of Herodotus' Cyrus as a penalty for his *hybris*, might well have formed part of Arrian's sources. It suited the contemporary Macedonian propaganda that blackened the portrait of Spitamenes creating the impression that his resistance was unjustified.

The second version of Spitamenes' death, as reported by Curtius, perhaps following Clitarchus, resembles Herodotus' account even more: Spitamenes' wife treacherously killed him while he was drunk and brought his head into Alexander's camp (Curt. 8.3.1–16; cf. *ME* 20–21). Contrary to the suggestion that the story flattered Seleucus' mother-in-law, as it emphasized that she was willing to surrender to Alexander's clemency (Tarn 1929, 140), one may conclude that it rather diminished Apama's status. She was represented as the child of a fanatic rebel and a treacherous woman ruthlessly betraying her husband, who was deeply in love with her. At least Curtius does not depict Spitamenes' wife as heroic but states that Alexander was repelled by a crime he regarded as an example of barbarian lawlessness (*licentiae barbarae exemplar*). 'Yet the atrocity of the deed prevailed over gratitude for the service, and he ordered notice to be given her to leave the camp' (Curt. 8.3.15, trans. J. C. Rolfe).

Thus, this description of Apama's family background might have been a piece of Ptolemy's propaganda in order to diminish the dynastic prestige of Seleucus' wife. A Macedonian and Greek familiar with Herodotus will not have missed the point. Perhaps, it could also be interpreted as a hint at the debated date of composition of Ptolemy's *History of Alexander*. Hence, it might be possible that Ptolemy wrote at least this part of his historiography after Ipsus when Seleucus and he began to alienate from each other.[20]

Giving Apama a public profile, Seleucus will have encountered a problem: as Alexander had excluded his Bactrian and Achaemenid wives from his political self-fashioning, there was no Argead role model available for an Iranian spouse. Hence, like the other Successors, Seleucus employed strategies developing in the early Hellenistic times. For instance, he founded at least three cities named after her (Fraser 2009, 337–41; Brosius 1996, 79). Symbolically, Apamea on the Euphrates was the twin city of Seleucia named after the king, and linked together by a bridge (Str. 16.2.4; Liv. 38.13.5; Plin. *Nat.* 6.132; App. *Syr.* 57).

In addition, Apama appeared as a dedicant and benefactress. She is attested epigraphically offering gifts to Leto, Artemis, and Apollo at Delos, and, therefore, being honoured by the Delians with a bronze statue (Macurdy 1932, 78–79). Her public concern for the allied Milesians and the sanctuary of Apollo at Didyma is testified to by a decree from Miletus dating from 298 (*Didyma* 480), the last year in which she was epigraphically attested. Set up by a Seleucid general and leading citizen, the text illustrates Apama's public role in support of Seleucus' interaction between the royal court and an important polis:

> Resolved by the council and the people, Lycus son of Apollodotus [moved] concerning the proposal submitted to the council by Demodamas son of [Aristeides], that Apama, wife of King Seleucus, should be honoured, resolved by the council and the people: since Queen Apama has previously displayed all goodwill and [zeal] for those Milesians who served in the army [with] king Seleucus, and now when [the] ambassadors came [into her presence], whom [king] Seleucus had summoned [from us], she [manifested] no ordinary devotion concerning the construction of the temple of [Apollo] at [Didyma], and Antiochus [her son], zealously following the policy of his father Seleucus (...) has announced] that he would build [a stoa] (...) for the God.
>
> (Austin 2006, no. 51, 108–09; Bielman 2002, 67–68)

Probably, Apama's goodwill for the Milesian soldiers in her husband's army meant that she financed rewards and additional supplies. The Milesian embassy might have been connected to the restoration of the temple she and her son had promised to finance (*OGIS* 213; *Didyma* 479; cf. Austin 2006, 108 n. 1).

Found in the Temple of Apollo at Didyma, the decree also illustrates the specific connection of the sanctuary with the Seleucids (Mehl 1986, 13), who thereby could imitate Alexander. His official court historian Callisthenes mentioned the oracle twice in a Panhellenic context. First, he claimed that the silent oracle returned to life when Alexander conquered Miletus in 331 and forecast his victory (Str. 17.1.43). Then, Callisthenes depicted Alexander as the avenger of Apollo in 329 when he slaughtered the Branchidae, whose ancestors Callisthenes falsely accused of having betrayed Miletus to Xerxes who plundered the sanctuary.[21] Seleucus, who is said to have restored the statue of Apollo that Xerxes allegedly had stolen (Paus. 1.16.3), established a special connection with the sanctuary at Didyma by dedications (Mehl 1986, 13). Since the reign of his son Antiochus I, it was even claimed that in fact Apollo was the founder of their family and father of Seleucus (Just. 15.4.3–6). This dynastic legend corresponded with the depiction of Apollo becoming the standard image on the reverses of Seleucid coins (Le Rider and Callataÿ 2006, 45–49).

Maybe Apama died before Seleucus married Stratonice, the daughter of Demetrius, in 299 (Heckel 2009, 39). However, it is also suggested (Brosius 1996, 79; Macurdy

1932, 78–79; Tarn 1929, 139) that she was still alive and respected, remained his wife throughout, and that he brought her back to prominence at his side after 293, when he had passed Stratonice on to his son Antiochus, 'the only anchor of our storm-tossed house' (Plu. *Demetr.* 38) to underline his designation and secure a smooth succession (Müller 2009, 20 n. 15; Schmitt 2005, 560; Bielman Sanchez 2003, 46).[22]

Perhaps, already in Alexander's lifetime, Seleucus had been one of Alexander's new men who supported his conciliatory policy towards the native population.

Lysimachus and Amastris

Lysimachus established the shortest-lived kingdom of the Successors. Although there is no hint in the ancient sources that he was among the bridegrooms at Susa (Arr. *An.* 7.5.6), it is suggested that he might have been one of those who abandoned their Persian wives (Heckel 2009, 155).

Interestingly, he did marry one of the brides from Susa in 302/1, more than twenty years after the mass wedding. His consort and second or third wife was Amastris, the niece of Darius III (Arr. *An.* 7.4.5; D.S. 20.109.7; Str. 12.3.10), who had been given to Craterus in Susa (D.S. 20.107.9; Memn. *FGH* 434 F 4.4; cf. Burstein 1976, 82). The latter dismissed her as soon as Alexander died to marry Phila, the daughter of Antipater, and passed Amastris on to Dionysius, the tyrant of prosperous Heraclea Pontica (Str. 12.3.10). After Alexander's death, Antigonus managed to exercise influence over Heraclea. When her husband died in 305, Amastris guarded the throne for her two minor sons (Heckel 2009, 21; Brosius 1996, 78). In 302, Lysimachus invaded northwest Anatolia to become her ally and husband (Seibert 1967, 93). This was a profitable political and practical step that provided him with the control of the strategically important port of Heraclea and supplies for his army in the winter quarters (*FGH* 434 F 4.9; Müller 2009, 33; Heckel 2009, 175; Seibert 1967, 94–95).

After Ipsus, Lysimachus summoned his consort to Sardis, where they resided together (Polyaen. 6.12; D.S. 20.104.7). Thus, in Asia Minor she was very visible at his side, although no children sprung from this union. As certainly her Achaemenid ancestry allowed him to display an elevated status, she was quite a good match in a time when the Successors had proclaimed their kingship and needed legitimization for this very new position, which they had not gained by hereditary right: 'Union with a Persian princess may have served to reinforce Lysimachus' claim to the territory which Alexander had 'inherited' from the Achaemenids' (Lund 1992, 75).

However, outside Asia Minor, in Thrace and Macedonia, Lysimachus does not seem to have given her a public profile. According to Memnon (*FGH* 434 F 4.9), he divorced Amastris in order to marry Arsinoe, the daughter of his ally Ptolemy, in about 300. Later on, she became the most visible of all of his wives (cf. *SIG* 381, l. 20–24).

As Lysimachus was polygamous (Plu. *Ant.* 91; cf. Ogden 1999, 58), he may have just sent Amastris back to Heraclea without any formal consequences. She made her residence at Amastris on the Paphlagonian coast (Brosius 1996, 78 n. 70), a city she had founded and named after herself (Str. 12.3.10). Her sons governed Heraclea under her authority while she stayed in touch with Lysimachus, who was a kind of 'supervisor'.

Only after her death, did Amastris become visible again in the context of Lysimachus' public image. Perhaps her prominence now reached its peak. In 285/84, she died under mysterious circumstances (Lund 1992, 30), and Lysimachus took advantage of the rumours circulating that she had been murdered by her sons (Heckel 2009, 21). Suddenly remembering his everlasting love for her, he made his way into Heraclea, proclaimed his intention to avenge her death, acquired her realm, and had her sons executed (Just. 16.3.2–3; Pomp.Trog. *Prol.* 16; *FGH* 434 F 5.2–3; cf. Carney 2000, 208; Lund 1992, 98, 105; Burstein 1976, 85).

His strategy to exploit the memory of their marital bond proved to be successful as Amastris seems to have been quite popular. To underline his claim to Heraclea, he carried on minting Heraclean coins that likely showed her head with a Phrygian headdress ornamented with wreath and star on the obverse to commemorate her (Callataÿ 2004; Burstein 1976, 143 n. 43; Mamroth 1949, 81–86).[23] During her lifetime, probably after they had split up, she had minted coins in her own right bearing the legend ΑΜΑΣΤΡΙΟΣ ΒΑΣΙΛΙΣΣΗΣ (Heckel 2009, 21; Forrer 1969, 2–3). Perhaps Amastris' coins inspired the coins of Arsinoe-Ephesus showing Arsinoe's veiled head or at least her portrait *sub specie deae* minted during the time of Lysimachus' influence over Ephesus (Müller 2009, 345–47; Forrer 1969, 4–6; cf. the image of the Amastris didrachm).

Results

After Alexander's death, most of the Macedonian bridegrooms who were forced to marry Iranian wives at Susa abandoned them as symbols of Alexander's controversial Asian policy and autocracy.

Seleucus took the risk to retain Apama. Later in his career, he probably profited from his decision endearing himself to the native population of eastern Iran.

Ptolemy took advantage of the traditional Egyptian hostility towards the Persians in order to adopt Alexander's policy in Egypt by claiming to be their liberator. Therefore, he could not afford living with a Persian woman at his side.

Lysimachus married Amastris for his political advantage in Asia Minor. However, her prominence at his side seems to have been limited to Asia Minor where her descent was still regarded as prestigious.

These cases shed further light on the efforts of the Successors to be accepted by Macedonians, Greeks and the native population in their realms.[24]

Bibliography

Alonso Troncoso, V. (2010) The Bearded King and the Beardless Hero: From Philip II to Alexander the Great. In E. D. Carney and D. Ogden (eds) *Philip II and Alexander the Great: Father and Son, Lives and Afterlives*, 13–24. Oxford.

Andreae, B. (2003) *Antike Bildmosaiken*. Darmstadt.

Atkinson, J. E. and J. C. Yardley (2009) *Curtius Rufus, Histories of Alexander the Great, Book 10*. Oxford.
Austin, M. M. (1993) Alexander and the Macedonian Invasion of Asia: Aspects of the Historiography of War and Empire in Antiquity. In J. Rich and G. Shipley (eds) *War and Society in the Greek World*, 197–223. London and New York.
Austin, M. M. (ed.) (2006) *The Hellenistic World from Alexander to the Roman Conquest*. 2nd. ed. Cambridge.
Baynham, E. (1998) *Alexander the Great. The Unique History of Quintus Curtius*. Ann Arbor.
Berve, H. (1926) *Das Alexanderreich auf prosopographischer Grundlage*. II. Munich.
Bielman, A. (2002) *Femmes en public dans le monde hellénistique*. Paris.
Bielman Sánchez, A. (2003) Régner au féminin. Réflexions sur les reines attalides et séleucides. In F. Prost (ed.) *L'Orient méditerranéen de la mort d'Alexandre aux campagnes de Pompée*, 41–61. Rennes.
Blasius, A. and B. U. Schipper (2002) Apokalyptik und Ägypten? In A. Blasius and B. U. Schipper (eds) *Ägyptische Apokalyptik*, 277–302. Leuven and Paris.
Böhme, M. (2009) Das Perserbild in den Fragmenten der Alexanderhistoriker. In M. Rathmann (ed.) *Studien zur antiken Geschichtsschreibung*, 161–86. Bonn.
Bosworth, A. B. (1972) Arrian's Literary Development, *Classical Quarterly* 22, 163–85.
Bosworth, A. B. (1995) *A Historical Commentary on Arrian's History of Alexander*. II. Oxford.
Bosworth, A. B. (2002) *The Legacy of Alexander*. Oxford.
Braund, D. (2005) After Alexander. In A. Erskine (ed.) *A Companion to the Hellenistic World*, 19–34. Oxford.
Briant, P. (2010) *Alexander the Great and his Empire*. Princeton.
Bringmann, K. (1993) The King as Benefactor. In Bulloch, A. *et al.* (eds) *Images and Ideologies*, 7–24. Berkeley.
Bröker, G. and W. Müller (2004) Aëtion, *Antikes Künsterlexikon (AKL)*, 5–6.
Brosius, M. (1996) *Women in Ancient Persia 559-331 BC*. Oxford.
Burstein, S. M. (1976) *Outpost of Hellenism. The Emergence of Heraclea on the Black Sea*. Berkeley.
Burstein, S. M. (ed.) (1985) *The Hellenistic Age from the Battle of Ipsos to the Death of Kleopatra VII*. Cambridge.
Burstein, S. M. (2000) Prelude to Alexander: The Reign of Khababash, *Ancient History Bulletin* 14, 149–54.
Burstein, S. M. (2004) *The Reign of Cleopatra*. Westport and London.
Callataÿ, F. de (2004) Le premier monnayage en argent de la cite d'Amastris (Paphlagonie), *Revue Suisse de Numismatique* 83, 57–80.
Carney, E. D. (1988) Eponymous Women: Royal Women and City Names, *Ancient History Bulletin*, 134–42.
Carney, E. D. (2000) *Women and Monarchy in Macedon*. Norman.
Carney, E. D. (2003) Women in Alexander's Court. In J. Roisman (ed.) *Brill's Companion to Alexander the Great*, 239–52. Leiden and Boston.
Carney, E. D. (2004) Women and Military Leadership in Macedonia, *The Ancient World* 35, 184–95.
Carney, E. D. (2006) *Olympias. Mother of Alexander the Great*. New York and London.
Carney, E. D. (2010) Putting Women in their Place: Women in Public under Philip II and Alexander III and the Last Argeads. In E. D. Carney and D. Ogden (eds) *Philip II and Alexander the Great: Father and Son, Lives and Afterlives*, 43–54. Oxford.

Collins, A. (2009) The Divinity of Alexander in Egypt: A Reassessment. In P. Wheatley and R. Hannah (eds) *Alexander and his Successors. Essays from the Antipodes*, 179–205, Claremont, CA.
Ellis, W. M. (2002) *Ptolemy of Egypt*. 2nd ed. London and New York.
Flower, M. (2000) Alexander the Great and Panhellenism. In A. B. Bosworth and E. Baynham (eds) *Alexander the Great in Fact and Fiction*, 96–135. Oxford.
Forrer, L. (1969) *Portraits of Royal Ladies on Greek Coins*. Chicago.
Fraser, P. (2009) *Greek Ethnic Terminology*. Oxford.
Goedicke, H. (1985) Comments on the Satrap Stela, *Bulletin of the Egyptological Seminar* 6, 33–54.
Grainger, J. D. (1997) *A Seleucid Prosopography and Gazetteer*. Leiden.
Greenwalt, W. S. (1988) The Marriageability Age at the Argead Court: 360–317 BC, *Classical World* 82, 93–97.
Gutzwiller, K. J. (1998) *Poetic Garlands: Hellenistic Epigrams in Context*. Berkeley.
Hammond, N. G. L. (1997) *The Genius of Alexander the Great*. Chapel Hill.
Heckel, W. (2009) *Who's Who in the Age of Alexander the Great*. Oxford.
Hölbl, G. (1994) *Geschichte des Ptolemäerreiches*. Darmstadt.
Hölscher, T. (2009) *Herrschaft und Lebensalter: Alexander der Große*. Basel.
Hoffmann, F. (2000) *Ägypten: Kultur und Lebenswelt in griechisch-römischer Zeit*. Berlin.
Holt, F. L. (1988) *Alexander the Great and Bactria*. Leiden.
Huß, W. (1994) *Der makedonische König und die ägyptischen Priester*. Stuttgart.
Huß, W. (2001) *Ägypten in hellenistischer Zeit 332–30 v. Chr.* Munich.
Klinkott, H. (2007) Xerxes in Ägypten. In S. Pfeiffer (ed.) *Ägypten unter fremden Herrschern zwischen persischer Satrapie und römischer Provinz*, 34–53. Frankfurt.
Koenen, L. (1993) The Ptolemaic King as a Religious Figure. In A. Bulloch *et al.* (eds) *Images and Ideologies*, 25–115. Berkeley.
Kosmetatou, E. (2004) Rhoxane's Dedications to Athena Polias, *Zeitschrift für Papyrologie und Epigraphik* 146, 75–80.
Kuttner, A. (1999) Hellenistic Images of Spectacle from Alexander to Augustus. In B. Bergmann and C. Kondoleon (eds) *The Art of Ancient Spectacle*, 97–123. Washington.
Ladynin, I. (2005) Adversary *Hšryš*: His Name and Deeds according to the Satrap Stela, *Chronique d'Égypte* 80, 87–113.
Le Rider, G. and F. de Callataÿ (2006) *Les Séleucides et les Ptolémées. L'héritage monétaire et financier d'Alexandre le Grand*. Paris.
Lloyd, A. B. (1982) Nationalist Propaganda in Ptolemaic Egypt, *Historia* 31, 33–55.
Lund, H. S. (1992) *Lysimachus. A Study in Early Hellenistic Kingship*. London and New York.
Macurdy, G. H. (1932) *Hellenistic Queens: A Study of Woman Power in Macedonia, Seleucid Syria, and Ptolemaic Egypt*. Baltimore and London.
Mamroth, A. (1949) Ein Bildnis der Königin Amastris auf Münzen des Lysimachos, *Berliner Numismatische Zeitschrift* 3/4, 81–86.
Mehl, A. (1986) *Seleukos Nikator und sein Reich*. Leuven.
Mehl, A. (1996) Apama, *Der Neue Pauly* 1, 823–24.
Merkelbach, R. (1954) *Die Quellen des griechischen Alexanderromans*. Munich.
Meeus, A. (2010) Kleopatra and the Diadochoi. In P. van Nuffelen (ed.) *Faces of Hellenism*, 63–92. Leuven.
Müller, S. (2007) Arsinoë III. als Artemis?, *Wiener Anzeiger* 142, 133–54.
Müller, S. (2008) Alexander's Relationship with Women as a *Topos* in Medieval Romance Traditions, *Medieval History Journal* 11, 259–87.

Müller, S. (2009) *Das hellenistische Königspaar in der medialen Repräsentation*. Berlin and New York.
Müller, S. (2011) Die frühen Perserkönige im kulturellen Gedächtnis der Makedonen, *Gymnasium* 118, 105–33.
Müller, S. (2012) Stories of the Persian Bride: Alexander and Roxane. In R. Stoneman *et al.* (eds) *The Alexander Romance in Persia and the East*, 295–309, Groningen.
Ogden, D. (1999) *Polygamy, Prostitutes and Death*. London.
Ogden, D. (2009) Alexander's Sex Life. In W. Heckel and L. A. Tritle (eds) *Alexander the Great. A New History*, 203–17. Oxford.
Olbrycht, M. J. (2009) Curtius Rufus, the Macedonian Mutiny at Opis and Alexander's Iranian Policy in 324 BC. In J. Pigon (ed.) *The Children of Herodotus*, 231–52. Newcastle.
Olbrycht, M. J. (2010) Macedonia and Persia. In I. Worthington and J. Roisman (eds) *A Companion to Ancient Macedonia*, 342–69. Oxford.
Pfeiffer, S. (2010) Das Dekret von Rosette. In G. Weber (ed.) *Alexandreia und das ptolemäische Ägypten*, 84–108. Berlin.
Pomeroy, S. (1982) Charities for Greek Women, *Mnemosyne* 35, 115–35.
Rathmann, M. (2005) *Perdikkas zwischen 323 und 320*. Vienna.
Schmitt, H. H. (2005) Ptolemaier, Ptolemaier(reich). In H. H. Schmitt and E. Vogt (eds) *Lexikon des Hellenismus*, 872–99. Wiesbaden.
Seibert, J. (1967) *Historische Beiträge zu den dynastischen Verbindungen in hellenistischer Zeit*. Wiesbaden.
Shabazi, A. S. (1987) Apama, *Encyclopaedia Iranica* 2, 150.
Stewart, A. (1993): *Faces of Power. Alexander's Image and Hellenistic Politics*. Berkeley.
Stewart, A. (2003) Alexander the Great in Greek and Roman Art. In J. Roisman (ed.) (2003) *Brill's Companion to Alexander the Great*, 31–66. Leiden and Boston.
Stoneman, R. (2008) *Alexander the Great. A Life in Legend*. New Haven and London.
Tarn, W. W. (1929) Queen Ptolemais and Apama, *Classical Quarterly* 23, 138–41.
Whitmarsh, T. (2005) *The Second Sophistic*. Oxford.
Wiesehöfer, J. (2005) *Das antike Persien um 550 v. Chr. bis 650 n. Chr.* Düsseldorf.
Wirth, G. (1959) Ptolemaios I. Soter, *RE* 23.2, 1603–45, 2467–84.
Wirth, G. (1985) *Philipp II. Geschichte Makedoniens*. I. Stuttgart.
Wirth, G. (1993) *Der Brand von Persepolis*. Amsterdam.
Yardley, J. C. and W. Heckel (1997) *Justin. Epitome of the Philippic History of Pompeius Trogus Books 11-12*. Oxford.

Notes

1 For example, Arsinoe II was portrayed as a military leader by the poet Posidippus (*Epigr.* 36 Austin-Bastianini col. VI 10–17). Cf. Gutzwiller 1998, 170–82; Müller 2009, 216–29. Berenice II is perhaps depicted as a naval warrior queen on a mosaic by Sophilus, cf. Andreae 2003, 35–36; Kuttner 1999, 111–13; Koenen 1993, 27.

2 Cf. Bielman 2002, 162; Burstein 1985, no. 36; Pomeroy 1982, 120–23.

3 Posidipp.Epigr. 116 Austin-Bastianini (*PLouvre* 7172); 39 Austin-Bastianini (col. VI 30–37); Athen. 11.497d; Call. *Epigr.* 5; Str. 17.1.16. Cf. Müller 2009, 215–16, 266–79.

4 Arr. *An.* 7.4.4–8; D.S. 17.107.6; Curt. 10.3.12; Plu. *Alex.* 70.3; Just. 12.10.9; Athen. 12.538b-539a. Cf. Briant 2010, 128; Ogden 2009, 207; Olbrycht 2009, 233–34; Carney 2003, 246–47; Brosius 1996, 76–78.

5 Curt. 8.4.23–30; 10.3.11; Arr. *An.* 4.19.5; 6.15.3; *ME* 29; Str. 11.11.4; Plu. *Mor.* 332e; *Alex.* 47. Diodorus' report is lost, but the content list to his book 17 mentions the marriage adding that Alexander persuaded numbers of Macedonian officers to marry Iranian women (cf. *ME* 31). This is probably the

case of a historical muddle. Diodorus or his source might have confused the event with the marriages in 324.

6 Cf. Olbrycht 2010, 359–60; Briant 2010, 116–17; Heckel 2009, 242; Wiesehöfer 2005, 151; Carney 2000, 99; Hammond 1997, 154; Yardley/Heckel 1997, 291; Holt 1988, 66–68.

7 Cf. Olbrycht 2009, 236–37, naming also Leonnatus and Perdiccas. See also Heckel 1992, 143–44.

8 Cf. Heckel 2009, 199. Hence, it is probable that Plutarch was mistaken in reporting that Roxane's second victim was Drypetis, Hephaestion's widow. Cf. Carney 2000, 110–11.

9 The inventory is dated to 305/4. The date of Roxane's offerings is uncertain: cf. Atkinson, Yardley 2009, 181; Heckel 2009, 338 n. 660; Kosmetatou 2004, 75–80; Berve 1926, 347 n. 2. Roxane offered a gold vessel, a gold rhyton, and a gold necklace. Alternatively, the dedications might be dated to the time when Roxane was in Macedonia supported by Olympias.

10 Arr. *Post.Alex.* 1.21,26; D.S. 18.23.1–3; Just. 13.6.4–6; Plu. *Eum.* 3.9. Cf. Heckel 2009, 199–201; Meeus 2010, 64–65; Carney 2006, 68–84.

11 D.S. 19.105.1–2; Just. 15.2.2–5; Paus. 9.7.2; Pomp.Trog. *Prol* 15. Cf. Braund 2005, 27.

12 Arr. *An.* 7.4.4–8; Just. 12.10.9; Plu. *Alex.* 70.3; D.S. 17.107.6; Curt. 10.3.12. Cf. Athen. 12.538b-539a. For the significance of the marriages, see Briant 2010, 128; Olbrycht 2010, 362; Ogden 2009, 207; Carney 2003, 246–47; Brosius 1996, 76–78.

13 Arr. *An.* 7.4.6; Plu. *Eum.* 1.7. Cf. Ellis 2002, 15; Heckel 2009, 55–56; Müller 2009, 22; Shabazi 1987, 150; Wirth 1959, 1607.

14 Plu. *Art.* 2.7.9; *Ages.* 3.3; *Alex.* 21.9; Curt. 3.13.13; 5.9.1; Arr. *An.* 3.23.7.

15 Curt. 5.7.3–4; Plu. *Alex.* 38.1; Str. 15.3.6; D.S. 17.72.1–4. Cf. Berve 1926, 175. According to Athen. 13.576d-e, they were even married: cf. Bielman 2002, 77. The children are mentioned in Just. 15.2.7; Athen. 13.576d-e.

16 Cf. Collins 2009, 203–05; Briant 2010, 104; Hölbl 1994, 9; Huß 1994, 129–33.

17 Paus. 6.3.1; Just. 13.6.18–20; D.S. 18.14.1. Cf. Huß 2001, 257; Austin 1993, 207. Tarn's suggestion that Ptolemy married an Egyptian princess shortly after his arrival in 323, is not widely accepted. It is based on an inscription recording a dedication by his daughter Ptolemais called 'daughter of Kheperkari', the solar name of Nectanebus II (Tarn 1929, 138–39). However, the document does not hint at the existence of an Egyptian wife. She probably would have not been that invisible. Ptolemy himself tried to commemorate Nectanebus II by adopting elements of his public profile (Huß 1994, 51 n. 111).

18 The time of the reign of Chababasch, who presumably ruled for two years, is uncertain. Mostly, it is assumed that he ruled under Artaxerxes III (338–336) and Darius III (Burstein 2000). Thus, the Persian king named Xerxes will have been Artaxerxes III (Ladynin 2005, 110–13: because of his alleged crimes in Egypt, cf. D.S. 16.51.2) or Arses-Artaxerxes IV. However, Klinkott (2007, 37–41) argues that he is to be identified with Xerxes I, as the knife hinted at his assassination and his hieroglyphic name, *Hšryš*, were very similar to his old Persian name Xšayaršan. Xerxes II is an unlikely candidate, as he reigned only a few weeks (424–423).

19 The suggestion in Seleucid circles that she was claimed to be an illegitimate daughter by Alexander and Roxane (Shabazi 1987, 150; Tarn 1929) is pure speculation based only on the tradition (App. *Syr.* 13) that a certain Alexander from Megalopolis falsely claimed to be a descendant of Alexander III. In order to give credibility to his story, he called his children Alexander and Apama.

20 I would like to thank Victor Alonso Troncoso and Edward M. Anson for this suggestion.

21 Str. 14.1.7. Cf. Curt. 7.5.28–35. Against Hdt. 6.19.1–3. Cf. Müller 2011, 127–28; Flower 2000, 118.

22 Plu. *Demetr.* 38; App. *Syr.* 59–61; V.Max. 5.7. The wedding characterized as a love match by the ancient sources is probably also connected with Antiochus' co-regency over the Upper Satrapies beyond the Euphrates as another strategy to underline his legitimization as heir apparent.

23 While it is suggested that her portrait with the Phrygian cap served to emphasize her Achaemenid descent (Brosius 1996, 78 n. 70; Mamroth 1949), it is also claimed that it was a portrait of Mithras (Forrer 1969, 4–6). See the illustration of the coin.

24 Acknowledgements: I am grateful to Victor Alonso Troncoso and Edward M. Anson for their kind support and helpful comments. I also like to thank Elizabeth Baynham, Brian Bosworth, Waldemar Heckel, Pat Wheatley and Gerhard Wirth.

ALEXANDER THE GREAT, PTOLEMY I AND THE OFFERINGS OF ARMS TO ATHENA LINDIA

Giuseppe Squillace

During his Asiatic campaign (*strateia*), Alexander sent bull heads (*boukephala*) and arms (*hopla*), as offering to Athena Lindia. The *Lindian Chronicle* describes the event in this way:

> King Alexander (dedicated) bull heads (*boukephala*), on which has been inscribed: 'King Alexander, having defeated in battle Darius and becoming 'Lord of Asia', sacrificed to Athena Lindia according to an oracle during the priesthood of Theugenes son of Pistocrateus'. The public records of the Lindians contain this news. And he also dedicated weapons (*hopla*), on which there is an inscription.
>
> (*Chron.Lind.* 38.103–109 Higbie)[1]

In 305, after Demetrius Poliorcetes' failed siege of Rhodes, Ptolemy Lagu offered twenty skulls of cattle to Athena Lindia. Again the *Lindian Chronicle* is the principal source:

> King Ptolemy (offered) twenty skulls of cattle (*prometōpidia boōn*) on which has been inscribed: 'King Ptolemy sacrificed to Athena Lindia during the priesthood of Athena (held) by Athenagoras', as the public records of the Lindians testify.
>
> (*Chron.Lind.* 39.110–13 Higbie)[2]

The parallelism of the gestures is obvious.[3] What is not so obvious are the aims of the two kings, which I will try to clarify.

Alexander the Great

Alexander's offerings of bull heads and weapons (perhaps weapons with an impressed cow-head on)[4] took place in 331, after the battle of Gaugamela.[5] Christian Blinkenberg proposed this date in his commentary on the *Lindian Chronicle*. He based it on the surrender of Rhodes to Alexander in 332 after the battle of Issus and during the siege of Tyre (Arr. *An.* 2.20.2; Curt. 4.5.11; Just. 11.11; see: Bosworth 1980, 242).

The chronology of Blinkenberg is generally accepted,[6] even though there have been other hypotheses. K. F. Kinch in his *Introduction* to Blinkenberg (1941, 92–94) dated the offerings after the battle of Issus, and Carolyn Higbie, in her recent edition of the *Lindian Chronicle* (2003, *comm. ad loc.* 135) and in *Brill's New Jacoby* (*comm. ad loc.*) remarked that an exact chronology is impossible. In her opinion, Alexander's offerings could be dated to many different phases of the Asiatic *strateia*.

The chronological problem, I think, has to be reconsidered. First, we can note that in the *Lindian Chronicle* Alexander, calling himself 'king' (*basileus*) as he did after the battle on Granicus in the inscription on the temple of Athena in Priene (*IPr.* 1), in a Priene decree (*IPr.* 156) and in two letters to the people of Chios (*SIG*[3] 283; *SEG* 12.506),[7] became - he says - 'Lord of Asia' (*kyrios tas Asias*) in accordance with a prophecy (*kata manteian*).

The offering of weapons to the gods from the booty was generally practiced in the ancient Greek world, and the sources mention Alexander doing so in 334 and in 331 after his victories respectively on the Granicus and at Gaugamela.[8] According to Arrian (*An.* 1.16.7) and Plutarch (*Alex.* 16.17–18), the Macedonian king sent 300 panoplies to Athens as an offering to Athena after his victory at Granicus (Squillace 1992–1994, 9–20). After the battle of Gaugamela, Plutarch says, Alexander was proclaimed 'King of Asia' (*basileus tēs Asias*). This time he offered sacrifices to the gods, wrote to the Greeks informing them that he was abolishing the tyrannies, giving every community its autonomy and rebuilding Plataea, which in the fifth century had fought against the Persians for Greek freedom. Alexander sent part of the booty to Croton because he wanted to honour the athlete Phäyllus who, unique among the Greeks of the West, captained a ship, which he supplied at his own expense, at Salamis (Plu. *Alex.* 34.1–3).

The sources record also two prophecies: one given before Alexander left for Asia, and the other before the battle at Gaugamela. In 335 Alexander had received a positive response from Delphi. The oracle declared him 'invincible' (Plu. *Alex.* 14.6–7). In 332, before Gaugamela, he received a similar endorsement at the oracle at Siwah. The priest declared him the 'son of Zeus' and prophesized the next victory and the conquest of the world (Callisth. *FGH* 124 F 14; Curt. 4.7.25–27; Plu. *Alex.* 26.12–27.9; Just. 11.11.2–10; see Squillace 2005, 307–13).

In both situations we can note prophecy, military success, sacrifices to the gods after the victory, and offerings of the booty. It would be unusual if Alexander, who always took care to perform ancient rituals and follow long-standing traditions, did not respect them after the battle of Issus. This victory was more important than the success at Granicus, because to the Greeks now Alexander was stronger than Darius and the Persian army, and could definitely pose himself as champion of Greek freedom and revenge (Sordi 1984, 23–30). Can we believe Alexander did not follow this ritual after Issus and did not send a part of the booty anywhere? We have to return to the offerings of the bull heads and the weapons registered in the *Lindian Chronicle*.

As I said, the offerings of the bull heads and weapons were based on a prophecy which predicted the victory over Darius and called Alexander 'Lord of Asia' (*kyrios tas Asias*). According to the sources, some months before the battle of Issus, Alexander visited Gordium.[9] Arrian (*An.* 2.3), who reports two versions of this episode, says Alexander went to Gordium out of curiosity. A local legend promised the power over Asia (*arxai tēs Asias*) to the person who untied the knot. Since Alexander was not able to untie the knot, he cut it, turning a possible perceived failure into a prophetic victory. Arrian refers also to Aristobulus' version, which is in contrast with the first one. According to

Aristobulus, Alexander took out the pin and in this way untied the wagon and fulfilled the prophecy (Bosworth 1980, 185–88).

The two versions are also found in Plutarch, who reports that whoever unties the knot will become 'King of the world' (Plu. *Alex.* 18.1–4: *basileus tēs oikoumenēs*). Marsyas of Pella says *basileus tēs Asias* (*FGH* 135–136 F 4 = Schol. Eurip. *Hipp.* 671). According to Curtius Rufus (3.1.14–18), Alexander went into the temple of Jupiter at Gordium, where the wagon was. Here he got acquainted with the prophecy (*oraculum*). It promised that whoever untied the knot would obtain the power over Asia (Curt. 3.1.16: *Asiae potiturum, qui inexplicabile vinculum solvisset*). In the same way, Justin (11.7.4) relates that ancient prophecies (*antiqua oracula*) had foretold dominion over all of Asia for any man (*eum tota Asia regnaturum*) who succeeded in untying the Gordian knot. Therefore, it was definitely a prophecy (*manteia*) which Alexander and his entourage used at Gordium to preserve the morale of the army before the next battle against the Persians.

Alexander (and his supporters) used the title 'Lord of Asia' (*kyrios tas Asias*) after Issus. This title suffuses the letter which the Macedonian king sent as a reply to Darius at Marathus in 332. Darius had asked for the release of his wife, mother and sons taken prisoners by Alexander and for a friendship and alliance treaty, but Alexander accused the Persian king and his ancestors of attacking the Greeks during the Persian wars, supporting Perinthus against Philip, conspiring in Philip's murder, becoming king of the Persians illegally, and backing the Spartans against Macedonia. Remembering these faults and his military successes of Granicus and Issus, he ordered Darius to obey him as 'Lord of Asia' (*tēs Asias hapasēs kyrios*). Alexander used the same title at the end of his letter, naming himself as 'King of Asia' (*basileus tēs Asias*) and stating that he had became lord (*kyrios*) of all things the Persian king owned (Arr. *An.* 2.14; but also D.S. 17.39.1; Curt. 4.1.10–14; Just. 11.12.1; see Squillace 2006, 355–65, with bibliography).

Therefore, Alexander in the inscription on the offerings to Athena Lindia repeated the content of the prophecy (*manteia*) which he received at Gordium and called himself by the title 'Lord of Asia' (*kyrios tas Asias*), which he employed in his letter to Darius in 332. At the same time the Rhodians surrendered to the Macedonian king (Just. 11.11.1), sent ten ships (Arr. *An.* 2.20.2), entrusted their polis and their harbours to him (Curt. 4.5.9) and offered to the king a precious mantle, Helicon's work, which he wore during the battle of Gaugamela (Plu. *Alex.* 32.11). Alexander garrisoned the island but, perhaps in the same year, freed it after his return from Egypt, accepting the request by a Rhodian embassy, as Curtius testifies (Curt. 4.8.12–13)[10].

If we date to 332 the offerings to Athena Lindia (some months after the battle of Issus and after the Rhodians' surrender), the act becomes very meaningful. Athena, the goddess of the Greeks in the Persian wars (Plu. *Arist.* 20; Paus. 9.4.1), had at the same time revenged Rhodes against the Persians. According to the *Lindian Chronicle* in 490, during the Persian wars, Datis, the Persian officer, by order of the king Darius, attacked Rhodes. The inhabitants of the island wanted to surrender because they were without water. Athena appeared in a dream to one of the Rhodian leaders and assured them that she would give the water. Informed about the dream, the Rhodians asked Datis for a five-days truce and promised to surrender if Athena did not fulfil her promise. A day later a strong storm hit the island. The Rhodians had the water and Datis was forced to retreat. Struck by the event, the Persian officer sent to Rhodes a mantle, a torque, and armlets as offerings to Athena (*Chron. Lind.* D 1–59 Higbie).

Alexander had underlined this theme already in 334 after the victory at Granicus when, as *hēgemōn* of the Greeks, he sent 300 panoplies (suit of armour) from the Persian booty to Athens and dedicated them with an inscription to Athena. He sent them to coincide with the Great Panathenaia (Arr. *An.* 1.16.7; Plu. *Alex.* 16.17–18). By the panoplies Alexander remembered the ancient role of the goddess as protector of the Greeks in the fifth century and brought the ancient tradition of the Delian League back to life: all the allies, during the Panathenaia, sent a cow and a panoply as gifts to the *hēgemōn* Athens (*IG* I^2 45; 63; Squillace 1992–1994, 17–18 n. 53–54).

Therefore, as with the 300 panoplies sent to Athens in 334, the bull heads and the arms offered to Athena Lindia (they were quite fitting for the *Boukopia* feast celebrated in Rhodes in honour of the goddess, during which cows were offered to her)[11] had an anti-Persian and philhellenic meaning. They made evident again the role of Athena in the war against the Persians and also the role of Alexander who, acquiring the power over Asia after the battle of Issus, now could present himself as 'Lord of Asia' (*kyrios tas Asias*), as predicted in Gordium, and again as avenger of the Greeks and champion of their freedom.[12]

Ptolemy

As stated earlier, Ptolemy offered also twenty skulls of cattle to Athena Lindia in 305 after Demetrius Poliorcetes aborted his siege of Rhodes. Demetrius had attacked the city with his sophisticated war machines for almost a year. The Rhodians, helped by Ptolemy, who (as had the other Diadochi) had proclaimed himself king a short time before (D.S. 20.53.1–4; Plu. *Demetr.* 18.1–4), were able to force Demetrius to make peace (D.S. 20.81–88; 91–100.5; but also Plu. *Demetr.* 20.9–21).[13] The islanders defended their freedom, mantained their economic revenues, became allies of Antigonus and Demetrius but remained in close friendship with Ptolemy (D.S. 20.99.3; Plu. *Demetr.* 22.8); furthermore, they gave to Demetrius 100 Rhodian citizens as hostages (see also Hauben 1977, 338–39; Ager 1996, 59–61; Braund 2003, 30).

At the end of the war the Rhodians honoured their allies during the siege. They erected statues of the kings Lysimachus and Cassander and, after receiving a positive response from the oracle of Ammon in Siwah, granted divine honours to Ptolemy, who had supported them with large resources. Furthermore, they dedicated in the city a sacred place with columns named *Ptolemaion* (D.S. 20.100.2–3; Habicht 1970, 109; Virgilio 1998, 151) and celebrated the victory by erecting a great statue of the Sun as symbol of the freedom of the island (*AP* 7.171; Musti-Pulcini 1996, 289–308).

As Alexander and the others mentioned by the *Lindian Chronicle* did, Ptolemy also celebrated a military success. The failure of Demetrius' siege, even if it was not a real defeat, it certainly constituted a victory for Ptolemy. And the latter presented it as a triumph, especially because he had been defeated by Demetrius one year before at Cyprus, had lost the island and had seen reduced his power in the Aegean (D.S. 20.47–53,2; Plu. *Demetr.* 15–17; Braund 2003, 28–9). After the Cyprus victory Antigonus and Demetrius proclaimed themselves kings (D.S. 20.53.2; Plu. *Demetr.* 18.1; Müller 1973, 78–105; Gruen 1985, 253–71; Billows 1990, 155–60; Adams 2010, 217).

In his dedication Ptolemy made an *imitatio Alexandri*. Ptolemy always identified with Alexander and wrote a history of Alexander's Asiatic *strateia*.[14] Furthermore, he, perhaps by Alexander's will, transported the king's body to Egypt in order to bury it (Curt. 10.5.4; Paus. 1.6.3; Just. 12.15.7)[15] and presented himself as of Argead descent and as an illegitimate son of Philip II.[16] Like Cassander, Lysimachus, and Antigonus, Ptolemy also tried to marry Cleopatra, Alexander's sister, in order to legitimate his succession to the Macedonian kingship (D.S. 20.37.3–7), being the first to mint coins with the portrait of Alexander (Lianou 2010, 127).

After Alexander's death, the Diadochi consistency used the theme of Greek freedom for propagandistic aims presenting themselves as champions of Greek freedom (Simpson 1959, 389–409; Seager 1981, 107). Especially Antigonus, Demetrius and Ptolemy transformed the power struggle into an 'ideological war'. According to Diodorus, in 315 Antigonus in Tyre issued a decree in which he declared all the Greeks free, without garrisons and autonomous. He did this because he hoped to obtain the support of the Greeks in the war against Cassander (D.S. 19.61.2–3; but also D.S. 19.74.1; 78.2).[17] When Ptolemy heard of Antigonus' decree, he issued his own version the same year. He wanted to make clear to the Greeks that he, no less than Antigonus, cared about their autonomy (D.S. 19.62.1; Simpson 1954, 25–31; 1959, 390; Billows 1990, 200). Both kings - Diodorus (19.62.2) concludes - tried to obtain the benevolence of the Greeks.

The freedom theme characterized also Antigonus' letter to Scepsis in 311, as well as the response of the polis (*OGIS* 5; 6; see Braund 2003, 25–26). Antigonus ascribed to himself the merit of defending Greek freedom and autonomy in the peace treaty he had concluded that year with Cassander, Lysimachus, and Ptolemy (*OGIS* 5, especially ll. 1–2; 53–55). An inscription from Miletus dated in 313 recalls the restoration of freedom, autonomy and democracy by Antigonus (*SIG*[3] 322). An inscription from Colophon of 311/306 says that Antigonus, following Alexander, granted freedom to that polis (Meritt 1935, 361 ll. 6–7; Welles 1934, 3–12; Simpson 1959, 393–94).

Ptolemy also employed the freedom theme for propagandistic aims. After his freedom decree in 315, in 310, accusing Antigonus to break the peace treaty of 311 garrisoning the Greek cities of Asia and violating their autonomy, he began to free the cities of Asia Minor (D.S. 20.19.3–5; 27.1–3; see Billows 1990, 206–07). In 309/8 he liberated Corinth and Sicyon from the garrisons of Polyperchon and Cassander and called upon the cities of the Peloponnese to join him in a freedom crusade. After these successes he summoned the delegates from the Greek states to hear a formal announcement of Greek freedom at the Isthmian games.[18]

The Greek freedom theme also characterized the later war between Demetrius and

Ptolemy (Suda, s.v. *Demetrios*). It was used for propagandistic aims and for obtaining the consent of the Greeks. In 307, Demetrius freed Athens from Demetrius of Phalerum and, together with his father, was honoured by the Athenians as 'king' and 'saviour-god' (Plu. *Demetr.* 8–10; D.S. 20.46).[19] The same year he freed the Greeks and won great consent (D.S. 20.102.1); in 302 he restored the Corinthian League and established the freedom of the Greeks as its principal aim (*ISE* 5; 7; 39),[20] and the same year, in the peace treaty with Cassander, he inserted a clause ensuring the autonomy of the Greeks (D.S. 20.111.2).[21]

Ptolemy's offerings to Athena should be placed in this 'propaganda war'. What did the king hope to get by his gesture? The *Lindian Chronicle* knows of another epiphany of Athena, besides the one during the Persian war mentioned earlier (*Chron.Lind.* D 1–59 Higbie): during Demetrius' siege the goddess appeared to the priest Callicles and urged him to order the *prytanis* Anaxipolis to write to Ptolemy and ask for his support (*Chron. Lind.* D 94–115 Higbie). So we get a coherent picture: Athena, who in the past had caused the failure of the siege of the Persians and had supported Alexander and his Asiatic *strateia* favoring his military success against Darius, now supported Ptolemy in helping free the Rhodians from Demetrius' siege.[22]

Therefore in his offerings Ptolemy used again the Greek freedom theme with propagandistic purpose against Antigonus and Demetrius. Recalling the Persian wars and Alexander's Asiatic *strateia*, Ptolemy could win a positive image after his defeat at Cyprus in 306:[23] now he was the new and authentic champion of Greek freedom, the true heir and successor of Alexander.[24]

Bibliography

Adams, W. L. (2010) Alexander's Successors to 221 BC. In J. Roisman and I. Worthington (eds) *A Companion to Ancient Macedonia*, 208–24, London.

Ager, S. (1996) *Interstate Arbitrations in the Greek World (337–90 BC)*. Berkeley.

Bearzot, C. (1992) Πτολεμαῖος Μακεδών. Sentimento nazionale e contrapposizioni etniche all'inizio del regno tolemaico. In M. Sordi (ed.) *Autocoscienza e rappresentazione dei popoli nell'antichità*, 39–53, Milan.

Bellen, H. (1974) Der Rachegedanke in der griechisch-persischen Auseinandersetzung, *Chiron* 4, 44–67.

Berthold, R. M. (1984) *Rhodes in the Hellenistic Age*. Ithaca.

Berve, H. (1926) *Das Alexanderreich auf prosopographischer Grundlage*. 2 vols. Munich.

Billows, R. A. (1990) *Antigonus the One-Eyed and the Creation of the Hellenistic State*. Berkeley, Los Angeles and London.

Blinkenberg, C. (1915) *Timachidas of Lindus. The Chronicle of the Temple of Athena in Lindus in Rhodes*. Bonn.

Blinkenberg, C. (ed.) (1941) *Lindos. Fouilles de l'Acropole (1902–1914). II: Inscriptions publiées en grande partie d'après les copies de K. F. Kinch par Chr. Blickenberg*. Tome I. Berlin and Copenhagen.

Bosworth, A. B. (1980) *A Historical Commentary on Arrian's History of Alexander. I: Commentary on Books I–III*. Oxford.

Braund, D. (2003) After Alexander: The Emergence of the Hellenistic World, 323–281. In A. Erskine (ed.) *A Companion to the Hellenistic World*, 105–20, London.
Burke, B. (2001) Anatolian Origins of the Gordian Knot Legend, *Greek, Roman and Byzantine Studies* 42, 255–61.
Campanile, M. D. (1998) La vita cittadina in età ellenistica. In S. Settis (ed.) *I Greci. Storia, cultura, arte, società*, II.3, 379–403, Turin.
Chugg, A. (2002) The Tomb of Alexander in Alexandria, *American Journal of Ancient History* 1.2, 75–108.
Collins, N. L. (1997) The Various Fathers of Ptolemy I, *Mnemosyne* 50, 436–76.
Erskine, A. (2002) Life after Death: Alexandria and the Body of Alexander, *Greece and Rome* 49, 163–79.
Faraguna, M. (2003) Alexander and the Greeks. In J. Roisman (ed.) *A Companion to Alexander the Great*, 99–130, Oxford.
Fraser, P. M. (1952) Alexander and the Rhodian Constitution, *La Parola del Passato* 7, 192–206.
Fraser, P. M. (1972) *Ptolemaic Alexandria*. I. Oxford.
Fredricksmeyer, E. A. (1961) Alexander, Midas and the Oracle of Gordion, *Classical Philology* 56, 160–68.
Fredricksmeyer, E. A. (2000) Alexander the Great and the Kingship of Asia. In A. B. Bosworth and E. Baynham (eds) *Alexander the Great in Fact and Fiction*, 73–85, Oxford.
Garoufalias, P. (1979) *Pyrrhus King of Epirus*. London.
Gehrke, H.-J. (1987) Die Griechen und die Rache. Ein Versuch in historischer Psychologie, *Saeculum* 38, 121–49.
Grana, F. and G. Mathiae (1959) Bucranio, *Enciclopedia dell'arte antica* II, 211, Rome.
Green, P. (1970) *Alexander the Great*. London.
Green, P. (1992) *Alexander of Macedon (336–323 BC). A Historical Biography*. Berkeley, Los Angeles and Oxford.
Gruen, E. S. (1985) The Coronation of the Diadochoi. In J. Eadie and J. Ober (eds) *The Craft of the Ancient Historian: Essays in Honor of C. G. Starr*, 253–71, Lanham.
Guarducci, M. (1969) *Epigrafia greca*. II. Rome.
Habicht, C. (1970) *Gottmenschentum und griechische Städte*. 2nd ed. Munich.
Hammond, N. G. L. (1997) *The Genius of Alexander the Great*. London.
Hammond, N. G. L. (2001) *Alexander the Great. King, Commander and Statesman*. 3rd edn. London.
Hauben, H. (1977) Rhodes, Alexander and the Diadochi from 333/332 to 304 BC, *Historia* 26, 307–39.
Heckel, W. (2006) *Who's Who in the Age of Alexander the Great. Prosopography of Alexander's Empire*. London.
Heisserer, A. J. (1980) *Alexander the Great. The Epigraphic Evidence*. Norman.
Heuss, A. (1938) Antigonus Monophthalmos und die griechische Städte, *Hermes* 73, 133–94.
Higbie, C. (2003) *The Lindian Chronicle and the Greek Creation of their Past*. Oxford.
Hiller von Gaertringen, F. (1897) Boukopia Theudaisia, *RE* 3.1, 1017–19.
Hiller von Gaertringen, F. (1931) Rhodos, *RE*, Suppl. 5, 731–840.
Lane Fox, R. (2004) *Alessandro Magno*. Turin (trans. from English).
Lévêque, P. (1957) *Pyrrhos*. Paris.
Lianou, M. (2010) The Role of the Argeadai in the Legitimation of the Ptolemaic Dinasty. In E.

Carney and D. Ogden (eds) *Philip II and Alexander the Great. Father and Son, Lives and Afterlives*, 123–33, Oxford.
Mastrocinque, A. (1976–1977) L'eleutheria e le città ellenistiche, *Atti dell'Istituto Veneto di Scienze, Lettere ed Arti, Classe di Scienze morali e Lettere* 135, 1–23.
Meritt, B. D. (1935) Inscriptions of Colophon, *American Journal of Philology* 56, 358–97.
Michel, C. (1900) *Recueil d'inscriptions grecques*. Bruxelles.
Müller, O. (1973) *Antigonos Monophthalmos und 'Das Jahr der Könige'*. Bonn.
Musti, D. and B. Pulcini (1996) La fiaccola delle Demokratia e la statua della libertà, *Rivista di cultura classica e medioevale* 38, 289–308.
Pearson, L. (1960) *The Lost Histories of Alexander the Great*. New York.
Pédech, P. (1984) *Historiens compagnons d'Alexandre*. Paris.
Poddighe, E. (2009) Alexander and the Greeks. In W. Heckel and L. A. Tritle (2009) (eds) *Alexander the Great. A New history*, 99–120, Malden, MA.
Prandi, L. (1983) Alessandro Magno e Chio: considerazioni su Syll.[3] 283 e SEG XII 506, *Aevum* 67, 25–32.
Prandi, L. (1990) Gli oracoli della spedizione asiatica di Alessandr', *Chiron* 20, 345–69.
Pugliese Carratelli, G. (1949) Alessandro e la costituzione rodia, *La Parola del Passato* 11, 154– 71.
Richards, G. C. (1915) Introduction to C. Blinkenberg, *Timachidas of Lindus. The Chronicle of the Temple of Athena in Lindus in Rhodes*, vi-xii, Bonn.
Richards, G. C. (1929) Timachidas. In J. U. Powell and E. A. Barber (eds) *New Chapters in the History of Greek Literature*, 76–87, Oxford.
Roller, L. E. (1984) Midas and the Gordian Knot, *Classical Antiquity* 3, 256–71.
Rouse, W. H. D. (1902) *Greek Votive Offerings*. Cambridge.
Seager R. (1981) The Freedom of the Greeks of Asia: From Alexander to Antiochus, *Classical Quarterly* 31, 106–12.
Sherwin White, S. (1985) Ancient Archives: The Edict of Alexander to Priene, a Reappraisal, *Journal of Hellenic Studies* 105, 69–89.
Simpson, R. H. (1954) The Historical Circumstances of the Peace of 311, *Journal of Hellenic Studies* 74, 25–31.
Simpson, R. H. (1957) Antigonus, Polyperchon and the Macedonian Regency, *Historia* 6, 371–73.
Simpson, R. H. (1959) Antigonus the One-Eyed and the Greeks, *Historia* 8, 385–409.
Sinn, U. (2005) Altar. In V. Lambrinoudakis and J. C. Balty (eds) *Thesaurus cultus et rituum antiquorum. 4: Cult Places, Representations of Cult Places*, 14–21, Los Angeles.
Sordi, M. (1984) L'orazione pseudodemostenica 'Sui patti con Alessandro' e l'atteggiamento dei Greci prima di Isso. In M. Sordi (ed.) *Alessandro Magno tra storia e mito*, 23–30, Milan.
Squillace, G. (1992–1994) Alessandro e l'offerta ad Atena di trecento panoplie, *Miscellanea di Studi Storici, Dipartimento di Storia, Università della Calabria* 9, 9–20.
Squillace, G. (2004) *Basileis o tyrannoi, Filippo II e Alessandro Magno tra opposizione e consenso*. Soveria Mannelli.
Squillace, G. (2005) Propaganda macedone e spedizione asiatica. Responsi oracolari e vaticini nella spedizione di Alessandro Magno tra verità e manipolazione (nota a Polyaen., Strat. IV 3,14), *Les Études Classiques* 73, 303–18.
Squillace, G. (2006) La voce del vinto? La lettera di Dario III ad Alessandro Magno a Marato nel 332 a.C. Nota a Diodoro XVII 39,1–2, *Mediterraneo Antico* 9.1, 355–65.

Squillace, G. (2010) Consensus Strategies under Philip and Alexander. The Revenge Theme. In E. Carney and D. Ogden (eds) *Philip II and Alexander the Great. Father and Son, Lives and Afterlives*, 69–80, Oxford.

Stevens, G. P. (1940) *The Setting of the Periclean Parthenon*. Cambridge, MA.

Stewart, A. (1993) *Faces of Power: Alexander's Image and Hellenistic Politics*. Berkeley.

Tarn, W. W. (1948) *Alexander the Great*. II. Cambridge.

Van Straten, F. T. (1981) Gifts for the Gods. In H. S. Versnel (ed.) *Faith, Hope, and Worship*, 65–151, Leiden.

Van Straten, F. T. (1992) Votives and Votaries in Greek Sanctuaries. In A. Schachter (ed.) *Le sanctuaire grec*, 247–90, Geneva.

Van Wees, H. (1998) Greeks Bearing Arms: The State, the Leisure Class, and the Display of Weapons in Archaic Greece. In N. Fisher and H. Van Wees (eds) *Archaic Greece: New Approaches and New Evidence*, 333–78, London.

Virgilio, B. (1998) Basileus. Il re e la regalità ellenistica. In S. Settis (ed.) *I Greci. Storia, cultura, arte, società*, II.3, 107–76, Turin.

Wehrli, C. (1968) *Antigone et Démétrios*. Geneva.

Welles, C. B. (1934) *Royal Correspondence in the Hellenistic Period. A Study in Greek Epigraphy*. New Haven.

Wheatley, P. (2009) The Diadochi, or Successors of Alexander. In W. Heckel and L. A. Tritle (eds) *Alexander the Great. A New history*, 53–68, Malden, MA.

Zahrnt, M. (2001) Alexander in Gordion und die Entstehung einer Legende. In S. Böhm and K. Valtin von Eickstedt (eds) *Ithake. Festschrift für Jörg Schäfer zum 75. Geburtstag am 25. April 2001*, 203–06, Würzburg.

Notes

1 *Chron. Lind.* 38.103–109 Higbie: Βασιλεὺς Ἀλέξαν[δ]ρος [β]ο[υκέφαλ]α, ἐφ' ὧν [ἐ]πιγέγραπται· / «βασιλεὺς Ἀλέξαν[δ]ρος μάχαι κρατήσας Δα/ρεῖον καὶ κύριος γε[ν]όμενος τᾶς Ἀσίας ἔθυ/σε τ[ᾶ]ι Ἀθάναι τᾶι [Λι]νδίαι κατὰ μαντείαν / ἐπ' ἱε[ρέ]ως Θευγέν[ε]υς τοῦ Πιστοκράτευς». πε/ρὶ [τ]ούτων το[ὶ] Λινδί[ων] χρηματισμοὶ περ[ι]έχοντι. / ἀν[έ]θηκε δὲ καὶ [ὅ]πλα, ἐφ' ὧν ἐπιγέγραπται.

2 *Chron. Lind.* 39.110–113 Higbie: Βασιλεὺς Πτ[ολ]εμαῖος προμετωπίδια βοῶν εἴ/κοσι, ἐφ' ὧν ἐ[πιγ]έγραπται· «Βασιλεὺς Πτολεμαῖος / ἔθυσε Ἀθά[ν]αι Λινδίαι ἐπ' ἱερέως Ἀθ[α]νᾶ τοῦ Ἀθανα/γόρα», ὡς μα[ρτ]υροῦ[ν]τι τοὶ Λινδ[ί]ων χρηματισμοί. Pyrrhus also offered bull heads and weapons to Athena Lindia, as the *Lindian Chronicle* (40.114–117 Higbie) testifies: Βασιλεὺ[ς] Πύρρο[ς] βουκ[έ]φαλα καὶ ὅπλα, οἷς / αὐτὸ[ς ἐ]χ[ρ]εῖτο ἐν τοῖς κινδύ[ν]οι[ς], ἀνέ[θηκε] κα/τὰ τὰν ἐκ Δωδώνας μαντείαν, ὡς περιέχοντι / τοὶ Λινδίων χρηματισμοί. Like the other Diadochi, he had Alexander as his model (Plu. *Demetr.* 41.4–5; *Pyrrh.* 8.1; Just. 18.1.2; see Lévêque 1957, 650; Garoufalias 1979, 34–35; Lianou 2010, 124) and in this circumstance made a clear *imitatio* of the Macedonian king. Pyrrhus offered bull heads and weapons in an indeterminable moment of his reign as the scholars remarked (see Blinkenberg 1915, 33, *comm. ad loc.*; Higbie 2003, 138, *comm. ad loc.*; Higbie, *Brill's New Jacoby*, *FGH* 532 F 3, *comm. ad loc.*). This chronology is too obscure to have a bearing on my argument.

3 *Chronicle* mentions also offerings to Athena by mythical figures like Cadmus (3.15–17 Higbie), Minos (4.18–22 Higbie), Heracles (5.23–36 Higbie), Tlepolemus (6.37–41 Higbie), Rhesus (7.42–47 Higbie), Telephus (8.48–53 Higbie), but also by historical figures like Phalaris tyrant of Acragas (27.21–28 Higbie), Deinomenes of Gela (28.30–35 Higbie), Amasis king of Egypt (29.36–55 Higbie), Hieron king of Syracuse (41.122–132 Higbie), and by cities like Phaselis (24.6–10 Higbie), Gela (25.11–14 Higbie), Acragas (30.56–59 Higbie), Soloi (33.75–79 Higbie).

4 *ThGL* s.v. *Boukephalos*. See Blinkenberg 1915, *comm. ad loc.*; Grana-Mathiae 1959, 211.

5 Blinkenberg 1915, 33, *comm. ad loc.* 104; 1941, 92–94, but also Richards 1915, xii; 1929, 82; Hiller von Gaertringen 1931, 777; Fraser 1952, 201 n. 1.

6 Pugliese Carratelli 1949, 167 n. 1; Fraser 1952, 201 and n. 1; Guarducci 1969, 136, 305; Hauben 1977, 315–16; Hammond 1997, 110; 2001, 150.

7 Heisserer 1980, 79–117, 142–68; Prandi 1983, 25–32; Sherwin White 1985, 69–89; Virgilio 1998, 115–16; Faraguna 2003, 114; Poddighe 2009, 111.

8 It is attested by the literary tradition (e.g. Th. 3.114.1) and by many inscriptions: e.g. Michel 1900, no. 1021, 1032. Many times part of the booty was dedicated to Athena: Hom. *Il.* 10.460; Paus. 5.14.5; see Rouse 1902, 95–148; Stevens 1940, 66; Van Straten 1981, 65–151; 1992, 247–90; Van Wees 1998, 333–78.

9 On the Gordian knot, Fredricksmeyer 1961, 160–68; 2000, 73–85; Roller 1984, 256–71; Prandi 1990, 357–62; Burke 2001, 255–61; Zahrnt 2001, 203–06; Squillace 2004, 144–47; 2005, 307–13.

10 Curt. 4.8.12–13: *Atheniensium deinde, Rhodiorum et Chiorum legatos audit. Athenienses victoriam gratulabantur et, ut captivi Graecorum suis restituerentur, orabant; Rhodii et Chii de praesidio querebantur. Omnes aequa desiderare visi impetraverunt.* See Green 1970, 152; 1992, 279–80; Hammond 2001, 130; Lane Fox 2004, 226. Arrian (*An.* 3.6.2) mentions only the Athenian embassy and Diodorus (18.8.1) states that Rhodes was freed after Alexander's death (on the disagreement of the sources, Fraser 1952, 199–201). Therefore, according to Hiller von Gaertringen 1931, 777; Tarn 1948, 215 and Pugliese Carratelli 1949, 146, Alexander freed Rhodes in 331 after the battle of Gaugamela; to Hauben 1977, 307–11 and Bosworth 1980, 242–43, only in 323.

11 *Boukopia/Bokopia*, Lindian fest: *IG* I 2 (I), 792; see *ThGL* s.v. *Boukopia/Bokopia*; *DGE* s.v. *Boukopios*; but also Hiller von Gaertringen 1897, 1018; Sinn 2005, 20–21. Offerings of cows to Athena are attested also in Homer (*Il.* 6.86–98) and in Herodotus (7.43: Xerxes sacrifices 1000 cows to Athena Ilias during the Persian wars).

12 On these slogans: Bellen 1974, 44–67; Gehrke 1987, 121–49; Squillace 2004, 62–71; 2010, 69–80.

13 See: Müller 1973, 78–105; Gruen 1985, 253–71; Berthold 1994, chap. 3; Campanile 1998, 398–99; Wheatley 2009, 62–63.

14 Arrian used fully Ptolemy's work: Arr. *An. Praef.* = Ptol. *FGH* 138 T 1. See Berve 1926, no. 668, 329–35; Pearson 1960, 188–211; Pédech 1984, 214–329; Heckel 2006, s.v. *Ptolemy* (6), 235–38.

15 Bearzot 1992, 41; Braund 2003, 23; Chugg 2002, 75–108; Erskine 2002, 163–79; Lianou 2010, 127.

16 His mother was Arsinoe, a Philip's concubine: Curt. 9.8.22; Paus. 1.6.2; but also Ael. fr. 285.7–9; Suda, s.v. *Lagos*. See Berve 1926, no. 668, 330; Bearzot 1992, 40–42; Collins 1997, 436–76; Heckel 2006, s.v. *Ptolemy* (6), 235–38; Lianou 2010, 129.

17 Simpson 1957, 371–73; 1959, 389–90; Wehrli 1968, 110–11; Billows 1990, 199–200.

18 They did not accept Ptolemy's appeal, who therefore garrisoned Corinth and Sicyon: D.S. 20.37.1–2. See Simpson 1959, 390–91; Billows 1990, 201–02; Braund 2003, 28.

19 On the freedom of the Greeks in the political and military strategies of Antigonus: Heuss 1938, 133–94; Simpson 1959, 385–409; Wehrli 1968, 103–29; Seager 1981, 107; Billows 1990, 197–236.

20 At Corinth, in 307, Demetrius was elected as *hēgemōn* of the Greeks as in the past Philip and Alexander: Plu., *Demetr.* 25.4. See Simpson 1959, 396–97; Braund 2003, 31.

21 Simpson 1959, 394. On the Greek freedom theme during the Hellenism: Mastrocinque 1976–1977, 1–23.

22 Witness also the Ptolemaic tetradrachms coined from 215 on or a bit ealier, featuring Athena on the reverse: see e.g. Stewart 1993, 231–43. On Athena in Alexandria, see Fraser 1972, 195.

23 Paschidis, in these proceedings (note 33), remarks that 'in the third epiphany of Athena in the *Lindian Chronicle* (*Lindos* II 2 D 95–115 [*FGH* 532 D 3]), the text speaks of a letter to *king* Ptolemy (l. 101), while denying the royal title to Poliorcetes (l. 95)'.

24 I would like to thank Prof. Victor Alonso Troncoso for inviting me to this congress and for his wonderful hospitality.

PROPAGANDA STRATEGIES AND POLITICAL DOCUMENTS: PHILIP III'S *DIAGRAMMA* AND THE GREEKS IN 319 BC

Elisabetta Poddighe

The ordinance (*diagramma*) promulgated in 319 by Philip III to free the Greek cities represents the longest document preserved by Diodorus (18.56) from the 4th century historian Hieronymus of Cardia, who probably gleaned it directly from the Macedonian royal archives (Rosen 1967, 64; Adams 1993, 202). The relevance of the document for research on forms of political communication is notable. Philip III's *diagramma* was the first royal ordinance issued after Alexander's death (323) to intervene in the political organization of the Greek cities and it was the first political act assumed by Philip III after the death of the regent Antipater (319), who had been the 'General in charge of the Macedonian and Greek affairs' from 334 (Just. 11.7.1; Curt. 4.11; D.S. 17.118.1; Arr. *FGH* 156 F 1.3). Since the *diagramma*'s main issues were, on the one hand, the political relationships with the Greek cities, and, on the other, Philip III's relationship with his predecessors' policies, it appears clear that the document's construction owed much to ideology and propaganda, the main concerns of this contribution.

Before examining the *diagramma*'s ideological significance, we should consider the institutional implications and political contents which Diodorus' account allows us to infer. The ordinance was promulgated by the royal chancellery, probably in autumn 319,[1] in the name of Philip III Arrhidaeus, Philip II's son, who is the sole representative of the kingship in this document (18.56.2 and 56.7). The co-ruler Alexander IV does not speak in the *diagramma* (Hatzopoulos 1996, 286; Arena 1999, 83; Habicht 2006, 83).[2] Polyperchon, appointed Antipater's successor as regent in Macedonia, was charged with the execution of the ordinance (18.56.7–8). As reproduced verbatim by Diodorus, the *diagramma* restored the Greeks to 'the peace and the constitutions that Philip II established (...) and the Greeks enjoyed under Philip II and Alexander' (18.56.2–3), invalidating the dispositions Antipater had made with the Greek cities beginning in 334, when Alexander left for Asia. It recalled the exiles 'that had been proscribed by the generals' (i.e. Antipater) after 334 (18.56.4), thus annulling Antipater's oligarchies en masse: those established in the Peloponnesian cities in the process of settling the Spartan war (333–331) ([Dem.] 17.7,10,16), and those imposed after the Hellenic war (323–322), when oligarchies were installed and garrisons were left in key positions in Greece.[3] The document makes one point clear: Antipater was responsible for all the misdirected policies towards the Greeks. Diodorus clearly defines the *diagramma*'s immediate finalities. It represented a means of defending Polyperchon's regency against the claims of Antipater's son Cassander, who had been appointed as chiliarch and did not consider Polyperchon a legitimate regent (18.48.5–49.1), and a way of gathering Greek support for the kings after Cassander's allies Ptolemy in Egypt and Antigonus in Asia had rebelled against them (18.49.3; 55.2). It was clear that 'Cassander would hold the Greek cities' against the kings, since 'some of the cities were guarded by his father's garrisons and dominated by Antipater's friends'; for this reason 'Polyperchon had summoned a council of all the commanders and the most important of the Macedonians' to decide 'how to fight' against the rebels and how 'to win for themselves many allies' amongst the Greeks (18.55.1–2).[4] The kings could not make an active contribution: Philip III was mentally infirm and Alexander IV was a child.[5] No hegemonic structure existed since the Corinthian league had been disbanded after the Hellenic war. The problem was solved with the council's resolution 'to free the Greek cities and to overthrow the oligarchies established in them by Antipater' (18.55.3). The *diagramma* was carefully designed to win allies for the king's cause (18.55.4) and to prevent the Greeks from declaring war against Macedon (18.56.7). It made no reference to terms like democracy (*dēmokratia*), freedom (*eleutheria*), or autonomy (*autonomia*), but the restoration of democracies was announced to the Greek envoys present at Pella (18.55.4), and freedom and autonomy were recalled in correspondence with the *diagramma*'s recipients (D.S. 18.64.3–5; 66.2; 69.3–4; Plu. *Phoc.* 34.4).

That the *diagramma* gained the expected support is undisputed, since many Greek cities adhered to Philip III's program of freedom and translated the *diagramma*'s provisions into their civic decrees (*dogmata*): it was these *dogmata* which reinstated democracies and spread word of the *diagramma* in the name of Greek freedom and autonomy.[6] It was foreseeable (and foreseen) that the *diagramma* would have circulated amongst the Greeks in the context of claiming their autonomy and freedom, and that the recipients would have acted in the communication network as the main actors in circulating freedom propaganda, as will be seen later. The adhesion was shortlived and in 318/17 many cities defected, passing over to Cassander' side.[7] However, the ephemeral character of the Greek adhesion is secondary here, since the analytical perspective adopted here is to evaluate the *diagramma*'s ideological meaning, namely the real significance of the repudiation of Antipater's policies. In this perspective the question is: how did reversing Antipater's policies serve Philip III in defining the king's relationship with his predecessors' policies? In other words: whose policies served as the model for the new program, those of Philip II or Alexander III? This question has implications for many others: i.e., did the *diagramma*'s provisions adhere to the proclaimed model? And were the propaganda's strategies functional for the declared political models?

As regards these issues, scholars' opinions differ. Several state that recalling Philip II's or Alexander's policies was a slogan lacking any concrete content (Green 1990, 18, 25) and that contrasting Antipater's policies to both Philip II's and Alexander's policies only served to ideologically legitimate the deposition of the oligarchies established in 322, as a return to the 'actual status' of 323 (Will 1984, 42–44; Hammond 1988, 134; Habicht

2006, 82). Other scholars propose that the *diagramma* restored the situation in Greece as in Alexander's last years (Billows 1990, 199) and that it amounted to a re-enactment of Alexander's exiles' decree of 324, a measure which several scholars construe as issued to destroy Antipater's power in Europe (Mendels 1984, 143–46; Blackwell 1999, 149–57). According to this interpretation, the *diagramma* was shaped as a 'sequel' to Alexander's exiles' decree (Heckel 1999, 489–98) and was meant to present Alexander as Philip III's political model (Wallace 2011). Finally, several scholars consider Philip II as the *diagramma*'s actual political model and the contrasting model to Antipater, but disagree on the degree to which the *diagramma* adhered to Philip II's settlements: if Polyperchon in the name of Philip III was trying to revive the League of Corinth and if the *diagramma* recognized the principles of autonomy and freedom granted by Philip II's peace (Rosen 1967, 64–68; Poddighe 2002, 179–87; Dixon 2007, 151–78). As in most research on the *diagramma*, however, little attention has been paid, even in the latter context, to the real function of the polarization between Philip II and Antipater, which is, in my opinion, the main ideological issue of the *diagramma*. My contribution to this far-reaching debate is to reconsider the function of this polarization: how refusing Antipater's policies served Philip III' party in defining the *diagramma*'s political purpose and its concrete provisions. As regards the political purpose, I contend that the *diagramma*'s priority was to present the Greeks with Philip II as a model for peace and Greek freedom and to focus their feelings of resentment on Antipater in order to conceal a decisive fact: infringements of the peace with Philip were largely ascribable to Alexander the Great's decisions. That result was gained by subsuming Alexander's policies in those of Philip and attributing Alexander's decisions from 334 to Antipater's policy. From this point of view, recalling Philip II's policies had an added value beyond the more evident meaning as a contrasting model to Antipater's. The analysis of the *diagramma*'s concrete provisions is consistent with this role for Antipater. What emerges is that Philip III's relationship with his predecessors' policies was carefully designed on the basis of a selective criterion which upheld those of Philip II's provisions capable of consolidating Greek consent and amended those of Alexander's dispositions which had caused Greek dissent. Polarization against Antipater was instrumental to express this 'selective relationship' and to overshadow the fact that the *diagramma*'s provisions often in reality corresponded to a rejection of Alexander's policies.

At this point, it is worthwhile considering the document at a textual level. I shall begin by considering the peculiarities already noted by scholars regarding the document's formal construction, generally regarded as the drafters' choice, and not Diodorus' adaptation (Rosen 1967, 64; Hammond 1988, 133–34; Adams 1993, 202). One aspect of the document is the heterogeneity in style and contents, which seem to fall into two sections on account of this discontinuity. What emerges is that in the document's first section (18.56.1–3), where Philip III declares his condemnation of Antipater's Greek policy after Alexander's death (323) and his intent to restore the policies of his predecessors (*progonoi*) Philip II and Alexander, the king's advisers use complicated constructions to define his relationship with his predecessors' policies, which are conflated apparently without distinction. On the contrary, in the second and normative section (18.56.4–8), they use short and clear sentences to define the regulatory interventions and to translate his program into concrete provisions. It is above all the 'general' (Adams 1993, 202–03) or 'vague' (Goukowsky 1978, 157; Will 1984, 42) character of the references to Philip III's predecessors' policies that scholars regard as the main textual peculiarity of the document. Regarding this vagueness, it is possible, as suggested by Rosen (1967, 64), that the royal chancellery faced greater difficulty in expressing the *diagramma*'s ideological contents than the normative section. There are, however, valid reasons to suspect that this vagueness was deliberate and instrumental, both to conceal the differences between Philip II's and Alexander's Greek policies and to mask Alexander's participation in Antipater's policy from 334 to 323. To differentiate *apertis verbis* Philip II's Greek policy from Alexander's meant undermining any dissociation from Antipater, since many of the infringements of Philip II's settlements, which the *diagramma* ascribed to Antipater, had been undertaken on Alexander's orders. In this context, I would argue that this vagueness in reference to the predecessors' policies is consistent with the choice of planning opposition to Antipater and in turn to his son Cassander in terms of the violation of Philip II's settlements.

The forms and purposes of this opposition differ within the *diagramma*. In the first section (18.56.1–3) the opposition is developed through an antithesis between Philip III's and Antipater's Greek policies in 323. This antithesis concealed the opposition between Philip II's and Alexander's Greek policies, and obscured the latter's responsibility for the Hellenic war in 323.

Philip III and the Greeks from 323: the Diagramma's Historical Review with Respect to Antipater's Role in Greek Affairs

The *diagramma*'s first section develops opposition to Antipater according to the following model: Philip III is presented as the sole heir of his father's policy and in the name of this continuity distances the king's political line from Antipater's. As regards the first aspect, one point is clear. The *diagramma* is proclaimed in the name of Philip III and twice makes reference to 'our father Philip' (18.56.2 and 56.7; Bosworth 1993, 424). If Christian Habicht (2006, 83) is right in affirming that there were no institutional reasons - such as a subordinate position for the younger Alexander IV – to proclaim an important ordinance from the period of joint rule in the name of one king, then we should explain this choice with the need to indicate the *diagramma*'s political authorship.[8] Consistent with this continuity is the antithesis between Philip III's resolution to act in conformity with his father's policy and Antipater's responsibility for not carrying out Philip III's (i.e. Philip II's) desires. There are two key passages. In 18.56.2, Philip III affirms with a *pluralis maiestatis* that in 323 he announced to the Greeks his resolution to revert to Philip's II policy: 'formerly, indeed when...the kingship descended upon us, since we believed it necessary to restore all to peace and to the forms of government that Philip our father established, we sent letters to all the cities in regard to these matters'. Opposition to

Antipater is developed in 18.56.3, where Philip III stresses that his resolution was not implemented because, while the king was 'far away' (sc. in Babylon) 'it happened that... certain of the Greeks, being misguided, waged war against Macedon and were defeated by the generals'. Here Philip III states that for the misdirected policies towards the Greeks (before and after the war) only the generals (i.e. Antipater) bore responsibility, while he decided to hold fast to his 'initial resolution'.

We shall return to Antipater's role as regards Philip III's resolution, but we first need to trace those aspects which indicate the readiness to construct a forceful text in terms of communication strategies. Firstly, by contrasting Philip III's resolution to revert to Philip II's policy as opposed to those of Antipater's policies, the king distinguished his message to the Greeks from the one implicitly sent by his present enemies, Cassander and his allies. The Greeks were told that the king and Polyperchon upheld Philip II's policy, as opposed to the generals who had rebelled against them. Relations with the Greeks represented just one aspect, albeit a decisive one, of the rhetoric of legitimacy adopted by the kings and Polyperchon against the rebels, a strategy that was based, even beyond the Greek question, on an opposition between those who conform to the kings' orders (D.S. 18.49.4; 57.2–3; 58.4; 59.3; 62.2–3) and those who rebel against them (D.S. 18.50.2; 54.3–4; 57.3–4; 62.2–3; 63.2–4). A second aspect is that the *diagramma* indicates Philip III's resolution to return to Philip II's policy as part of an *idem sentire* of the king and the Greeks with respect to Alexander's policies in Greece. This was the reason why the *diagramma* recalled Philip III's earlier letters 'sent to all the cities' in 323 (D.S. 18.56.2): as the main proof of Philip III's dissociation from Alexander's policies.

Historians agree on the authenticity of these letters (Rosen 1967, 65; Hammond 1988, 133), but their true authorship and their juridical form remain debated. Who induced Philip III to address the Greeks? The hypothesis that it may have been Adea-Eurydice, his wife (Bengtson 1987, 40), lacks evidence. More plausible is that Perdiccas, the guardian (*epimelētēs*) and regent of the king (Anson 2009, 283–84), was behind Philip III's announcement (Goukowsky 1978, 157; Bosworth 1988, 228), but in this case, what might Antipater's role have been, since the European parts of the empire were ruled over by Antipater and Craterus after the Babylon settlement?[9] Even the juridical form of this communication is unclear: a 'circular letter' (Bosworth 1988, 228), representing the abstract of a *diagramma* (Mari 2006, 211), or a general announcement (Goukowski 1978, 157)? Although nothing is certain as regards this communication, its objective is clear: it was the dissociation of Philip III from Alexander's policies in favor of those of Philip II's.[10] The expectations of Philip III's advisers in 323 are also clear. The proposal to revert to Philip II's settlements was an attempt to avoid the Hellenic war that the Greeks prepared against Macedon. Contemporary and later sources construed this war as fought for Greek freedom against Alexander's despotism, and namely against his exiles decree of 324.[11] Alexander's decree (presumably a *diagramma*) had ordered the return of the long-term exiles (except those guilty of sacrilege and murder) and required the Greek cities to apply the measures under threat of military reprisal (D.S. 17.109.1; 18.8.2–4). Its impact on life in the city-states was predictable and its role in motivating the Greek revolt is undisputed. Since the exiles' return would have altered the political equilibrium recognized in 337, the Greeks thought that it amounted to a total abrogation of the Common Peace. Those directly affected, the Athenians (whose cleruchies on Samos were threatened) and the Thessalian cities, reacted to Alexander's decision and decided, after Alexander's death, to start the Hellenic War (Bosworth 1988, 227). Since Alexander's responsibility in the origination of the revolt was clear, Philip III had predictably to dissociate himself from Alexander, after the latter's death, in the effort to avoid the conflict. This proposal to revert to Philip II' policies was thus instrumental in making Philip III himself a party in Greece against Alexander's despotism without expressly referring to him.

What was Antipater's role in 324 when the Exiles' Decree was issued? What was Antipater's role in 323, when the Greeks protested against the Exiles' Decree? And what has the *diagramma* to say on the whole matter? The *diagramma* had to define carefully Antipater's role towards the Greeks, since it was functional to represent Antipater as responsible for prompting the Greeks to revolt and to gloss over Alexander's responsibility.

Firstly, it is worth considering Antipater's role with respect to Alexander's decree. Antipater was the general charged to enforce its application (D.S. 18.8.4), but scholars discuss whether Antipater's power was affected by Alexander's decree (Heckel 1999, 489–98), if Antipater created obstacles in its application (Mendels 1984, 149; Blackwell 1999, 149–57), and if the decree was somehow connected to Alexander's plan of 324 to replace Antipater with Craterus as his general for Greek affairs (Arr. *An.* 7.12.4; Heckel 1999, 498). What can be inferred from Philip III's *diagramma* is that Alexander's Exiles' Decree did not amount to a repudiation of Antipater's policies, and this inference is in agreement with external evidence on Alexander's *diagramma*. Diodorus (18.8.4), quoting Alexander's decree from Hieronymus, states that the recipients of the decree were exiles whose sentences were not ascribable to Alexander's decisions. Diodorus' account is confirmed by contemporary evidence attesting that people to be restored in 324 were long-term exiles who had been generations in exile: this was the case for the Samians exiled since 365 (*SIG*^{3} 312) and for the largest group of Tegeans restored in 324 who were proscribed during the civil war that brought the establishment of the Arcadian *koinon* (Rhodes-Osborne no. 101).[12] Philip III's *diagramma* is consistent with this evidence, since its recipients were those condemned by Antipater after 334 and not restored by Alexander in 324 (D.S. 18.56.4). We shall return to this clause, but it is important to stress here that, while the 319 *diagramma* annulled the decrees of exile handed down by Antipater, Alexander's *diagramma* apparently did not. Evidence of Alexander's resentment against Antipater is often traced in Alexander's plan to move Antipater to Asia and the program entrusted in 324 to Craterus to 'take charge of Macedonia, Thrace, Thessaly and the freedom of the Greeks' (Arr. *An.* 7.12.4; Mendels 1984, 146; Heckel 1999, 489–98). But that plan is not clear. Arrian (*An.* 7.12.5) does not say what role Alexander had in mind for Antipater in Asia, observing that 'perhaps his recall was not meant in fact to disgrace him' (cf. Baynham 1994, 345). In this framework it is possible, as Ashton (1993, 126) suggested, that 'Alexander intended to install Antipater as overall commander and king's representative in Asia'. We should also take into account that Alexander's plan to replace Antipater with Craterus 'undoubtedly influenced ancient views' as to a possible rift occurring between Alexander and his regent (Baynham 1994, 343). Anyway, whatever the suspicions between the two recorded by the sources (Curt. 10.10.14–15; D.S. 17.118.1), Arrian (*An.* 7.12.7) states that 'no overt act was recorded of Alexander' against Antipater. Ultimately, while there is clear and concrete evidence of an anti-Antipatrid political line in 319, this is less evident in 324 or earlier (see below).

Antipater's loyalty can be traced considering his role as the enforcer of Alexander's decree, either before or after Alexander's death. Regarding this role, several scholars have suggested that Antipater acted unloyally, creating obstacles to decree implementation (Blackwell 1999, 157) and vowing not to enforce it (Mendels 1984, 146). According to this view, Antipater's secret activity caused the Aetolians to defect from the Hellenic war; directly affected by the Exiles Decree they had had to return the occupied Oeniadae to the Acarnanians (D.S. 18.8.6; Plu. *Alex.* 49). As a matter of fact, Antipater's real involvement in the Aetolian affair is unclear (Baynham 1994, 345–46) and it is quite difficult to see Antipater's interest in the matter, considering that the Aetolian contribution to the revolt was insignificant and could not be 'the focus of a general rising against Macedon' (Bosworth 1988, 227). What can be inferred from the *diagramma* is that Antipater acted in keeping with Alexander's resolutions as regards the Exiles' Decree even after Alexander's death, which leads us to consider the problem of Antipater's responsibility for not carrying out Philip III's program in 323. After the Babylon settlement, which confirmed Antipater as general with powers extending over Greece, he must have played a role in conveying Philip III's proposal to the Greeks. This opens two possible scenarios: either Antipater was incapable of realizing the king's resolution to revert to Philip's II settlements or Antipater created obstacles in its realization. Whatever Antipater's responsibility, the *diagramma* clearly states that the king was 'far away' when the controversy with the Greeks led to war (18.56.3), and it seems to make Antipater responsible for not having reconciled the Greeks with the king. Also the lack of awareness on the part of the Greeks, who faced with the choice of either beginning or avoiding war, made a bad decision – probably after being misled – could be attributed to Antipater's responsibility. In 323, Antipater was responsible for relations with the Greeks, and since the Greeks protested against Alexander's Exiles' Decree and Antipater probably had the authority to amend the decree in Philip II's name, the responsibility for not having done so falls to Antipater. Alexander's role as the originator of the Exiles' Decree is completely obscured.

Antipater's responsibility for the Hellenic war is a key point. It has been observed that Athenian propaganda re-interpreted the Hellenic war – once democracy was reinstated (May 318) – as presented in the *diagramma*, i.e. as a 'pre-emptive war' against Antipater. Shane Wallace has extensively explored this issue in epigraphical evidence, namely in the second Euphron decree of 318 (*IG* II^2 448 b), and shown how the Hellenic war was recast as a struggle against Antipater 'both in origin and action' (Wallace 2011). In this same framework, I suggest that it was the need to ascribe the responsibility for not being able to conduct the Greeks to a peaceful solution to Antipater, which led the king to recall his earlier letters to the Greeks in the *diagramma*. In this sense, I would not consider the quotation of those letters as merely a 'point' of the *diagramma*'s 'historical review' (Rosen 1967, 64). This reference had a broader significance: it meant that the 319 resolution was consistent with the previous one, or plausibly communicable as such. Thus, just as the initial resolution was to be understood as 'a reaction against the despotism of Alexander's last months' (Bosworth 1988, 228), its recall was also meant in this sense.

The 'historical review' outlined in the first section of the *diagramma* was for propaganda purposes. Sources do not record any conflict either between Philip III and Antipater or between Antipater and Polyperchon until 319. The Babylon settlement with the elevation of Philip III to the kingship was a victory for Antipater (Bosworth 2002, 50), as was the settlement at Triparadeisus, in 321, when Antipater became the guardian of the kings (Baynham 1994, 351–53). Also clear is that Polyperchon was content to follow the Antipatrid 'party line' up to 319 (Heckel 1999, 497). But while it is an established fact that the changed official attitude of Philip III as dictated by his regent was useful in 319 for undermining Antipater's son, Cassander, and gaining popularity, less considered by scholars is the surplus value of this reversal of Antipater's policies, i.e. that with this reversal, Philip III rejected Alexander's resolutions without having to indicate Alexander as responsible. This refusal was a tool in the new regime's 'selective relationship' with Philip III predecessors' Greek policies.

Philip III's Selective Relationship with his Predecessors' Policies and Antipater's Role in that Selection

The *diagramma*'s second section revoked *de facto* Alexander's dispositions, while re-establishing Philip II's decisions (D.S. 18.56.4–8). However, even in this section, the formal wording does not distinguish between Philip's or Alexander's Greek policy. Philip III's stated resolution was to prepare for the Greeks 'the peace and governments enjoyed under Philip and Alexander' and to permit the Greeks 'to act in all other matters according to the decrees (*diagrammata*) formerly issued by them' (18.56.3–4). These *diagrammata* did not belong to the treaty of 337 and 336, and were, in the case of Philip II, those measures previously taken with the individual states dealing with territorial disputes (as shown in 18.56.6–7), in Alexander's case, those provisions he had made with the Greeks after 336 (Rosen 1967, 67–68). As regards these latter decisions, Philip III's *diagramma* suspended those of Alexander's dispositions in which Antipater was directly involved, without attributing any responsibility to Alexander.

In this second section, the *diagramma* develops opposition to Antipater in relation to Antipater's own violation of Philip II's settlements which the *diagramma* recalled formally referring twice to the 'peace' (18.56.2 and 56.3). That peace recognized Greek autonomy and freedom, and prevented the Greeks from declaring war on the

Macedonian kingdom (Rhodes-Osborne no. 76; Dem. 17.8). Against the eventuality of a war against Macedon, Philip III's *diagramma* obliged the Greeks 'to pass a decree that no one shall engage in war or in public activity in opposition to us' and stated that all who opposed the king were to be banished (18.56.7). It did not mention the guarantee clause, found in the settlements of 337 ensuring that transgressors would be punished with a federal war (Rhodes-Osborne, no. 76, ll. 17–22; Poddighe 2009, 105). This clause's omission suggests that no hegemonic structure existed in 319 and shows that there was no immediate intention to reform the Corinthian league (Poddighe 2002, 187; *contra* Dixon 2007, 151–78), since the threat of Polyperchon's military action cannot be likened to federal intervention (18.56.7). Except for the League, the terms of the treaty were fully recalled, namely its central principles – the freedom and autonomy of the Greeks. There is no reason to believe that the *diagramma* excluded those very principles, even if they are not explicitly mentioned (see below). The formal oath taken by the Greeks to uphold the terms of the 337 treaty does not mention either the terms autonomy or freedom, and only mentions 'the peace', while reference to these principles only appears in the speech *On the treaty with Alexander*, delivered by an anonymous Athenian orator and preserved in the Demosthenic corpus ([Dem.] 17.8).[13] To make the *diagramma* explicit was unnecessary, since its provisions had to be made into laws by civic decrees (18.56.7) and there reformulated with an explicit lexicon. This is confirmed by correspondence between the Athenians and Polyperchon, where it is affirmed that the *diagramma* sanctioned the autonomy from garrisons, and that ignoring this principle meant violating (*paranomein*) a formal act, i.e. both the *diagramma* and the following Athenian *dogma* (D.S. 18.65.6–66.2). That reference to 'the peace' included Greek autonomy is, moreover, testified to by the *diagramma*'s provisions which recalled the exiles, granting them the recovery of property and civic rights, i.e. the political and social status in force at the time of the peace agreements.

The exiles' return was meant to reverse the infringements dating up to 334 (D.S. 18.56.4). They were assigned to Antipater's decisions, even though they followed from Alexander's orders. According to the anonymous Athenian orator, Alexander was responsible for constitutional changes in the Peloponnesian cities in the years 333–331. They were justified by the need to ensure control over Greece, when Agis of Sparta was preparing war against Macedonia, and were coordinated by Antipater on Alexander's orders. At Messene in around 333, the Philiades, tyrants overthrown in the disorders following Philip's death, were brought back ([Dem.] 17.7); at Sicyon Alexander returned an anonymous tyrant from exile ([Dem.] 17.16); finally, at Pellene, Alexander replaced a democratic regime with the tyrant Chaeron ([Dem.] 17.10). After the Spartan war, when compliant regimes and garrisons had been installed in the cities involved in the revolt (Tegea and Megalopolis were among them), Antipater entrusted all decisions to the federal *synedrion* and avoided any autocratic approach to the question. In this case too Alexander had the last word (Curt. 6.18–19; D.S. 17.73.5; Poddighe 2009, 115). That Alexander was in disagreement with Antipater's policy in the Peloponnese, as often suggested (Mendels 1984, 143–46; Blackwell 1999, 147–57), has no concrete evidence

(Billows 1990, 194; Baynham 1994, 339–42). Contemporary sources blamed Alexander as being responsible for these constitutional upheavals and later sources attest that Alexander sent Antipater money to finance his operations (Arr. *An.* 3.6.3; 3.16.10). Whatever Alexander's opinion as regards Antipater's policy after 334, he endorsed it up to his death. On the contrary, Philip III's *diagramma* stated that exiles sentenced by Antipater after 334 had to be restored (D.S. 18.56.4). Apparently, the *diagramma* did not concern Alexander's orders in which Antipater had no role, i.e. those concerning Lesbos and Chios during the Aegean war (333–332).[14] In these last cases, however, the exiled people were convicted of treason (medism) and thus fell within the ambit of the exclusion clause envisaged both by Alexander's decree of 324 (D.S. 18.8.2) and by Philip III's *diagramma* (18.56.5).[15]

The recall of people sentenced by Antipater after 334 did not quite end matters. In order to gain popularity Philip III had to be seen to amend Alexander's recent dispositions which prompted the Greeks to the Hellenic war, i.e. Alexander's Exiles' Decree of 324 and obviously Antipater's provisions following that war. The *diagramma* differentiated the long-term exiles allowed to return under Alexander's decree from those who were offered this opportunity in 319: only the latter ('those who are restored by us') were granted 'a complete amnesty' and allowed to recover 'the full possession of their property' and citizenship rights (18.56.4). The return of the exiles – who had to be received back by their cities before the thirtieth day of Xanthichus (March) 318 – was accompanied by the reinstatement of democracies where they had been deposed in favour of compliant regimes (tyrants or oligarchies). The reinstatement of democracy in Messene should be probably dated within this context, since the alliance with the Macedonian kingdom, preserved by a Messenian inscription, presumably dating to 318, is signed for the *dēmos* (*SEG* 43.135; Matthaiou 2001, 226). In 318, democracy was reinstated in Athens (D.S. 18.66.3–67.6; Plu. *Phoc.* 34.1–35.1), Argos (D.S. 18.57.1), Eretria (*IG* 12.9.196; Knoepfler 2000, 599), and Sicyon (*IG* II^2 448 b) where oligarchies had been installed after the Hellenic war.

That the *diagramma*'s purpose was to amend Alexander's decree of 324 is most clear where it defines 'those to be not restored' (D.S. 18.56.5), since the exceptions were made, at least in some cases, along the lines established by Philip II and against Alexander's resolutions. Philip III's expressed priority was the following: to make adjustments and exceptions to the categories restored by Alexander in 324 in order to compensate the Greeks most affected by the Exiles' Decree of 324. The most obvious case is Samos. Alexander's decree had obliged Athens 'to return Samos to the Samians' (*SIG*^{3} 312, ll. 11–14), who had been expelled by Athenian cleruchs established on the island beginning in 365, and the Athenians' opposition to this return originated the Greek revolt in 324 (D.S. 18.8.7; Poddighe 2007). In 319, against Alexander's resolution and in favor of Philip II's decision, the *diagramma* returned the island to the Athenians.[16] Equally indicative are the exceptions of Pharkadon, Trikka, and Amphissa in Thessaly. Traditional interpretation is that Philip III confirmed Antipater's sentences against the Thessalian cities involved in the Hellenic war (Adams 1993, 204–05). This version, however, conflicts with the following evidence. Firstly, Diodorus attests that all the Thessalian cities (except Pelinna and Larissa) had fought against Antipater and he does not record a reason why these cities should be singled out for a harsher punishment (18.11.1–3; 12.3; 15.4–6; 17.4). A second argument is that the 319 *diagramma* recalled *en masse* the exiles condemned by Antipater after the Hellenic war, since the exceptions envisaged for bloodguilt, impiety, or treason, the latter being the stated reason for the exclusion of the Megalopolitans, were explicitly expressed (18.56.5). Most importantly it would not have been diplomatic to endorse Antipater's decisions against the Thessalians. As we read in the Athenian decree, to be dated in 321 or 320, which honoured the Thessalians exiled by Antipater, they represented the most popular victims of Antipater' antidemocratic policies (*IG* II^2 545+2406; Poddighe 2002, 166–69). Philip III's resolution to confirm the exiles in those Thessalian cities becomes comprehensible when considered in light of Philip II's decisions, not Antipater's. These exiles reconfirmed in 319 probably dated back to Philip's intervention in Thessaly during the conflict between the Thessalian league and the tyrants of Pherae and during the Third Sacred war against the Phocians (356–346). Diodorus and Polyaenus report that Onomarchus, the Phocian general, forced the cities of Amphissa (D.S. 16.33.3), Pharkadon (Polyaen. 4.2.18) - and possibly Trikka - to surrender, while Justin (8.3.1–5) affirms that in 352, Philip exiled people who had betrayed the Thessalian cause. On this occasion, Philip was unable to advance into central Greece since he was blocked at Thermopylae and Heraclea, which was probably involved in the initiative (this is possibly why the exiles from Heraclea were reconfirmed).[17] In this framework, the reconfirmation of these exiles receives a double explanation: Philip III suspended Alexander's resolution of 324 to restore those long-term exiles and upheld Philip II's measures. The issue in both cases was Greek freedom. Philip II returned freedom to the Thessalian cities (D.S. 16.14.2; 38.1), thus, enforcing in 319 Philip's sentences of exile meant reaffirming the restitution of freedom to the Thessalians (Squillace 2004, 54, 59), and at the same time compensating them after Alexander's Exiles' decree.

Philip III's right to amend his predecessors' policies was legitimated by two final clauses. Philip III had the right to reconsider his predecessors' rulings dealing with 'political organisations (*politeumata*) declared hostile' for which the cities concerned were invited to present themselves before the king (18.56.6). It has been suggested that this provision dealt with Alexander's order regarding the Achaean, the Arcadian and possibly the Boeotian leagues (Hyp. *Dem.* fr. 5, col. 18; Goukowsky 1978, 158), a measure probably ordering the leagues' dissolution and conceived to ensure the return of the exiles in 324 (Poddighe 2009, 118); this would mean that Philip III suspended even this last Alexander's ruling. This aim is consistent with epigraphical evidence attesting that the Arcadian *koinon* was operative after 323 (*IG* IV 616), but we cannot be sure, as Piérart suggests (1982, 134, 137), that the *koinon* had been reconstituted in 318, when Polyperchon was discussing the question of the alliance against Cassander with the Peloponnesian cities (D.S. 18.69.3–4).[18] It also remains unclear whether Philip III's right to amend his predecessors' resolutions concerned those of Philip's and Alexander's regulations which were 'inconsistent with each other', as suggested (Bencivenni 2003, 34–35). The latter case is nonetheless contemplated by the *diagramma*'s provision which regarded Athens' territorial possessions. In this case too, Alexander's resolutions were to be suspended, and Philip's restored: this was evident for Samos, as seen, but also likely for Oropus. The *diagramma* granted autonomy to Oropus (18.56.7) possibly against Alexander's resolution, if it had been Alexander, not Philip (as Pausanias erroneously affirms), to assign Oropus to Athens in the aftermath of the Theban revolt (Paus. 1.34.1; Knoepfler 2001, 371–85).[19] The *diagramma* granted autonomy to the Oropians 'as at present', i.e. in recognition of the status gained during the Hellenic war, and this recognition was the perfect conclusion to the normative section. The *diagramma* would only win the support of the Greeks against Cassander in recognition of the demands that had accompanied this war, i.e. Greek autonomy and freedom. This is consistent with Diodorus' account stating that Polyperchon's council decided that the most effective means to counter Cassander was 'to give freedom to the cities through Greece' (18.55.3).

The Greek Cities, the Freedom of the Greeks, and the Perceived Historical Role of Antipater

The role of the Greek cities in spreading word of the *diagramma*'s contents is a central issue. The basic rules of political communication dictate that the recipients of a message have to play a key role in disseminating its contents. The originators of the *diagramma* were aware of these rules. They debated using terminology that was typical of Greek assemblies (D.S. 18.55.3; Landucci 2008, 230)[20] and immediately informed the Greek envoys present at Pella that democracy would be reestablished, returning them to their cities to quickly report the *diagramma* to their assemblies (D.S. 18.55.2–4). Once the *diagramma* had been dispatched, Polyperchon sent instructions to Athens, Argos and 'the other cities' regarding the deposition of the oligarchies (D.S. 18.57.1; Plu. *Phoc.* 32.1). The key passage was the 'translation' of these instructions into the civic decrees which reorganized the *diagramma*'s provisions in communicative canons familiar to the Greeks (Bertrand 1990, 105; Ceccarelli 2005, 362). The recipients would have then acted in the communication network as the main actors in circulating freedom propaganda, which explains Polyperchon's close contacts with traditionally sound democratic cities like Athens (D.S. 18.64.3–5; 66.2; Plu. *Phoc.* 34.4), Argos (D.S. 18.57.1), or Eretria (*IG* 12.9.196; Knoepfler 2000).

Appreciating the role played by the *diagramma*'s recipients within the communication network may help to solve the main debated problems concerning the strategies adopted for disseminating the *diagramma* and the role assigned in this context to the issue of Greek freedom. The *diagramma* allocated a decisive role to the label of Greek freedom, since it was this very demand that had inspired the Hellenic war. In such a context, it is difficult to believe that the *diagramma* did not mention Greek freedom because this would have been acknowledging the legitimacy of the Hellenic war (Will

1984, 43), nor is it plausible that Polyperchon adopted freedom propaganda only in 318, to fit the Greek reception of the *diagramma* (Dixon 2007, 168). It is instead possible that these terms entered Athenian propaganda once democracy was restored and that in the same context the Hellenic war was re-cast as a war for which Alexander had no responsibility (Wallace 2011), which was a result of the *diagramma*'s propaganda. That this was successful propaganda is suggested by epigraphic evidence, revealing the centrality of the polarity between Antipater and Greek freedom in Athenian civic decrees (Kralli 1999) and the emergence of a contemporary (albeit ephimeral) positive memory of Alexander.[21]

The polarity between Greek freedom and Antipater's actions may also explain Polyperchon's decision not to use the Panhellenic festivals to announce the *diagramma*. Manuela Mari (2002, 194) has called attention to the fact that Philip III could have used the Nemean games, held in autumn of 319, and suggests that he chose not to do so because there was no hegemonic structure like the Corinthian League. While it is true that there was no league, it is easy to recognize that the control of the city of Cleonai over the Nemean games in 319 would have made them an inappropriate place to present a program of liberty to the Greeks after the Hellenic war. Using the Nemean games to announce the *diagramma* would have brought back memories of Antipater's favour for Cleonai, a policy that his son Cassander also pursued after 316 (D.S. 19.64; Miller 1982, 103–05). Cleonai had abandoned the Greek alliance against Antipater and had then joined the general's side during his campaign in the Peloponnese, after the fall of Athens. According to Plutarch (Plu. *Dem.* 28.4; *Phoc.* 29.1; *Mor.* 849b-c), the Athenian orator Hypereides was executed on Antipater's orders at Cleonai, which thus represented the place where Greek liberty had been symbolically murdered. Since the theme of Greek freedom was often evocated with the image of Freedom buried with the bodies fallen for the cause of common liberty, it was predictable that Cleonai and the Nemean games, which in 319 were under Cleonai's control, had no role in the proclamation of Greek liberty in 319 (Lyc. *C.Leocr.* 50; Dem. *Epith.* 23–24; Culasso Gastaldi 2003, 78). Polyperchon's desire to distance himself from Cleonai may also be the reason behind the restructuring of the city, which led to the city losing both its control over the Nemean games and its status as a polis (it became a *kōmē* of Argos) in 318.[22] It is possible that in 318, when Polyperchon discussed the question of the alliance against Cassander with the Peloponnesian cities (D.S. 18.69.3–4), he decided to gather at Corinth the delegates from the Greek cities in order to reconstitute the Corinthian league (Dixon 2007, 168). But there is no trace of this project in 319 (Poddighe 2002, 187).

To conclude, we might ask what role Alexander's propaganda played in this program of Greek freedom in 319? Waldemar Heckel has correctly observed that Polyperchon was influenced by Alexander's program on Greek freedom of 324 (Arr. *An.* 7.12.4; see above) when he was dispatched as the officer next in seniority to Craterus (Heckel 1999, 498). It is plausible that in 324 Polyperchon became more familiar with these slogans, and I agree with Heckel that the slogan for Greek liberty was supposed to add an ideological foundation to the 319 *diagramma* through the fundamental connection with the rejection of Antipater's policies. But while in Heckel's view that connection first arose in 324, I think it was a peculiar issue of the 319 *diagramma*. With respect to the question of any continuity between Alexander's and Polyperchon's regard for the policies of Antipater I find two aspects problematic: while Alexander's decree confirmed Antipater's resolutions, Polyperchon's *diagramma* suspended these very resolutions, and while in 319 the rejection of Antipater's policies was in turn linked to the project of returning to Philip's policies, in 324 there was no trace of this link (Bosworth 1988, 224). Thus, while it is worthwhile underlining the continuity between the slogans and the propaganda, it is also important to recognize the discontinuity between the political models. That Philip III's *diagramma* contrasted *de facto* Antipater's policies with Philip II's, not Alexander's, is the result of this discontinuity.

The effectiveness of the *diagramma*'s ideological constructions is evident, since Greek propaganda re-echoed them with the result of temporarily obliterating Alexander's responsibilities for the Greek grievances. With respect to the success of the communicative strategy, also significant is the reuse that one of the Diadochi, namely Antigonus, made of the ideological models experimented with in Philip III's *diagramma*, i.e. the role of Philip II as the referent for policies favorable towards the Greeks (see Billows 1990, 230, 322; Poddighe 2002, 182–83) or the rhetoric of legitimacy and obedience to the kings (D.S. 19.61.1–3). This later reuse of the *diagramma*'s ideological constructions is perhaps worth more than the ephemeral character of the Greek adhesion to the cause of Polyperchon and Philip III.

Bibliography

Adams, W. L. T. (1993) Cassander and the Greek City-States (319–317 BC), *Balkan Studies* 34.2, 197–211.

Alonso Troncoso, V. (2010) The Bearded King and the Beardless Hero: From Philip II to Alexander the Great. In E. Carney and D. Ogden (eds) *Philip II and Alexander the Great: Father and Son, Lives and Afterlives*, 13–24, Oxford.

Ameling, W. (1994) The Inscriptions of Heraclea Pontica. In L. Jonnes (ed.) *Inschriften griechischer Städte aus Kleinasien*. Vol. 47. Bonn.

Anson, E. M. (2009) Philip II, Amyntas, Perdicca, and Macedonial Royal Succession, *Historia* 58, 276–86.

Arena, E. (1999) La titolatura regale nella Macedonia ellenistica: i βασιλεῖς Filippo III e Alessandro IV nelle fonti letterarie ed epigrafiche (323–317 a.C.), *Ancient Macedonia* 5, 77–98.

Ashton, N. G. (1993) Craterus from 324 to 321 BC, *Ancient Macedonia* 5, 125–31.

Baynham, E. (1994) Antipater: Manager of Kings. In I. Worthington (ed.) *Ventures into Greek History*, 331–56, Oxford.

Bencivenni, A. (2003) *Progetti di riforme costituzionali nelle epigrafi greche dei secoli IV–II a. C.* Bologna.

Bengtson, H. (1987) *Die Diadochen. Die Nachfolger Alexanders des Grossen*. Munich.

Bertrand, J. M. (1990) Formes des discours politiques: décrets des cités grecques et correspondance des rois hellénistiques. In C. Nicolet (ed.) *Du pouvoir dans l'antiquité: mots et réalités*, 101–15, Geneva.

Billows, R. A. (1990) *Antigonos the One-Eyed and the Creation of the Hellenistic State*. Berkeley.

Blackwell, C. W. (1999) *In the Absence of Alexander*. New York.

Boiy, T. (2007) *Between High and Low. A Chronology of the Early Hellenistic Period*. Frankfurt.

Bosworth, A. B. (1988) *Conquest and Empire. The Reign of Alexander the Great*. Cambridge.

Bosworth, A. B. (1993) Perdiccas and the Kings, *The Classical Quarterly* 43.2, 420–27.

Bosworth, A. B. (2002) *The Legacy of Alexander. Politics, Warfare, and Propaganda under the Successors*. Oxford.

Ceccarelli, P. (2005) Forme di comunicazione e ideologia della polis: discorso in assemblea, decreto ed epistola ufficiale. In U. Bultrighini (ed.) *Democrazia e antidemocrazia nel mondo greco*, 345–69, Alessandria.

Culasso Gastaldi, E. (2003) Eroi della città: Eufrone di Sicione e Licurgo di Atene. In A. Barzanò, C. Bearzot, F. Landucci, L. Prandi and G. Zecchini (eds) *Modelli eroici dall'antichità alla cultura europea*, 65–98, Rome.

Dixon, M. (2007) Corinth, Greek Freedom, and the Diadochoi. In W. Heckel, L. Tritle and P. Wheatley (eds) *Alexander's Empire: Formulation to Decay*, 151– 78, Claremont, CA.

Green, P. (1990) *Alexander to Actium. The Historical Evolution of the Hellenistic Age*. Berkeley.

Habicht, C. (2006) *The Hellenistic Monarchies. Selected Papers*. Ann Arbor.

Hammond, N. G. L. and F. W. Walbank (1988) *A History of Macedonia*. III. Oxford 1988.

Hatzopoulos, M. B. (1996) *Macedonian Institutions*. 2 vols. Athens.

Heckel, W. (1999) The Politics of Antipatros: 324–319 BC, *Ancient Macedonia* 6, 489–98.

Knoepfler, D. (2000) Décrets d'Eretria pour des Macédoniens, *Ancient Macedonia* 6, 599–612.

Knoepfler, D. (2001) *Décrets érétriens de proxenie et de citoyenneté*. Lausanne.

Kralli, J. (2000) Athens and the Hellenistic Kings (338–261 BC): The Language of the Decrees, *The Classical Quarterly* 50.1, 113–32.

Landucci Gattinoni, F. (2008) *Diodoro Siculo. Biblioteca storica, libro XVIII. Commento storico*. Milan.

Mari, M. (2002) *Al di là dell'Olimpo. Macedoni e grandi santuari della Grecia dall'età arcaica al primo ellenismo*. Paris and Athens.

Mari, M. (2006) L'activité legislative du roi et des cités en Macédoine. In A.-M. Guimier-Sorbets, M. B. Hatzopoulos and Y. Morizot (eds) *Rois, cites, nécropoles. Institutions, rites et monuments en Macédoine*, 209–23, Athens.

Matthaiou, A. P. (2001) ΔΥΟ ΙΣΤΟΡΙΚΕΣ ΕΠΙΓΡΑΦΕΣ ΤΗΣ ΜΕΣΣΗΝΗΣ. In V. Mitsopoulos-Leon (ed.) *Forschungen in der Peloponnes*, 221–31, Athens.

Mendels, D. (1984) Aetolia 331–301: Frustration, Political Power, and Survival, *Historia* 33, 129–80.

Miller, S. G. (1982) Kleonai, the Nemean Games, and the Lamian War, *Hesperia* Suppl. 20, 100–08.

Piérart, M. (1982) Argos, Cléonai et le koinon des Arcadiens, *Bulletin de Correspondance Hellénique* 106, 123–37.

Poddighe, E. (2002) *Nel segno di Antipatro. L'eclissi della democrazia ateniese dal 323/2 al 319/8 a.C.* Rome.

Poddighe, E. (2004) Atene e le lotte tra i diadochi nell'anno dell'arconte Archippo II (318/7 a.C.), *Ancient History Bulletin* 18.1–2, 1–24.

Poddighe, E. (2007) La questione samia tra Alessandro e Atene: 'libertà dei Greci', *Quaderni di Storia* 66, 29–45.

Poddighe, E. (2009) Alexander and the Greeks: the Corinthian League. In W. Heckel and L. Tritle (eds) *Alexander the Great. A New History*, 99–120, Malden, MA.

Rhodes, P. J. and R. Osborne (eds) (2003) *Greek Historical Inscriptions: 404–323 BC*. Oxford.

Rosen, K. (1967) Political Documents in Hieronymus of Cardia (323–302 BC), *Acta classica* 10, 41–94.

Squillace, G. (2004) *Filippo II e Alessandro Magno tra opposizione e consenso*. Soveria Mannelli.
Wallace, S. (2011) History and Hindsight. The Importance of the Hellenic War and Euphron of Sikyon for the Athenian Democracy in 318/7. In H. Hauben and A. Meeus (eds) (forthcoming) *The Age of the Successors (323-276 BC)*. Leuven.
Will, E. (1984) From the Death of Alexander to Triparadeisos (323–321), *CAH* 3.1, 23–48.

Notes

1 There are serious difficulties with the chronology of the early Hellenistic period, but high and low chronology agree on the date of the events between spring 319 and autumn 318 (Boiy 2007, 118, 152). For autumn 319 as the date of the *diagramma*'s publication see Poddighe 2002, 185.
2 Alexander's son was associated in the kinghip by the summer of 322 (Bosworth 1993, 423–26).
3 For the Hellenic war see D.S. 18.8–17; Just. 13.5; Plu. *Phoc.* 23–26; Paus. 1.25.3–5; Hyp. *Epit.* 1–20. Regarding the dispositions of the Macedonian garrisons in Greece after the war, the garrison in Athens is the only one mentioned (Plu. *Phoc.* 28.4; D.S. 18.64.3–5; 66.2), but this was almost certainly the case for Argos (D.S. 18.57.1), Megalopolis (D.S. 18.68.3), Sicyon (*IG* II^2 448b). See below.
4 It is not evident if this was 'the Council' i.e. a formal body (Hatzopoulos 1996, 341–42, 487–96), or rather a council summoned ad hoc by Polypercheron and composed by his *philoi*: Macedonian notables and military commanders. Diodorus implies that it was rather an ad hoc meeting.
5 Discussion of sources and scholarship on Arrhidaeus' psychiatric disorders in Bosworth 2002, 30 n. 9.
6 For the *diagramma*'s process of enactment through the civic *dogmata* see below.
7 For the details of negotiations with Cassander and discussion of the main factors which led the Greek cities to defect, see Poddighe 2004, 11–13.
8 For the differing opinion that only the older king was competent to act in official documents, see Arena 1999, 77–98, who discusses previous scholarship (78 n. 4).
9 D.S. 18.2–3; Curt. 10.6–10; Arr. *FGH* 156 F 1.1–4. For a comprehensive discussion of the source tradition on the Babylon settlement, see Bosworth 2002, 29–63.
10 The study of Philip III's royal portrait suggests that he attached Philip II's image (bearded) rather than Alexander's (beardless) and that he inaugurated the earliest *imitatio Philippi* (Alonso 2010, 21).
11 Hyp. *Epit.* 10–11, 16, 19, 24, 34, 37, 40; D.S. 18.8–10; Curt. 10.2. Just. 13.5.2.
12 Part of the Tegeans who were restored were those sentenced in the aftermath of the Spartan revolt (330) and exceptionally allowed to return by Alexander for strategic reasons (Poddighe 2009, 118).
13 The traditional chronology of Demosthenes' speeches dates the oration in 336/5, but scholars think 333 more probable or 331, in the context of the debate following the Spartan revolt (*status quaestionis* in Poddighe 2009, 103 n. 19).
14 Alexander's interventions are recorded in the cities of Eresus (Rhodes-Osborne no. 83), Mytilene (Rhodes-Osborne no. 85 a–b), and Chios (Rhodes-Osborne no. 84 a–b). See Poddighe 2009, 109–12.
15 That explains why Philip III in 319 upheld Alexander's resolution of 324 not to restore the tyrants exiled from Eresus (Rhodes-Osborne no. 83, ll. 95–102; Bosworth 1988, 224; *contra* Bencivenni 2003, 76 n. 19, 95).
16 Alexander's resolution had been upheld by Antipater and Perdiccas in 321 (D.S. 18.18.9).
17 Ameling 1994, 56, identifies the Eraclea mentioned in the *diagramma* with Heraclea Pontica (but see Poddighe 2004, 15 n. 80).
18 Playing the 'Arcadian league card' was useful for freedom propaganda in 319, since the case for Greek freedom had been successfully defended by Demosthenes before the Arcadian *koinon* on the eve of the Hellenic war (Plu. *Mor.* 846d; Pierart 1982, 133).
19 Philip II promised Oropus to the Athenians but never upheld his promise (Dem. 5.9–11; 6.30).
20 Differing are Dixon (2007, 168) and Wallace (2011) who think that Diodorus was applying later terminology to the creation of the Edict.
21 See Wallace 2011 (forthcoming). On the transient nature of this memory cf. *IG* II^2 457, ll. 9–19; Plu. *Mor.* 852c–d, with Culasso Gastaldi 2003, 73–81.
22 For a comprehensive discussion of the evidence see Mari 2002, 266–67.

THE ALEXANDRIAN FOUNDATION MYTH: ALEXANDER, PTOLEMY, THE *AGATHOI DAIMONES* AND THE *ARGOLAOI*

Daniel Ogden

The anguiform deities of the Greek world tended to have little by way of myth, but Agathos Daimon did enjoy a starring role in the foundation myth of Alexandria preserved by the *Alexander Romance* (the A text of which dates to c. 300 AD).[1] According to this, Alexander's architects marked out the projected city to extend between the rivers 'Serpent' (*Drakōn*) and 'Agathodaimon' (Ps.Callisth. 1.31.7; the latter name is given to the Canopic branch of the Nile in several inscriptions, e.g. *OGIS* 672, and at Claudius Ptolemy *Geography* 4.5). Then:

> They began to build Alexandria from the Middle plain and so the place took on the additional name of 'Beginning', on account of the fact that the building of the city had begun from that point. A serpent (*drakōn*) which was in the habit of presenting itself to people in the area kept frightening the workmen, and they would break off their work upon the creature's arrival. News of this was given to Alexander. He gave the order that on the following day the serpent should be killed wherever it was caught. On receipt of this permission, they got the better of the beast when it presented itself at the place now called the Stoa and killed it. Alexander gave the order that it should have a precinct there, and buried the serpent. And he gave the command that the neighbourhood should be garlanded in memory of the sighting of Agathos Daimon. He commanded that the soil from the digging of the foundations should all be deposited in one particular place, and even up until this day a large hill is there to be seen, called the 'Dung Heap'. When he had laid the foundations for most of the city and measured it out, he inscribed five letters, alpha, beta, gamma, delta, epsilon: alpha for 'Alexander', Beta for 'king', gamma for 'scion', delta for 'of Zeus' and epsilon for 'founded this unforgettable city'. Beasts of burden and mules were at work. When the foundations of the *hērōon* had been laid down <he set it [i.e. the stele on which he had inscribed the letters] in on a pillar>.[2] There leaped out from it a large host <of snakes>, and, crawling off, they ran into the four [?] houses that were already there. Alexander, who was still present, founded the city and the heroon itself on the 25th Tybi. From that point the doorkeepers admitted these snakes (*opheis*) to the houses as Agathoi Daimones. These snakes are not venomous, but they do ward off those snakes that do seem to be venomous, and sacrifices are given to the hero himself <, as serpent-born>. They garland their beasts of burden and give them a holiday since they helped in the foundation of the city by carrying loads. Alexander ordered that the guardians of the houses be given wheat. They took it and milled it and made porridge [?] and gave it to the snakes in the houses. The Alexandrians preserve this custom until today. On the 25th of Tybi they garland their beasts of burden, make sacrifice to the Agathoi Daimones that look after their houses and make them gifts of porridge.
>
> Ps.Callisth. 1.32.5–7 and 10–13 (A) ~ Armenian §§ 86–8

This text implies the establishment both of a civic cult for a singular Agathos Daimon as special protector of Alexandria, and of private cults for plural *agathoi daimones* as protectors of individual homes within the city. The public cult of Agathos Daimon was almost certainly established already during the reign of the first Ptolemy, and we may assume that a mythology, which presumably resembled this one in broad outline, was developed for the serpent at the same time. The Agathos Daimon serpent was integrated into the Alexander Aegiochus statue type that was developed in Alexandria as early as ca. 320–300 and that decorated Alexander's tomb there.[3] Secondly, Diodorus and Curtius tell of a miraculous serpent that appeared to Alexander in a dream at the siege of the Brahmin city of Harmatelia in 326/5. According to this, the Indians had inflicted fatal wounds on Alexander's men by shooting them with arrows dipped in a poison made from the rotting carcasses of a local venomous snake. But it was over Ptolemy that Alexander grieved in particular. As he slept the serpent appeared to him and carrying a special herb in its mouth: the serpent demonstrated its curative properties and showed him where it grew. Upon waking Alexander found the plant at once and applied it to Ptolemy, thus healing him. The normal assumption is that a tale found in both these authors derives from Clitarchus, who worked in Alexandria itself, and is usually believed to have published under Ptolemy, soon after 310.[4]

The private cult is attested in a fragment of Phylarchus, whose history finished in 219 with the death of Cleomenes III of Sparta. He speaks of the Egyptians keeping asps in their houses: these come when called by a click of the fingers to receive gifts of barley in wine and honey, retreating at a second click (*FGH* 81 F 27 = Ael. *NA* 17.5). Plutarch subsequently gives us a vignette of two Egyptian neighbours fighting for possession of an Agathos Daimon snake they find in the road (*Mor.* 755e).

Despite the obscurities relating to the first lacuna and insertion in the *Romance* passage quoted, we are presumably intended to think that the host of *agathoi daimones* snakes that somehow emerges from an inscribed tablet in the *hērōon* of Agathos Daimon are, in some fashion, the great serpent redivivus. Such a revivification indeed puts the seal on Agathos Daimon's heroic status: a dead entity that somehow contrives to live on and continue to exercise influence in the world. Whilst it does not seem that we are being told that the host of small snakes was born directly from the carcass of the large one, it is nonetheless worth noting the ancient Greek belief that the spirits of heroes could indeed emerge from their corpses in the form of snakes (Plin. *Nat.* 16.234). On some wonderful archaic vases Ampharaus and Patroclus, amongst others, emerge from their barrows in the form of snakes.[5] Diogenes Laertius, quoting second- and first-century BC sources, tells how Heraclides of Pontus aspired to be believed to have joined the gods after his death, and so ordered those loyal to him surreptitiously to replace his corpse with a serpent as he was being carried out to burial, which then obligingly crawled out before the assembled mourners.[6] Virgil's account of Anchises' manifestation of himself at his tomb in the form of a serpent to Aeneas is well known (*A.* 5.95–96). And sometimes, it seems, the corpses of heroes could turn into multitudes of snakes, as in the *Romance* case. It is surely the implication of Hyginus' tale that

Medea delivered the people of Absoris from a plague of snakes by hurling them into her brother Apsyrtus' tomb and confining them there on pain of death and that it was from this very tomb that they had originated (*Fab.* 26). But of particular relevance in this Alexandrian context is Plutarch's tale of the death of the Spartan king Cleomenes III in Alexandria itself. As his body hung on public display after his suicide a huge serpent manifested itself and coiled around his head, keeping the birds away. Ptolemy Philopator panicked at this, and the women of Alexandria followed his lead, making offerings to Cleomenes and declaring him a hero and a son of gods (*Agis.* 60). No doubt the Alexandrians panicked so greatly precisely because they had the model of their own Agathos Daimon before their eyes.

Christian tradition preserves, albeit awkwardly, a narrative related to this latter part of the *Romance*'s narrative, in that it also has Alexander presiding over the killing of bad snakes and the introduction of good snakes into Alexandria. A ps.-Epiphanian narrative of the third century AD survives in two recensions of its own, and is reflected, in on the whole better, though not perfect, condition, in the seventh-century AD *Chronicon Paschale.* The three texts differ from each other only by variation in omission. The following translation merges them to produce an almost fully intelligible text:

> Jeremiah was of Anathoth, and he died in Daphnae in Egypt when he was stoned to death by the local people. He was laid to rest in the region of the Pharaoh's palace, because the Egyptians held him in honour, since he had done them good service. For he prayed for them, and the asps left them alone, as did the creatures of the waters, which the Egyptians call *menephōth* and the Greeks call crocodiles, which were killing them. The prophet prayed and the race of asps was averted from that land, as were the attacks of the creatures from the river. Even to this day the faithful pray in the place he lay, and by taking earth from the site of his tumulus they heal bites inflicted upon people, and many avert even the creatures in the water. We heard from some old men, descendants of Antigonus and Ptolemy, that Alexander the Macedonian visited the tomb of the prophet and learned the mysteries pertaining to him. He transferred his remains to Alexandria, and arranged them, with all due honour, in a circle. The race of asps was thus averted from that land, as similarly were the creatures from the river. And thus he threw in [sc. inside the circle] the snakes called *argolaoi*, that is 'snake-fighters' (*ophiomachoi*), which he had brought from Peloponnesian Argos, whence they are called *argolaoi*, that is, 'right-hand-men (*dexioi*) of Argos'. The sound they make is very sweet and of all good omen.
>
> [Epiph.Const.] *De prophetarum <vita> et obitu* first recension, p. 9 Schermann
> ~ second recension, pp. 61–62 Schermann
> ~ *Chronicon Paschale* p. 293 Dindorf[7]

The final sentences appear to mean that Alexander took Jeremiah's deterrent remains from Daphnae and arranged them in a circle around the city of Alexandria. Snakes (and crocodiles) outside the circle were thus prevented from entering it. He then threw his other-snake-fighting *argolaoi* snakes inside the circle, where they will presumably have destroyed the other snakes marooned inside it, and taken their place. Alexander may have made the circle by distributing the prophet's limbs, but we should almost certainly think rather of him sprinkling the remains in the form of a fine line of cremation ash.

This would then align neatly with the tradition, first found in Strabo, that Alexander had initially marked out the circle of Alexandria for his architects by sprinkling a line of barley meal that was then devoured by birds, in an act of good omen (Str. 17.1.6 C792; Plu. *Alex.* 26.)

At first sight the *Suda* gives us an interesting variation on the final part of this account:

> *Argolai*: a kind of snake (*opheis*), which Alexander the Macedonian brought from Pelasgian Argos to Alexandria, and he threw them in the river to kill the asps, when he transferred the bones of the prophet Jeremiah from Egypt to Alexandria [regarded as technically outside the land of Egypt]. The same prophet also killed these asps. *Argolai* derive their name from the left-hand men (*laioi*) of Argos.
>
> *Suda*, s.v. *argolai*[8]

Which river? The Drakon or the Agathodaimon river of the *Alexander Romance*? Alas, neither. On closer inspection the notion that Alexander threw his Argive snakes into a river is revealed merely to derive from an over-hasty repackaging of an original text akin to the Epiphanian one, where the throwing-in of the snakes (sc. into the circle) follows a reference to creatures from the river (i.e. the crocodiles of the Nile). And indeed it makes little sense to speak of snakes living in rivers, water-snakes aside.

That said, the *Suda* does help us to understand in part the baffling etymology of *argolaoi* supplied by the Epiphanian version. A folk-etymology deriving *argolai* or *argolaoi* from *argo-laioi* is just about imaginable at verbal level, though what 'the left-hand men of Argos' might actually be remains a mystery. A redactor in the Epiphanian tradition, no doubt puzzled himself, at least found the negative connotations of the left-hand side unsatisfactory for such good snakes, and so corrected the explanation to invoke rather the positive connotations of the right-hand side, throwing the verbal baby out with the bathwater in the process. *Dexios* also carries the particular connotation of good omen, and this could be why the further justificatory contention is made that the snakes have a good-omened voice. If this archaeology is correct, it implies that the *Suda* must depend on an account resembling these Epiphanian ones, but prior to them, because 'left' had not yet been substituted for 'right' in it. And it must be conceded that *argo-laioi* makes a better folk-etymological ancestor to the term *argolaoi* of the Epiphanian tradition than to the *Suda*'s own *argolai*. On the other hand, from the perspective of possible genuine etymologies, the *Suda*'s version of the term, *argolai*, seems much more satisfactory, simply signifying as it does 'Argives', *Argolas* being an ancient term for Argive, found first in Euripides.[9] The Epiphanian term *argolaoi* ought in reality to have meant either 'peoples (*laoi*) of Argos' or 'shining/white/idle [all possible meanings of the adjective *argos*] peoples'.

Like the *Romance*'s myth, this one accounts for the arrival, alongside Alexander, of a host of good snakes in Alexandria, which we may assume were to be identified with those that became the object of private cult: we note the Romance's contention that its Agathoi Daimones 'are not poisonous, but they do ward off those snakes that do seem to be poisonous': these, clearly, are 'snake-fighters' too. The tale also efficiently salutes the Argeads' and thereby the Ptolemies' claim to derive their stock ultimately from Argos.[10]

Jeremiah was evidently a St Patrick avant-la-lettre, and he is associated with the phenomenon known to folklorists (in consequence of St Patrick) as 'Irish earth',[11] that of the soil of a certain place being repellent to certain venomous or pestilential creatures, which is well attested elsewhere in Graeco-Roman culture, at least from the age of the elder Pliny in the first century AD onwards: the earth of Crete was fatal to venomous snakes, that of the island of Astypalaea and of the Balearic island of Ebusus drove snakes away, whilst that of the Tunisian island of Galata drove away scorpions; Sicilian achate stones cured wounds inflicted by spiders and scorpions, whilst Sicilian stones in general deprived scorpions of their venom; Lemnian earth had cured Philoctetes' famous snakebite, could do the same for others too, and could even function as an emetic for those who had swallowed poisons.[12] Much closer to home, Aelian preserves an interesting aetiology for the plant *helenion* that has all the appearance of being Alexandrian in origin. After the Egyptian king Thonis attempted to force himself upon the refugee Helen, his queen Polydamna, the 'all-conquering' witch, sent her off, in their common interest, to live on the then snake-infested island of Pharos, giving her a herb to protect her from the snakes. Helen planted it, and in time it covered the island, producing seeds the snakes could not abide and so rendering it free of them.[13]

The Jeremiah tale also salutes a familiar motif of snake-control stories, that of deployment of a 'magic circle' against them, as in the following ps.-Aristotelian tale:

> In Thessaly they say that the sacred snake (*hieros ophis*) kills all not just if it bites them, but even if it just touches them. Therefore, whenever it appears and they hear its voice (and it appears only rarely), the snakes and the vipers and all the other beasts flee. In size it is not great but moderate. They say that once in Tenos, the city in Thessaly, a sacred snake was killed by a woman.[14] The killing took place in the following fashion. The woman drew a circle, laid down herbs (*pharmaka*) and entered the circle, together with her son. Then she imitated the voice of the creature. The creature sang in response and approached.[15] As it sang, the woman fell asleep, and then it came closer still, with the result that she was not able to resist sleep. But her son lying beside her roused her by pummelling her at her own bidding, for she explained to him that if she fell asleep, both she herself and he would perish. But, she explained, if she compelled and drew on the beast, they would be delivered from it. And when the beast came into the circle, it was immediately drained of moisture.
>
> [Arist.] *Mir.* 845b

We also learn from Lucan that the Psylli, the snake-mastering race of Libya (of whom more anon), protected Cato's camp from Africa's terrible snakes by carrying a number of burning substances, including noxious deer-horn, around its perimeter;[16] he further tells us that they similarly contain the effects of snake-bites by isolating the area of the wound with a circle of their saliva (Luc. 9.922–37). And in Lucian's *Philopseudes* (11–13) a Babylonian Chaldaean purifies a farm infected with snakes by going out at dawn, reciting seven sacred names from an old book and purifying the place with a torch, encircling it three times.

It is hard to suppose that the Jeremiah material as we have it, with its motif of martyrdom, antedates the Christian era, even though Ptolemaic Alexandria's large and proud Jewish population could have constituted a ready audience for it. However, the motif of the transfer of a great man's remains from the land of Egypt proper to Alexandria is so strikingly reminiscent of Ptolemy's historical transfer of Alexander's own tomb from Memphis to Alexandria, that we can only assume that the tale of Alexander's transfer of Jeremiah's remains has supplanted an original one of Ptolemy's transfer of Alexander's. Thus, as Alexander in life delivered the site of Alexandria from the bad snakes, so Jeremiah in life delivered the people of Egypt from dangerous reptiles. And then as Ptolemy subsequently transferred Alexander's remains to Alexandria to confer continuing protection on the city, so Alexander was then held to have transferred Jeremiah's remains to the city. It is unlikely that any original story relating to Alexander's body subjected it to dispersal in the fashion of Jeremiah's, given that it famously lay intact inside his tomb in Alexandria, at any rate, up until the point at which Octavian gazed upon it before breaking off its nose (Suet. *Aug.* 2.18; D.C. 21.16; cf. in general Saunders 2006). And if this was indeed the original tale, then it would gratifyingly have put Ptolemy himself exactly where he has long been suspected of being: at the heart of the Agathos Daimon myth and cult. Perhaps his original role is remembered in the attribution of the Epiphanian tale to his sons (though the parallel role of the sons of Antigonus is admittedly harder to explain).[17]

Let us refer back to the key but curious sentence in the *Romance*: 'These snakes are not poisonous, but they do ward off those snakes that do seem to be poisonous, and sacrifices are given to the hero himself <, as serpent-born>'. This is a somewhat puzzling non-sequitur, in context, and it is not immediately clear whether the 'hero' concerned is Agathos Daimon, whose heroisation has just been described, or to Alexander himself. But the primary reference must nonetheless be to Alexander. On the one hand, only in the most curious and restricted circumstances is it meaningful to describe a serpent, such as Agathos Daimon, as 'serpent-born'. On the other, Alexander was of course famously serpent-born, with Plutarch and others preserving the myth of him being sired upon Olympias by a gigantic snake.[18] More sense can be made of it when we link Alexander's serpent-birth specifically to the notion in the Epiphanian tradition of the good snakes warding off the bad snakes, and also to beliefs about peoples known as Ophiogeneis, 'Snake-born'. The phrase 'as serpent-born' does not exist in the Greek A text of the *Romance* but is restored from the Armenian translation, which is held to reflect the original of the α tradition rather better than the poor quality A, and in which the word translated as 'serpent' is *višap*. The standard term for 'serpent-born' in Greek is *ophiogenēs*, and Kroll's (and subsequently Stoneman's) proposed restitution of *hōs ophiogenei* is therefore wholly plausible.[19] But since we cannot completely depend upon this having been the Greek's ipsissimum verbum, the following case is mounted on the basis of the qualities one could have expected of a man born from a snake in the ancient Greek thought-world rather than upon the application of the specific term itself.

We know of three groups of Ophiogeneis, snake-born peoples, in the Greek world. The

Phrygian Ophiogeneis mentioned by Aelian had an origin myth that was gratifyingly similar to Alexander's birth myth:

> As Halia the daughter of Sybaris was passing into a grove of Artemis (the grove was in Phrygia) a divine snake manifested itself before her, enormous to see, and it had sex with her. And from this derived the so-called Ophiogeneis (Snake-born) of the first generation.
>
> Ael. *NA* 12.39[20]

The other two groups of Ophiogeneis bring us closer to Alexander in his snake-deterring role. Strabo speaks of the Ophiogeneis of Parium on the Hellespont:

> Here, they preserve the myth that Ophiogeneis have a kinship with serpents. They say that the males of the Ophiogeneis cure those who are bitten by vipers (*echiodēktoi*) by continuously massaging them, like sorcerers (*epōidoi*), first bringing the discoloration across into themselves and then putting a stop to the inflammation and the pain. They tell the myth that the founder of the race transformed into a human hero from having been a snake. Perhaps he was one of the Psylli of Libya, and his power endured amongst his descendants for a time.
>
> Str. 13.1.14 C588

Pliny knew of a group of Ophiogeneis living in Cyprus, seemingly a family rather than a race as such, of whose bodies serpents were frightened. He compares them to the Italian snake-bursting Marsi and <the> Psylli (again) in this regard, like whom they can cure snake-bites with a mere touch or suck. An ambassador of this family, Euagon, came to Rome only to be thrown by the consuls into a great pot of snakes so that they could test his powers. The snakes merely licked him all over. Pliny notes that not only the saliva of this family (sc. in common with that of the Marsi and the Psylli), but also their sweat had medicinal properties (sc. against snake-bites). Perhaps it was this unique sweat that was the cause of the virulent smell they emitted in the spring. And perhaps, at a different level, it was their own serpent-stock that was the ultimate cause of this stench, since the emission of a stench was a quality typical of serpents and dragons. Pliny also suggests that this miraculous family may have died out in his own day (*si modo adhuc durat*).[21]

It is a curiosity of both Strabo's and Pliny's reports that the Ophiogeneis should be antithetical to serpents and yet born of them. But the paradox can be resolved if we recall the ideal symmetricality to which ancient dragon-fights and serpent-fights tended from the point at which, already in Hesiod, Zeus answered Typhon's fiery breath with his fiery thunderbolts (Hes. *Th.* 826–28, 844–47, 853–56; see Ogden 2007, 79–86). It stands to reason, therefore, that those best equipped to fight serpents should be those that partake of their nature. And so it makes perfect sense that Alexander should have been worshipped as snake-born precisely in the context of his dismissal of snakes.

As we have seen, the ancient notices on the Ophiogeneis often align them with the Psylli of the Libyan Syrtes (as well as the Italian Marsi), and the Psylli are credited with a 'magic circle' technique for snake-banishing similar to that attributed to Alexander.[22] It is likely that the lore of the Psylli also had an impact upon this tale. They were mentioned first by Hecataeus (*FGH* 1 F 331–32; his 'Psyllic Gulf' was doubtless related to the Syrtes), whilst for Herodotus they were an already long-vanished race, one that had been buried in desert sands when they made war on the South Wind (Hdt. 4.173; this material is resumed at Gel. 16.11.3). But for the authors of the third century BC and onwards they were alive again, and from this point they were defined by their relationship with snakes. Agatharchides of Cnidus knew, in indirect response to Herodotus, that the Psylli had been brought to the brink of extinction not by the South Wind but by the neighbouring Nasamones, and that the race had then been repopulated by its straggling survivors (but at any rate, the survival-status of the race is in question, as with Pliny's Ophiogeneis). Agatharchides also knew that the Psylli could not feel the bites or stings of deadly snakes or scorpions, that their blood was fatal to them, and that their very touch or odour inflicted an enervating drowsiness on the creatures, as if it were a sleep-inducing drug (a great achievement, since it was normally held in antiquity that snakes, which cannot close their eyes, were by nature unsleeping). He knew too that they subjected their children to a trial of legitimacy (more strictly a trial of Psyllus-paternity) by throwing them into a chest of snakes; the snakes wilted away before the child of Psyllus-blood, instead of attacking him (cf. the ordeal to which the Ophiogenes Euagon was subjected in Rome).[23] One Callias, the author of a multi-volume work on the Syracusan tyrant Agathocles (who died in 289), knew that a Psyllus could cure a snakebite in its early stages by spitting on it and 'bewitching' (*kategoēteuse*) it with saliva, in its middle stages by swilling water in his mouth, spitting it out and giving it to the victim to drink, and in its late stages by lying down naked with the victim and rubbing skin against skin (*apud* Aelian *Nature of Animals* 16.28). And this last method was known to Nicander of Colophon too (*Fr.* 32 Gow and Scholfield, *apud* Ael. *NA* 16.28). The paradoxographer Antigonus also knew in this century that the Psylli could not feel snakebites (Antig. *Mir.* 16b). These themes are frequently resumed and sometimes finessed in the later Greek and especially the Latin traditions, with particularly elaborate contributions from Lucan in the context of his description of Cato's march through Libya and Silius as he describes the backgrounds of several of the Carthaginian Hannibal's local allies.[24] Amongst later novelties is the more explicit assertion that the Psylli were sorcerers.[25] Dio (51.14) makes an important logical clarification in relation to the legitimacy test: only men can be Psylli, not women, so the test cannot produce a false positive on the basis of blood inherited from the mother (cf. Str. 13.1.14 C588, where it is only the males amongst the Ophiogeneis of Parium that have the power to cure snakebites). Pliny (on occasion) and Pausanias speak of Psylli almost in the way that imperial texts speak of 'Chaldaeans', that is as denoting groups of technical specialists abroad and perhaps itinerant in the Roman empire with little ostensible connection to the place indicated by the ethnic used to designate them. Pliny (*Nat.* 11.89) tells that Psylli had imported pests from all countries into Italy, to profit from them, but had failed to be able to keep their scorpions alive, save in Sicily.[26] He seems to say too that the Psylli test themselves against poisonous toads which they first irritate by warming them in pans, which is suggestive of some sort of travelling show (*Nat.* 25.123; however the text appears to be corrupt). Pausanias

(9.28.1) tells that the Psylli find it easier to cure men bitten on Helicon because the roots and herbs the snakes eat (!) there are less poisonous than elsewhere.

Another point made – uniquely – by Agatharchides is of particular interest: the Psylli derived their name from king Psyllus, whose tomb is situated in the Greater Syrtes (*FGH* 86 F 21a = Plin. *Nat.* 7.14). Stephanus of Byzantium also makes a passing reference to this originating Psyllus, albeit without mention of his tomb (s.v. Ψύλλοι). It is tempting to suppose that the race derived not only its name but also its defining qualities from this king (much as the Phrygian Ophiogeneis derived their qualities from a single individual), and to compare Psyllus' tomb with those of Jeremiah and Alexander. Were the ideas attaching to Jeremiah and to Alexander derived from the lore of the Psylli? Or was the lore of the Psylli rather derived from the serpent mythology generated in early Alexandria in connection with Alexander and the transfer of his tomb? It may be significant that the Psylli only acquire their snakes in the literary record the course of the third century BC. The gravitation of Psyllus-type lore to Egypt is attested by Strabo and Pliny, both of whom explicitly compare the inhabitants of the island of Tentyra/ Tentyrus (Dendera) to the Psylli. Strabo tells that as the Psylli have a natural resistance to snakes, the people of Tentyra have a natural resistance to crocodiles, so that they have no fear in entering the river with them and in manhandling them. Pliny tells that the islanders are small of stature and ride on the crocodiles' backs, putting a staff through their mouths, which they use as a bridle. By shouting alone they can compel them to flee or disgorge the bodies of those they have recently swallowed. So the crocodiles stay away from the island, repelled by the very scent of its inhabitants, as are snakes from the Psylli. This is of particular interest when we note that crocodiles are also singled out as repulsed alongside snakes in the Jeremiah material.[27] As it happens, the Psylli were introduced in their own right into the mythology of the fall of the Ptolemaic dynasty. Suetonius and Dio tell us that Octavian called in Psylli in an attempt to revive Cleopatra from her asp-bite, but that it was too late, for she was already dead (Suet. *Aug.* 17; D.C. 51.14).

Abbreviations

LIMC *Lexicon Iconographicum Mythologiae Classicae* (1981–1999). 9 vols in 18 parts. Zurich and Munich.

PGM Preisendanz, K. and A. Henrichs (1973–1974) *Papyri Graecae Magicae. Die griechischen Zauberpapyri.* 2nd edn. 2 vols. Stuttgart.

TrGF Snell, B., R. Kannicht and S. Radt (1971–2004) *Tragicorum Graecorum Fragmenta.* 5 vols. Göttingen.

Bibliography

Amsler, F., F. Bovon and B. Bouvier (1996) *Actes de l'apôtre Philippe.* Turnhout.

Amsler, F., F. Bovon and B. Bouvier (1999) *Acta Philippi.* 2 vols. (I: *Textus*; II: *Commentarius*). Corpus Christianorum, Series Apocryphorum nos 11–12. Turnhout.

Cook, A. B. (1914–1940) *Zeus. A Study in Ancient Religion.* 3 vols. Cambridge.
Dunand, F. (1969) Les représentations de l'Agathodémon. À propos de quelques bas-reliefs du Musée d'Alexandrie, *Bulletin de l'Institut français d'archéologie orientale* 67, 9–48.
Dunand, F. (1981) Agathodaimon, *LIMC* 1.1, 277–82. Zurich.
Errington, R. M. (1990) *A History of Macedonia.* Berkeley (transl. from German).
Fontenrose, J. (1959) *Python. A Study of the Delphic Myth and its Origins.* Berkeley.
Fraser, P. M. (1972) *Ptolemaic Alexandria.* 3 vols. Oxford.
Ganschinietz/Ganszyniec, R. (1918) Agathodaimon, *RE Suppl.* 3, 37–59.
Ganschinietz/Ganszyniec, R. (1919) *De Agatho-daemone.* Warsaw.
Gantz, T. (1993) *Early Greek Myth. A Guide to Literary and Artistic Sources.* Baltimore. Continuous pagination.
Grabow, E. (1998) *Schlangenbilder in der griechischen schwartzfiguren Vasenkunst.* Münster.
Harrison, J. (1899) Delphika, *Journal of Hellenic Studies* 19, 205–51.
Harrison, J. (1912) *Themis.* Cambridge.
Harrison, J. (1922) *Prolegomena to the Study of Greek Religion.* 3rd ed. Cambridge.
Hasluck, F. W. (1909–1910) Terra Lemnia, *Annual of the British School at Athens* 16, 220- 31.
Jakobsson, O. (1925) *Daimon och Agathos Daimon.* Lund.
Jouanno, C. (2002) *Naissance et métamorphoses du Roman d'Alexandre. Domaine grec.* Paris.
Krappe, A. H. (1941) Irish Earth, *Folk-Lore* 52, 229–36.
Krappe, A. H. (1947) St Patrick and the Snakes, *Traditio* 5, 323–30.
Kroll, W. (ed.) (1926) *Historia Alexandri Magni (Pseudo-Callisthenes). I. Recensio vetusta.* Berlin.
Mitropoulou, E. (1977) *Deities and Heroes in the Form of Snakes.* 2nd ed. Athens.
Ogden, D. (2007) *In Search of the Sorcerer's Apprentice.* Swansea.
Ogden, D. (2009a) Alexander's Snake Sire. In P. Wheatley and R. Hannah (eds) *Alexander and his Successors: Essays from the Antipodes*, 136–78, Claremont, CA.
Ogden, D. (2009b) Alexander, Scipio and Octavian: Serpent-siring in Macedon and Rome, *Syllecta Classica* 20, 31–52.
Ogden, D. (2011) *Alexander the Great: Myth, Genesis and Sexuality.* Exeter.
Phillips, O. (1995) Singing away Snakebite: Lucan's Magical Cures. In M. Meyer and P. Mirecki (eds) *Ancient Magic and Ritual Power*, 391–400, Leiden.
Pietrzykowski, M. (1978) Sarapis-Agathos Daimon. In *Hommages à Maarten J. Vermaseren*, III, 959–66, Leiden.
Quaegebeur, J. (1975) *Le dieu égyptien Shaï dans la religion et l'onomastique.* Leuven.
Rohde, E. (1925) *Psyche.* London.
Sarian, H. (1986) Erinys, *LIMC* 3.1, 825–43.
Saunders, N. J. (2006) *Alexander's Tomb.* New York.
Schermann, T. (1907) *Prophetarum vitae fabulosae.* Leipzig.
Schwarzenberg, E. (1976) The Portraiture of Alexander. In E. Badian (ed.) *Alexandre le Grand. Image et réalité*, 223–67, Geneva.
Sfameni Gasparro, G. (1997) Daimon and Tyche in the Hellenistic Religious Experience. In P. Bilde, T. Engberg-Pedersen, L. Hannestad and J. Zahle (eds) *Conventional Values of the Hellenistic Greeks*, 67–109, Aarhus.
Shaw, I. and P. Nicholson (eds) (1995) *The Dictionary of Ancient Egypt.* London.
Stewart, A. (1993) *Faces of Power. Alexander's Image and Hellenistic Politics.* Berkeley.
Stoneman, R. (1994) Jewish Traditions on Alexander the Great, *Studia Philonica Annual* 6, 37–53.

Stoneman, R. (2007) (ed. and trans.) *Il romanzo di Alessandro*. I. Milan.
Stoneman, R. (2008) *Alexander the Great. A Life in Legend*. Yale.
Tarn, W. W. (1928) The Hellenistic Ruler-Cult and the Daemon, *Journal of Hellenic Studies* 48, 206–19.
Taylor, L. R. (1930) Alexander and the Serpent of Alexandria, *Classical Philology* 25, 375–78.
Wolohojian, A. M. (trans.) (1969) *The Romance of Alexander the Great by Pseudo-Callisthenes. Translated from the Armenian Version*. New York.

Notes

1 Dunand 1981, 281 goes too far in asserting that Agathos Daimon had no mythology. For Agathos Daimon in general see Harrison 1912, 277–316; Cook 1914–1940, II 2, 1125–29; Ganschinietz/Ganszyniec 1918 and 1919; Jakobsson 1925, especially 151–75; Rohde 1925, 207–08 n. 133; Tarn 1928; Taylor 1930; Fraser 1972, I, 209–11, with associated notes; Quaegebeur 1975, 170–76 and *passim*; Mitropoulou 1977, 155–68; Dunand 1969; 1981, with bibliography; Pietrzykowski 1978; Sfameni Gasparro 1997; Jouanno 2002, 75–76, 105–08; Stoneman 2007, 532–34; 2008, 56–58.

2 This is supplied from the Armenian translation, for an English translation of which see Wolohojan 1969. The Greek A MS is both lacunary and corrupt at this point. For the phrase that survives, '+ ἐπὶ ἓν ἐπιστύλιον...' (as printed by Kroll 1926 and Stoneman 2007), I would conjecture, on the basis of the Armenian, 'ἐπέθηκεν ἐπὶ στυλίον', 'he set on a pillar'. The β recension has a slightly more elaborate tale: when the gatehouse to the shrine was being built, a huge, ancient tablet full of letters fell out of it, and it was out of this that the snakes emerged. Presumably the notion was that a piece of ancient Egyptian masonry was being reused. But this tablet full of letters would seem to be a doublet of the tablet that Alexander himself has just inscribed with his own five letters.

3 Schwarzenberg 1976, 235 with fig. 8; with Stewart 1993, 247; Stoneman 2007, 533. The case for the Agathos Daimon serpent having been integrated into the Aegiochus statue is considerably strengthened by the limestone-statuette model of it in the new Museo Bíblico y Oriental in León. This statuette is in roughly the same state of preservation as that of Schwarzenberg fig. 8 and, like it, incorporates the supporting tree-trunk with snake. But in this case the open-mouthed snake is represented more crudely, as a sort of low-relief figure on the side of the trunk. I thank Professor Alonso Troncoso for bringing this object to my attention.

4 D.S. 17.103.4–8; Curt. 9.8.22–8 (cf. 9.1.12); sanitised versions of the story at Str. 15.2.7 C723; Iust. 12.10.2–3; Oros. *Hist.* 3.19.11. Ptolemy's role in the generation of serpent lore around Alexander is discussed in Ogden 2009a; 2009b; 2011.

5 Amphiaraus: Tyrrhenian amphora of ca. 575–550, *LIMC* Erinys 84 = Alkmaion 3 (where illustrated) = Grabow 1998 K103; discussion at Harrison 1922, 236 (with fig. 55 and importantly superseding Harrison 1899, 214–15, also with illustration); Sarian 1986, 841; Gantz 1993, 526, 679; note also *LIMC* Alkmaion 9. Patroclus: Athenian black-figure hydria of ca. 510, *LIMC* Achilleus 586. Further examples: Grabow 1998, K96a, 96b, 97, 104, with discussion at p. 147–70.

6 D.L. 5.89–91, incorporating Heraclid.Pont. F 16 Wehrli, Demetr.Magn. *FHG* IV p. 382 (first-century BC) and a fragment of Hippobotus (c. 200 BC).

7 For the Epiphanius recensions, see Schermann 1907. Brief discussion at Stoneman 1994, 2007, 533, 2008, 57.

8 The note is repeated at [Zonar.] s.v. ἀργόλαι (thirteenth century AD).

9 E. *TrGF* F 41 and 630. The *Suda* also repeats a baffling series of phrases to the effect that 'He [who? Alexander?] seeks the sacred bones of the prophet Jeremiah in (the) Argolas': *Suda* s.vv. Ἱερεμίας, Ὀστᾶ Γιγάντων, Ὄφις.

10 Curt. 9.8.22; Paus. 1.6.2,8; Ps.Callisth. 3.32 (A); unpublished Ptolemaic inscription at Errington 1990, 265 n. 6 (Ἡρακλείδας Ἀργεάδας).

11 See Krappe 1941 and 1947 with a great many parallels. Indeed the snake-repellent effects of Irish

earth are attested prior to St Patrick's act of snake-cleansing, first in Bede's *Ecclesiatical History of the English People*, 1.1 (completed c. 731 AD). St Patrick's cleansing is first attested in Gerald of Wales' *Topography of Ireland*, 1.23 (completed in 1187 AD). The tale's international fame is founded upon the fleeting reference to it in Jacobus de Voragine's *Golden Legend*, 50 (1263–1267 AD).

12 Plin. *Nat.*3.78 (Ebusus; so too Mela 2.7); 5.7 (Galata); 37.54 (Sicily, including the achate); Dsc. 5.113 (Lemnian earth an emetic for poisons); Gal. *De Simplicium Medicamentorum Temperamentis et Facultatibus* 12.169 Kühn (Lemnian earth cures poisonous snakebites in general); Philostr. *Her.* 6.2 (Lemnian earth cures Philoctetes); Ael. *NA* 5.2 (Crete); 5.8 (Astypalaea). See Hasluck 1909–10 and Krappe 1941, 233–34.

13 Ael. *NA* 9.21; cf. Hom. *Od.* 4.219–34 for Helen, Thonis, Polydamna and the latter's herbs, both healing and deleterious. I thank Professor Alonso Troncoso for bringing this text to my attention.

14 There is no Tenos in Thessaly, and doubtless the tale was originally attached to the well-known island of that name. The role of the witch in the story will have attracted it to Thessaly, witches typically being conceptualised as Thessalian in the Greek world. Plin. *Nat.* 4.66 and Stephanus of Byzantium s.v. Τῆνος know that the island of Tenos was of old known as Ophioussa, 'Snake-land'.

15 It is interesting to note that the terrible snake described here is also distinguished, improbably, by its voice, as are the friendly *argolaoi* of the Epiphanian story.

16 Luc. 9.915–21 (*ultima castrorum medicatus circumit ignis*, 915). The burning of powdered deer horn is recommended as a fumigation against snakes also at Ael. *NA* 2.9. Plin. *Nat.* 28.100 attributes to 'the mages' the claim that one can put snakes to flight by burning the fat of the hyena.

17 I note, however, that Ptolemy and Antigonus appear together as Alexander's closest pair of lieutenants in the later stages of Ps.Callisth. <,> 3.18–23 (A); cf. Armenian version, §§225–46 Wolohojian.

18 Cic. *Div.* 2.135; Liv. 26.19.7–8; Plu. *Alex.* 2–3; Ptolemy son of Hephaestion at Phot. *Bibl.* no. 190 (148a); Gel. 6.1.1; Iust. 11.11.2–5, etc. Discussion at Ogden 2009a; 2009b; 2011.

19 Ps.Callisth. 1.32.11 (A): καὶ θυσία τελεῖται αὐτῷ τῷ ἥρωι <ὡς ὀφιογενεῖ>, as reconstituted by Kroll 1926 and accepted by Stoneman 2007. The Armenian translation: §87 Wolohojian. However, Taylor 1930, 376–77 would prefer the term *višap* to reflect some version of the term δράκων.

20 Could Aelian be referring to the Parium Ophiogeneis of Str. 13.1.14 C588 (as below)? This seems unlikely. Although it had once been regarded as part of Hellespontine Phrygia, in Aelian's day Parium belonged to Bithynia, and the origin myth does not match Strabo's. It has been suggested that the name Halia, which might be construed as 'woman of the sea', indicates that the action takes place somewhere on the Phrygian seaboard. It has also been suggested that the name should rather be read as Alia, and that the woman should be understood to be the eponym of a city of that name in central Phrygia. Both are possible: see Fontenrose 1959, 120. But it is also just possible that Aelian has in mind a people supposedly living in or around Phrygian Hierapolis, and that these are refracted in the Ophianoi of Hierapolis that take centre-stage in the later fourth-century AD apocryphal *Acts of Philip* (8.15 ABB = 96.3 LB, for the name). For the identification of Philip's Hierapolis with the famous Phrygian Hierapolis, see Amsler, Bovon, Bouvier 1996, 69–72; 1999, I, 244; II, 17–20, 374, 520–45.

21 Plin. *Nat.* 28.30–31. For the snake-bursting of the Marsi, see Lucil. *Book* 20 F 7 Charpin (575–76 Marx); Verg. *Ecl.* 8.71; Hor. *Epod.*17.29; Ov. *Med.* 39. For the stenches emitted by serpents and dragons in various contexts, see, e.g., Hes. *Th.* 861–2 (Typhon); [Hom.] *h.Ap.* 300–6, 352–73 (Delphic dragon); Ov. *Met.*3.49 and 75–76 (Serpent of Ares); V.Max. 1.8 ext. 19 (Bagrada dragon, recycling Livy); Hyg. *Fab.* 30.3 (Hydra).

22 Explicit comparisons or connections between Ophiogeneis and Psylli at Var. *Antiquitates Rerum Humanarum et Divinarum* apud Prisc. *Gramm.* 10 p. 524; Str. 13.1.14 C588 (Ophiogeneis of Parium descended from a Psyllus?); Plin. *Nat.* 28.30. For the Psylli in general see (the often inaccurate) Phillips 1995.

23 Agatharch. F 21a (= Plin. *Nat.* 7.14), F 21b (= Ael. *NA* 16.27; the more extensive treatment of the Psylli at 1.57 evidently derives from the same source). The full extent of Agatharchides' material on the Psylli is evidently unknown to Phillips 1995, who proclaims that the Psylli's famous legitimacy-test is found first in Varro. The notion of paternity-testing with snakes originated in a variant the myth of

baby Heracles. According to the version of Pherecyd. F 69 Fowler (*apud* Apollod. 2.4.8), Amphitryon wished to know which of the twins Heracles and Iphicles had been sired by him and which by Zeus, and so he cast *drakontes* into their bed. When Iphicles fled whilst Heracles stood his ground, he knew that he was his own.

24 Var. *Antiquitates Rerum Humanarum et Divinarum* apud Prisc. *Gramm.* 10 p. 524 (legitimacy test); Cinna F 10 Courtney *apud* Gel. 9.12.12 (a Psyllus renders an asp drowsy); Str. 17.1.44 C814–15 (Psylli resistant to snakebites); Cels. 5.27 (Psylli suck out venom); Luc. 9.890–937 (the Psylli's voice has the power of a drug over a snake; they are protected by their blood; their legitimacy test; their circular fumigation techniques; their spittle contains the venom within the wound, or they will suck it out, and can tell from the taste of the venom what variety of snake has inflicted the bite); Plin. *Nat.* 8.93 (snakes repelled by the scent of the Psylli), 21.78 (Psylli resistant to snakebites), 28.30 (Psylli suck out venom); Sil. 1.411–13 (Athyr disarms serpents of their poison, sends them to sleep with his touch, and performs the legitimacy test), 3.300–2 (the Marmaridae make snakes forget their poison with their incantations, and relax them by their touch), 5.352–5 (Synalus of the Garamantes, neighbours of Cyrenaica, send snakes to sleep by touching them); Plu. *Cat.Mi.* 56 (the Psylli suck out the poison and bewitch the snakes with incantations); D.C. 51.14 (Psylli cannot feel snakebites; they can suck out venom; the legitimacy test, in which the snakes fall asleep when they crawl under the child's clothes); St. Byz. s.v. Ψύλλοι (Psylli's immunity to snakebites).

25 E.g. Hsch. s.v. Ψυλλικὸς γόης: ὁ τῶν Ψύλλων. Οἱ δὲ Ψύλλοι ἔθνος Λιβύης.

26 This is curious: *Nat.* 37.54 (on the affects of Sicilian stones, especially the achate, on scorpions, discussed above) might have led us to expect the opposite.

27 Str. 17.1.44 C814–15 (further passing reference to the Psylli at 2.5.33 C 131; 17.3.23 C 838); Plin. *Nat.* 8.92–93; 28.30. It was a commonplace that Egyptian magicians and priests could ride on the backs of crocodiles: *PGM* XIII.282–86 (magical recipe text: 'If you wish to cross on top of a crocodile, sit on it and say: 'Hear me, you that live in the water. I am the one that passes his time in heaven and I travel on water, in fire, in air and on land''); Luc. *Philops.* 34 (the priest-sorcerer Pancrates, he of apprentice fame, rides on crocodiles amongst other wondrous feats); Ael. *NA* 17.6 (Amometus told of a city in Libya [NB] in which the priests charmed [καταγοητεύοντες] sixteen-cubit crocodiles out of their lake with incantations [ἐπαοιδαῖς]); behind these fantasies may lurk the fact that the god Horus/Harpocrates was often represented standing on a pair of crocodiles, for which see Shaw and Nicholson 1995, 133. See further Ogden 2007, 244, 265.

THE DIADOCHI AND THE ZOOLOGY OF KINGSHIP: THE ELEPHANTS

Víctor Alonso Troncoso

The horse, embodied in Bucephalus, is the emblematic animal of Alexander's kingship, while the eagle on his coins evokes a more common paradigm of celestial majesty (see Price 1991, 103–04, pl. 14). On the contrary, dogs do not seem to have featured prominently in his lifetime, in spite of the fact that Plutarch (*Alex.* 61.3) mentions Peritas, which had been reared and was loved by the Macedonian conqueror, adding that the king founded a city and gave it the animal's name (Le Bohec-Bouhet 2011, 494–95). With regard to the Successors, horses and dogs continued to be associated to their careers in different ways, although it remains difficult to gauge the extent to which these domestic species, without further qualifications, can be labelled as specifically royal emblems. Were they not signs of aristocratic power and leisure in general? Or could they not have been remembered just for their qualities, such as bravery and fidelity? This seems to be at least the story about Lysimachus' dead body, protected by his hound at Corupedium (see Pownall, this volume), which inspired a true *logos* in ancient historiography (Landucci 1990). Yet we hear about the Nesaean royal mares inherited from the Persian kings by the new conquerors, hence the interest of Eumenes in capturing the royal herds of horse that were pasturing about Mount Ida (Plu. *Eum.* 8.3; Anson 2004, 117). We are told that in 315 Seleucus barely managed to escape from Antigonus' agents in Babylon thanks to the speed of his mount (D.S. 19.55.5–7; Malal. *Chron.* 8.202 Dindorf). Did the providential steed inspire the recurrent motif of a horned horse head on his coins, a royal emblem as it were of divine favour? According to Malalas, the king later set up at Antioch a statue of the head of a horse with a gilded helmet next to it, with an inscription recalling the animal's service: 'On this Seleucus escaped to safety from Antigonus' (see Babelon 1890, xxiii). At any rate, one thing is certain: animals emerge or reinforce their position as icons of royal and dynastic pre-eminence among the Successors. The lion played a central role in Lysimachus' royal imagery, as numismatic evidence shows (Mørkholm 1991, 81), thereby giving colour to the story about his heroic origins as lion-tamer (Lund 1992, 6–8); the bull's horns belonged to the standard portraiture of Demetrius Poliorcetes, probably recalling a kind of assimilation to Poseidon Taurus (Pollit 1986, 32; Mørkholm 1991, 79); the eagle, symbol of Zeus and king of birds, appeared associated to the warrior life of Pyrrhus (Plu. *Pyrrh.* 10.1); the serpents arose from the Egyptian earth to animalize the Ptolemaic iconography of

Alexander (see Ogden, this volume), alongside the ram's horns of Ammon; even the panther of Dionysus entered the zoological repertoire of the candidates for the new *basileia*, and no wonder a contemporary mosaic at Pella depicts the god riding the elegant feline (Pollit 1986, 213 fig. 225).

The bestiary of Greek mythology, therefore, may have shaped the new royal portraiture, probably to proclaim the king's extraordinary qualities, if not to suggest or to assert his divinity. In other words, zoology is likely to have played a role in the process of constructing the king's identity and public persona.

If self-fashioning among the Diadochi involved special relationships to certain animals, could we detect the manipulations of the images and even the polemical intention of the iconographies? Did the contenders wage battles of images (say, *iconomachiae*) making use of a bestiary ad hoc? Another question pertains to ethnicity and ethnic boundaries: might a creature from an exotic country become an acceptable symbol of political power in a Greco-Macedonian milieu? As a long term phenomenon, kingship has normally established a strong bond with the forces of nature, beginning with the animals (see, v.g., Franco 2005; Belozerskaya 2006). To what degree was it the case among the Successors and to what degree would we be entitled to speak of an animalization of the kingly idea and image? Did the nature essentially charismatic of the new *basileia* favour this trend?

These and other related problems guide my research agenda for the future, but in the present paper I would like to restrict my analysis to one case study: that of elephants.

From Perdiccas to Ptolemy

Probably the earliest testimony about the relationship between animals and kingship under the Successors is provided by Alexander's hearse. According to Diodorus (18.3.5; 26.1), Perdiccas and the marshals assigned its preparation to Arrhidaeus (Berve 1926, no. 145; Heckel 2006, 53), apparently a regent's man or at least under his control (Rathmann 2005, 35; Stewart 1993, 218). Perdiccas must have been in the end the supervisor of the whole work, including its iconographic program. No doubt the design of the hearse reflected the official representation of Alexander's empire at the court at that given moment, comprising Greco-Macedonian and Asian elements in artful combination.[1] Its hybrid and ecumenical conception was reinforced by the animal imagery chosen for the outer decoration of the carriage, which included Persian goat-stags and lions (D.S. 18.26.5; 27.1). In addition, two other species, horses and elephants, formed part of a series of historical representations. Four long painted tablets exhibited the four arms of the imperial army: infantry, cavalry, navy, and elephants. The latter were no doubt Indian elephants, shown arrayed for war and carrying native mahouts in front and Macedonians fully armed behind them (D.S. 18.27.1). The appearance of the pachyderms certainly introduced an unprecedented and striking image in the history of Greek art and representation of royal power. With Perdiccas' fiat, Arrhidaeus bore witness to the recent incorporation of the Indian beasts into the Macedonian army (Scullard 1974, 75; Alonso, forthcoming) and, at the same time, he set up a model that would prevail in Hellenistic iconography for many years: a whole body elephant carrying his mahout along with a couple of warriors. The chiliarch himself had employed the elephants alongside the cavalry in order to intimidate the infantry of Meleager (Curt. 10.9.11–18), and then he had inaugurated an exotic and terrifying method of capital punishment against the leaders of the rebels, the execution by elephant.[2] The elephant, in effect, was to be accepted as an emblem of the king's power, mainly among Seleucids and Ptolemies, to the extent that regular troops are to be seen mounting these beasts on reliefs, terracottas, paintings, and coins (Scullard 1974, pls. 7, 12, 21b, fig. 15). But, unlike Indian rajas or later Kushan monarchs, the Greco-Macedonian *basileus* is never featured riding or mounting the animal.[3] No legends or myths of elephants providentially associated to royal figures are attested in Hellenistic literature either, contrary to Sassanid (see, v.g., *Book of the Deeds of Ardashir, Son of Papag* 1.10,13). As far as I know, there is no record of any Hellenistic king, including Alexander the Great, fighting a battle on one of his elephants, with the exception of Ptolemy Ceraunus. According to Memnon of Heraclea (*FGH* 434 F 88), he was killed in Macedonia by the Celts, 'who had captured him alive after the elephant on which he was riding was injured and threw him off'.[4] Should we rule out the possibility of finding any iconography of a Hellenistic king mounting the great pachyderm?[5]

Elephants appear on the coins issued by Ptolemy in Alexandria (Zervos 1967, series B-v). The chronology of issue v, introducing a new obverse type with the head of the deified Alexander in an elephant headdress, has been slightly lowered by Lorber (2005, 62) to c. 320 (Macedonian year 320/19). The revised dating, accepted by Arnold-Biucchi (2006, 60) and Stewart (2007, thus rectifying 1993, 233), reinforces the claim that the new money's inauguration followed not only the hijack of the hearse and the funeral in Memphis, but also the failure of Perdiccas' invasion of Egypt, as first Svoronos (1904, 54) and later Kuschel (1961, 17) had supposed (cf. Brown 1984, 406–09; Dahmen 2007, 10 n. 5; Le Rider, Callataÿ 2006, 100).

Ptolemy's tetradrachms are famous for their being the first official portrait of Alexander minted by any of the Successors and – provided that the gold double daric allegedly from the Mir Zakah Deposit is not authentic[6] – for their inaugural image of the king wearing an elephant scalp and Ammon's horns; from series C-xii and D-xiii on, dated by Lorber (2005) to 313/12 and 312/11, a scaly aegis and the Dionysian *mitra* will be incorporated.[7] I would like to add to the previous research interpretations that the animal's meaning is not the same in the imperial iconography of the regent as on the coinage of the satrap. While in Perdiccas' rendering the Indian pachyderms strengthened the idea of Alexander's multiethnic military superpower, being featured as one of its redoubtable weapons, the elephant scalp must be read for what it was, a war trophy, an icon of a formidable beast that was nevertheless defeated by the Macedonian phalanx. There is no need to insist on Ptolemy's separatist agenda from the very beginning of his governorship, to which his monetary policy bears ample witness too (Reden 2007, 43–48; Caroli 2007, 232–35). Unlike the imperial ideology of the hearse, ethnicity operated on the Ptolemaic coinage polemically and centrifugally, as it proclaimed Macedonian superiority over the emblematic - and royal - zoology of India, at the same time as it rooted Alexander's apotheosis on the Egyptian and Libyan soil. Moreover, specialists have pointed out that the satrap's new coinage was introduced to supplant Alexander's own Heracles tetradrachms, the semiotic implication being this: as the lion scalp was to his ancestor, so was now the elephant scalp to Alexander.[8] In the aftermath of the Nile battle, the innovative type with the *exuviae elephantis* could make full sense: it was to celebrate Ptolemy's victory over Perdiccas' 200 elephants by invoking Alexander's triumph over Porus' elephants – and remember that the satrap himself repulsed the beasts with Alexander-like élan, personally blinding the lead beast with a long spear and wounding its mahout (D.S. 18.34.2; cf. Svoronos 1904, 54; Kuschel 1961, 17; Brown 1984, 409; Bosworth 2007, 20–21). The demoralized invaders realized too late that Perdiccas at the Nile would play the role, not of Alexander, but of the Indian Porus at the Hydaspes.[9]

The hypothesis that this peculiar numismatic type derived from some cult-statue of the dead conqueror at Alexandria,[10] need not be incompatible with the interpretation of the tetradrachms as a message of victory. If the monument was set up before the regent's invasion, on the occasion of Alexander's funeral in Memphis, it would have anticipated the idea that the Indian beasts were not invincible; the ensuing imitation of the *exuviae elephantis* by the coin engravers would have confirmed the validity of that prediction once Perdiccas was defeated. In the event that the supposed statue was made after the Nile battle, both sculptor(s) and engraver(s) would have worked as part of a coordinated plan that aimed at designing an image of Alexander befitting the new satrap's political situation.

On an intertextual analysis (see Allen 2000, 174–81, for the non-literary arts), we may conclude that Ptolemy's emissions not only refuted the unionist program advocated by the regent, but they even departed from the neutral iconography of the Porus coins, especially the smaller tetradrachm specimens with the bowman and chariot types (Holt 2003, pls. 6–12; Price 1991, pl. CLIX, i–j). Without denying the possibility that both the decadrachms and the tetradrachms may have commemorated Alexander's victory over the Indian armies (Holt 2003, 139–65), it is equally true that their devices do not seek to belittle the enemy (Lane Fox 1996, 99–100), leaving ample room for different readings (the most idealistic of which has been probably that of Price 1982). If the single combat scene of the tetradrachms conveyed the idea of a certain military and zoological parity (Alonso, forthcoming), with the raja on his imposing pachyderm facing the Macedonian king on his famous horse, this compromise has disappeared in Ptolemy's coins. To reinforce the Ptolemaic hierarchy of zoology, series C and D featured on the reverse an eagle standing on a thunderbolt, the personal badge of Ptolemy, next to Zeus or Athena – series B had already presented the father god holding his own eagle.

No departure from this fundamental stance is to be seen in the satrap's successive emissions, series C-xii to D-xvii (c. 313/12–295, according to Lorber 2005). I think that the military developments can provide us with a context to explain the continuity of significance of the *exuviae elephantis*. Whether Ptolemy managed to organize an elephant corps with the exemplars taken from Perdiccas (so Epplet 2007, 223; *contra* Scullard 1974, 97 and Bosworth 2007, 20), and whether this contingent was further reinforced or consolidated with the animals captured at Gaza from Demetrius (D.S. 19.84.4), is perhaps an open question. Judging from the aforementioned battle, where Ptolemy and his ally Seleucus had to counteract the enemy's 43 elephants (D.S. 19.82.3–4), not with the same beasts, but with a mine-field of iron-spiked devices (D.S. 19.83.2), one could reach the conclusion that the booty of 320, if substantial in Indian reinforcements, had became useless eight years later. It cannot be a coincidence that after this victory Ptolemy struck at Sidon, in the now occupied Phoenicia, an issue of tetradrachms with the new types, dated to 312–11 (Zervos 1967, 7–8; Mørkholm 1991, 65), while as soon as Demetrius and his father recaptured the city, its mint reverted to Alexander standard types (Wheatley 2003, 274). Ptolemy certainly could boast of having beaten the fearsome animals of the young Antigonid, yet the satrap's counsellors dissuaded him from confronting the father's army, 'which was many times stronger and had a larger number of elephants' (D.S. 19.93.6). Again, in 306, the satrap thwarted an invasion by Antigonus, commanding a strong army that included no fewer than 83 pachyderms (D.S. 20.73.2), largely by the expedient of offering the enemy soldiers generous bribes if they would desert and by implementing an effective coastal defence (D.S. 20.75.1–3). Of local elephants opposing the Antigonids Diodorus says nothing. It is no surprise, therefore, that in the Lagid's ideology of victory, at least during his satrapal period, the great pachyderms held a negative connotation, as spoils of war and ethnic emblem of military defeat. This initial orientation should not rule out the possibility, hinted by Scullard (1974, 81), that Ptolemy may have liked to reserve some of these animals for festive and ritual celebrations in honour of Alexander at the capital (see below on his gold staters with the Argead in elephant quadriga). At any rate, the Ptolemaic policy in this regard will begin to change with the second member of the dynasty, Philadelphus, who is reported to have undertaken the systematic hunting of African beasts for war uses (see, v.g., Casson 1993).

Seleucus' innovations

We should expect some degree of polysemy when interpreting the *exuviae elephantis*, particularly if we bear in mind that this icon formed part of a variable set of attributes (horns, forehead band, aegis, beardlessness, long hair, expressive eyes, *anastolē*), not to speak of the correlated obverse or reverse type, which should be understood as complementary and interrelated. Obviously the variations introduced in Alexander's portraiture depended on the political intentions of the issuing authority. From the very beginning the impressive headdress became a symbol of evident superiority, probably with several overlapping evocations: invincibility, universal hegemony, apotheosis, conquest of India, mystical identification with the ruler responsible for the minting, and very soon association with Dionysus (Smith 1988, 41). It was, therefore, a symbol easy to use and manipulate. Evidence of this is that, hardly ten years after the first Ptolemaic emission in 320, Agathocles of Syracuse coined a gold stater that had on the obverse a head wearing an elephant scalp, with Ammon's horns and aegis, and on its reverse a striding, winged Athena, helmeted and brandishing shield and spear, with the legend *agathokleos* (Stewart 1993, fig. 87). This victory-coin is usually connected with the tyrant's great success outside Carthage in 310 and is supposed to depict Alexander in imitation of the Lagid types (see Maritz 2004, 42–46). However, unlike Ptolemy, Agathocles did not have to fight elephants, for the Carthaginians acquired them later, and he lacked them too. Consequently, the use of the elephantine icon became in his coinage a pure metaphor of triumph, with an evocative yet not narrative function.

On the other side of the Hellenistic world, from Syria to the Upper Satrapies, our zoological icon will experience more important changes, both in form and connotation. The military underestimation of the Indian beasts, according to the Ptolemaic reading, does not seem to have disappeared on the coinage of Seleucus bearing Alexander clad in elephant's skin - though, not by chance, without the ram's horns of Ammon, an Egyptian god (cf. Goukowsky 1978, 127). A coordinated special emission of gold darics and double darics, assigned to the eastern mints of Babylon (*SC* no. 101), Susa (*SC* no. 183) and Ecbatana (*SC* no. 219), carries an obverse type with a head of the deified king in the new headdress and a reverse with a Nike holding wreath and *stylis*. These gold series, on the Persian standard, were accompanied by bronze issues at Susa and Ecbatana, reproducing the same obverse types (*SC* nos. 188–190, 222–223) and adding the legend *Alexandrou* on the reverse. No doubt the Seleucid elephant scalp imitates Ptolemy's silver coinage, with which Seleucus must have become very familiar while exiled from Babylonia at Alexandria, as Newell (*ESM* 112) already pointed out. The legend 'of Alexander' may have been influenced by the Lagid precedent too, though ultimately both reverse designs derived from Alexander's own Heracles/Zeus tetradrachms and Athena/Nike gold staters. Traditionally, the political context for these emissions had been placed in the years immediately after Seleucus' campaign against Chandragupta in 305/4, that is, c. 303/2, supposing that these gold staters and bronzes would be celebrating the Seleucid triumph by evoking Alexander's conquest of India.[11]

More recently, however, Kritt (1997, 108–18) has established a lower date c. 300–298 for the Alexander/Nike bronzes of Susa, based on their control connections and their inverted anchor symbol, and hence he has also concluded that their Ecbatana counterparts could be dated to the same years. The author has further hypothesized that the new iconographic type of Alexander in elephant-skin was first introduced to all Seleucid coinage in this period (see also *SC* 48, 74–75, 87, following him). On his reasoning, only the trophy coins from Susa (*SC* nos. 173–76) would commemorate the military triumph over Chandragupta, judging by their reverse legend *Seleukou* and the clear victory type, whereas the subsequent bronze and gold coinage would refer exclusively to the Indian campaign of Alexander. In my opinion, Kritt may be perfectly right as regards the bronze denominations minted in the two Iranian capitals, but I would not rule out altogether a dating before Ipsus for some of the gold emissions; more so if we consider that the latter may have worked as a presentation issue and the bronze as an imitation (Stewart 1993, 315).[12] Certainly, we have good reasons to think that the Indian campaign was far from being a full military success (yet, contrast Mehl 1986, 183–86 with Grainger 1990a, 108–09), but the Seleucid propaganda had no need to speak the language of the historical truth, and the least to the native populations of Babylonia, Persia and the other Iranian satrapies. *Exuviae elephantis* meant, again, celebration of victory against the fabulous beasts from the Far East, that is, against their royal owners; and, once again, they implied evocation of, and identification with, Alexander. Furthermore, if the latter returned from India with about 200 elephants (Arr. *An.* 6.2.2; *Ind.* 19.1), his successor could claim to have got from the Maurya more than twice that amount (Str. 15.2.9).

It is my contention that the great shift in the symbolism of this animal on the Seleucid coinage can be detected after Ipsus. From that moment text and images addressed a very different situation. Ipsus had not been an ordinary battle according to Greek standards. As Mehl (1986, 206) has rightly pointed out, the scale in the use of elephants and the profit Seleucus made of them were unprecedented and had no equivalent in the history of Hellenistic warfare. Powerful *Tyche* had decided that the 'master of elephants' (Plu. *Demetr.* 25.4), rather than his colleague Lysimachus, would become the moral victor and the charismatic figure of the moment. His feelings are not difficult to imagine, especially regarding the architects of triumph: pride of owning such animals and gratitude towards them. At least for once in the Hellenistic age a Greco-Macedonian ruler may have made his the words of the Mauryan *Arthaśāstra* (2.2.13): 'The victory of the king is in principal a matter of the elephant' (see Sick 2002, 131–32).

In effect, the key role of Seleucus in the defeat of Antigonus and Demetrius was duly signaled by different royal mints that introduced, for the first time among the Successors, the image of an impressive elephant standing alone. The coin type in itself was no novelty, if we remember the tetradrachm series from Babylonia associated with the Porus decadrachms, bearing the sole pachyderm on the reverse (Holt 2003, pls. 6–10). The programmatic dimension of the Seleucid emissions did not involve great innovations either: Seleucus, in fact, was retaking Perdiccas' iconographic treatment of the Indian beasts as one of the four arms of the multiethnic imperial army, and above all he was giving visual manifestation to the Seleucid shock force. Nevertheless, if the new iconography depicting an elephant head was not particularly significant in itself, the appearance of the same head with horns involved a qualitative change, for it aimed to strengthen the animal's status within the zoology of early Hellenistic kingship. And in case any doubt remained, the legend *basileōs seleukou* on the reverse of these pieces made clear enough the royal origin of the message delivered to all the peoples of Asia.

Susa produced at least two series of silver staters with elephant type on the reverse (*SC* no. 187; cf. *ESM* nos. 323, 330), dated c. 288/7, in addition to an issue of silver drachms with elephant head type (*SC* no. 181; cf. *ESM* no. 317) and a lesser denomination of silver obols featuring the same type with horns (*SC* no. 182; cf. *ESM* no. 325), respectively ascribed by Kritt (1997, 33, 61–65) to the years 291–288/7 and 287–281. The mint of Seleucia on the Tigris, for its part, had already coined two bronze denominations (B and C) c. 296/5 or later (*SC* nos. 128–129; cf. *ESM* nos. 15–18); from c. 296/5 they were followed by a (C) bronze denomination featuring the head of a horned elephant accompanied by a beardless Heracles on the obverse (*SC* no. 147). Bactria, so close to India, could not miss either, and there operated an uncertain mint that issued royal bronze coinage (A, B and C), showing a bearded Heracles as the main type and a standing horned and belled beast on the reverse (*SC* nos. 264–66). However, the initiative of using the elephant as a coin type since about the year 300 might have been taken by Apamea on the Orontes (see Hadley 1974, 62), a military centre that stabled the 500 war elephants of Seleucus (Str. 16.2.10). Newell (*WSM* 156–57) assigned to this mint one of the bronze denominations based on its Syrian fabric and martial types (*WSM* no. 1128, c. 300–280), noting that a hornless pachyderm, unlike the horned horse featured on the reverse, conveyed no mythological meaning, but directly alluded to the actual arsenal of elephants stationed at Apamea. If there seems to be full agreement on the explicitness of this elephantine type, as well as on the general chronology of the emission (cf. *SC* no. 35, more accurately c. 300–281), the interpretation of the equine's symbolism is more open (compare Babelon 1890, xxiii–xxv with *WSM* 156–57 and Mørkholm 1991, 75–76).

The growing importance and popularity of the elephant as a triumphant weapon in the Diadochi wars, especially after Ipsus, are shown by the fact that the animal emblem did not remain confined to the satrapies east of Apamea. As it happens, the numismatic iconography of the Indian beasts reached the westernmost domains of the first Seleucid. Further west in Syria, the mint of Antioch seems to have coined a silver hemiobol highly illustrative in terms of military propaganda: the Macedonian shield featured on the obverse, image and symbol of the conquerors' phalanx, was accompanied by an elephant head on the other side of the coin (*SC* no. 14, from c. 300). And at Pergamum, once reconfirmed in the governorship of the city by Seleucus, Philetairus emitted a splendid commemorative coinage with types honouring his new king, dated to 281 (*SC* no. 1; cf. *WSM* nos. 1528–29). Again a steed head with bull's horns figured on the obverse of the tetradrachms, while on the reverse an impressive pachyderm pointed openly to the elephant power of the Seleucid royal house. There is also some evidence that at least one other mint in Asia Minor issued the same denomination employing the Pergamene types (*SC* no. 2). Why this tribute to the new animals among the Greek subjects in 281? It has been maintained by Houghton and Lorber (*SC* 15) that the Attalid's aim was to celebrate Seleucus' reconquest of India and presumably also the role of his elephant corps at Corupedium. I find the Indian expedition too remote and too distant an event for celebration by a governor on the coast of Asia Minor, while the battles of Ipsus and above all Corupedium lay much closer in time.[13] There is no account of the course of the latter, but it would be strange if Seleucus did not put his elephant corps to good use against the troops of Lysimachus (see Scullard 1974, 99). This had been the case of his last battle against Demetrius, in 285 (Polyaen. 4.9.3; cf. Bar-Kochva

1976, 78). Note, at any rate, that the relevance of the pachyderm became stronger in the emissions from Apamea than in those from Pergamum, since the former exhibits the elephant as obverse type. For a purely Greek milieu an equine, either the divinized Bucephallus or the mount whose speed saved Seleucus' life, was more important than an exotic beast without any mythic pedigree (on which, see Wellmann 1905, 2252; Alonso, forthcoming).

Ptolemy and Seleucus: a battle of images?

Finally, coinciding with the second part (2nd phase) of the last issue (xvii) of series D (Jenkins group c), still featuring the elephant-capped Alexander, and perhaps one or two years later than the first post Ipsus emissions from Apamea with the standing elephant (*SC* no. 35, c. 300), another iconographic innovation took place in the Alexandria mint. Once again the Ptolemaic initiative proved to be daring, both in the realm of political ideology and artistic design. After having assumed the diadem, the Lagid became the first Successor to put his portrait on his coins, on gold staters, from c. 304 onwards, maybe in a date as late as 298 or even 297 (cf. Lorber 2005, for the lowered chronology). The reverse shows a chariot drawn by four elephants bearing a deified figure of Alexander, who stands armed with aegis and thunderbolt, and over the type the legend *ptolemaiou basileōs*.[14] On my reading, the image signifies not only the triumph of the apotheosized king over the Indians (cf. *SC* 7; Dahmen 2007, 12), but also his supernatural power over the forces of nature, symbolized in the huge strength of the two pairs of pachyderms – 'they submit mildly to his direction' (Bosworth 2007, 18). It is interesting to compare the Ptolemaic type with its Seleucid imitation and reinterpretation (*ESM* 38–39; *SC* 7), the elephant chariot series, mainly on silver denominations. They are tetradrachms, drachms and hemidrachms minted at Seleucia on the Tigris, from c. 296/5 (*SC* nos. 130–33, 155), with barbarous imitations after 296/5 (*SC* nos. 156–58); at Susa, from c. 295 (*SC* nos. 177–80), including a unique Artemis in elephant *biga* gold stater c. 287 (*SC* no. 163); at Aï Khanoum, from c. 285 (*SC* nos. 276–83, Ad19); and at two uncertain Bactrian mints, from c. 290/86 to 281, perhaps Bactra (*SC* nos. 259–63), with the same exceptional Apollo/Artemis type on the gold (*SC* no. 257), and Aï Khanoum (*SC* nos. 272–75). The Seleucid remake, the obverse of which presents a laureate head of Zeus – not the king's portrait –, inserts on the reverse a warlike goddess in a chariot, generally Athena, holding a shield and a spear in a gesture of attack, or Artemis, shooting an arrow from her bow, and it has the elephants horned, implying their divinity. Seleucus' appropriation of the design is completed by the addition of an anchor symbol, his personal badge, and the legend *basileōs seleukou*.

I think that the image modifications redefine the relationship of the Diadoch not so much with Alexander, as with the gods and the Indian beasts. The processional Alexander of Ptolemy in a quadriga – redolent of the Alexander in Philadelphus' Great Pompe (*FGH* 627 F 2.34) –[15] has disappeared in favour of a combatant Athena/Artemis in a quadriga or a biga, who not only commands over the elephants, as the Ptolemaic

Alexander does, but who fights with them too. Rather than an expression of the king's physical strength (so Sherwin-White and Kuhrt 1993, 23), which cannot be denied, but which is a message more explicit on Seleucus' coinage with the charging bull type (cf. Hadley 1964, 40; *WSM* 380; *SC* 8–9), we should see in this whimsical imagery a very personal exaltation of the animal servants, blessed by their association with two Olympians. The preeminence achieved by the beasts in the eyes of Seleucus and their ensuing appearance in the numismatic iconography after Ipsus seem to be consistent with their divinization, that is, with their insertion in the realm of mythology – Greek and Asiatic mythology. The Seleucid propaganda aimed at exploiting the power of images to carve a new space for the exotic creatures on a celestial level. As the winged steeds were to Zeus and to some other Olympians when riding their chariots, so were the horned elephants to Athena and Artemis according to the Seleucid version. The visual prompt must have been intelligible and appealing above all to the Greco-Macedonian mercenaries and settlers of the eastern cities, though without forgetting that many Iranians were the users of these coins and the potential readers of their types according to their own cultural codes.[16] The large horns, in effect, had served as symbols of supernatural power and apotheosis in the Mesopotamian tradition (at least from Naram-Sin of Akkad), which does not preclude recognizing that they now formed part of a general Dionysian symbolism, pervasive in Seleucus' coinage from the victory tetradrachms to the Dionysus/anchor bronzes of Aï Khanoum and the special horseman issue from Ecbatana (see Iossif, Lorber 2010, 156–60). But probably the entire semiotic power of these images will be missing if the modern viewer does not bear in mind the intertextual and polemical intention that also inspires them. For in the variations on the zoology of kingship we can reasonably guess a very conscious effort on the part of the emerging Nicator to detach his public persona from the old friend and protector, Ptolemy, now his rival because of the Ipsus booty (D.S. 21.1.5).

The symbolic elevation of the elephant's status in Seleucus' ideology of kingship went beyond the fine arts and the art of war, as if all this were not enough. In effect, Libanius (*Or.* 11.90) preserves a precious account dealing with the foundation rites of Antioch on the Orontes, of which there is no reason to distrust (see Mehl 1986, 207). 'In drawing out the limits of the city' - the orator narrates -, 'he [Seleucus] had elephants stationed around the area at places where he intended towers to be' (cf. also Downey 1963, 32 and Grainger 1990b, 56).

That said, it is to be noted that the official acceptance of the elephant in the zoology of the 'dynastic identity' - to use the lucky expression of Sherwin-White and Kuhrt 1993, 22 - took place not without certain limitations. Restrictions on the animal supply from India precluded the full generalization of elephants in the war scenarios of the *Diadochenzeit*, while ethnic prejudices surely prevented these beasts from reaching the high status they already enjoyed among the Indian rajas (see Alonso, forthcoming). A key case in point may be the so-called *elephantarchēs* bronze of Seleucus (*SC* no. 25), first studied in detail by Newell (*WSM* 102, no. 929). It shows on its obverse a figure seated on a rock holding an elephant goad (*ankh*) and on its reverse a horned head of the same animal. The great American numismatist had suggested that the seminude and bearded male might be an idealized representation of the Seleucid king as 'master of elephants', in the context of a victory issue celebrating Lysimachus' defeat in 281 with the involvement of the elephant corps. Recently, however, Iossif and Lorber (2010) have proved that the figure corresponds to Dionysus, among other more positive reasons, because 'it would be unthinkable that, for instance, a great owner of elephants such as Seleucus would have represented himself in the guise of an ordinary elephant handler, a profession far below the rank of king' (148). Letting aside the fact that Seleucus belongs to a new generation of sovereigns that are portrayed unbearded in imitation of Alexander (Alonso 2010), I agree that even the mere iconographic rendering of a Macedonian *basileus* as *elephantarchēs* in the strict sense - an official position in the Seleucid army (Bar-Kochva 88, 90–91; Sick 2002, 134) – would have been unacceptably underestimating, let alone the possible connotations of Indian identity. Yet, what might be unworthy of a living Macedonian king – being the rider of an elephant or even the driver of an elephant chariot – was allowed to a god or to an apotheosized mortal (see in general Matz 1952).

Final remarks

There is a Spanish proverb that runs: *dime con quién andas y te diré quién eres.* Applied to our case study, it could perhaps turn out this way: tell me how you get along with the elephants, and I'll tell you the kind of Diadoch you are. It may not be by chance that the two most successful among the Successors, Ptolemy and Seleucus, defined their public persona by constant reference to these animals - the Seleucid conqueror in more direct and positive terms than the cautious Lagid, whose attitude was much more ambivalent. After Alexander, Perdiccas had led the way, and who knows if his premature death may have frustrated the development of new roles at the court and additional iconographies for the fourth arm of the imperial army.

A military and pragmatic approach toward the Indian beasts, apparently without further ideological pretentions, seems to have prevailed among the other contenders.[17] If Lysimachus ever got some elephants (cf. D.S. 21.1.2), they seem to have left no mark in history, and at any rate the king of Thrace preferred the forepart of an attacking lion as his distinctive badge on coinage (Landucci 1992, 19–20, 46). Furthermore, his splendid Alexander tetradrachms and drachms issued after Ipsus, in 297/96, maintain the ram's horn of Zeus Ammon (Mørkholm 1991, nos. 178–82), in tune with Ptolemy's image of the great conqueror, though at variance with Seleucus', that omits the Egyptian symbol; but, at the same time, Lysimachus' reinterpretation diverges equally from the Ptolemaic and Seleucid Alexander, in that the arrogant *exuviae elephantis* – still present in the last phase of Ptolemy's series D-xvii, c. 298–295 – are not incorporated to the new design. As regards Demetrius, he proved to be imaginative and daring when designing his royal image (Newell 1927, 169; Smith 1988, 38–39, 52), but the Indian beasts were no longer a relevant part of his army after Ipsus, while his personal memories of Gaza may not have helped a lot to love them; in fact, there is an anecdote in Plutarch (*Demetr.* 25.4) that recalls the Antigonid mocking Seleucus as the *elephantarchēs*. Cassander, who came to possess a non-negligible herd (D.S. 19.35.7), embodied a European ethos too distant from the Asiatic sources of these animals. Of course, there also operated the members of the older generation, such as Antipater, Antigonus, Polyperchon and, perhaps in the same vein, Philip Arrhidaeus. If it is true that they had no prejudices at all concerning the use of elephants in battle, it seems equally true that they overlooked the symbolic potential of this zoology as an emblem of kingship or leadership, probably because the seniors did not feel the need to develop a new public image for themselves (Alonso 2010). In this sense, the case of Antigonus is particularly striking, bearing in mind that his campaigns and his victories owed so much to the new weapon of war, even to the extent of being credited by Polyaenus (4.6.7) as 'the only general who used those beasts', in about 319 (see Billows 1990, 78, 353–54, with the figures), and by Pausanias (1.12.3) as the Successor who got 'more [elephants] than any' other king; or considering that he may have followed the custom of adorning his beasts with coloured (purple) trappings, perhaps after the rajas' fashion (compare Plu. *Eum.* 14.4 with D.S. 17.86.5). Yet, the posthumous Alexanders of Monophthalmus' coinage reveal a conventional stance, I dare to say typical of the seniors, like Antipater's, or Arrhidaeus' himself, rooted in the Macedonian motherland. For his part, Eumenes could be as imaginative as any other among the Successors, and there it is the device of the ceremonial tent dedicated to the Alexander cult from 318 (D.S. 18.61.1; Plu. *Eum.* 13.3–4; cf. Anson 2004, 150–52, 165). Revealingly, however, the Cardian is not reported to have arrayed any elephant unit around this magnificent tent, contrary to the precedent set up by the Argead for his own pavilion (*FGH* 81 F 41; Polyaen. 4.3.24), and in spite of the fact that he received a year later a contingent of 120 pachyderms directly from India (D.S. 19.15.5). A younger contemporary of the Diadochi, Pyrrhus, cultivated a martial style closely associated with the elephant force, and the Roman people kept very much alive the souvenir of his intimidating strike force on Italian soil (Scullard 1974, 101–13). The elephantine elements, nonetheless, are lacking in the Epeirote's known portraiture (Smith 1988, 64–65; Brown 1995, 31–22), it being significant that the elephants and other weapons carved in relief on his funeral monument at Argos are not said to be accompanied by any representation of the royal person, neither as rider nor as commander (Paus. 2.21.4).

Ptolemy Ceraunus, probably more impressed by Seleucus' warrior achievements than by his own father's, seems to have shared the same passion for these animals as his protector. Justin (17.2.14) even makes him lend 50 elephants to Pyrrhus for the Italian campaign (see Heinen 1972, 72–74). But, Ptolemy's eldest son clearly lacked the virtues of Nicator, and I wonder whether his death in combat riding an elephant might have been interpreted not only as an extravagance, but also as a bad omen for every king to come who preferred a mount like his to the noble horse. After all, nobody had ever seen the invincible Alexander engaging in battle on one of his Indian beasts.[18]

Abbreviations

ESM Newell, E. T. (1978) *The Coinage of the Eastern Seleucid Mints: From Seleucus I to Antiochus III.* New York.

SC Houghton, A. and C. Lorber (2002) *Seleucid Coins: A Comprehensive Catalogue. Part I: Seleucus I through Antiochus III.* 2 vols. Lancaster/London.

WSM Newell, E. T. (1977) *The Coinage of the Western Seleucid Mints: From Seleucus I to Antiochus III.* New York.

Bibliography

Allen, G. (2000) *Intertextuality*. London and New York.

Alonso Troncoso, V. (2010) The Bearded King and the Bearded Hero: From Philip to Alexander the Great. In E. Carney and D. Ogden (eds) *Philip II and Alexander the Great: Father and Son, Lives and Afterlives*, 13–24, Oxford.

Alonso Troncoso, V. (forthcoming) Para una zoología de la realeza: Alejandro Magno y los elefantes. In M.-J. Werlings and J. Zurbach (eds) *Melanges en mémoire de Pierre Carlier*. Rennes.

Anson, E. M. (2004) *Eumenes of Cardia. A Greek among Macedonians*. Leiden.

Arnold-Biucchi, C. (2006) *Alexander's Coins and Alexander's Image*. Cambridge, MA.

Babelon, E. (1890) *Catalogue des monnaies grecques de la Bibliothèque Nationale. Les Rois de Syrie, d'Arménie et de Commagène*. Paris.

Bar-Kochva, B. (1976) *The Seleucid Army*. Cambridge.

Belozerskaya, M. (2006) *The Medici Giraffe and Other Tales of Exotic Animals and Power*. New York.

Berve, H. (1926) *Das Alexanderreich auf prosopographischer Grundlage*. II. Munich.

Bieber, M. (1964) *Alexander the Great in Greek and Roman Art*. Chicago.

Billows, R. A. (1990) *Antigonos the One-Eyed and the Creation of the Hellenistic State*. Berkeley and Los Angeles.

Bopearachchi, O. and P. Flandrin (2005) *Le portrait d'Alexandre le Grand. Histoire d'une découverte pour l'humanité*. Monaco.

Bosworth, A. B. (2002) *The Legacy of Alexander. Politics, Warfare, and Propaganda under the Successors*. Oxford.

Bosworth, A. B. (2007) Rider in the Chariot: Ptolemy, Alexander and the Elephants. In K. A. Sheedy (ed.) *Alexander and the Hellenistic Kingdoms. The Westmoreland Collection*, 17–22, Sydney.

Brown, B. R. (1984) Art History in Coins: Portrait Issues of Ptolemy I. In M. Bonacasa and A. Di Vita (eds) *Alessandria e il mondo ellenistico-romano*, II, 405–17, Roma.

Brown, B. R. (1995) *Royal Portraits in Sculpture and Coins: Pyrrhos and the Successors of Alexander the Great*. New York.

Caroli, C. A. (2007) *Ptolemaios I. Soter. Herrscher zweier Kulturen*. Constance.

Casson, L. (1993) Ptolemy II and the Hunting of African elephants, *Transactions of the American Philological Association* 123, 247–60.

Dahmen, K. (2007) *The Legend of Alexander the Great on Greek and Roman Coins*. New York.

Downey, G. (1963) *Ancient Antioch*. Princeton, NJ.

Epplett, C. (2007) War Elephants in the Hellenistic World. In W. Heckel, L. Tritle and P. Wheatley (eds) *Alexander's Empire. Formulation to Decay*, 209–32, Claremont, CA.

Fischer-Bossert W. (2006) 'Review' of Bopearachchi and Flandrin 2005, *American Numismatic Society* 5.2: http://ansmagazine.com/Summer06/Portrait.

Franco, C. (2005) L'animale e l'eletto: Segni di regalità nel mondo antico. In E. Cingano, A. Ghersetti and L. Milano (eds) *Animali tra zoologia e letteratura nella cultura classica e orientale*, 233–47, Padua.

Goukowsky, P. (1978) *Essai sur les origines du mythe d'Alexandre (336-270 av. J.-C.)*. I. Nancy.

Grainger, J. D. (1990a) *Seleukos Nikator: Constructing a Hellenistic Kingdom*. London and New York.

Grainger, J. D. (1990b) *The Cities of Seleukid Syria*. Oxford.

Hadley, R. A. (1964) *Deified Kingship and Propaganda Coinage in the Early Hellenistic Age: 323-280 BC.* Diss. Pennsylvania.

Hadley, R. A. (1974) Royal Propaganda of Seleucus I and Lysimachus, *Journal of Hellenic Studies* 94, 50–65.

Hazzard, R. A. (1995) *Ptolemaic Coins: An Introduction for Collectors*. Toronto.

Heckel, W. (2006) *Who's Who in the Age of Alexander the Great*. Malden, MA.

Heinen, H. (1972) *Untersuchungen zur hellenistischen Geschichte des 3. Jahrhunderts v. Chr. Zur Geschichte der Zeit des Ptolemaios Keraunos und zum chremonideischen Krieg*. Wiesbaden.

Holt, F. L. (2003) *Alexander the Great and the Mystery of the Elephant Medallions*. Berkeley and Los Angeles.

Holt, F. L. (2006) Ptolemy's Alexandrian Postcript, *Saudi Aramco World* 57.6, 4–9 (= http://www.saudiaramcoworld.com/issue/200606/ptolemy.s.alexandrian.postscript.htm).

Hoover, O. D. (2011) Never Mind the Bullocks: Taurine Imagery as a Multicultural Expression of Royal and Divine Power under Seleukos I Nikator. In P. P. Iossif, S. Chankowski and C. Lorber (eds) *More than Men, Less than Gods: Studies on Royal Cult and Imperial Worship*, 197–228, Leuven.

Hurter, S. (2006) Review of Bopearachchi and Flandrin 2005, *Swiss Numismatic Review* 85, 185–95.

Iossif, P. (2004) Les monnaies de Suse frappées par Séleucos Ier: Une nouvelle approche, *Numismatica e Antichità classiche* 33, 249–71.

Iossif, P. and C. Lorber (2010) The Elephantarches Bronze of Seleucos I Nikator, *Syria* 87, 147–64.

Jenkins, G. K. (1990) *Ancient Greek Coins*. 2nd rev. ed. London.

Kritt, B. (1997) *The Early Seleucid Mint of Susa*. Lancaster.

Kuschel, B. (1961) Die neuen Münzbilder des Ptolemaios Soter, *Jahrbuch für Numismatik und Geldgeschichte* 11, 9–18.

Landucci Gattinoni, F. (1990) La morte di Antigono e di Lisimaco. In M. Sordi (ed.) *Dulce et decorum est pro patria mori. La morte in combattimento nell'antichità*, 111–26, Milan.

Landucci Gattinoni, F. (1992) *Lisimaco di Tracia: Un sovrano nella prospettiva del primo ellenismo*. Milan.

Lane Fox, R. (1996) Text and Image: Alexander the Great, Coins and Elephants, *Bulletin of the Institute of Classical Studies* 41, 87–108.

Le Bohec-Bouhet, S. (2011) Les chiens en Macédoine dans l'Antiquité. In N. Badoud (ed.) *Philologos Dionysios: Melanges offerts au professeur Denis Knoepfler*, 491–515, Geneva.

Le Rider, G. and F. de Callataÿ (2006) *Les Séleucides et les Ptolémées. L' héritage monétaire et financier d'Alexandre le Grand*. Monaco.

Lorber, C. L. (2005) A Revised Chronology for the Coinage of Ptolemy I, *Numismatic Chronicle* 165, 45–64.

Lund, H. S. (1992) *Lysimachus: A Study in Early Hellenistic Kingship*. London and New York.

Mariotta G. (2004) La cerimonia del trasporto in Egitto del corpo di Alessandro: il carro funebre del re (Diod. 18.26–28). In H.-D. Heimann, S. Knippschild and V. Mínguez (eds) *Ceremoniales, ritos y representación del poder*, 89–108, Castellón de La Plana.
Maritz, J. (2004) The Face of Alexandria - the Face of Africa? In A. Hirst and M. Silk (eds) *Alexandria Real and Imagined*, 41–66, London.
Matz, F. (1952) Der Gott auf den Elephantenwagen, *Abhandlungen der Geistes- und Sozialwissenschaftlichen Klasse* (Akad. Wiss. Lit. Mainz) 10, 720–63.
Mehl, A. (1986) *Seleukos Nikator und sein Reich*. Leuven.
Mørkholm, O. (1991) *Early Hellenistic Coinage: From the Accession of Alexander to the Peace of Apamea (336–188 BC)*. Cambridge.
Newell, E. T. (1927) *The Coinages of Demetrius Poliorcetes*. Oxford.
Olbrycht, M. J. (2004) *Aleksander Wielki: i świat irański*. Rzeszów.
Pal, P. (1986) *Indian Sculpture. I: Circa 500 BC–AD 700*. Los Angeles.
Pollit, J. J. (1986) *Art in the Hellenistic Age*. Cambridge.
Price, M. J. (1982) The Porus Coinage of Alexander the Great: A Symbol of Concord and Community. In S. Scheers and J. Quaegebeur (eds) *Studia Paulo Naster oblata*, I, 75–85, Leuven.
Price, M. J. (1991) *The Coinage in the Name of Alexander the Great and Philip Arrhidaeus*. 2 vols. Zurich and London.
Rathmann, M. (2005) *Perdikkas zwischen 323 und 320. Nachlasser des Alexanderreiches oder Autokrat?* Vienna.
Reden, S. v. (2007) *Money in Ptolemaic Egypt. From the Macedonian Conquest to the End of the Third Century BC*. Cambridge.
Scullard, H. H. (1974) *The Elephant in the Greek and Roman World*. Cambridge.
Sherwin-White, S. and A. Kuhrt (1993) *From Samarkhand to Sardis. A New Approach to the Seleucid Empire*. Berkeley and Los Angeles.
Sick, D. H. (2002) An Indian Perspective on the Graeco-Roman Elephant, *The Ancient World* 33, 126–46.
Smith, R. R. R. (1988) *Hellenistic Royal Portraits*. Oxford.
Stähler, K. (1993) Alexanders Leichenwagen. Archäologische Kommentierungs- und Interpretationsversuche. In Idem (ed.) *Form und Funktion. Kunstwerke als politisches Ausdrucksmittel*, 59–31, Münster.
Stewart, A. (1993) *Faces of Power. Alexander's Image and Hellenistic Politics*. Berkeley and Los Angeles.
Stewart, A. (2007) Review of Arnold-Biucchi 2006, *Bryn Mawr Classical Review* 08.58 (= http://bmcr.brynmawr.edu/2007/2007-08-58.html).
Svenson, D. (1995) *Darstellungen hellenistischer Könige mit Götterattributen*. Frankfurt.
Svoronos, J. N. (1904) *ΤΑ ΝΟΜΙΣΜΑΤΑ ΤΟΥ ΚΡΑΤΟΥΣ ΤΩΝ ΡΤΟΛΕΜΑΙΩΝ*. Vols. 1 and 3. Athens.
Tafazzoli, A. (1975) Elephant: A Demotic Creature and a Symbol of Sovereignty, *Acta Iranica* 5, 395–98.
Tarn, W. W. (1930) *Hellenistic Military and Naval Developments*. Cambridge.
Tarn, W. W. (1966) *The Greeks in Bactria and India*. Cambridge.
Wellmann, M. (1905) Elefant, *RE* V.2, 2248–57.
Wheatley, P. (2003) The Year 22 Tetradrachms of Sidon and the Date of the Battle of Gaza, *Zeitschrift für Papyrologie und Epigraphik* 144, 268–76.
Zervos, O. H. (1967) The Early Tetradrachms of Ptolemy I, *ANS Museum Notes* 13, 1–16.

Notes

1 For good discussions on the iconography and decoration of the carriage, with the previous bibliography, see Stähler 1993; Stewart 1993, 216–21; Goukowsky 2002, 137–40; Mariotta 2004; and Olbrycht 2004, 311–13.

2 For centuries it was a method of capital punishment in South and Southeast Asia, and particularly in India. Among the Diadochi, Eumenes proclaimed before his army that he would rather die that way than be delivered to Antigonus (Plu. *Eum.* 17.5).

3 As Pal 1986, 71 has noticed, Kushan king Vidma Kadphises is shown on his coins riding an elephant, in 'a representation for which there is no Indo-Greek or Scytho-Parthian prototype'. Later, under the Gupta dynasty, Kumagupta I is featured on the obverse of one of his coins fighting a lion while riding an elephant (Pal 1986, 112 fig. C 30b). For the prominent role of the pachyderm in the Mauryan iconography, cf. Sick 2002, 132–33.

4 Compare with G. Syncellus, *Ecloga Chronographica* 507, p. 322 Mosshammer (= *FHG* III Porphyrius Tyrius 3.6). Heinen 1972, 88–89 and Scullard 1974, 99, 120 refer to Ceraunus' manner of death, but without remarking its exceptional character in the history of the Hellenistic royal warfare. This seems to be a general trend in modern research.

5 We do have a relief of a king, perhaps a Ptolemy, featured as a pharaoh riding on an elephant (Scullard 1974, fig. 11), but it comes from Meroe (Musaw-warat es-Sofra), not from Hellenistic Egypt. Even at Ipsus, if the elephants may well have been under Seleucus' personal command (Bar-Kochva 1976, 108 with n. 16; Mehl 1986, 206; Billows 1990, 184), he must have fought on foot, among the infantry battalions (see Sherwin-White and Kuhrt 1993, 14), and/or on horseback (see Plu. *Demetr.* 29.3, with Bar-Kochva 1976, 248 n. 15, and Grainger 1990a, 120). As regards the story told by Aelian (*NA* 7.41) about the philanthropic behaviour of an elephant of Pyrrhus at Argos, it must be interpreted in the light of Plutarch's testimony, which has the Epeirote fighting on horseback and refers the anecdote to the rider of Nicon (*Pyrrh.* 33.4–5; 34.1).

6 See Bopearachchi and Flandrin 2005, with Holt 2006. The authenticity of the coin has been questioned, at least, by Fischer-Bossert 2006; Arnold-Biucchi 2006, 84; Hurter 2006; and Dahmen 2007, 9 n. 13. Stewart 2007 seems to remain undecided.

7 See Kuschel 1961, 15–17; Brown 1984, 408–09; Svenson 1995, 106–07, 112–13; and exhaustively Stewart 1993, 233–43, for a discussion about the meaning of all these attributes. Svoronos 1904, pls. I-VI and Hazzard 1995, figs. 36, 103–105 are useful to illustrate the different portrait types.

8 Hadley 1974, 53 n. 9; Goukowsky 1978, 206; Stewart 1993, 235; Brown 1995, 22 with n. 35; cf. also Smith 1988, 40–41; Brown 1984, 408; Svenson 1995, 107, 113; Bosworth 2007, 20.

9 Stewart 1993, 236 misunderstood all this as he dated the new issue before Perdiccas' invasion (like Goukowsky 1978, 206, and Hadley 1964, 8) and considered the prominence of the elephants on the new series 'sheer bravado', supposing that the Lagid used their image as 'the invulnerable instrument and symbol par excellence of the invincible world conqueror', in spite of the fact that he had no elephant corps in 321. See more correctly Scullard 1974, 81. It is also wrong to make the generalization, as Kritt (1997, 153 n. 203) does, that the elephant-skin headdress on Ptolemaic coins should be associated with Alexander's conquest of Africa (Egypt). Stewart's (1993, 234–35) discussion on this point may be a bit misleading too.

10 See Bieber 1964, 53, followed by Mørkholm 1991, 63 and Jenkins 1990, 125. Hesitantly, Brown 1984, 411 n. 27 and Reden 2007, 35–36. On the contrary, Stewart 1993, 243–52 does not list this statue type among the freestanding portraits of Alexander that stood in Alexandria.

11 Cf. Tarn 1966, 131; Hadley 1964, 38–39; 1974, 52–54; *ESM*, 20–21, 112, 174–75; Goukowsky 1978, 127 n. 199, 207; Mehl 1986, 182; Stewart 1993, 237, 314–15; Bosworth 2007, 21.

12 Iossif 2004 has questioned Kritt's chronology for Susa's trophy series (c. 305/4–295), placing it after Ipsus. If so, no special types would have commemorated the Indian campaign, something perhaps a bit strange. The assumption that at least some emissions with Alexander in elephant-scalp predate 301 would solve the problem.

13 See *WSM* 316–17; Hadley 1974, 63; Le Rider, Callatay 2006, 44; Iossif, Lorber 2010, 157. Mehl 1986, 299, remains undecided.

14 Svoronos 1904, pls. 4a 1–7, 4b 18–22; Jenkins 1990, C28; Mørkholm 1991, pl. 96; Hazzard 1995, figs. 1, 38, 106. For the iconography and political interpretation, see Bosworth 2007.

15 Cf. Pollit 1986, 28; Price 1991, 35; Stewart 1993, 260; Bosworth 2007, 17–18; Reden 2007, 39.

16 See now Hoover 2011, who also notes that on the bulk of Seleucus' coinage featuring elephant types the *Daevic* (evil) animal is commonly supplied with horns, an *Ahuric* (good) attribute. On the pachyderm as a creature of Ahriman in Zoroastrianism, cf. Tafazzoli 1975.

17 For the role of the animals in the military history of this period, see Scullard 1974, 76–100 and Epplett 2007, 216–32. Tarn 1930, 92–98 and Bosworth 2002, 98–168 are not without interest.

18 This paper is part of the research project *Iconografía de la realeza e identidad cultural en el Oriente helenístico* (HUM2006-00980), financed by the Spanish Ministry of Education and Science. I am very grateful to Catherine Lorber for her valuable criticisms and the bibliographical orientations. However, any shortcomings naturally remain my responsibility.

INDEX